Eng[d] by G.E. Perine & Co N.Y.

BEFORE THE BA

WOMEN OF THE WAR.

MRS FANNY RICKETTS.

S. S. SCRANTON & CO.

WOMEN OF THE WAR;

THEIR

HEROISM AND SELF-SACRIFICE.

BY

FRANK MOORE,

AUTHOR OF "THE REBELLION RECORD," "DIARY OF THE AMERICAN REVOLUTION," ETC., ETC.

Illustrated with Steel Engravings.

Hartford, Conn.:
S. S. SCRANTON & CO.
R. C. TREAT, CHICAGO, H. H. BANCROFT & CO., SAN FRANCISCO.
NATIONAL PUBLISHING COMPANY, CINCINNATI.
1866.

Electrotyped at the Boston Stereotype Foundry,

No. 4 Spring Lane.

INTRODUCTION.

The histories of wars are records of the achievements of men, for the most part: the chroniclers have had to record that women, by their intrigues or their fatal gift of beauty, have been the cause of strifes innumerable; and it is confessed that they have inspired heroism and knightly deeds, but they have had small share in the actual conflicts. It has been their portion to suffer in silence at home, and to mourn the dead. For them it has been to hear of sufferings which they could not alleviate, to grieve or rejoice over results to which they had contributed only sympathy and prayers.

It has been different in our Conflict for the Union. Other wars have furnished here and there a name, which the world delights to repeat in terms of affection or admiration, of some woman who has broken through the rigidity of custom, and been conspicuous, either among armed men, like the Maid of Saragossa, or in the hospitals, like the heroine of Scutari. But our war has furnished hundreds as intrepid as the one, and as philanthropically devoted as the other. Indeed, we may safely say that there is scarcely a loyal woman in the North who did not do something in aid of the cause — who did not contribute, of time, or labor, or money, to the comfort of our soldiers and the success of our arms. No town was too remote from the scene of war to have its society of relief; and while the women sewed and knit, and made delicacies for the sick, and gathered stores, little girls, scarce old enough to know what the charitable labor meant, went from house to house, collecting small sums of money, — the fruitful energy of all keeping the storehouses and treasury of the Sanitary Commission full, and pouring a steady stream of beneficence down to our troops in the field.

Everywhere there were humble and unknown laborers. But there were others, fine and adventurous spirits, whom the glowing fire of patriotism urged to more noticeable efforts. These are they who followed their husbands and brothers to the field of battle and to rebel prisons; who went down into the very edge of the fight, to rescue the wounded, and cheer and comfort the dying with gentle ministrations; who labored in field and city hospitals, and on the dreadful hospital-boats, where the severely wounded were received; who penetrated the lines of the enemy on dangerous missions; who organized great charities, and pushed on our sanitary enterprises; who were angels of mercy in a thousand terrible situations. There are others who have illustrated, by their courage and address in times of danger, by their patience in suffering, and by adventures romantic and daring, some of the best qualities in our nature. Like the soldiers of the armies, they were from every rank in life, and they exhibited a like persistence, endurance, and faith. There are many hundreds of women whose shining deeds have honored their country, and, wherever they are known, the nation holds them in equal honor with its brave men.

The story of the war will never be fully or fairly written if the achievements of women in it are untold. They do not figure in the official reports; they are not gazetted for deeds as gallant as ever were done; the names of thousands are unknown beyond the neighborhood where they live, or the hospitals where they loved to labor; yet there is no feature in our war more creditable to us as a nation, none from its positive newness so well worthy of record.

It is the object of this book to gather and present narratives of the services in the war of some of the women who shared its perils, and ought to inherit its glories. Their experiences are varied, and include both sufferings and adventures, the narration of which cannot fail to warm the heart and excite admiration wherever they are read. They may be taken as representatives of the thousand others whose good deeds are a crown to the national glory.

CONTENTS.

KADY BROWNELL.

MRS. P. B. HURD.

MARGARET E. BRECKINRIDGE.

MRS. ELIDA RUMSEY FOWLE.

BRIDGET DIVERS.

MRS. ISABELLA FOGG.

WHAT WE DID AT GETTYSBURG.

MRS. MARY W. LEE.

WOMEN OF THE WAR.

MRS. FANNY RICKETTS.

NO page in the history of the bloody war which has just now come to an end is so brilliant as that illuminated by a record of the noble sacrifices and exploits of heroic women.

The historian of other wars can point to affecting though isolated cases of courage and devotion, but no annals are so rich as ours in those deliberate acts of unquestioning self-sacrifice, which at once ennoble our estimate of human nature, and increase the homage we pay to the virtues of woman.

American mothers, with more than Spartan patriotism, sent forth their sons to fall by rebel bullets, or to languish in rebel prisons. Many loyal women along the vexed border, and within the lines of the enemy, exhibited a more than human courage for the Union and its glorious banner, in the face of persecution and danger. In the hospital, and amid the stormy scenes of war, they displayed a heroism as brilliant as that of Grace Darling, surpassed the charity of Florence Nightingale, and repeated the humility and gentle sacrifices recorded of Mary in the sacred Scriptures.

Every one, thoughtful and true, must admire and appreciate the memorable conduct of the young wife Gertrude, of mediæval times; who knelt at the foot of the wheel upon which her unfortunate husband hung in excruciating torture, praying for the wretched sufferer, whispering words of consolation, and sustaining him with exhortations to look at the joys beyond. "He had ceased to try to send her away," says the historian, "and still she watched when morning came again, and noon passed over her, and it was verging to evening when for the last time he moved his head, and she raised herself so as to be close to him. With a smile, he murmured, '*Gertrude, this is faithfulness till death,*' and died."

Mrs. Hemans, in her exquisite way, has given utterance to this elevated sentiment of self-sacrifice in the beautiful lines, —

"I have been with thee in thine hour
  Of glory and of bliss;
Doubt not its memory's living power
  To strengthen me through this.
And thou, mine honored love and true,
  Bear on, bear nobly on;
We have the blessèd heaven in view,
  Whose rest shall soon be won."

Similar in intensity and fortitude was the spirit manifested by the lady whose name heads this chapter. More than once was her husband mangled under the iron wheel of battle.

Once he was reported dead, and his dying words and his sword were brought to the agonized wife. But she overcame all obstacles, penetrated the hostile lines, reached the side of his bloody stretcher, went into captivity with him, and made his spared life and recovered health the monument of her unwavering and heroic devotion.

The father of Mrs. Ricketts, Mr. J. Sharpe Lawrence, was an Englishman of wealth, possessing large estates in the Island of Jamaica, where he met Miss Ricketts, the youngest daughter of Captain Ricketts, of the British army, and Sarah Livingston, whose American connections have been celebrated in our history from colonial times.

The father and mother of Mrs. Ricketts were married at Elizabeth, New Jersey, where, after some years of migratory life between England and the West Indies, they decided to remain, and where their third daughter, Fanny Lawrence, was born.

Her education was principally conducted by that best of all teachers, her mother, who brought to the delightful and sacred task not merely the love of a mother, but a mind of uncommon clearness, which had been admirably trained and stored by life-long habits of close observation and wise reading.

In January, 1856, Miss Lawrence was married to a distant relative on her mother's side, James B. Ricketts, then a captain in the First artillery U. S. A., and immediately went with him to the distant south-western frontier of the republic, on the Rio Grande, where his company was stationed.

Here she remained with him for more than three years,

till that grand mustering of all the powers of the republic to the long-contested battle-grounds along the Potomac. Their life on the Mexican frontier was full of interest, novelty, and adventure. The First artillery was often engaged in repulsing the irregular and roving bands of Cortinas, who rode over the narrow boundary river in frequent raids and stealing expeditions into Texas. When in camp, Mrs. Ricketts greatly endeared herself to the men in her husband's company by constant acts of kindness to the sick, and by showing a cheerful and lively disposition amid all the hardships and annoyances of garrison life at such a distance from home, and from the comforts and refinements of our American civilization.

She was a spirit of mercy as well as good cheer; and many a poor fellow knew that, if he could but get her ear, his penance in the guard-house for some violation of the regulations would be far less severe on account of her gentle and womanly plea.

In the spring of 1861 the first artillery was ordered to Fortress Monroe, and her husband, together with the gallant and accomplished Greble, who fell a few weeks after at Bethel, carried on an artillery school of practice, where the future heroes of the Chickahominy, and Fredericksburg, and Chancellorsville, and Gettysburg were taught to handle, with fatal skill, the engines of warlike art. A few weeks before the first advance under McDowell, Captain Ricketts was ordered to Alexandria, to command a battery of light artillery. Mrs. Ricketts was constantly with him, both here and while on the Peninsula. The brave boys were so accustomed to her presence at headquarters, and had so many cheerful and grateful reminiscences of her graceful charities away on the distant Rio Grande, that she remained with them until the eve of the grand advance in the middle of July, 1861, when she was, for the first time, separated from her husband by military rules; and while he and the company moved on to Centreville, and thence to "battle's magnificently stern array" on the plains of Manassas, she returned, crushed with a nameless foreboding, to her temporary home in Washington, to do all that woman can when she sends her chosen one, and her other self, into the untold and innumerable dangers of war. She could only do what thousands of others did — watch, and hope, and pray, listening with heavy hearts to the far-off roar, and grasping with wild avidity at every fragment of news from the hotly-contested field.

On the evening of the 21st, rumors, and then messengers came hurrying to her room, confirming the very worst fears of an agonized wife. Persons hitherto unknown to her called to give her the most harrowing details of the wounds her husband had suffered; and then his death was announced. All these accounts she persistently refused to credit, clinging to the mighty hope that nothing but absolute conviction can quench in the loving heart. At last what seemed to be fatal evidence was adduced. Lieutenant E. D. Baker, then aid-de-camp to General Franklin, brought her the captain's sword, and repeated in her ears his dying words — "Give this to my wife; tell her I have done my duty to my country, and my last words are of her and our child."

This was soon afterwards confirmed by the tearful sympathy of Captain Ricketts' junior lieutenant, the gallant

Kirby, who recited the story of his long but fruitless search for the captain's body. At this the agonized wife was plunged into an abyss of despair, and of painful clinging to hope against hope, almost as heavy as desperation; and this dreadful state lasted through two nights, when the lingering flame of hope was roused into a mighty and controlling motive, by a telegram from General Wadsworth, stating that an officer, who met his flag of truce, informed him that Captain Ricketts was alive, but dangerously wounded and a prisoner.

Without a moment's hesitation, she determined, at all hazards and despite all obstacles, to reach his side. Repairing at once to Captain (now General) Beckwith, of the subsistence department, he procured for her a light carriage, drawn by two horses, and a driver, whose southern sympathies were such as to make him more than willing to pass within the rebel lines. General Scott gave her a pass valid to the extent of the Union lines, and thus equipped, and wholly unattended, she started on the search for her wounded and perhaps dying husband. She drove on, without material delay, till halted by the rebel pickets; and she was obliged to remain lingering in an agony of suspense and doubt, till a note, written by her to the cavalry leader, Stuart, whom she had known in sunnier days on the Rio Grande, had been carried to him, and was returned with the permission indorsed to advance within the southern lines as far as Fairfax.

Here, on learning the nature of her errand, he demanded her signature to a written parole of honor that she would not act the part of a spy. Notwithstanding her extreme anxiety to avoid detention, she indignantly tore the paper in pieces before his eyes, replying, "I am no spy, but the wife of a wounded officer, and will go as your prisoner, but never sign a parole."

Ex-Senator Wigfall, of Texas, here remonstrated, and some discussion followed, when Stuart rudely told her to drive on at once. But she knew too well the difficulties into which she would be plunged if she drove on as ordered on a road crowded with rebel soldiers, or through a country swarming with exultant and straggling cavalry.

She knew the usage to which, by the rules of honorable warfare, she was entitled, and insisted on being supplied with a pass and a guide to the headquarters of General Joseph E. Johnston. This request was at length unwillingly acceded to, and she was soon face to face with the rebel hero of Bull Run, who, without much hesitation, allowed her to drive to a house situated on a part of the field still crimsoned with the streams of battle, where her husband had been carried. What fearful and ghastly scenery now surrounded this young and delicately-reared woman! The first vision of that terrible picture was stamped on her brain, to be effaced only by death. Corpses, swollen by incipient decomposition, stripped of every shred of clothing, were sweltering all around, under the heat of a July sun. In the court-yard of the house where she was informed that her husband could be found, lay rows of the wounded and the dead. On the door-step, as she entered, lay an arm, all mangled and bloody, which a surgeon had just amputated and tossed down there as carelessly as though it had been a chicken's leg; while under the window she glanced at a fearful pile of human limbs, the accumulation of two days' amputation. The hall was narrow and nearly obstructed by a large mahogany dining-table, on which was lashed a wretched victim, who was writhing in almost mortal agony under the knife and saw of the operator. Blood was over the floor and on the walls, and had spirted from severed arteries, so that the very ceiling was spotted with scarlet.

Passing on up stairs, she found six wounded men in a small chamber, five ranged along the wall on the floor, and one, more pallid than the rest, very still, on a bloody stretcher. This was her husband!

At first he was unconscious, but at length feebly murmured in her ear, "*I knew you would come.*"

A Union surgeon who was in attendance, and whose unremitting and skilful care saved the limb and the life of Captain Ricketts, Dr. Lewis, of Michigan, urged upon her the importance of self-control, and the removal from the enfeebled sufferer of everything calculated to excite or alarm; and from that moment on, through all the anxieties and sufferings that followed, she armed herself in a fortitude that seemed almost stoical and unnatural.

Though her husband's life was hanging as by a thread, so that a little neglect might be fatal to him, her woman's heart could not resist the appeals that all night long came up from the different rooms of that house of suffering and of horror for *water*. She rose from the floor beside her husband, and taking a part of the small supply that a surgeon had brought for his hot and swollen leg, from a spring half a mile distant, she groped her way among the groaning and prostrate forms, moistening their parched lips. Once she was startled by the fearful announcement, made in a clear voice, that rose above the groaning, "He is gone, our brave corporal! The Lord gave and the Lord hath taken away." This called her attention to the speaker, whom she learned to be Prescott, of the Fourteenth Brooklyn regiment. He, too, poor fellow, was "taken away," but not without passing through a furnace of suffering so terrible that he had occasion to envy the earlier and less painful death of the brave corporal. His leg was hopelessly shattered, and was amputated above the knee three times within a week; and then he was transported to Richmond in a box-car, where the stump was so bruised that the artery was opened, and he bled to death at last.

For two weeks Mrs. Ricketts remained with her husband in the house where she found him. The means furnished for rendering the sufferers comfortable were of the lowest possible order, and that, too, in a country abounding in the luxuries of old civilization, and within a few hours' ride of the national capital. No food was furnished but raw bacon and hard-tack, with some coffee and sugar, captured at Centreville; no cooks, or facilities for cooking, the surgeons, after their long toils with the wounded during the day, being obliged to bring water a half mile, and prepare the food as best they could.

The effluvium from the battle-field was such that the rebel camps were removed. Finally, the odor became so intolerable that the guards left. Then appeared that loathsome curse and epidemic of army hospitals, *gangrene*, and it was determined to break up the field hospitals, and remove all the wounded prisoners to Richmond; and an order to that effect was issued on the 3d of August.

Captain Ricketts' wounds were more dangerous, and his situation more critical, in the early part of August, when he was removed to Richmond, than at any time since the battle. He had been hit in three places; but the wound which gave him the greatest pain, and which for weeks rendered his recovery doubtful, was from a ball that had entered his left leg, near the knee joint, shattering the bone, and followed by such pain and swelling, that mortification was constantly feared.

So great was the danger from this latter source, that twice Mrs. Ricketts had expostulated, with all the earnestness of woman, with the surgeons, who insisted that amputation was absolutely necessary. But considering the heat of the season, the discomforts and privations under which he was suffering, and the amount of corruption and the gangrene which abounded among all the wounded, she was satisfied that his chances of recovery would not be improved by the dreaded operation.

In the removal to Richmond Mrs. Ricketts was able to secure for him a hospital car, instead of the rude box cars, which gave fatal jolts to many a poor fellow who might otherwise have recovered.

In praiseworthy contrast to the rudeness and indifference generally manifested by the rebel officers, and the insults of rebel women heaped upon them at the different stations, the conduct of Wade Hampton, and of Stonewall Jackson, and of Major Webb, of North Carolina, was considerate and generous. Colonel Hampton brought ale and refreshments to the wounded officer and his heroic wife; and months after, Mrs. Ricketts was able to repay the civilities of Major Webb, by procuring his pardon and release from Johnson's Island, where he was confined as a prisoner.

Notwithstanding the sea of horrors into which this devoted pair had been plunged by the results of the battle, and the ghastly surroundings of the battle-field, where they had remained for two weeks, they found their situation worse, if possible, in Richmond.

The wounded prisoners were taken to the city poor-house. Crowded into those dreary and cheerless rooms, between bare brick walls and the roof unceiled, these sufferers lay on the dirty floors, and pined, and languished, and felt hope and life die out in their breasts, when comfortable surroundings might have saved most of them.

The fare was coarse and unpalatable to the last degree, even to persons in health, and utterly revolting to the patients, whose systems were reduced by loss of blood and by the nervous prostration of unceasing pain. Captain Ricketts grew worse, and the gloomiest forebodings pressed like lead upon the brave heart of the heroic wife. Again the surgeons consulted over his dreadfully swollen leg, and prescribed amputation; and again it was spared to the entreaties of his wife, who was certain that his now greatly enfeebled constitution would not survive the shock. Much of the time he lay unconscious, and for weeks his life depended entirely on the untiring patience and skill with which his wife soothed down the rudeness of his prison-house, cheering him and other prisoners who were so fortunate as to be in the room with him, and alleviating the slow misery that was settling like a pall upon them.

Yet none of the prisoners, at least in the daytime, had the luxury of being private in their sorrow. At all hours crowds of curious and listless gazers were permitted to come and feast upon this spectacle of suffering, as though these wounded officers and the solitary woman that was sharing their prison life were savages caught in the act of cannibalism in the Feejee Islands.

The daily papers of the city were constantly pandering to this savage taste, by suggesting greater cruelty and worse hardships as the proper desert of men who had "polluted the sacred soil of Virginia by the foot of the invader."

To the credit, however, of some whose public acts were thoroughly disunion, it must be admitted that in private they discharged some of the duties of humanity towards these wounded prisoners. The wife of Adjutant-General Cooper and the sister of James M. Mason, both repeatedly sent Mrs. Ricketts and her husband baskets of delicate and palatable food; and both these ladies, in defiance of the bitter and vulgar prejudice which was nourished by the daily press, paid them visits of respect, and manifested a womanly kindness and regard.

There was also, in the lower walks of life, a touching instance of womanly sympathy which deserves respectful mention, even as the charity of Mary Magdalene has been forever rescued from oblivion by the pen of the sacred historian.

There was a woman who had formerly lived in New York, and at that time was living with a well-known gambler in Richmond, who daily and regularly ministered to these unfortunate prisoners, until at length her kindness came to the ears of the officials, who forbade her sending them any more food. But, with the wit and perseverance of a woman, she at length obtained such a modification of the order as would allow her once a week to send a basket to Mrs. Ricketts. This basket, which came each Sabbath morning, was packed with the most substantial viands, and gave Mrs. Ricketts the pleasure of providing her husband, who had now commenced slowly to recover, with food that he could relish, and, with the rest, broke, at least for one day, the dreary and tasteless monotony of prison fare.

But the abyss of wretchedness was not sounded yet. Nearly three months of imprisonment had elapsed while these suffering patriots were languishing, yet hoping that the great republic, in whose invincible might and perpetual integrity they never lost confidence, would turn upon her enemies, and burst their prison doors, with a grand and decisive victory. But, in the last days of October, they heard the tramp of the prisoners taken at Ball's Bluff passing through the streets of Richmond, and the jeers and taunts of the rebel mob that followed at their heels.

There now came an order breaking up the little group of fellow-sufferers, whose sorrows had united them in a deep, though sombre friendship. Colonel Willcox, who was now nearly well of a terrible wound in the arm, was sent to Charleston, and the other convalescents were to be confined in Libby Prison. Soon after this removal to that abode of nameless horror, that has since become famous in its infamy, Mrs. Ricketts was reclining at night upon the narrow cot beside her husband's stretcher, when she heard the voice of a messenger beside her, who stood there in the darkness, and coolly announced that Captain Ricketts had been selected as one of the thirteen officers of highest rank in possession of the Confederate government, as hostages for the thirteen privateersmen held in New York. He was to go to the condemned cell, and be liable at any moment to execution, whenever the rebel government might learn of the execution of their imprisoned sailors. Conceive the mental suffering of that devoted wife during the long hours of that dreadful night!

After four months of untold suffering, and having much of the time hung insensible on the verge of life, he was now beginning to gain strength, and with fair treatment might live and be strong again. But on the morrow he was to be carried away from her, and beyond all her ministrations or visits, and locked in the felon's cell — a dungeon reserved for prisoners convicted of infamous crimes, and liable any day to be dragged out to a cruel death.

But Mrs. Ricketts was not a woman to yield to a disaster so appalling without using every possible means to avert the blow. In Mrs. Cooper she thought she had a friend whose husband had influence at rebel headquarters, and as soon as daylight enabled her to trace the lines, she composed a letter, such as only such a wife could write in such a crisis. Mrs. Cooper was moved, and the rebel secretary, who on the 11th of November had issued the fearful order that included Captain Ricketts, on the 12th instructed General Winder that "all the wounded officers had been exempted as hostages." The motive which Mrs. Cooper brought to bear upon his mind was not any suggestion of humanity, but the fear that such cruelty to wounded officers might damage the fair name of the Confederacy in the eyes of the people of Europe.

When the name of Captain Ricketts was first read, there occurred one of those instances of prompt and manly self-sacrifice, that elevate our estimate of human nature, and deserves record and perpetual remembrance. Captain Thomas Cox, of the first Kentucky volunteers, exclaimed at once, "*What, that wounded man, attended by such a devoted wife? Let me go in his place!*"

The constant draught upon the vital powers made by such a long series of watchings, sufferings, and by anxiety so acute and agonizing, at length began to appear in the shattered health of Mrs. Ricketts; and permission was asked, and, after long delay, granted, for her to drive out daily, and for a little while to breathe air purer than that of Libby Prison.

But before this little boon could be of any practical advantage, the exchanged officer arrived in Richmond, and the pallid but now convalescent invalid dragged his still painful limb across the threshold of Libby Prison, and with his heroic wife took the first train for Fairfax. It was now the last week of December, 1861. Some months elapsed before Mrs. Ricketts recovered her health; but Captain Ricketts recovered very rapidly, and had the satisfaction of knowing that government recognized his services and his sufferings; for in the spring of 1862 he received the commission of a brigadier-general, and was assigned to duty in McDowell's corps, at Fredericksburg. Mrs. Ricketts remained with him for some months that followed, until, in the fall of 1862, when campaigning against Jackson in the Valley, General Ricketts commanded the second division first army corps, and the corps being constantly on the march or in battle, she was obliged to retire for a few weeks to her home in Washington.

But Antietam gave him back to her society again, as Bull Run had the year before, though not under circumstances quite so painful. He was wounded in the same leg as in the former battle, by his horse being shot and rolling upon him. The injury thus occasioned confined him during the fall of 1862, and in the winter of 1862–'63 he was on duty at Washington, as president of the military commission.

When the battle at Chancellorsville was fought, in May, 1863, Lieutenant Kirby, who had been a brother officer with General Ricketts when both were in the First artillery, was brought to Washington in a very feeble state, having suffered the amputation of a limb., The poor fellow was carried to the general's house in Washington, where Mrs. Ricketts took care of him with that patient kindness which is so unspeakably grateful to a sufferer. But care and skill could not save him. He did not live to read his commission as brigadier. Other officers and sufferers of every grade now claimed her attention, for Gettysburg soon followed; and during all that summer and fall she continued her labors among those who seemed most to require her attentions, her husband having recovered his health and returned to participate in all the battles in which his corps was engaged.

In the summer of 1864, when Grant advanced on Richmond, General Ricketts distinguished himself greatly in the battle of Cold Harbor, and received the public thanks of General Meade; and, a few weeks after, his division fought the battle of Monocacy, the effect of which was to delay the last rebel invasion, and give the Union troops time to concentrate for the final repulse of Ewell from Maryland.

Soon after, in September, 1864, the Sixth corps went up the Shenandoah Valley with Sheridan, and in October the battle of Cedar Run was fought; and there General Ricketts received his third serious wound, which came nearer being fatal than any former injury. A ball pierced his right breast, and the report came to Washington that his wound was mortal. His wife's fidelity, and the story of her sufferings at Richmond, had become known to government, and she obtained not only a pass, but a mounted escort, who went with her up the valley, to protect her from the attacks of Mosby's guerrillas, who were swarming, everywhere in the rear of the battle-field. She found General Ricketts far more comfortably situated than on that memorable occasion three years before. The ball had been extracted; but the nature and situation of the wound rendered his recovery a long time doubtful, and for four anxious and weary months she was hanging over his couch, and doing everything that love and skill could suggest to save a life that had now become doubly precious to her for the sufferings and the anxieties which had been devolved upon both by stern demands of the country. At length, as spring opened in 1865, and when Sherman had wheeled, in the magnificent curve of his grand march, from Atlanta to Savannah, and northward to the rear of the long-beleaguered city, the generals knew the gigantic game was nearly ended, and General Ricketts was among those who, having suffered so long and so much, desired to "be in at the death." The wish was not denied him. In April he was with his old corps, and chased the routed and crumbling rebel column to Danville, where the effect of cold and exposure made both his wounds very painful, and he was obliged to quit the field. Again, and now for the last time, the devoted wife hurries along the familiar roads, and presses forward to where the suffering hero needs her cheerful presence and her skilful care.

The war is now over. The great events of April crowd in quick succession—the capture of Richmond, the surrender of Lee, and the murder of Lincoln; but General Ricketts and his wife still linger in camp, for his wounds are still painful. But at length the Sixth corps, that had marched, and suffered, and fought so many hard battles on the soil of Virginia, moves off northward, crosses the Potomac; and then, but not till then, the duties of the heroic general and his no less heroic wife are ended.

With the first boom of the deadly thunder at Manassas, she had been called away from her life of joyous ease and peaceful love, and so long as the noise of that long war lasted, she had known no rest nor intermission in her labors of womanly care and devotion.

It was not until she had left the soil of Virginia, peaceful now, but all scarred with battles and drenched in blood, that she could fully realize that that precious life was now no longer at hazard in the fierce storms of battle.

Does not every reader join in the prayer that years of

deep calm and blessed union may reward fidelity so heroic and suffering so great? May we not apply to her the dying words of the Suabian nobleman to his wife, "Gertrude, this *is* faithfulness to the end," and the wish of the English poet for his friend, whom he compares to "that fair Syrian shepherdess," —

"After this thy travel sore
Sweet rest seize thee evermore"?

MRS. MARY A. BRADY.

AN old Greek writer, in reflecting how his nation had been roused from luxury and stimulated to actions that made Greece heroic by the stress of the Persian invasion, exclaimed, in his enthusiasm, "War is the father of all things."

In like manner, we of America, looking at all the latent heroism that was developed during those four years of national agony and national glory, may, in no accommodated sense, hail our great war as the father of a great national peace, before impossible; and the nurse of magnanimous acts, and lives of saint-like devotion to the good of others.

While, among those who composed our armies, there were men who fought from very different motives and incitements, — some for love of glory, some from hatred of national injustice, some for a splendid name, and some for an undivided nation, — so, among the heroines, some followed their husbands, and were ready to dare everything and suffer everything for them and their cause; others sought the field out of a generous rivalry not to be outdone in sacrifices by the sterner sex; others were incited by pure patriotism; while a few moved and acted from motives rarer and purer, perhaps, than all these — a simple and unmixed desire to alleviate human suffering, a philanthropic kindness of soul, and the swelling of a large-hearted charity, that was willing to labor anywhere, and in any manner, to relieve the wants of those who were suffering pain and privations in a worthy cause.

Prominent among this numerous class must be placed the record of the lady whose name is written at the head of this memoir.

Mrs. Brady was not an American by birth. She had no son, or brother, or husband in the war. Born in Ireland, in 1821, and having married, in 1846, an English lawyer, twelve years of quiet residence in this country had, no doubt, sufficed to impress her with American love and pride; but she had no such stake in the issue, no such incentives to do all and suffer all that woman can in such a struggle, as might have impelled the exertions of thousands who did far less than she.

What demand of mere patriotism could have made it her duty, as an American citizen merely, to forego all the comforts of her home in Philadelphia, leave a family of five little children, push her way through all embarrassments and delays, through all the army lines, and sometimes in spite of general orders, to the very front, or to those hospitals where the men were brought in with clothing red with the fresh-flowing gore of battle, and spend days and weeks at the field hospitals just in the rear of the great battle-fields, and return home only to restore her wasted energies, and start out again on her errands of tireless philanthropy? Yet such is the outline of Mrs. Brady's life, and such the summary of her charities from the summer of 1862, when the sick and wounded from McClellan's Peninsular army were brought to the northern hospitals, till the summer of 1864, when, by reason of her exertions, exposures, and excitements, the silver cord of life was strung too tightly, and in the midst of her labors, while planning fresh sacrifices and new fields of exertion, it snapped, and she ceased to live, except in the hearts of survivors, and in the memory of thousands of soldiers, who

> "Shall tell their little children, with their rhymes,
> Of the sweet saint who blessed the old war-times."

Up to the summer of 1862 the life of Mrs. Brady was unmarked by other than the domestic virtues and the charities of home. Her life was that of an industrious, kind-hearted woman, finding her chosen and happy sphere in the duties of wife and mother. She merited the eulogy which the Greek orator bestowed on that woman, who, most intent upon home duties, was least talked of abroad, whether for praise or blame.

It was on the 28th of July, 1862, that Mrs. Brady and a few others met at her husband's law office, to take into consideration the condition of the soldiers who had been brought from James River, and were then languishing in various hospitals in and around Philadelphia, but principally at the Satterlee Hospital, in West Philadelphia, not far from Mrs. Brady's home.

There alone was an ample field for all their labors, and objects to absorb all the contributions of charity and patriotism that could be made to pass through their organization as a channel of sanitary relief. Here were three thousand soldiers, a mutilated fragment of the grand army with which McClellan had advanced up the peninsula, and which had floundered in the mud and rain, and through the battles of the Chickahominy, and been reduced by the six hard fights of that terrible campaign. True, the worst cases of the wounded were in hospitals nearer the front, at Washington, or Norfolk, or on James River; but here were hundreds and hundreds languishing with that low, dull fever that overcame so many who shared in that campaign, and which was called in the army the "James River fever." Here, too, were the mutilated men, nursing the painful stumps from which an arm or a leg had been amputated. The absolute physical necessities of these patients were, to a reasonable degree, met by the customary appliances of an army hospital. The patient had a bed, narrow and hard, indeed, but clean. His food was such as the hospital surgeon prescribed—now a plate of boiled rice, now a slice of beef, or a dish of soup. But moral and social restoratives he had none. To wrestle in grim patience with unceasing pain; to lie weak and helpless, thinking of the loved ones on the far-off hill-side, or thirsty with unspeakable longing for one draught of cold water from the spring by the big rock at the old homestead; to yearn, through long, hot nights, for one touch of the cool, soft hand of a sister or a wife on the throbbing temples,—this was the dreary routine of suffering and cheerlessness in the great hospital before Mrs. Brady and her associates commenced their labors of wise and systematic kindness.

The object of their organization was declared to be to create committees, who, in turn, should visit the different wards of the United States Hospital, for the purpose of ameliorating the condition of the sick and wounded soldiers, and to establish a depot of sanitary supplies, whose location should be generally known; to have their organization officially recognized by the governor and the military and medical authorities of the United States; and eventually, that members of the association should visit the hospitals at Washington and the army in the field, to learn the wants of sick soldiers, and do all in their power to relieve them.

Mrs. Brady was elected president of the association; and from that day to the hour of her death — not quite two years after — her labors were unceasing, her devotion unbounded, and her discretion unerring in the great enterprise of the sanitary well-being of the soldiers of the republic.

For some months their labors were confined to the hospital at West Philadelphia. A committee of these ladies regularly, each day, went the round of the hospital wards, distributing the delicacies and the various articles of comfort that were now daily arriving in a steady stream at the depot for their hospital supplies on Fifth Street.

But the ministries of Mrs. Brady and her corps were not confined to the mere distribution of currant jelly, preserved peaches, flannel shirts, and woollen socks. They carried with them a moral cheer and soothing that were more salutary and healing than any of the creature comforts. The patient, suffering hero of Williamsburg or Malvern Hill was assured, in tones to whose pleasant, home-like accents his ear had long been a stranger, that his efforts in behalf of his country were not ignored or forgotten; that they too had a son, a brother, a father, or a husband in the field. Then the pallid face and the bony fingers were bathed in cool water, and sometimes a chapter in the New Testament, or paragraph from the morning papers, read, in tones low, but distinct, and in such grateful contrast to those hoarse battle-shouts that had been for weeks, perhaps, ringing through his feverish brain — "*Column, forward — dress on the colors — aim low, and make your shots tell — file right, march!*"

Then the painful and inflamed stump was lifted, and a pad of soft, cool lint fitted under it; and the thin, chalky lips would move slowly, and say that he "felt easier."

Here a poor fellow, who had an armless sleeve, was enjoying the services of a fair amanuensis, who in graceful chirography wrote down, for loving eyes and heavy hearts, in some distant village of Vermont or Michigan, the same old soldier's story, told a thousand times, by a thousand firesides, but always more charming than any story in the Arabian Nights — how, on that great day, he stood with his company on a hill-side, and saw the long gray line of the enemy come rolling across the valley; how, when the cannon opened on them, he could see the rough, ragged gaps opening in the line; how they closed up and moved on; how their general came along, and made a little speech, and told them to aim low and then give them the bayonet; how he rushed on at the command to "charge;" how this friend fell on one side, and poor Jimmy —— on the other; and then he felt a general crash, and a burning pain, and the musket dropped out of his hand; then the ambulance and the amputation, and what the surgeon said about his pluck; and then the weakness, and the pain, and the hunger; and how much better he was now; and how kind the ladies in Philadelphia had been to him; that he didn't care much about the loss of his arm, so far as he was concerned, only he couldn't do as much for his father and mother as he had hoped; but he lost it in the line of his duty, and would lose the other one rather than have the government broken up.

Who would not sew, knit, make currant jelly, write letters for a hospital full of brave, patient battle heroes like that?

After their recovery and return, Mrs. Brady received numerous letters from those she had visited in the hospitals, thanking her and blessing her for her good deeds.

The following, from a Pennsylvania volunteer, is selected from a score equally interesting: —

CAMP NEAR BELLE PLAIN, VA., *January* 19, 1863.

MRS. MARY A. BRADY.

Dear Friend: There is one of my comrades in the West Philadelphia Hospital (Ward H) by the name of Harry Griffin. I wish you would be so kind as to call and see him as you make your daily rounds.

You are engaged in a good work in visiting the afflicted, and by contributing to their wants; and surely you will reap your reward in good season, and God will bless you. Every true soldier you have helped shall remember you with respect and gratitude. I shall always remember you myself with deep feelings of gratitude, and I shall never forget the kindness bestowed on me by the ladies. "A friend in need is a friend indeed." My arm is still sore.

Believe me to be, madam, yours truly,

JOSEPH A. WINTERS,
Co. B, 7th Reg. Pa. Vol.

Late in the fall, at the time of the annual Thanksgiving, Mrs. Brady and the other ladies determined that those who still remained — some sixteen hundred — should not lack the material supplies on which to celebrate the day.

Mrs. Brady and Miss Lydia C. Price were the efficient committee on Thanksgiving Dinner. They appealed to the cities and towns around Philadelphia in behalf of the brave fellows, and Mrs. Brady showed her characteristic kindness and thoughtfulness by applying to Dr. Hayes for the release on that day of all the boys who for any indiscretion had found their way to the guard-house. The good surgeon granted her request, and Mrs. Brady had ready for them, at the appointed dinner hour, seventy-five turkeys, one hundred chickens, twenty geese, sixty ducks, eight hundred and fifty pies, eighty-five rice puddings, and fifteen barrels of eating apples. Two bakers' establishments were placed at their disposal, and the food brought up warm to the hospital in covered wagons.

The number of patients in this hospital now rapidly diminished, and, in December, Mrs. Brady began to arrange plans for more extended and arduous labors for the soldier. At their depot there was a constantly increasing supply of various articles, such as the soldiers were supposed most to need.

Soldiers' aid societies had sprung up all over the state, and Mrs. Brady was widely known as president of the mother society in Philadelphia.

Numerous boxes had been sent to her care, and she regarded herself as the authorized trustee of the charities of large communities.

She determined not to trust the distribution of these goods to careless or unknown agents, but after consultation with others of the association, it was decided that Mrs. Brady was to go to the field in person, and distribute the contents of the boxes from tent to tent, as she found the men in camp who most required them.

While at Alexandria she prepared and sent home to the association in Philadelphia a charming narrative of her journey and all its incidents, and how the contents of the boxes were given out, and how the boys received them, and how she could have distributed twenty times as much without giving to any who did not require aid.

When she went to Fairfax and the camps between the Potomac and the Rapidan our national fortunes were at ebb tide. It was the Valley Forge of the war. The Peninsular campaign had been magnificent, but a failure. Then Jackson, and soon after Lee with him, had advanced to the Potomac, driving Pope before him into Washington city. Then at South Mountain and Antietam the invading tide had been met and rolled back; but Lee was not pursued. Then Burnside had taken the army across the Rappahannock, and fought a superior force under able generals, on the worst ground he could have chosen, with such results as might have been expected. The army was greatly used up and demoralized, and the sick list was fearful.

Beyond Alexandria, in the direction of Falmouth, where the army lay, Mrs. Brady came upon one camp of twelve thousand six hundred convalescents; a little beyond, a sick camp of eight thousand, and in the forty military hospitals in and around Washington she visited thirty thousand sick and wounded. Of course the sixty boxes she took from Philadelphia were but a mouthful to a hungry man; but she gave out the articles herself, with true English thoroughness and perseverance, making numerous inquiries, and faithfully striving to give to those who were most in need.

While travelling among this army of the sick, she was overtaken one evening by a snow storm, and was obliged to fare like the soldiers, shivering all night under one gray blanket, in a tent without a fire, and listening to a dreary chorus of coughing, which suggested all the grades and varieties of pulmonary disease. But her thoughts were not on her personal discomforts, rather on the twelve thousand sick soldiers, in the midst of whom she was passing but a single cheerless night; and she hurried home to ply her needle, and stimulate by her pen the activities of others, and collect as soon as possible additional supplies. She only stopped to pay a flying visit to the sick in Washington, and describes, in affecting language, how, in every ward she entered, all who were not too sick or badly wounded would rise up in their beds in astonishment at seeing a lady visitor.

At several of the Alexandria hospitals the doctors and nurses told her no other lady had ever before called.

In about a month Mrs. Brady, and the other ladies of the association, had sixty large boxes full of flannel shirts, socks, butter, dried fruit, wine, jelly, preserves, farina, soap, towels, combs, and several packages of smoking tobacco, apples, and onions. Her second trip was much like the first, except that now she penetrated to the extreme front, and heard the rebel drums tattoo in the camps on the other side of the Rappahannock, and the church clocks striking in Fredericksburg.

Here she took a four-mule wagon, and went through the army, stopping wherever a little red flag indicated a sick tent. She saved a number of boxes for the Alexandria hospitals, and the convalescents would file by her stand, and receive each an apple, a lemon, a handful of smoking tobacco, or a pair of socks, and what was about as good, and cost nothing, a cheerful word, a smile, a pleasant joke, or a wish that she had more for each.

Returning home, the month of April was passed in active preparations for another trip. Yet her family was not neglected. In camp or on the cars she was knitting for them, or making a dress, and at home divided her time between the demands of her family and the army, working now on a child's frock and now on a soldier's shirt.

May came, and with it Chancellorsville and its ten thousand wounded. This time she took forty-five packages, and they were filled with articles suited to the sick and suffering. With a view to immediate and practical efficiency, she took two cooking stoves, and proceeded at once to the great field hospital of the Sixth corps, where she soon had a tent pitched, her boxes piled around for a wall, her stoves up, and a little squad of the slightly wounded to get wood and water, open her boxes, and take her cooked articles to the different hospital tents.

Reporting to the division surgeons, and working under them, she received "requisitions" that looked almost appalling, as she saw the rapidly diminishing pile of boxes, and the two cooking stoves.

She writes to the association at Philadelphia that "fifty dozen cans of condensed milk, a hundred dozen fresh eggs, thirty boxes of lemons, ten boxes of oranges, one hundred and fifty pounds of white sugar, two hundred jars of jelly, and twelve dozen of sherry are needed. "*Everything is wanted*," she adds, earnestly. "Send us linen rags, towels, and some cologne; some red and gray flannel shirts, and limb pillows for the amputated."

But her labors were not confined to her little extemporized kitchen. At night she could hardly sleep for the groans from the tents where the worst cases lay, and she often passed several hours, moving softly through those tents of pain, going to those who seemed to suffer most, and soothing them by words, and by little acts of kindness; fitting a fresher or softer pad under some throbbing stump, talking with some poor fellow whose brain was full of fever, and who thought the battle was not yet over; moistening lips, stroking clammy foreheads, and helping another soldier to find his plug of tobacco.

Then, at five o'clock, she had the fires started, and honored as many requisitions for rice pudding, blanc mange, custard, and milk punch, as the draught upon her boxes could supply. This life lasted till some time in June, when the rapid invasion of Lee required corresponding movements on the part of Hooker, and the hospitals on Potomac Creek were broken up. Mrs. Brady had barely reached her home, and resumed for a little time the old and sacred round of domestic life, when she felt herself summoned to sanitary and hospital labors by a voice louder and nearer than any before — by the thunder of those five hundred cannon at Gettysburg, that for three fearful days piled the ground with bleeding wrecks of manhood.

Operating in her usual homely but effective and most practical manner, she at once sought a camping ground near a great field hospital, reported for duty to the division surgeon, and had a squad of convalescents assigned to assist her. Her tents were erected, the empty boxes piled so as to wall her in on three sides, and the stoves set up and fuel prepared; so that in two or three hours after reaching Gettysburg, the brigade and division surgeons were pouring in their "requisitions," and the nurses were soon passing from her tent with tubs of lemonade, milk punch, green tea by the bucketful, chocolate, milk toast, arrowroot, rice puddings, and beef tea, — all of which were systematically dispensed in strict obedience to the instructions of the medical men. Whenever during the day she could, for a short time only, be relieved from these self-imposed kitchen duties, and for many hours after nightfall, she was sure to be among the cots, beside the weakest and those who suffered most. Her frequent visits to the army had made her face familiar to a great number of the soldiers, so that she was often addressed by name, and warmly greeted by the brave fellows. "To see the face of a lady does us good, madam." "We are very glad you are come." "You cheer us up, Mrs. Brady."

When she remarked how grateful the stay-at-homes ought to feel to the brave hearts that fought so gallantly for them, and drove back the rebel hordes from the great cities along the border, simultaneously a chorus of voices exclaimed, "Why, Mrs. Brady, we would all have died, to the very last man, right here on the battle-field, before we would have let the Confederates win, or move on Philadelphia."

There we find the true reason of the national success at Gettysburg. It was not that Lee's abilities were clouded; not that Stonewall Jackson was dead. The Confederate force was never greater, never more resolute, or wielded with more masterly vigor; but they had never before met an army that was raised to the heroism of martyrs by the determination to "die to the very last man right there," rather than let the rebels win.

Speaking of her first day at these hospitals, Mrs. Brady says, "We shortly found ourselves rubbing away the pain from mutilated limbs, and bathing the feet of others, speaking cheerful words to them all, which latter we believed to do good like a medicine. In the daytime we cook and fill requisitions for all sorts of things, and personally distribute our miscellaneous stores to the men with our own hands, conversing cheerfully with the patients. Thus we spend our days as well as our nights."

These labors continued till August, when the field hospitals at Gettysburg were mostly broken up. For the remaining portion of the year 1863, as there were no battles in Virginia, Mrs. Brady remained at home, and continued her hospital labors in Philadelphia, and in receiving and preparing supplies for the approaching winter. She was now well known in Philadelphia, and became the almoner of numerous but private charities, funds being placed in her hands to be used according to her discretion in aiding soldiers or their families. The most of this money she gave in a private manner, but regularly, to the widows of those who had fallen in the great battles. On one occasion, as she entered a street car, crowded with passengers, she noticed that a soldier was looking very steadily in her face. His sleeve was empty. Presently the maimed warrior called out, with some emotion, "Don't you know me, Mrs. Brady?" "Really," she replied, "I can't quite recollect you, I see so many of Uncle Sam's brave boys." "Not recollect me, Mrs. Brady?" said the soldier, his eyes now filling with tears: "don't you remember the day you held my hand while the doctors cut my arm off? You told me to put my trust in God, and that I should get well over it. You said I was sure to recover; and here I am, dear madam, thank God!"

It seems that he had felt a natural revulsion when the amputation was suggested, but asked the surgeons to send for Mrs. Brady, and he would do just as Mrs. Brady said. She came, took the poor fellow's hand, and spoke a few low, kind words. "Now put up the sponge," said he to the surgeon; and the chloroform reduced him to insensibility as his pallid, bloodless hand still lay in hers. But, with the sensibility of her sex, she was obliged to turn away just as the operator took up the long, glittering knife.

Early in the year 1864, when Meade, in command, was manœuvring unsuccessfully against Lee for the occupation of the south bank of the Rapidan, in what is known as the Mine Run campaign, Mrs. Brady made her fifth and last visit to the front. She was now so well and so favorably known, that every facility was afforded her in the transportation of her boxes, and she penetrated to the front, and made herself useful in the primary field hospital that was established in consequence of the action at Morton's Ford, on the 6th of February. Her ministrations were of the same nature with those described above, except that here she saw the wounded just as they were brought from the field, and shared in the deep excitements and agitations of battle. She was just in the rear of an engagement that threatened at one time to become general and bloody. Most of the time she could secure no better bed than a bundle of wet straw. As a natural consequence of such hardships and exposures, we find her reaching home on the 15th of February, "completely worn out." An examination of her condition by physicians revealed the grave fact that rest and quiet alone could never restore her. An affection of the heart, which had existed for some time, but which, on account of her strong health and fine powers of constitution, had never before caused any uneasiness, had been rapidly developed by the last few weeks of uncommon excitement and fatigue.

Yet in March and April her health rallied somewhat, and she continued to collect and prepare the stores for another mission to the camp.

May now came on, and with it the grand advance of

the army of the Potomac, now strongly reënforced, and wielded by a fresh champion, just come from his great victories in the West; and the nation was tiptoe with expectation. Then followed the battles of the Wilderness and Spottsylvania, with their necessary and ghastly sequel, the long rows of hospital tents, acres of wounded, and suffering, and sick, with the demand for everything that can assuage pain, and reinvigorate the languid or exhausted currents of life. But Mrs. Brady could not respond to this call, as she had done when other battles were fought. Disease had seated itself at the fountains of her life. The abnormal action of the heart grew worse and worse, causing now the most acute suffering. Skilful physicians were summoned; but science was baffled, and the appalling announcement fell with unexpected and crushing weight upon the inmates of that home of which she was the centre and the sun, that no human skill could prolong that life, but within a few weeks those five little children must be motherless.

On the very day that sealed the fate of Virginia, — the 27th of May, 1864, — when Lee gave up the open contest with his too powerful antagonist, and fell sullenly back to his intrenchments at Petersburg and Richmond, she, whose mind even then was turned from the solemn surroundings of the death-bed, and the tearful faces of her children, to the suffering heroes of those great fights, — she was summoned away from all stormy scenes and arduous labors, into the kingdom of perpetual peace.

The burial of her remains took place on the 1st day of June. Hundreds of soldiers and officers of the army of the Potomac sent to the surviving members of the family their fervent tributes to the worth, beauty, and strength of her character, and expressions of gratitude for the kindness they had experienced at her hands.

A very large number of sorrowing friends, and poor people, and widows of soldiers, and five ministers of that religion of love and charity which she had so eminently practised, were in attendance at her funeral, and paid abundant, yet not undue, honor to the memory of the dead; for, during the forty-two years of her earthly existence, as long as life and strength remained to enable her to labor for the good of others, had she not followed closely in the steps of Him who always went about doing good, and reproduced the virtues of that Scripture heroine, the woman that was "full of good works and alms-deeds, which she did continually"?

KADY BROWNELL,

THE HEROINE OF NEWBERN.

ALL our revolutionary historians are eloquent in their praises of the bold heroine of Monmouth, "Captain Molly." They tell us how she was carrying water to the men of Proctor's battery on that hot and bloody afternoon in July, when a ball crushed in the skull of her husband, just as he was ramming a charge into his field piece, and he fell at her feet a bloody corpse. "Lie there, my darling, till I avenge your death!" exclaimed Molly, and seizing the rammer, she went on with the work which death had cut short, while the men cheered her all along the line. All through that afternoon, till night covered the landscape and closed the battle, Molly stood by her gun, and made good her husband's place, swabbing the piece, and forcing home the successive charges with the vigor and coolness of the bravest soldier. The next morning she was presented to General Wayne, all soiled and bloody as she had fought; and Washington gave her a commission as sergeant, and by his recommendation her name was placed on the list of half-pay officers for life.

The annals of our great war for the Union are not wanting in similar instances where the wife of the soldier has

Eng^d. by G.E. Perine & Co. N.Y.

KADY BROWNELL

IN ARMY COSTUME.

Engraved Expressly for the Women of the War.

gone with her husband, experienced all the hardships of the camp, stood in the line with sword at her side, carried the colors into the thickest of the fight, and then, when the bloody work was over, devoted herself, with the delicate tenderness of her sex, to mitigating the horrors of the battle-field.

Such was the brave young wife whose name stands at the head of our sketch; and such were her courage, her bearing, and her services on the plains of Manassas and at the battle of Newbern. Her father was a Scotchman, and a soldier in the British army. He was stationed far away on the African coast, in Caffraria; and there, in the year 1842, in the regimental barracks, and surrounded by the rude but kind old soldiers, her father's companions in arms, little Kady was born.

Accustomed to arms and soldiers from infancy, she learned to love the camp; and it was not strange, years later, when she had come to America and married a young mechanic in Providence, that the recollections of the camp fire in front of her father's tent, as well as the devotion of a newly-married wife, and loyalty to the Union, prompted her to follow her husband, stand beside him in battle, and share all his hardships.

Her husband, Robert S. Brownell, was made orderly sergeant of a company in the First Rhode Island infantry, one of the earliest regiments of three months' men who responded to the first call for troops, the day after national colors were run down the flag-mast at Fort Sumter.

The First Rhode Island infantry was soon full to overflowing. It had eleven full companies of a hundred each;

and as ten were enough for a complete organization, the eleventh was formed into a company of carbineers or sharp-shooters, and the brave young wife of the orderly was made the color-bearer of this company.

When the regiment went into camp in Maryland, early in the summer of 1861, this Daughter of the Regiment was resolved not to be a mere water-carrier, nor an ornamental appendage. She would be effective against the enemy, as well as a graceful figure on parade, and applied herself to learn all the arts and accomplishments of the soldier. When the company went out to practise daily at the target, she carried her rifle, as well as the colors; and when her turn came, the men seldom restricted her to the three shots which were allowed to each. So pleased were they by her skill and coolness with the weapon, that she was allowed as many shots as she chose, and thus became one of the quickest and most accurate marksmen in the regiment. Nor was the sergeant's straight sword, which hung at her belt, worn as an idle form. She practised daily with her husband and his friends in camp, till she felt herself as familiar with its uses as with the carbine.

When the regiment moved she sought no indulgences on account of her sex, but marched in line beside her husband, wearing her sword and carrying the flag.

The middle of July came, and the Union army was at length moving southward from the Potomac, its face set towards Richmond. She marched with her company, and carried her flag. On the day of the general action she was separated from her husband, the carbineers with whom she was connected being deployed as skirmishers in the skirt of pine woods on the left of the line. About one o'clock on that eventful day the company was brought under fire. She did not carry her carbine that day, but acted simply as color-bearer. The men, according to skirmish tactics, were taken out by fours, and advanced towards the enemy. She remained in the line, guarding the colors, and thus giving a definite point on which the men could rally, as the skirmish deepened into a general engagement. There she stood, unmoved and dauntless, under the withering heat, and amid the roar, and blood, and dust of that terrible July day. Shells went screaming over her with the howl of an avenging demon, and the air was thick and hot with deadly singing of the minie balls. About four o'clock, far away on the right, where the roar had been loudest, a sudden and marvellous change came over the scene. The Union line was broken, and what was a few moments before a firm and resolute army, worn and bleeding, but pressing to victory, became a confused and panic-stricken rout.

The confusion now ran down the line, from right to left, and the sharpshooters of the First Rhode Island, seeing the battle lost and the enemy advancing, made the best retreat they could in the direction of Centreville. But so rapidly spread the panic, that they did not rally on their colors and retreat in order. She knew her duty better, and remained in position till the advancing batteries of the enemy opened within a few hundred yards of where she stood, and were pouring shells into the retreating mass. Just then a soldier in a Pennsylvania regiment, who was running past, seized her by the hand, and said, "Come, sis; there's no use to stay here just to be killed; let's get into the woods." She started down a slope with him towards a pine thicket. They had run hardly twenty steps, when a cannon ball struck him full on the head, and in an instant he was sinking beside her, a shapeless and mutilated corpse. His shattered skull rested a moment on her shoulder, and streams of blood ran over her uniform.

She kept on to the woods, where she found some of the company, and before long chanced upon the ambulance, into which she jumped; but the balls were flying too thick through the cover. She sprang out, and soon after found a stray horse, on which she jumped, and rode to Centreville. Here and at Arlington Heights, for more than thirty hours, she was tortured by the most harassing stories about her husband.

One had seen him fall dead. Another had helped him into an ambulance, badly wounded. Another had carried him to a hospital, and the enemy had fired the building, and all within had perished. Then, again, she learned that his dead body was left in the skirt of pine woods in front of where she stood. So fully did she believe this at one time, that she had mounted a horse, and was starting back from Alexandria, in hope of getting through the lines and finding him, when she was met by Colonel Burnside, who assured her that Robert was unhurt, and she should see him in a few hours.

The first Rhode Island was a three months regiment, and its time expired on the 1st of August.

She returned with it to Providence, where she received a regular discharge; but it was only to reënlist with her husband in the Fifth Rhode Island. The fall of 1861 was a time of inaction in the army. McClellan had taken command, and for months the great Union army, with a spirit and intelligence never equalled in any military organization, and abounding in zeal for "short, sharp, and decisive" work, was month after month getting ready to move. Meantime Burnside, who was a colonel at Bull Run, had been made a brigadier, and placed in command of the Burnside expedition, whose duty it was to penetrate the country south of Richmond, and at the opportune moment to advance on Richmond from that direction, while the grand army should march upon it from the north.

The Fifth Rhode Island was in his force. In January Roanoke Island was taken, and the first blow struck at the rebel power. Early in March he was in Neuse River, and advancing on Newbern. In the organization of the regiment Kady was not now a regular color-bearer, but acting in the double capacity of nurse and daughter of the regiment. When the force debarked, on the thirteenth, she marched with the regiment fourteen miles, through the mud of Neuse River bottom, and early the next morning attired herself in the coast uniform, as it was called, and was in readiness, and was earnest in the wish and the hope that she might carry the regimental colors at the head of the stormers when they should charge upon the enemy's field works.

She begged the privilege, and it was finally granted her, to go with them up to the time when the charge should be ordered. Here, by her promptness and courage, she performed an act which saved the lives of perhaps a score of brave fellows, who were on the point of being sacrificed by one of those blunders which cannot always be avoided when so large a proportion of the officers of any force are civilians, whose coolness is not equal to their courage.

As the various regiments were getting their positions, the Fifth Rhode Island was seen advancing from a belt of wood, from a direction that was unexpected. They were mistaken for a force of the rebels, and preparations instantly made to open on it with both musketry and artillery, when Kady ran out to the front, her colors in hand, advanced to clear ground, and waved them till it was apparent that the advancing force were friends. The battle now opened in good earnest. Shot and shell were flying thick, and many a brave man was clinching his musket with nervous fingers, and looking at the bristling line of bayonets and gun-barrels which they were about to charge with anything but cheerful faces, when Kady again begged to carry her colors into the charge. But the officers did not see fit to grant her request, and she walked slowly to the rear, and immediately devoted herself to the equally sacred and no less important duty of caring for the wounded.

In a few moments word was brought that Robert had fallen, and lay bleeding in the brick-yard. That was the part of the line where the Fifth Rhode Island had just charged and carried the enemy's works. She ran immediately to the spot, and found her husband lying there, his thigh bone fearfully shattered with a minie ball; but, fortunately, the main femoral artery had not been cut, so that his life was not immediately in danger from bleeding.

She went out where the dead and wounded were lying thick along the breastwork, to get blankets that would no longer do them any good, in order to make her husband and others more comfortable.

Here she saw several lying helpless in the mud and shallow water of the yard. Two or three of them she helped up, and they dragged themselves to dryer ground. Among them was a rebel engineer, whose foot had been crushed by the fragment of a shell. She showed him the same kindness that she did the rest; and the treatment she received in return was so unnatural and fiendish that we can hardly explain it, except by believing that the hatred of the time had driven from the hearts of some, at least, of the rebels, all honorable and all Christian sentiments.

The rebel engineer had fallen in a pool of dirty water, and was rapidly losing blood, and growing cold in consequence of this and the water in which he lay.

She took him under his arms and dragged him back to dry ground, arranged a blanket for him to lie on, and another to cover him, and fixed a cartridge box, or something similar, to support his head.

As soon as he had grown a little comfortable, and rallied from the extreme pain, he rose up, and shaking his fist at her, with a volley of horrible and obscene oaths, exclaimed, "Ah, you d—— Yankee ——, if ever I get on my feet again, if I don't blow the head off your shoulders, then God d—— me!" For an instant the blood of an insulted woman, the daughter of a soldier, and the daughter of a regiment, was in mutiny. She snatched a musket with bayonet fixed, that lay close by, and an instant more his profane and indecent tongue would have been hushed forever. But, as she was plunging the bayonet at his breast, a wounded Union soldier, who lay near, caught the point of it in his hand; remonstrated against killing a wounded enemy, no matter what he said; and in her heart the woman triumphed, and she spared him, ingrate that he was.

She returned to the house where Robert had been carried, and spreading blankets under him, made him as comfortable as he could be at a temporary hospital. The nature of his wound was such that his critical time would come two or three weeks later, when the shattered pieces of bone must come out before the healing process could commence. All she could do now was simply to keep the limb cool by regular and constant applications of cold water.

From the middle of March to the last of April she remained in Newbern, nursing her husband, who for some time grew worse, and needed constant and skilful nursing to save his life. When not over him, she was doing all she could for other sufferers. Notwithstanding her experience with the inhuman engineer, the wounded rebels found her the best friend they had. Every day she contrived to save a bucket of coffee and a pail of delicate soup, and would take it over and give it out with her own hands to the wounded in the rebel hospital. While she was thus waiting on these helpless and almost deserted sufferers, she one day saw two of the Newbern ladies, who had come in silks to look at their wounded countrymen. One of them was standing between two beds, in such a position as to obstruct the narrow passage. Our heroine politely requested her to let her pass, when she remarked to the other female who came with her, "That's one of our women — isn't it?"

"No," was the sneering response, "she's a Yankee ——," using a term which never defiles the lips of a *lady*. The rebel surgeon very properly ordered her out of the house.

It is but justice, however, to say that in some of her rebel acquaintances at Newbern human nature was not so scandalized.

Colonel Avery, a rebel officer, soon after he was captured, said something to her about carrying the wrong flag, and that "the stars and bars" was *the* flag. "It won't be *the* flag till after your head is cold," was her quick reply. The colonel said something not so complimentary to her judgment, when General Burnside, who was standing near, told him to cease that language, as he was talking to a woman. Immediately the colonel made the most ample apologies, and expressed his admiration of her spirit and courage, and afterwards insisted on her receiving from him sundry Confederate notes in payment of her kindness to the wounded among his men. There was one poor rebel, who died of lockjaw from an amputated leg, whom she really pitied. He said he "allus was agin the war — never believed Jeff Davis and them would *suc*ceed no how," and talked about his poor wife and his seven children, who would be left in poverty, and whom he would never see again, in a way so natural and kindly that she forgot all about the brutal engineer and the insulting woman in silk, and did all she could to make the poor old man comfortable. He was fond of smoking, and in the terrible pain he suffered, the narcotic effect of the tobacco was very soothing. Kady used to light his pipe for him at the hospital fire, and go and give it to him.

In April Robert could bear removal, and was made as comfortable as possible on a cot on the steamship. Arriving in New York, he lay a long time at the New England Rooms; and his faithful wife, as tender as she is brave, thought only of his life and his recovery. But it was eighteen months before he touched ground, and then the surgeons pronounced him unfit for active service; and as his soldier days were over, Kady had no thought of anything more but the plain duties of the loving wife and the kind friend. The colors she so proudly carried she still keeps, as well as her discharge, signed A. E. Burnside, and the sergeant sword, with her name cut on the scabbard, and sundry other trophies of the Newbern days. An excellent rifle, which she captured, she gave to a soldier friend, who carried it back to the front, and fought with it till the war was ended.

THE HEROINE OF SHETECK LAKE.

A STORY OF BORDER SUFFERING.

THE indirect and remote sufferings occasioned by the great civil war in America have been almost as great as the direct miseries produced by battles. The greater part of our standing army is, in time of peace, stationed along the western frontier, and in a long series of outposts that extend from the cool and lonely lakes of Western Minnesota on the north to the haunts of the savage Camanches on the Mexican border.

When the great demands of the crisis fell upon the country in the spring of 1861, the first and most obvious result was the calling eastward of all, or nearly all, the regiments of the regular army who had been for the long years of peace interposed as a barrier of steel between the painted and treacherous barbarians of the mountain and the prairie and the ever-advancing line of industrious civilization. Lyon and Sedgwick, the heroic Lander, and the indomitable Colonel Cross, with some who enlisted on the southern side, and the rank and file, making an aggregate of nearly thirteen thousand troops, were suddenly withdrawn from the frontier; and this left a long line of pioneer settlement wholly unprotected from the treacherous and savage foe.

The result might easily be imagined, if it were not a part of our national history.

Naked Camanches were creeping through the high grass of Western Texas, and shooting ploughmen and shepherd boys almost within sight of the state capital. The western settlements of Arkansas and Kansas were unsafe; and farther north, on the western line of Iowa and Minnesota, the Sioux, friendly and peaceable only when utterly crushed, were raising their heads, and perpetrating a series of atrocities and murders which recall the old story of Wyoming, and the early settlement of Kentucky. About the 17th of August a party of two hundred and fifty or three hundred Indians proceeded to the agency at Yellow Medicine, and commenced an indiscriminate slaughter of all the whites, young and old, male and female. Then the marauders, flushed with success, pressed on with their work of death, murdering, with the most atrocious brutalities, the settlers in their isolated farm-houses, violating and then killing women, beating out the brains of infants, or nailing them to the doors of houses, and practising every species of atrocity which their fiendish natures prompted.

The following account of the sufferings of Mrs. Hurd and her children was elicited from her in an examination before the United States commissioners at Davenport, in Iowa; and during the recital of her story the audience were many times melted to tears, and for a little while business was suspended, and the hall of justice turned into a house of mourning. The narrative is somewhat condensed, but the simple words in which Mrs. Hurd told it are retained as far as possible.

"I was born in the western part of the State of New York, and removed with my parents to Steuben County, in Iowa, where I passed my childhood. I was married, in 1857, to Phineas B. Hurd, and we went to live in La Crosse, Wisconsin, and remained there about two years; and then we started west, and settled, with a few others, on Sheteck Lake, in Murray County, about a hundred miles west of Mankato, on the Minnesota River. It was a beautiful lake, and the lands around were excellent for grass and wheat. There were not many of us; but we were contented, and thought we had a permanent and happy home. The Indians hung around the lake, as it was an old hunting-ground of theirs; but they had sold out their title, and appeared to be very friendly. I knew a good many of them, for they would often come in and ask for something to eat, and I always treated them well. Some time in June, Mr. Hurd and another man left home on a trip to Dacotah, taking a span of horses and a wagon, expecting to be gone about a month. We had two children, and Mr. Voight was living with us, and had charge of the farm.

"He had been gone over two months, and I began to grow very anxious about him. One morning, the 20th of August [1862], — it was about five o'clock in the morning, — and I had just gone out to milking, and left my two children asleep in the house, when about twenty Indians rode up and jumped off their horses. I saw that one of the horses was in the span that Mr. Hurd had when he started on his trip. As soon as I got to the house, the Indians went in, and commenced to light their pipes and smoke. Pretty soon my youngest child woke up, and was frightened at seeing so many Indians, and began to cry. Mr. Voight took him up and carried him out into the front yard, when one of the Indians stepped to the door, and shot him through the body, so he fell dead, with the child in his arms. As soon as this shot was heard, ten or fifteen more Indians and squaws rushed into the house, and began to destroy everything they could lay their hands on. We had a good stock of cows, and I had worked hard, and had on hand about two hundred pounds of butter and twenty-three cheeses. All this the Indians destroyed; and while it was going on, some of them told me they would not kill me and the children if I would not give any alarm, but go east, by a very blind road, to the nearest settlement. They started me off just as I was, without even a sun-bonnet on, and would not let me dress either of the children.

"They went out with me about three miles. I took the youngest in my arms, and led the other, a little boy, between three and four years old. There were seven of them who started with me; and I took just one look at what had been our prosperous and happy home, now full of naked and painted savages.

"Before they left me they repeated the condition on which they would spare me and the children: that we were to keep straight east, across the open prairie; that all the whites were to be killed, but I might go to my mother. I was bareheaded, the children almost naked, and we had not a mouthful of food, nor a blanket to shelter us in the cool nights or in a storm. We took the unfrequented road into which the Indians had conducted us. It was clear, and the sun shone uncommonly bright; but the dew on the grass was cold and heavy. William Henry was barefoot, and dressed very thin, and he clung close to me, and begged me to go back to the house. He did not know of the death of Mr. Voight, as I kept him from seeing the body; and he cried piteously at first, but, after a while, pressed my hand, and trudged manfully along by my side. The little one was asleep in my arms, unconscious of our situation. About ten o'clock in the forenoon a thunder-storm came on, and the rain and wind were violent for about three hours. I heard two guns fired, and I knew that my neighbor, Mr. Cook, was killed.

"During the storm I lost the trail, and all that afternoon walked on, not knowing whether I was right or wrong. Water stood on all the lower parts of the prairie, and I kept looking for a dry place where we could spend the night. At last I came to a sand hill, and sat down on the top of it, to rest for the night. I laid my children down, and leaned over them, to keep the rain off their faces and protect them from the cold wind. Hungry, and tired, and wet as he was, William fell asleep, and slept nearly all night; but the little one worried a good deal, and the night wore away slowly. As soon as I could see, I took up the little ones, and moved on. About seven o'clock I heard guns, and then I knew I had lost my way, and was still in the vicinity of the lake. I changed my course, and went away from the direction in which the guns were heard. But no trail was visible. I was not conscious of hunger myself, but it was so distressing to hear my precious little boy crying for his bread and milk, and moaning with hunger and weakness! It was wet and misty all that day. Towards night William grew sick and vomited, and it seemed impossible for him to keep up any longer. The youngest still nursed, and did not seem to suffer materially.

"About dark, the second day, I struck a road, and saw, to my sorrow, that I was only four miles from what had been my home, and had not yet commenced my terrible journey across the prairie.

"Then, for a little while, my heart sank in me, and I thought it would be some satisfaction to die right there, and end our weary journey on this travelled road, over which I had passed with my husband in happier days. But this feeling was but for a moment. I took courage, and started on the road to New Ulm. When it was quite dark I stopped, and passed the night as I had the former, without sleep. In the morning I started on. It was foggy, and the grass wet; the road, being but little travelled, was grown up with grass. William was so faint and sick that he could not walk much of the time; so I was obliged to carry both. I was now much reduced in strength, and felt very hungry. My boy no longer asked for food, but was thirsty, and drank frequently from pools by the road-side. I was too weak to carry both my children at the same time, but took one a distance of a quarter or half a mile, laid it in the grass, and went back for the other. In this way I travelled twelve miles, to a place called Dutch Charlie's, sixteen miles from Lake Sheteck. I arrived there about sunset, having been sustained in my weary journey by the sweet hope of relief. What was my consternation and despair when I found it deserted and perfectly empty! The house had not been plundered by the Indians, but abandoned by the owner. My heart died within me, and I sank down in despair. But the crying of my boy aroused me. I had promised him food when we got there; and when none could be found, he cried bitterly. But I could not shed a tear. I found some green corn, which I tried to eat; but my stomach rejected it. I found some carrots and onions growing in the garden, which I ate raw. My oldest child continued to vomit. I offered him some carrot, but he could not eat it. That night I staid in a cornfield, and in the morning, at daylight, continued my search for food.

"To my great delight, I found the remains of a spoiled ham. Here I may say my good fortune began. There was no more than a pound of it, and that much decayed; and I saved this for my boy, feeding it to him in very small quantities. His vomiting ceased, and he revived rapidly. I gathered more carrots and onions; and with this store of provisions, about eight o'clock on the morning of the third day, I again set forth on my weary road for the residence of Mr. Brown, twenty-five miles distant, and reached it in two days. Under the effects of the food I was able to give my boy, he gained strength, and was able to walk all the last day. When within two or three miles of Mr. Brown's house, two of our old neighbors from Lake Sheteck settlement overtook us, under the escort of the mail-carrier. Both of them had been wounded by the Indians, and left for dead. Thomas Ireland had been hit with eight balls, and, strange to say, was still able to walk, and had done so most of the way. Mrs. Estleck was utterly unable to walk, having been shot in the foot, in the side, and through the arm. The mail-carrier had given her his seat in the buggy, and was walking beside the horse. At first I thought they were the Indians, and that I and my little ones, after five days of such fearful suffering and hunger, must die by the hands of the savages. I did not dare to look around, but kept on my way till overtaken; and then my joy was so great at seeing my friends alive, that I sank to the earth insensible. We staid at Mr. Brown's house ten days, living on potatoes and green corn. Mr. Ireland and the carrier went on to New Ulm, and found the settlement in ashes, the Indians having burned nearly two hundred houses. A party of twelve men, with a wagon, was sent to our relief, and we were made comfortable; but the sad and sickening thought was now fully confirmed in my mind that my husband had been killed in the general massacre of all the remote settlements, and my fatherless children and myself left beggars."

It is some gratification to know that the government has been very kind to these unhappy border sufferers, restoring to them the value of their property destroyed. Governor Ramsay considers that not less than five hundred persons were murdered by the savages, and that between twenty thousand and thirty thousand persons fled for their lives, leaving everything behind them. For some months between seven thousand and eight thousand persons, mostly in the sad condition of Mrs. Hurd, were dependent upon the charity of their friends. The property thus lost and destroyed was between two and three millions, most of which was restored by confiscating the annuity paid these Minnesota Sioux. It is also a satisfaction to know that in about a month after the date of these atrocious barbarities, the whole of these Indians were met by our troops in a battle at Wood Lake, on the 22d of September, and utterly defeated. Five hundred were taken prisoners, of whom three hundred were sentenced to be hanged; but the sentence was finally executed on thirty-eight only of the ringleaders. Little Crow, the chief who instigated the whole insurrection, succeeded in making his escape into the wilds of Dacotah.

Mrs. Hurd now finds a home with her brother, in La Crosse, Wisconsin; and though the government has dealt generously with her, and abundant sympathy has been manifested in her sufferings, nothing can bring back to her the murdered husband, the beauty, the loveliness, and the sunny future opening before her on that pleasant August morning, when, like the leap of a tiger, that storm of savage desolation swept upon her, and in a brief half hour left her to the awful consciousness of being a widow, houseless, and without food, with two almost naked children in an open prairie.

The great Latin poet has touched a chord of universal sympathy in his elegant description of the flight of his hero from burning Troy, bearing his aged father on his shoulders, and leading his little boy, who trotted along beside him, his little steps all unequal to the warrior's stride.

Our heroine bore her two children during a part of her fearful flight, but having been without food for nearly sixty hours, and all the time sustaining the little one on her arm by food from her bosom, was compelled to deposit half her precious cargo in the grass, and return for the other; thus, on the two days when she travelled, advancing twelve miles each day, herself walking thirty-six. Could the force of nature go farther? Do our annals anywhere contain a more remarkable instance of the wonderful sustaining power which maternal love can inspire in the delicate frame of woman?

MARGARET E. BRECKINRIDGE.

IN the midst of the tedious and disheartening siege of Vicksburg, when hundreds and thousands of our brave boys in blue were floundering in the mud of the Sunflower Swamp, and pneumonia and typhoid fever were slaying more than fell by the bullet, two ladies were standing on the deck of a steamer, in the rear of the beleaguered city.

One was unusually slender in figure; and, in the fine, strong lines of her nobly-modelled head, and the steady brightness of her dark eye, it was easy to read the marks of superior character, uncommonly fine natural abilities, and that heroic self-forgetfulness, which, since the days when the sand of the Roman amphitheatre was red with the blood of saints, has decorated the annals of Christianity with the long roll of holy martyrs. Even the devoted band of women who had gone down to nurse the sick and suffering soldiers in that dreary place, felt that she was, fatally to her own life, foremost in her devotion, and was, all too soon for those who loved her here, winning her celestial crown.

One present chided her eagerness for hospital labor, and said, "You must hold back; you are going beyond your strength; you will die if you are not more prudent."

Instantly the slender form dilated, and the dark eye glittered with the intense enthusiasm of her soul, as, with a voice of impressive earnestness, she exclaimed, "Well, what if I do! Shall men come here by tens of thousands, and fight, and suffer, and die, and shall not some women be willing to die to sustain and succor them?"

In a little more than a year from the time when Margaret Breckinridge uttered those thrilling and memorable words, she made good her utterances by her deeds; and the rich young life, full of promise, polished with the finest culture, and warm with beautiful affections, had been offered on the altar of patriotic zeal.

The blood that this noble girl carried in her veins, and the name she bore, were guarantees of a fine character. Her grandfather was John Breckinridge, of Kentucky, who in 1806 was taken from a high position in the national Senate to fill the office of Attorney-General of the United States, and died ere his faculties and his fame had reached their meridian, soon after taking his seat in the cabinet of Jefferson. His son, John Breckinridge, D. D., the father of Margaret, while a student at Princeton, in 1815, gave up the brilliant political career to which his great abilities and the name of his father in a manner committed him, and consecrating his talents to Christian virtue and the church, became the Ajax of Orthodox Christianity in the southwest, and afterwards a great light among the churches of Baltimore and of New Jersey.

Mrs. Breckinridge was the daughter of the Rev. Dr. Samuel Miller, who, though dead, yet speaketh to the churches through those great theological writings, which, with the productions of his colleague, Dr. Alexander, have become classics in the American church. When Margaret was six years old her mother died, and three years after, her gifted father, so that her tutelage and education fell to her grand-parents, at Princeton, in whose family she grew up to womanhood, though making long visits to Kentucky; and, after the marriage of her sister Mary, in 1852, having her home mostly in the family of that brilliant and patriotic martyr in the war, her brother-in-law, Colonel Peter A. Porter, of Niagara, who fell before Richmond, in the summer of 1864, leading his regiment in the deadly charges at Cole Harbor.

With so much in her family history and surroundings to breathe of patriotism, zeal, and devotion, it is not strange that, from the outset of the war, Margaret Breckinridge was possessed with the idea of becoming a hospital nurse while the war lasted. To do what she could, and all that she could, to aid in the fierce struggle against rebellion, was the object ever before her eyes, and filling her heart.

But the delicacy of her health, and an unwillingness to brave the kind dissuasion of all her friends, induced her to remain in Princeton till the spring of 1862, when the vast proportions and evident duration of the struggle became apparent to all.

But during this first year she did all she could with her pen, as well as her needles, to advance the common cause. The Princeton Standard has several articles by Miss Breckinridge, which compare favorably with the finest utterances of that stirring time.

Though the lips of a girl were at the mouthpiece of the

clarion, it gave no uncertain or feeble note. Take the following: —

"England has her standing army ready at her sovereign's call, but England never saw what we have seen. She never saw the hills and valleys start to life with armed men; and from the eastern seaboard, the northern hills, the western prairies, and the sunny plains and mountain sides which rebellion thought to claim, saw the growing streams pour inward to a common centre, leaving in their track the deserted workshop, the silent wheel, the idle tool, and the ungathered harvest. All was forgotten but the danger threatening the country in which each man was a sovereign, the city which belonged alike to all, and the rulers whom the right of suffrage had proclaimed the people's choice. Is not this as it should be? Surely they only who govern themselves can fight heartily and bravely for the preservation of that noble right of self-government.

"There is a legend of a holy man, to whom God spoke at midnight, and said, 'Rise, and write what I shall tell thee;' but he answered, 'Lord, I have no light.' And God said, 'Rise, and write as I bid thee, and I will give thee light.' So he obeyed. His fingers sought the pen, and as he touched it to the parchment, his hand glowed with light that streamed from under it, and illumined all the chamber. So it has been with us. It was the voice of God that roused us to see the peril which menaced liberty and union. It was only for the rescue of such liberty and such a Union as ours that a nation could have been so roused; and therefore from this very uprising come new light and strength; for that Union must be worth our lives and fortunes the possibility of whose destruction has called a nation to its feet. Yes, good seceding brothers, the Union is worth all that we can give; 'there are many things dearer to a nation than even blood and treasure;' and we must bring you home like the prodigal, and restore to you all that you have madly flung away, whatever it may cost us. You may hug to your bosoms the narrow liberties and loose-twisted union of your new Confederacy for a little while, but your waking will come as surely as ours. O, if he who stirred the people with his war-cry a hundred years ago, could come back now, and, standing where he stood then, gaze upon the ruins you have made, do you not think he would lift his hand to Heaven once more, praying, 'If this is liberty, O give me death!'"

In April, 1862, Miss Breckinridge left her home in Princeton for the West, and with the full intention of devoting herself to the soldiers for the war.

Remaining some weeks in Baltimore, she there commenced her hospital labors; and the letters she wrote from that place show the hearty satisfaction she took in the work, and the deep interest she felt in the individual cases committed to her care.

Here she contracted measles from some of the wards which she constantly visited, so that during this summer her health, never firm, received a serious shock. But in Lexington, Kentucky, where the summer and fall were passed, she resumed her work in the hospitals of that place.

Her pen, too, was busy, and she has left several incidents of Jack Morgan's and Kirby Smith's invasions, that are charmingly told, and throw much light on the real state of things in Kentucky that summer. One is too good to be omitted.

"On Tuesday, the 2d of September, Kirby Smith and his body-guard rode into Lexington, and took formal possession of the town without the firing of a gun. 'Lor, massa,' said one of his negro attendants, 'dis de easiest took town we got yet.' Flushed with his success, he issued an order for the observance of Jeff Davis' Thanksgiving Day, and notified the different clergymen that their churches must be opened. Perplexity sat upon reverend faces when the day came. But two churches were opened, and in one a secretly delighted pastor sat gazing at empty pews, and in the other a dismayed congregation sat gazing at an empty pulpit. At last they sent for General Smith to come and officiate in person.

"He went with a great deal more reluctance than he did into the first Bull Run battle, where his opportune arrival gave Johnston the victory; and when he reached the pulpit his embarrassment was not diminished to find them all Presbyterians, while what religion he had was of the Episcopal type. But he drew the prayer book from his pocket, read most of the service wrong, and without being sustained by any very prompt or hearty responses from the audience. At length, dismissing his little flock of goats, he came out of church a sadder and a wiser man, and found the good people of Lexington crowding around a train of Union ambulances, that were taking the wounded from the battle at Richmond, Kentucky, on to Cincinnati, — bidding them good by, filling their haversacks and canteens, and whispering to them, 'Every one of you, bring a regiment with you when you come back.'

"He confessed that he was not prepared for such a demonstration over Union soldiers, and such an utter lack of interest in Jeff Davis' Thanksgiving Day.

"'Where does General Smith preach this morning?' said a lovely Union lady to the sentinel at headquarters, the next Sunday.

"'You are mistaken, ma'am,' replied the obtuse sentinel. 'General Smith *isn't a preacher at all.*'"

In the fall of 1862 Miss Breckinridge left Kentucky to spend the winter in St. Louis with her brother, Judge Breckinridge, whose house was her western home. Immediately on her arrival she commenced her visits at the hospitals in that city. After two days spent at Jefferson Barracks, she says, "I shall never be satisfied till I get right into a hospital to live till the war is over. If you are constantly with the men, you have hundreds of opportunities and moments of influence in which you can gain their attention and their hearts, and do more good than in any missionary field."

In December, 1862, Grant commenced the movements that in July following gave Vicksburg to the Union arms and opened the Mississippi from its source to its mouth. Throughout this winter, from December to March, Miss Breckinridge realized her wish, being constantly with the men in the hospital, for she passed her whole time on the transports or at the great hospitals at Young's Point and at Helena, where five thousand died from disease, and there were at one time twelve thousand sick.

Mrs. J. C. Hoge, of Chicago, one of her colaborers in that field, has given, in a few paragraphs and incidents, a fine picture of Miss Breckinridge as a hospital nurse:—

"It has been my privilege to know many devoted women in our American hospitals; but I can truly say, no one has impressed me as she did. Her fragile form, beaming face, musical voice, and youthful appearance, were wonderfully fascinating to the soldiers. Her transparent purity and simple dignity awed them, and as I have visited them, from cot to cot, I have heard, after she had passed, the outburst of a soldier's enthusiastic gratitude again and again.

"'Ain't she an angel?' said a gray-haired veteran to me, as I followed her on the steamer City of Alton, to assist her in giving the boys their breakfast. 'She never seems to tire; she is always smiling, and don't seem to walk. She flies all but. God bless her!'

"Said another, a fair boy of seventeen summers, as she smoothed his hair, and told him, with glistening eyes, he would soon see his mother and the old homestead, and be won back to life and health,—'Ma'am, where do you come from? How could such a lady as you are come way down here to take care of us poor, sick, dirty boys?' Said she, 'I consider it an honor to wait on you, and wash off the mud you've waded through for me.'

"Said another, 'Lady, please write down your name, and let me look at it, and take it home, and show my wife who wrote my letters, and combed my hair, and fed me. I don't believe you are like other people.'

"And then, as she passed on, they would fold their hands, and say, 'God bless her, and spare her life.' Thus her days passed; and though God soon took her to himself, her weeks of army labor might count as years for the usefulness and the blessings with which they were crowded.

"In her tour of a week with me through the north-west to visit the Aid Societies, her earnestness and whole-souled devotion to the soldiers' interests overcame her timidity, and she was induced to tell some interesting facts concerning the sufferings of the soldiers and loyal people in the border states. Her memory is fragrant now among these simple-hearted, patriotic people. She stirred them up to increased labor, and the mention of her name, and allusion to her death, bring forth tears from those who only saw and heard her once, but they loved her. She pleaded her own cause eloquently when admonished to rest from hospital work. She had counted the cost, and stood ready to die, if need be, as the hero in the front ranks of battle. Methinks the crown she now wears must be richly studded with immortal souls, for in all her army work she preached Christ, and him crucified."

The letters of Miss Breckinridge, written on board the transports, from Helena, and St. Louis, are full of the most touching accounts of sick and dying soldiers. The following is, no doubt, one that she related with effect to the various ladies' Aid Societies which she visited with Mrs. Hoge: —

"Soon after the capture of one of the rebel forts in the west, a lady went into the hospital where the wounded had been taken. She was much attracted by two young men, lying side by side, all splintered and bandaged, so that they could not move hand or foot, but so cheerful and happy-looking, that she said, —

"'Why, boys, you look very bright to-day!'

"'O, yes,' they said, 'we're all right now. We've been turned this morning.'

"And she found that for six long weeks they had lain in one position, and for the first time that morning had been moved to the other side of their cot.

"'And were you,' she asked, 'among those poor boys who were left lying where you fell that bitter morning, till you froze fast to the ground?' 'Yes, ma'am,' they said, 'we were lying there two days. You know they had no time to attend to us; they had to go and take the fort.' 'And didn't you think it was very cruel in them to leave you to suffer so long?' '*Why, no, ma'am; we wanted them to go and take the fort.*'

"'But, when they took it, you were in too much agony to know or care for it?'

"'O, no, ma'am!' they answered, with flashing eyes, and faces glowing with the recollections of that day; 'there were a whole lot of us wounded fellows on the hill-side, watching to see if they would get the fort. When we saw they had it, every one of us that had a whole arm waved it in the air, and we hurrahed till the air rang again.'"

In a letter published in the Princeton Standard, and describing a trip on a hospital transport from St. Louis to Young's Point, and back to Memphis, she says, "There's a soldier's song of which they are very fond, and which I will copy for you some day, one verse of which often comes back to me: —

'So I've had a sight of drilling,
And I've roughed it many days;
Yes, and death has nearly had me;
Yet I think the service pays.'

"Indeed, it does — richly, abundantly, blessedly; and I thank God that he has honored me by letting me do a little and suffer a little for this grand old Union, and the dear, brave fellows who are fighting for it.

"Just before we parted with our boat-load of sick at Memphis, one of my convalescents, a fine, trustworthy fellow, came to me with a little note, which he handed me without a word. 'Read it at your leisure,' he said, when I asked him what it was. It contained a few honest, touching, simple words of thanks, written in the name of all the sick in my ward, and you may well imagine it is a greater treasure to me than an autograph letter from the greatest man on earth would be.

"I don't know that I have ever told you how much I am amused by the curiosity of people as to *how much salary I get*, and how often I am assailed with the question, 'How much do you get a month?' At first I was indignant; now I laugh over it."

In March her health was found too much impaired to allow her to make any more trips on the transports; but in St. Louis she continued to visit the hospitals, and labor among the refugees and freedmen. She was busy also with her pen, and in sewing and knitting for the soldiers. The natural wondering as to who might wear the socks upon which her fingers were occupied, she has expressed in the following graceful lines, published at the time in the Princeton Standard: —

"Here I sit, at the same old work,
Knitting and knitting from daylight till dark;
Thread over and under, and back and through,

Knitting socks for — I don't know who;
But in fancy I've seen him, and talked with him too.

"He's no hero of gentle birth,
He's little in rank, but he's much in worth;
He's plain of speech, and strong of limb;
He's rich in heart, but he's poor of kin;
There are none at home to work for him.

"He set his lips with a start and a frown
When he heard that the dear old flag was shot down
From the walls of Fort Sumter, and, flinging away
His tools and his apron, stopped but to say
To his comrades, '*I'm going*, whoever may stay;'
And was 'listed and gone by the close of the day.

"And whether he watches to-night on the sea,
Or kindles his camp-fire on lone Tybee,
By river or mountain, wherever he be,
I know he's the noblest of all that are there,
The promptest to do, and the bravest to dare,
The strongest in trust, and the last to despair.

"So here I sit at the same old work,
Knitting socks for the soldiers from daylight till dark,
And whispering low, as the thread flies through,
To him who shall wear them, — I don't know who, —
'Ah, my soldier, fight bravely; be patient, be true·
For some one is knitting and praying for you.'"

She remained in St. Louis until about the middle of May, when she visited Chicago, and made those visits to the various Aid Societies alluded to in the letter of Mrs. Hoge. She then proceeded to Niagara, her health steadily declining, and passed the summer, fall, and winter at Princeton, the sea-side, and Philadelphia, cherishing all the time the hope that she would be able to resume her work in hospitals very soon; but she only saw these successive hopes end in disappointment, like receding phantoms before the traveller in Arabia.

She received no permanent benefit from anything. The subtle miasmatic poison of the Mississippi swamps lurked in her system, and was slowly bringing her to the grave. Yet in the spring of 1864, while at Philadelphia, she was in frequent attendance at the Episcopal Hospital, and begged of the surgeons to allow her to go with them in their round of the surgical wards, that she might become more skilled and useful to wounded men.

A Christian friend and co-laborer has furnished the following beautiful account of her labors here, in a letter written after Miss Breckinridge's death, and directed to one of her near relatives: —

"Besides her desire to acquire experience in surgical cases, she expressed an earnest wish to do what she could for the spiritual welfare of the patients in our hospital, hoping in the time spent there to acquire more facility in speaking for Christ.

"She came to the hospital early in May, 1864, lovely in form and feature, full of animation and enthusiasm, overflowing with sympathy and tenderness. In her presence there was always sunshine, and her bright spirit tinged and influenced all about her. Immediately she began to interest herself in the patients, spending an hour or two in the morning, following the surgical nurse, who instructed her in the best mode of bandaging and treating the various wounds. She was not satisfied with *seeing* this, but often washed and dressed the wounds with her own hands, saying to me, with her bright smile, 'I shall be able to do this for the soldiers when I get back to the army.' The patients could not understand this, and would often expostulate, and say, 'O, no, miss! that is not for the likes of you to be doing;' but she would playfully insist, and have her way.

"Her attention in the wards was constant. With her little Testament in her hand, she went from one bedside to another, a ministering angel to all there, cheering the desponding, encouraging the timid and doubtful. While I write I have been interrupted by a visit from an old colored woman, who was in the hospital last spring. I asked her if she remembered Miss Breckinridge. She looked surprised at the question, and said, 'Yes, indeed; I never could forget her. She was so good to old Sidney. Why, she never went to her bed without looking in on me to see how I was getting on. O, I never saw her like. She used to sing to me, too. Now she is singing Jesus' praise in heaven. She was *my* lady!'

"At twilight it was her custom to sing hymns in the ward, and long after she had left us, her sweet voice was spoken of as a blessing lost by the sick and suffering. A universal favorite with officers, nurses, patients, and lady visitors, many a tear was shed when the intelligence of her death reached us."

In June, just as she was expecting and preparing to go out to Virginia, to resume her army labors, and while suffering from a severe attack of erysipelas, there came the appalling news that her beloved brother-in-law, Colonel Porter, had been killed at Cold Harbor. The blow fell upon her with overwhelming force. There was one wild cry of agony, — one hour of unmitigated agony, — and then a saintly submission to the will of her heavenly Father.

"I saw her last," says Mrs. Hoge, "in Philadelphia, in June, 1864. The frail tenement of her soaring spirit was tottering; the fastenings were being removed surely, but noiselessly. Her great grief was that she was laid aside from her work just, as she said, when she was learning to do it so much better.

"Her great desire to recover was, that she might labor till war was over. None of us realized that she was so near the final rest. Her Christ-like self-abnegation and devotion sealed her frequent exhortations to the patients that she visited, as long as her health permitted. God grant the beautiful, inspiring lesson of her life and death may not be lost to us, her fellow-workers who survive."

After the great blow of Colonel Porter's death, she for a time abandoned her efforts to resume army labor, saying, quietly, "I can do more good at Niagara than anywhere else just now."

After a little rest in Baltimore, she accompanied the sad family party to Niagara, and apparently bore the journey with comfort and safety; but the night after her arrival at the house of her cousin, Miss Porter, she became alarmingly ill, and lay down never to rise again.

The inroads of disease soon reduced that intellectual vivacity and earnestness which characterized her talk and the productions of her pen while strength remained. Five weeks her life hung trembling in the balance; and if unwearied attentions and practised skill could have averted the stroke of death, so fair a light had not been quenched.

But that could not be; and, on the 27th of July, the blessed vision, of which she had often caught glimpses, became for her a grand and permanent reality.

Beside the ashes of her beloved sister and brother, the vast Niagara, roaring its sublime monotone as her dirge, sleeps now the fragile casket of this "gem of purest ray serene;" and her voice, no longer now uttering hymns of Christian cheer beside the cots of dying soldiers, chimes with that chorus that John heard in the Apocalypse, saying, "Blessing, and honor, and power, forever and ever, be unto Him that washed us, and made our robes white in the blood of the Lamb."

MRS. ELIDA RUMSEY FOWLE.

LATE in the fall of 1861, an irregular and wretched-looking crowd of Union soldiers moved slowly up one of the broad avenues of the national capital. Coming from a great number of regiments, without proper organization or *esprit du corps*, emaciated, sallow-looking, and ragged, how fearfully had they changed from that gay, confident, and shouting army, that in July had moved out from Arlington Heights, with "On to Richmond!" for their watchword! Yet they were the same men. Only these poor fellows had been captured in the disastrous rout of Bull Run; had been marched, in the midst of taunts and jeers, into the rebel capital; had been confined in that wretched and filthy slaughter and tobacco house in Richmond, over which the sign "A. Libby & Co." had been fastened — a name now infamous in military history. During the long, hot months of August, September, and October, the poor fellows had sweltered in that reeking pen, breathing foul air, eating miserable rebel army rations, and apparently forgotten by that great government for which they had so freely fought, and which they had thought abundantly able to reach and protect her citizen-soldiers in all parts of the world. Yet, in the city that once rang with the eloquence of Patrick Henry, a city that had given to America such men as Jefferson, Madison, and John Marshall, they had been jeered at, insulted, and starved for the crime of having volunteered to save the national ensign from dishonor, and the national unity from destruction.

They halted for some time before one of the government buildings, these rough, unhappy looking men. They were conscious of being dirty and seedy looking. They had been captured in a battle which loyal Americans were nowise proud to mention; and though they had done their duty, and done it nobly, and borne their insults and discomforts with soldier-like patience, yet, standing thus crestfallen under the towering dome of the Capitol, the enthusiasm with which they had enlisted was all gone; the proud Americanism that had swelled in their bosoms was dull and cold. In short, these exchanged prisoners were demoralized by disaster and suffering, and had for a time become indifferent to the glories and traditions of their country.

As they stood or sat there on the ground, a pleasant-spoken gentleman — a clerk at one of the desks of the navy department — stepped among them, and said, "Boys, how would you like to hear a little song this morning?" "O, very well, I guess," was the somewhat languid response.

He retired for a moment, and returned with a young lady, whose modest manner and flushed face told, better than any words, how entirely unaccustomed she was to making any public exhibition of her vocal powers. She sang the first stanza of "Star-spangled Banner." As the almost forgotten strains of that great national song rang out on the cool autumnal air, every soldier started up from his attitude of languor and indifference, and came nearer to the fascinating singer.

They formed a circle around her, and as those on the outside of the ring complained that they could not see her, some one said, "Make a stand for her." Instantly, as though a command had been given, fifty knapsacks were unslung, and piled in a rude pyramid before her. She stepped upon it flushed, and still more animated by this sudden and novel mode of expressing their high appreciation of her effort, and sang the remaining stanzas with a warmth and enthusiasm that surprised her as much as it delighted the soldiers. The effect upon the men was marvellous.

> "The present scene, their future lot,
> Their toils, their wants, were all forgot;
> Cold diffidence and age's frost
> In the full tide of song were lost."

The pleasant memories of singing schools and sleigh rides were revived. They thought of their sisters, and "the girls they left behind them." The bloody afternoon at Bull Run, and the long, dreary days within the loathsome walls of Old Libby, the suffering, the blood, and deaths were all forgotten. They only remembered that the glorious old flag still floated from the top of the "imperial dome," and that America was still the "land of the free and the home of the brave."

Miss Rumsey stepped down from that little rostrum of soldiers' knapsacks animated with patriotic enthusiasm, and inspired with a new and noble purpose.

Others might idly regret that they were women, and could not take the sword or bayonet in the holy cause. Others, again, might follow the camp, and minister in person to the wounded and dying. She, too, had a gift and a mission. There was good for her to do in soothing, cheering, and sustaining the soldiers. The rare and beautiful gift of *voice* could now be consecrated on the altar of patriotism, and the songs which she had learned and practised to please her father and enhance the attractions of his home, might now fan the dying flame of patriotism in a thousand war-weary bosoms; they might ring along the wards of the great hospitals, bring joy back to many a faded eye; or, breathed low and sweet at the pillow of the dying, they would smooth the ruggedness of the dark valley, and awaken holy aspirations for the

> "undisturbed song of pure concent
> Aye sung before the sapphire-colored throne,
> To Him that sits thereon."

From that time on, till after the battle of Gettysburg, and near the close of the war, Miss Rumsey gave herself unremittingly to labors for the good, the comfort, the social, moral, and mental well-being of the soldier. She was as wholly devoted and absorbed in such voluntary labors as though she had enlisted, and was in duty bound, and under a military oath of consecration.

Her father's house was opposite Judiciary Square, and several hospitals were situated within a short distance. Of these she became a frequent, and, in many cases, a regular and constant visitor. And in all the wards she visited, she never hesitated to afford the soldiers the benefit of her vocal powers whenever she was requested; and very often she volunteered to sing for those who were strangers and unacquainted with her gifts, and with her promptness to comply with that request when made. On Sabbath afternoons, and often during the week, she, in company with Mr. Fowle and other Christian gentlemen, visited various hospitals, and held soldiers' prayer meetings in different wards, singing the most familiar and widely-known songs of religious love and worship.

Yet these labors, important and valuable as they were, are regarded by her and her friends as secondary and incidental merely, as compared with the great and admirable enterprise with which her name was chiefly associated, and for which she is held in grateful remembrance by tens of thousands of soldiers.

It was mainly by the exertions of Mr. Fowle and Miss Rumsey that the Soldiers' Free Library, on Judiciary Square, in Washington, was established, the building erected, the books contributed and arranged, and the library conducted. During some epochs in the war, Washington city contained as many as twenty thousand sick, wounded, or convalescent soldiers. By far the greater portion of these men could read, and two thirds or three fourths of them were in such health as to be able to move or hobble about on crutches; and thus, above all things, they needed some wholesome and moral amusement during convalescence.

A library free to all soldiers, and well supplied with papers, magazines, and all sorts of valuable and entertaining, yet moral books, was an institution of the utility of which there could be no doubt, and whose power to cheer, elevate, and entertain could not be over-estimated. Miss Rumsey had numerous friends, in different villages in the north, who were known as soldiers' friends, and who knew her as an efficient and constant hospital visitor. She was the almoner of the various comforts and delicacies which had been contributed by various soldiers' Aid Societies in Connecticut, Massachusetts, and New York. To these societies Miss Rumsey now applied, and very handsome returns of books and papers were made. During the year 1862 these books and magazines were distributed by Miss Rumsey and Mr. Fowle in their hospital visits. In a little more than a year they distributed two thousand three hundred and seventy-one Bibles and Testaments, one thousand six hundred and seventy-five books and magazines, forty thousand tracts, thirty-five thousand papers, twenty-five reams of writing paper, nine thousand envelopes; and of "creature comforts," over three thousand shirts and drawers, great quantities of towels, sheets, gowns, slippers, wines, and jellies.

During this period, they conducted nearly two hundred singing meetings at hospitals, or in camp. In the fall of 1862, the arrangements then in operation were found inconvenient and inadequate to supply the literary demands at the hospital, and the plan was conceived of raising a sum sufficient to erect on some public ground a building of sufficient size and proper construction, to be used as the Soldiers' Free Library.

To carry forward this worthy enterprise, Miss Rumsey

and Mr. Fowle gave in Washington, Boston, and various other places, a number of vocal concerts, the proceeds of which were to be devoted to the purchase of the necessary lumber, and procuring labor for constructing the library.

These concerts were a success. Their principal feature was the songs of Miss Rumsey, and particularly those stirring and patriotic airs which she sang to so many of the soldiers. "The Star-spangled Banner,"as sung by her, was always received with rounds of applause, and every mark of the warmest enthusiasm. "The Young Recruit" and the "Battle Cry of Freedom" were also favorite and effective. Another song, of soft and pathetic character, met with great success, and had a touching private history. It was called "The Dying Soldier Boy." In May, 1862, soon after the bloody action at Williamsburg, Miss Rumsey, in her hospital visits, found a poor boy, only seventeen years of age, at the Patent Office Hospital, who had suffered from typhoid fever, and this was followed by consumption. Day by day he grew paler and weaker, till at last he could speak only in whispers. Yet the dear little fellow was conscious that he was about to die, and was prepared to go. Miss Rumsey was much interested in his case, and at twilight she would often visit him, and at his request would, in a low, soft voice, sing in the ear of the dying soldier boy songs of Jesus and of heaven that he loved to hear. One evening, just as the sun had set, she found him failing rapidly; and, "I want to hear a hymn," he whispered. That charming little melody, called "Nearer Home," was his favorite. It begins thus: —

"One sweetly solemn thought
  Comes to me o'er and o'er:
Nearer my parting hour am I
  Than e'er I was before."

A group of sympathizing soldiers gathered around his bed-side. Her voice choked and faltered, and the tears stood upon her cheeks, as she sang the first, second, and third stanzas. Before commencing the fourth she glanced down at the pallid face, and saw that a fearful change had come over the marble features. King Death had stolen upon him as he listened, and stamped his royal signet on the countenance of the boy soldier. The last human sounds he had heard were the plaintive tones of that sweet vocalist, singing to him of the heavenly home and the starry crown. A poetical version of this affecting scene was made by Mr. Fowle, in the following stanzas, which Miss Rumsey sang to the tune of "Annie Laurie:"—

THE DYING SOLDIER BOY.

Sing me a song before I go,
  Said the dear and dying boy;
"Nearer Home" is the one I love;
  O, sing of heavenly joy.
Sing, for "I'm going home,"
  Over the "crystal sea;"
I'm going to join the angel throng,
  And spend eternity.

With faint and trembling voice we sang
  Of "laying my burden down;"
We sang the sweet, sweet words,
  "Wearing my starry crown;"

And then the soldier smiled.
  As his spirit soared above,
He left "*his* cross of heavy grief,"
  To spend a life of love.

Brave boy! we mourn your fate;
  Your life was nobly given;
Far from home, and far from friends,
  You gave up earth for heaven.
No stone may mark the spot
  Where our Soldier Boy is laid,
But in our hearts he has a place,
  A spot in memory made.

Our country mourns for heroes brave,
  Who've died to save our land.
Our hearts, how oft they bleed
  For many a noble band!
And at their hallowed graves
  We *all* shall pilgrims be;
We'll shed a tear for those who've died
  For RIGHT and LIBERTY!

Another favorite piece of Miss Rumsey, which she gave in nearly all the concerts, was composed by the same gentleman, at the time when the first rebel flags which had been captured at Fort Donelson and Roanoke Island were exhibited at the Capitol in Washington, on the anniversary of the birth of the Father of his Country, February 22, 1862. Miss Rumsey usually sang it to the air of "Bunker Hill."

THE REBEL FLAGS.

Sadly we gazed upon the flags
  Torn from our brothers' hands,
And shed a tear for those once loved,
  Now joined to traitor bands.

They've put our flag beneath their feet,
They've trailed it in the dust,
And to the breeze their flag unfurled,
And placed in it their trust.

Mark what a treacherous deed it was,
From the good old flag to turn;
With us they dwelt beneath its folds,
And now its stars they spurn.
They've left the flag of Washington,
The flag our fathers gave;
A richer boon was never given,
Or prouder flag to wave!

But when the traitors raised their flag,
And marshalled for the fight,
Six hundred thousand freemen rose
To battle for the right.
Then to our God the prayer went up,
"Protect our noble band;"
God blessed our cause; our flag now waves
Within the traitors' land.

Then down, down with the rebel flags;
Tread them beneath your feet;
And gayly to the breeze unfurl
The flag we love to greet.
Wave on, ye glorious "STARS AND STRIPES!"
And still our song shall be —
Long live, long live the good old flag;
Three cheers, three cheers for THEE.

Two of these concerts realized the sum of three hundred dollars, and this was immediately expended in the purchase of lumber for the building of the Soldiers' Free Library. Upon the opening of the next session of Congress, in December, a joint resolution passed both Houses, appropriating the ground necessary for the erection of the building. Early in January the following note was handed to Miss Rumsey.

SENATE CHAMBER, *January* 7, 1863.

MISS ELIDA B. RUMSEY, 423 FIFTH STREET.

Madam: The joint resolution of the House of Representatives authorizing the Secretary of the Interior to grant permission to erect a building on Judiciary Square for the purpose of a library for the use of the soldiers, &c., has *just passed the Senate.*

Very respectfully, SOLOMON FOOTE.

Other concerts were now given, and the proceeds appropriated to the same purpose, so that within a few weeks, in the early part of the year 1863, Mr. Fowle and Miss Rumsey had the gratification of seeing their most laudable and self-sacrificing efforts crowned with success. A building sixty-five feet long, and twenty-four feet wide, was erected, containing a library-room, a room for hospital stores, and a reading-room, which, with appropriate ceremonies, was dedicated to the free use of the soldiers. After the building was completed and dedicated, a circular was issued to the friends of soldiers everywhere, requesting contributions of magazines, pictorial papers, and books.

The results of this appeal, and the proceeds of several concerts given in Boston and vicinity, were so handsome in pecuniary returns and in books, that soon after the library opened it contained twenty-five hundred volumes. This number was soon swelled to three thousand, and before the war closed there were six thousand volumes of good reading matter on the shelves of the institution. For some time Miss Rumsey acted as librarian. But afterwards convalescents, not able to return to line duty, were successively detailed for this purpose. One who acted for some time in this capacity was a loyal Virginian from the valley of the Shenandoah.

The following letter from him conveys the sentiments of at least one soldier on the value of the Soldiers' Free Library: —

BERKELEY COUNTY, VA., *October* 29, 1864.

TO MR. AND MRS. JOHN A. FOWLE.

Kind and highly-esteemed Friends: Though two, yet I will address you as *one*, for you are *one* in every good work, and in devotion to the interests of the soldier.

How often have I blessed you in my heart for originating and getting up the Soldiers' Free Library! How I enjoyed the meetings there! I fear you overrate my services as librarian, and give me more credit than I deserve; for I only did what was my duty to do. My most pleasant hours in Washington were spent in the library, and if I should ever visit it again, it will be the most attractive place to me in the capital.

Matters are very quiet in the valley now, and have been since the late fight. I tell you, Sheridan gave the rebs Hail, Columbia, and Yankee Doodle combined on the 19th of this month, and I do not think their army will trouble us again this winter.

For your kind wishes, so happily expressed, please accept my sincere thanks. May Heaven bless and reward you, both in this life and that which is to come, for your kindness and labors of love in behalf of our soldiers.

Your sincere Friend.

During all the time that Miss Rumsey was laboring thus persistently and nobly to found the library, the visits to hospitals and camps, and the Sabbath exercises in the Representatives' Hall, and among the soldiers, were by no means discontinued.

In that dark and calamitous campaign of August and September, 1862, she at one time went out into the primary hospitals, and labored among the wounded and dying of a disastrous battle-field. It was just after the second battle of Bull Run, fought August 30, 1862. Mr. Fowle obtained an ambulance, and Miss Rumsey loaded it with some four hundred and fifty loaves of bread, meat, spirits of all kinds, bandages, lint, shirts, and other descriptions of stores. Leaving Washington late on Saturday afternoon, they drove out by way of Bailey's Cross-Roads, and reached Centreville very early on Sunday morning.

They halted at a little building near the road, which was already nearly full of the wounded. As others arrived, or were brought in, they were laid on those first brought, care being taken, however, to lay a wounded arm upon a sound leg, and a mutilated leg upon a body where its weight would not give pain. The stacks of wounded were thus laid up on all sides of the little room, and the blood that flowed from so many open veins ran down and stood in a deep crimson pool all over the middle of the room. For some time Miss Rumsey remained in the ambulance, giving out bread to the famishing boys, who crowded around as soon as it was known there was anything to be eaten there. Most of them had eaten nothing for twenty-four hours, and were hopelessly separated from their supply trains. After she had given out most of the bread and other edibles, she stepped down from the ambulance, and went inside, to see if she could be of use to the sufferers there.

Certainly there was enough to be done, and she felt that the only way to keep from being overcome by such an accumulation of horrors was to plunge at once into active usefulness. She offered to dress the arm of the first man she saw. He had received a ball directly through it the day before, and a field surgeon had dressed it, and wrapped it so tightly that it was now paining him terribly. Miss Rumsey knelt beside him, and slowly undid the bandage. The flesh was entirely colorless, and the pain was relieved as the pressure was removed. She then brought some water and a sponge, and began to wash the wound.

The contact of water and the gentle pressure of the sponge soon removed the dried and coagulated blood, and the wound commenced to bleed afresh. Soon the blood began to flow in little spouts, and as there was no surgeon present, she became alarmed. Some of the crimson stream fell upon her dress, and the floor was everywhere red. It was a hot summer morning, and she had been travelling all night. The room, too, was crowded, and the smell of human blood was strong. All these, operating together, were too much for Miss Rumsey. All at once she found her consciousness failing her, and in a moment she was as helpless as any of the wounded that lay upon the floor. She was taken out to the ambulance, and the usual restoratives of cold water and fresh air applied. With the return of consciousness she began to chide herself—"To think that I have come all the way from Washington to bind up the wounds of these soldiers, and here the first case of running blood I see I have to become faint and helpless! I won't faint. I will go back, and work among those poor fellows; that's what I came here for, and I'm determined to accomplish something." So in a few moments she was back again among the bleeding men, a little paler than before, but resolute. She went on binding up wounds, bathing them with water, cooling parched lips, and giving stimulants to those who had lost much blood, laboring thus all day till nearly nightfall. Two or three other parties, that had come out from Washington on similar errands of mercy, seeing her thus efficient and useful, left their hospital supplies with her, and thus she was kept busy throughout the day. The good things were given out to privates and officers without discrimination, the only requirement being that they needed something. Their little hospital would hold about fifty, and as fast as their wounds were dressed they were sent off in ambulances to Washington. Only two soldiers died under their care: one, whose name and regiment were unknown, wandered in from the battle-field, fell down speechless from sheer exhaustion, and died in a few moments. His body was searched in vain for papers that might disclose his name and regiment, but no clew was ever obtained. A grave was dug beside the little hospital on Sunday evening, his body was decently interred, and the grave marked with that saddest of all inscriptions, "UNKNOWN."

The other who died was a non-commissioned officer in a New York regiment. He had been struck in the breast, and the severe concussion produced inward bleeding, of which he died, unable to speak; but a letter from home was found in his pocket, and proved that he was a dutiful and good son. A small sum of money was found with the letter, of which Miss Rumsey took charge; and immediately upon reaching Washington she wrote a full and feeling account to his distant and stranger friends. She had the gratification of receiving a prompt and grateful answer from his father, and her first letter was published in connection with a funeral sermon preached at Springwater, N. Y., in commemoration of the virtues of Corporal James F. Snyder.

A few months later, as she was nursing in one of the hospitals on Judiciary Square, and near her home as well as the Soldiers' Free Library, in which she took so great and constant interest, she found one of the patients in a very dangerous state. He had been wounded at Chancellorsville, and hopes were entertained that he would recover. But the injury was close to a main artery, and the suppuration extended so as to involve its tissues, and he suddenly commenced to sink from internal bleeding.

When he found his strength failing, he desired to have the Bible read and prayer offered at his bedside. Then turning to Mrs. Fowle, he said there was one thing more that he would like to say before he died. "Will you, kind lady, write to Miss ——, to whom I have been engaged for the last two years, and break to her the sad news? Tell her all I have said; send her my pocket memorandum, my gold pen, and the twelve dollars in the book." A few moments after, he added, in a clear but faint voice, "Tell Deming," — a wounded comrade from the same town, —

"if he ever gets well, to tell my friends *that I was wounded bravely fighting for my country, and die happy.*"

The sacred duty of carrying out the last wish of this dying patriot was carefully performed.

This was but one of many similar instances, and a great number of letters have been received by her from the friends of deceased soldiers, assuring her of their esteem and gratitude, in language like the following: "My Bible teaches there is a reward in store for you, aside from the present satisfaction of having done what you could to relieve the sufferings of a fellow-mortal, for Christ said, 'Inasmuch as ye have done it unto one of the least of these my brethren, ye have done it unto me.'"

In the spring of 1863, after the completion and opening of the Soldiers' Free Library, and as there was much less demand for constant hospital labor, Miss Rumsey was united for life with the gentleman whose name has several times appeared on these pages, and who labored constantly and most effectively with Miss Rumsey for the physical and moral well-being of the soldier.

As Mr. Fowle and Miss Rumsey had acquired almost a national reputation by their admirable and extensive labors, and as they had long been connected with the Capitol choir, their marriage was celebrated in the House of Representatives, and by their old and intimate friend and associate in every good work, Chaplain Quint.

Though retaining a constant and lively interest in the Union and its defenders, the duties and enjoyments of Mrs. Fowle, since the close of the war, and for a year previous, have been the blessed and womanly enjoyments of a home made sacred by love and enriched by the sweetest fireside melodies.

In the midst of these pleasures, the richest memories of her life are of those active and crowded months when the national fortunes were lowest, and she was laboring with hands and feet, with needle, pen, and voice, to relieve, to sustain, to cheer, and to soothe the weary, destitute, or dying Union soldier.

BRIDGET DIVERS.

THE Heroines of the Great War for the Union, like its heroes, have come from every class of society, and represent every grade in our social scale. Ladies of the highest refinement and social polish have left homes of luxury, and devoted themselves, week after week, and month after month, to daily labor and nightly vigils in the wards of great hospitals.

No less praiseworthy and admirable have been the devotion and self-sacrifice of those who were born in less favored circles, and brought with them to the work, if not the elegance of the boudoir, the hearty good will, the vigorous sense, and the unwearied industry of the laboring class.

If the antecedents and manners of Bridget Divers, whom Sheridan's men commonly knew as "Irish Biddy," were not those of what the world calls "a lady," she proved herself possessed of the heart of a true, brave, loyal, and unselfish woman, who devoted herself, from the beginning to the end of the war, to the good of the soldier, with such uncalculating generosity, that she deserves and enjoys the grateful remembrance and the unfeigned respect of every patriot who saw anything of her admirable labor.

In the commencement of the war, she went out with the First Michigan cavalry, and through the war continued to act with and for that organization. But as she became familiar with the army, and well known in it, she extended her labors so as to reach the wants of the brigade, and even the division to which the First Michigan belonged.

She knew every man in the regiment, and could speak of his character, his wants, his sufferings, and the facts of his military record. Her care and kindness extended to the moral and religious wants, as well as the health, of the men of her regiment, as she always called it. In the absence of the chaplain she came to the Christian Commission for books and papers for the men, saying that she was the acting chaplain, and appearing to take a very deep interest in the moral and religious well-being of them all.

It made no difference to her in what capacity she acted, or what she did, so be it was necessary for the good of the men.

Acting now as *vivandière* or daughter of the regiment, now as nurse, hospital steward, ward master, and sometimes as surgeon, she was invaluable in each capacity. From her long experience with wounds and disease, her judgment came to be excellent, and her practical skill equal often to that of a physician. In drawing various supplies from the Sanitary and Christian Commission she showed good judgment, and knew just what the men really wanted, never encouraging waste or recklessness in distribution, while she was really very kind and tender-hearted.

Her whole soul was in the work of aiding and sustaining the soldier. No day was too stormy or too cold to check her in an errand of mercy. She overcame all obstacles, and battled successfully with all sorts of rebuffs and discouragements in the prosecution of her duties.

When the Christian Commission received letters from home, which was very frequently the case, inquiring for a soldier, if the man was believed to be even in the division to which she was attached, Bridget was the first person to whom application was made. If it was in "her brigade," as she called it, she could tell all about him. If in the division, she was more likely to know than the commanding officer or the adjutant, and could generally give all the desired information. Her memory of names and places was truly wonderful.

When the brigade was in active service she was with it in the field, and shared all its dangers. She was a fearless and skilful rider, and as brave as the bravest under fire.

In actual battle she had two or three horses killed under her, and in the course of the war lost eight or ten in various ways.

In the battle of Cedar Creek she found herself at one time cut off and surrounded by the enemy, but managed, by an adroit movement, to escape capture.

As to making something out of the war, she was utterly indifferent to that. At one time a purse of some three hundred dollars was made up and presented to her; but in a few weeks the most of it was gone, having been expended in various purchases for the comfort of her boys. Any money given to her was sure to find its way back again into the regiment, as she would expend it for the benefit of some sick, or wounded, or unfortunate man, or for the purchase of hospital supplies.

Her personal appearance is not prepossessing or attractive. Sleeping on the ground like a soldier, and enduring hardships like the rest, her face has become browned by exposure, and her figure grown athletic by constant exercise and life in the open air. But the heart that beats under her plain cassock is as full of womanly tenderness as that of any princess in purple velvet; and, though her hand is strong and brown, it is as ready to do an act of generous kindness as that of Florence Nightingale herself.

Not even with the close of the war did her self-imposed duties end. She has become attached to the free and spirited life of the cavalry soldier, and preferring camp life, with its hardships and adventures, to the comfort and tameness of villages, she is now with the detachment that has crossed the great plains and the Rocky Mountains for Indian service on the distant western frontier.

MRS. ISABELLA FOGG.

WHEN the boom of the great guns in Charleston harbor, in the spring of 1861, went rolling across the continent, their echo penetrated to the border town of Calais, in Maine, on the extreme eastern verge of the Union, and there summoned men from their ships, and lumber mills, and farms, to the heroic duty of sustaining the government, threatened by half a continent in arms against it.

Nor did that summons reach the ears of men only. The lady whose name is written above felt that she was called, also, to go out, to leave the quiet and seclusion of her home, and do all that a woman may do to sustain the hands and the hearts of those who had the great battle of freedom to fight.

In the spring of 1861 the family duties by which she was bound seemed to make it impracticable for her to leave at once. But in July, Bull Run, with its disastrous issue, ran like a mingled cry of agony and of shame over the land, and the demand of April was repeated in a tone sterner and more imperative than before.

About this time changes occurred in the family of Mrs. Fogg, which seemed to release her from pressing obligations to remain at home; and her schoolboy son, like ten thousand others in those arousing times, followed the twofold impulse of loyalty and youthful enthusiasm, and exchanged the playground for the camp, and his grammar for Scott's Tactics.

When her son enlisted, Mrs. Fogg thought her duty no longer obscure, and offered her services, without compensation, to the governor and surgeon-general of the state, and under their direction spent several weeks in preparing and collecting sanitary and hospital stores.

Early in the fall of 1861 she went out with one of the Maine regiments, and proceeded with it to Annapolis, where she remained several months, acting at first as the nurse of those who fell sick in the regiment, and afterwards was connected with the General Hospital. When the coast expedition, under General Sherman, was organized, she was of course very desirous of going with the regiment. But this was not found practicable. A duty less romantic, but equally important, was now brought home to her, and right nobly did she discharge it. The spotted fever appeared in the post hospital, and as one or more fell victims to it daily, much alarm existed, and it was difficult to obtain nurses for the sufferers. In this exigency Mrs. Fogg and another lady volunteered their services, and for week after week, all day, and often for a considerable part of the night, were on duty in the fever ward, constant in their devotion to the patients, and indifferent to the danger of infection.

This duty lasted till the spring of 1862, when those campaigns against the enemy were inaugurated and carried to a consummation by which the first serious and eventually fatal blows were inflicted on the defiant monster of Treason.

Early in May came the first bloodshed on the Peninsula. The mutilated heroes of Williamsburg were brought in — one great, bloody cargo of suffering humanity — to the northern hospitals, on the Elm City; and a shudder of horror and agony ran over the nation. We began to see the fearful price by which the Union was to be redeemed. Mrs. Fogg was now more anxious than ever to be constantly and actively employed in labors to assuage sufferings so immense as were likely to be the price of captured Richmond. Hastening to Washington, she placed herself under the direction of the Sanitary Commission, and when the Elm City returned she went, in company with several other ladies, and some gentlemen of the Christian and Sanitary Commissions, to labor on the hospital transports in the York and James Rivers. These transport labors are described elsewhere, in the rehearsal of the labors and sacrifices of Miss Bradley, Miss Ethridge, Mrs. Harris, and Miss Hall.

On the last day of May came the bloody field of Fair Oaks, after which there was a broad and unbroken stream of the wounded and the sick pouring steadily to the rear from the active and warlike front, along the Chickahominy and around Richmond. The charge of these removals was in the hands of Dr. Swinburne, who, observing the skill and activity of Mrs. Fogg in attending those who were brought on the cars to the White House, asked her if she would be willing to go up to the front and labor. The application was made to Mrs. Fogg through Mr. Knapp, of the Sanitary Commission, and her prompt reply was, "Mr. Knapp, that is just where I would like to go."

A branch of the Sanitary Commission was accordingly established at Savage Station, two miles from the front; and, during the long, hot days of June, Mrs. Fogg was here laboring throughout the day, protecting herself from sunstroke by a wet towel, worn in her hat, distributing cooling drinks, food, and stimulants to the sick, as they arrived in long trains from Fair Oaks, and as they were collected from the different parts of the great army. Just before the campaign culminated in the seven days' fight, her son came down to Savage Station, and gave a moving account of the sufferings of his comrades at the extreme front, where he was stationed. The next morning found Mrs. Fogg in an ambulance, loaded with supplies for the sick, making her way through the Chickahominy Swamp, to where Keyes was posted, on the extreme left, and within sight of the spires of the rebel capital.

On reaching the camp of the Sixth Maine, which was in Hancock's brigade of Smith's division, she found from sixty to seventy brave fellows, who, though sick, had refused to be sent to the brigade hospital, partly from the soldier's dislike of all hospitals as long as he can stand, but mainly because they hoped to be well enough to march through the streets of Richmond, which they confidently expected that great army, then having nearly one hundred and twenty thousand men fit for duty, would enter in a few days.

Here, protected from the burning midsummer sun and the malarious night air by nothing better than little shelter and "dog" tents, they were languishing with typhoid fever and chronic diarrhœa; their bed the earth, their fare salt pork and "hard-tack." The medical officers of the regiment were neither unskilled nor inattentive. Her labors for that day were wholly for these brave sufferers, dispensing the stores which she had brought, cooking palatable food, quenching the fever thirst, cheering the sinking heart with kind and sympathetic words. Their smiling or tearful gratitude was a reward and a stimulus which dispelled fatigue, and made her heedless of the occasional shot or shell that went screaming over the lines.

Returning in the evening to the station, she consulted with the agents of the Christian and Sanitary Commissions as to the possibility of bringing constant relief to such cases as she had just been attending. But the day following all such plans were cut short by the rapid and disastrous culmination of the campaign. The battle of Gaines' Mill had been fought, the rebel army being concentrated on the north side of the Chickahominy, and McClellan's force divided by the stream. The north bank of the stream was lost, his communications cut: it only remained for McClellan to force his way across to the James River, and establish there a new base of operations.

Innumerable woes and horrors of war now crowded about Savage Station. The country was full of sick, and wounded, and stragglers. The roar of the artillery grew louder as it advanced. Trains of sick and wounded, which had been started for White House, were coming back. It was announced that Jackson had cut the communications of the army, and that Savage Station, with its thousands of helpless sick and wounded, must be abandoned, and all that could must take up their line of march for James River.

Through all these fearful scenes and agonizing fears,

while the very existence of the army seemed to be threatened, and ignorant whether her son might not be at that moment stiff on the battle-field, or stretched on an amputation table, Mrs. Fogg continued her labor for the sick till the last moment, and then retreated with the rest to Harrison's Landing. On the way she was able, by giving out from her sanitary supplies in the ambulance, to earn the blessing of many who were ready to perish.

Her special duty at the landing was assigned her by Dr. Letterman — the charge of preparing food for amputation cases, who must, for a time at least, have only the simplest diet. Occasionally, as opportunity offered, she would take an ambulance and go out through the regiments, distributing stores furnished by the Sanitary Commission to the soldiers in their tents or in the trenches, only sorry that her supplies were not twenty-fold more abundant.

These labors were continued through July and a part of August, till the hospitals were broken up, and the army began to return to the Potomac. She then went in the steamer Spaulding, with a load of wounded, to Philadelphia, and after seeing the last of the peninsula sufferers comfortable in an amply-furnished hospital, she returned to Maine for a little rest, having been absent then just one year.

Little repose, however, took this unwearied worker for the soldier. In Portland she waited on the mayor, and obtained letters from him and prominent citizens to the governor of the state, who listened with interest to all her plans and explanations, and wrote her a long reply, embodying his views as to measures of sanitary relief to be taken by the state. The result was the appointment of a state agent in the person of Colonel Hathaway.

With supplies collected through her efforts, and in company with Colonel Hathaway and another co-laborer, — one of the most esteemed ladies of Portland, — she started again for Washington, on the 4th of October, the primary object being to supply pressing demands in the Maine regiments, but with no such exclusive charity as passes unnoticed the needy soldiers wherever they may be found.

Wide indeed, and white for harvest, did she find the field of sanitary labor. The wrecks of the campaign, whose only feature that was not wholly disastrous was the bloody field of Antietam, were strewn widely over Maryland, filling the ill-supplied hospitals, crowding the deserted cabins, and packed beneath shelter-tents. At no time during the war was there so much suffering that might have been saved by an effective sanitary system as in the fall of 1862. During October and November Mrs. Fogg labored incessantly at numerous hospitals, her efforts being fully appreciated and seconded by the medical officers. Following the flag, she advanced with the army into Virginia, and as the winter promised to be one of great activity, her labors were especially directed to supplying the Maine boys with clothing suitable for winter and a winter campaign.

In December she penetrated to the front, and every facility was afforded her by General Hooker, in whose corps she found most of the Maine soldiers. A few days after she witnessed that brave but unavailing attempt under Burnside, and immediately found abundant work in the hospitals that were established after the battle, and in the great camps of sick and convalescents which were scattered all the way from the Rappahannock to the Potomac.

Let us from her diary select the labors of a single day, and remember that such trips were repeated daily almost throughout that winter: —

"Started with ambulance filled with necessary stores of all kinds, such as bread, soft crackers, canned chicken, oysters, dried fruit, preserves, condensed milk, dried fish, pickles, butter, eggs, white sugar, green tea, cocoa, broma, apples, oranges, lemons, cordials, wines, woollen underwear, towels, quilts, feather pillows, all invaluable among so many sufferers so far from home and its comforts. My first visit was directed to those regiments where the wants were most pressing; but my special mission was to those who languished under bare shelter tents, they being entirely dependent upon their rations, and seldom or never reached by sanitary and hospital stores. In company with the surgeons, who always welcomed us, we made the tour of the camp, going from tent to tent, finding from one to three in each of those miserable quarters, suffering from camp diseases of every form, distributing our stores at the surgeons' suggestion. We left reading matter generally in each tent. Then we would hasten away to the General Hospital, and pass the latter part of the day in reading the Bible to some dying soldier, or write out his words of final and touching farewell to the loved ones at home, then bathe fevered brows, moisten with water and refresh with cordials mouths parched with fever, and, adjusting pillows under aching heads, bid our patients farewell. Weary, but glad at heart for having it in our power to do so much for our boys, we sought our tents, which scarce protected us from snow and rain; but we were happy in a sense of duty discharged, and in enjoying the grateful love of our sacrificing heroes."

This routine of noble and most useful labor was now and then interrupted by a visit to Washington, where Mrs. Fogg went to receive and forward to the camps along the Rappahannock and Acquia Creek, the sanitary stores which were being regularly shipped from Portland and other places in Maine.

But labors and exposures like these could hardly be continued through that gloomy winter without interruption from disease; and early in March Mrs. Fogg was prostrated with a severe attack of pneumonia, by which her sanitary labors were interrupted for several weeks, until the sun and winds of April had dried the deep mud of a Virginia winter, and General Hooker advanced across the river to establish his lines at Chancellorsville. At the time of the great battle which followed, Mrs. Fogg and the lady who had accompanied her from Portland spent five days and nights of almost incessant work at the United States Ford, feeding and reviving the wounded as they came pouring from the field, as they were too much exhausted to proceed without some refreshment.

About daylight on Monday morning, the 4th of May, she and her companion, exhausted by their labors, and vigils, and excitement, crept to an unoccupied corner of a low attic, to obtain an hour of sleep, when a terrific storm of shells and round shot came smashing through the roof. The enemy had, during the night, pushed forward a battery, and opened upon their position at daylight. A terrible scene of confusion and excitement now followed. The screaming and hissing messengers of death were falling thick and fast all around, and piercing the little hospital crowded with the wounded. All who could walk or crawl were leaving for the rear. As she passed one heroic young soldier, she remarked, "You have been left, poor boy." He looked up with a calm smile, and replied, "Don't call me poor; I have laid one arm on the altar of my country, and am ready to sacrifice the other also." A soldier, whose wounds she had just dressed, was this moment killed by a shell which burst immediately over their heads.

As this sudden attack became known, some general officers, who knew the importance of the sanitary stores at this hospital, took active steps for their defence, and the hostile battery was silenced or withdrawn.

Two weeks later, General Lee sent a flag of truce, and offered protection to such detachments as might be sent within his lines to bring away some fifteen hundred wounded.

A train of ambulances was accordingly started, and Mrs. Fogg took all her sanitary stores, which were the only supplies on the spot and available, and established a temporary Rest, or way-side hospital, on the north bank of the river, near the ford, where fires were made, and large quantities of palatable food prepared and given to the sufferers in each ambulance as it reached the bank. For five days the train of ambulances was active in these removals, and numerous lives were saved by the refreshment thus timely administered in the middle of the agonizing journey from the rebel lines to the Union hospitals.

The sufferings and labors of Chancellorsville were quickly followed by the glorious but bloody days at Gettysburg.

Mrs. Fogg left her stores to be forwarded as soon as might be, and she pressed to the scene of action, arriving in Gettysburg on the 4th of July.

As there was a lack of sanitary stores and of food of all kinds, she took a team and made an extensive circuit among the farmers, collecting from them all that she could. The Baltimore fire company also placed at her disposal a large amount, which they had brought forward, and she labored for some ten days or two weeks with her accustomed zeal and patience among that great host of sufferers, estimated by General Meade, when all that were left on the field from both armies are included, at nearly twenty-two thousand men.

But the corps of workers was soon found to be proportionably large. Nurses, matrons, lady superintendents, special cooks, and every class of persons who can ameliorate suffering and make themselves useful at such a time, came in great numbers from the adjacent cities; and Mrs. Fogg was convinced that she could be of more service by following the flag, and keeping with the heroic men whose stubborn courage had won that all-important battle.

During the fall of 1863 she was at Warrenton, Culpepper, Bristow Station, Rappahannock Station, Kelly's Ford, and Mine Run, and bestowed the same attention on the sick and wounded that she had the year before on nearly the same ground.

During the winter of 1864 she again visited Maine, and the legislature of that state, much to their credit, voted a handsome sum of money to be appropriated and placed at her disposal for disbursal, according to her knowledge and judgment of the wants of the soldiers. Hurrying back to the front, she saw those great movements inaugurated by the new commander of the army of the Potomac, and of all the forces of the United States, which, after a series of battles unparalleled in obstinacy and extent, at last broke the rebel force, and closed the war.

Then followed that ever-memorable second week of May, with hard fighting for seven consecutive days, and Grant "determined to fight it out on that line, if it took all summer." Twelve thousand wounded were reported at Rappahannock Station and at Fredericksburg. Leaving her son sick at Alexandria, Mrs. Fogg drove to Fredericksburg, taking Miss Dix in her ambulance, and found that old, war-blasted city one great hospital. In all her experience she had seen nothing so terrible.

"It was indescribable," she writes, "in its enormous woes, a sight demanding the tears and prayers of the universe — the awful price of a nation's existence." Laboring here in the manner described above for two or three weeks, she passed on with the army to Front Royal, and thence to the James, crossing it on the great pontoon bridge. Hospitals were now established at City Point, and as the summer advanced, and the army appeared to be stationary around Petersburg, and the hospitals well supplied and easy of access, she sought a scene of duty more arduous. Returning north to Boston, and then to Calais, she was successfully engaged in organizing new and more extensive plans of usefulness, when there came the terrible news that her son, who had gone back to his regiment (from which he had been for a time detailed to drive his mother's ambulance) and been with Sheridan in the battle of Cedar Run, had been mortally wounded.

The anxieties of the mother now triumphed over the thoughts of philanthropy, and she flew to Martinsburg, in Virginia, to make inquiries for her boy. She was about to leave the place and press forward to the scene of the recent action, when she happened to meet a delegate of the Christian Commission, who to her inquiries was enabled to reply that her son had been in Martinsburg, that he had suffered amputation of his leg, survived the operation, been carefully attended, and forwarded to a hospital in Baltimore. She reached that city in a few hours, greatly exhausted by the long journey and the deep anxiety, but found her boy doing well. She attended him for two weeks, when she was herself prostrated, and remained sick more than a month. Recovering her health, in November she went to Washington, and reported to the Christian Commission. As there was no longer the same demand as before for the class of labor in which she had been so persistent and successful, she reported to Mrs. Wittenmeyer, who, as special agent of the Christian Commission, had charge of the special diet kitchens in a great number of hospitals. By her she was assigned to duty in Louisville, Kentucky.

While laboring here on a hospital boat, in January, 1865, she stepped through an unseen opening in the deck, and received very serious and permanent injuries from the fall.

Unable to return to the state for whose brave patriots

she had labored so long and so successfully, the close of the war found her a permanent invalid among strangers. But this affliction was as nothing in her estimation. Her son was a cripple for life. She would never enjoy health again. But, to use the language of her diary, she is daily solaced and penetrated with deep gratitude to God that he so long preserved her in health and strength, to witness the triumph of the right, and the dawn of peace, and the days when the patriot, no longer languishing in camp nor agonizing on the field, will not suffer for what woman, in her tenderness, can do for him.

WHAT WE DID AT GETTYSBURG.

THE roar of another great battle has at last died away. For three long, hot days in July the ground has jarred with the fearful concussion of three hundred cannon, and trembled under the tread of immense hosts of fighting men.

The "long tormented air" is quiet at last. The fierce enemy having for three days dashed his long gray lines, like great ocean waves, against the firm battalions that awaited him so sternly on the crests of the hills around the town, has moved sullenly away, defeated, but dangerous still. He has hurried back to the Potomac, and abandoned all thought of planting his defiant banner on Battle Monument, or dictating terms of settlement to the loyal states from Independence Hall. The Union army, after its herculean struggle, succeeding as it did a series of forced marches, has gone into camp, and is reposing a little on its hard-earned and blood-sprinkled laurels. And now, from the great cities that were so recently threatened, come pouring to the relief of the vast multitude of sufferers, the noble army of charity, the Christian Commission, the Sanitary Commission, representatives of Ladies' Aid Societies and Soldiers' Relief Societies; and they are welcome all, and all needed, for the amount of work to be done is stupendous.

The invader has left eight thousand wounded to the tenderness and mercy of those whose homes a few days ago they were threatening to burn, and whose government, and priceless liberty, and constitution they hoped to see toppled to the dust. More than thirteen thousand loyal soldiers are wounded; so that here lie over twenty-two thousand suffering, bleeding, dying men.

They are in want of everything than can conduce to comfort, assuage pain, or lift and illuminate the ever-deepening shadow that covers them as they go down into the dark valley. The wounded of both armies had marched, for many a long, hot day, under a broiling sun, and through clouds of dust. From the 15th June, when the Federal general broke camp at Falmouth, till the 4th of July, when the issue had been met and decided, it had been one swift succession of long, forced marches, growing longer and more strenuous, to end only in the forces being plunged into the bloodiest battle of the war. The sun smote fierce on all the torn and dusty landscape; there was no shade on the battle-field, no food, no rest, or help, or cheer of any kind. The medical corps had moved southward with the army, expecting another great battle near the Potomac, and the greater part of the immense duty of caring for all these wounded devolved on voluntary charity, the unpaid goodness of those hundreds of noble souls, both men and women, who were seeking no reward but an approving conscience, and the final benediction, "Inasmuch as ye have done it unto the least of these my brethren, ye have done it unto me."

While the battle was raging these wounded were gathered into field hospitals, without reference to organization. In a few days these were broken up, and all who could bear transportation brought to the railroad station, and others collected into corps and division hospitals. At the depot, the Sanitary Commission, anticipating the wants of the case, had come prepared from Baltimore, and a spacious lodge or rest was erected. Large store tents were at hand, filled with all manner of supplies, for the preparations to meet this emergency were commensurate with the magnitude of the work. A cook-house was put up, with caldrons and stoves, and a steam apparatus, and these were all kept in full operation, day and night.

These preliminary arrangements were completed by the 9th July, and then the labor could be systematic and effective. Day after day, and frequently for a great portion of the night, these labors continued for four months. At length the various smaller hospitals, in and near town, were broken up, and the wounded that could not be removed farther were collected at Camp Letterman, on the hills east of the Gettysburg; and here these sanitary labors were continued till the 17th November, when the last car-load of mutilated men took its departure for Pittsburg, in the railway ambulance.

Nearly all who had ever labored for the soldiers in the east came here; and representatives of a hundred delightful homes, whose family names had been known and honored in the northern cities and colleges since the Mayflower landed, might be seen devoting themselves, in the heartiest cheerfulness and good will, to the noble work.

One there was — her name is not to be written on these

pages, but it is well known to the recording angel — the excellence of whose work is equalled only by the charming simplicity and grace of her narrative. One of her own sex, herself a noble worker, thus eulogizes the fair authoress of the story below, known perhaps already to some of our readers, under the title of "What we did at Gettysburg:" —

"She is now (1863) in a far distant hospital, and it is therefore not improper that this allusion to her should be made. Her sense, energy, lightness, and quickness of action, her thorough knowledge of the work, her amazing yet simple resources, her shy humility, which made her regard her own work with impatience, almost with contempt; all this, and much else, has made the memory of —— a source of strength and tenderness, which nothing can take away."

"What we did at Gettysburg, for the three weeks we were there, you will want to know. 'We' are Mrs. —— and myself, who, happening to be on hand at the right moment, gladly fell in with the proposition to do what we could at the the Sanitary Commission Lodge after the battle. There were, of course, the agents of the Commission, already on the field, distributing supplies to the hospitals, and working night and day among the wounded. I cannot pretend to tell you what was done by all the big wheels of the concern, but only how two of the smallest ones went round, and what turned up in the going.

"Twenty-four hours we were in making the journey between Baltimore and Gettysburg, places only four hours

LEAVING THE HOSPITAL TENTS FOR THE BATTLE FIELD.

apart in ordinary running time; and this will give you some idea of the difficulty there was of bringing up supplies when the fighting was over, and the delays in transporting wounded. Coming towards the town at this crawling rate, we passed some fields where the fences were down, and the ground slightly tossed up. 'That's where Kilpatrick's cavalrymen fought the rebels,' some one said; 'and close by that barn a rebel soldier was found, day before yesterday, sitting dead;' no one to help, poor soul, 'near the whole city full.' The railroad bridge, broken up by the enemy, government had not rebuilt as yet, and we stopped two miles from the town, to find that, as usual, just where the government had left off, the Commission had come in. There stood their temporary lodge and kitchen, and here, hobbling out of their tents, came the wounded men who had made their way down from the corps hospital, expecting to leave at once in the return cars.

"This is the way the thing was managed at first: The surgeons, left in care of the wounded three or four miles out from the town, went up and down among the men in the morning, and said, 'Any of you boys who can make your way to the cars, can go to Baltimore.' So off start all who think they feel well enough, anything being better than the 'hospitals,' so called, for the first few days after a battle. Once the men have the surgeon's permission to go, they are off; and there may be an interval of a day, or two days, should any of them be too weak to reach the train in time, during which these poor fellows belong to no one, the hospital at one end, the railroad at the other, with far more than chance of falling through between the two. The

Sanitary Commission knew this would be so of necessity, and, coming in, made a connecting link between these two ends.

"For the first few days the worst cases only came down in ambulances from the hospitals; hundreds of fellows hobbled along as best they could, in heat and dust, for hours, slowly toiling, and many hired farmers' wagons, as hard as the farmers' fists themselves, and were jolted down to the railroad at three or four dollars the man. Think of the disappointment of a soldier, sick, body and heart, to find, at the end of this miserable journey, that his effort to get away, into which he had put all his remaining stock of strength, was useless; that 'the cars had gone,' or 'the cars were full;' that while he was coming others had stepped down before him, and that he must turn all the weary way back again, or sleep on the roadside till the next train 'to-morrow.' Think what this would have been, and you are ready to appreciate the relief and comfort that was. No men were turned back. You fed and you sheltered them just when no one else could have done so; and out of the boxes and barrels of good and nourishing things, which you, people at home, had supplied, we took all that was needed. Some of you sent a stove (that is, the money to get it), some of you the beef-stock, some of you the milk and fresh bread; and all of you would have been thankful that you had done so, could you have seen the refreshment and comfort received through these things.

"As soon as the men hobbled up to the tents, good hot soup was given all round; and that over, their wounds were dressed, — for the gentlemen of the Commission are cooks or surgeons, as occasion demands, — and, finally, with their blankets spread over the straw, the men stretched themselves out, and were happy and contented till morning, and the next train.

"On the day that the railroad bridge was repaired we moved up to the depot, close by the town, and had things in perfect order; a first-rate camping ground, in a large field directly by the track, with unlimited supply of delicious, cool water. Here we set up two stoves, with four large boilers, always kept full of soup and coffee, watched by four or five black men, who did the cooking under our direction, and sang (not under our direction) at the tops of their voices all day, —

'O darkies, hab you seen my massa?'

'When this cruel war is over.'

Then we had three large hospital tents, holding about thirty-five each, a large camp-meeting supply tent, where barrels of goods were stored, and our own smaller tent fitted up with tables, where jelly-pots and bottles of all kinds of good sirups, blackberry and black currant, stood in rows. Barrels were ranged round the tent walls; shirts, drawers, dressing-gowns, socks, and slippers (I wish we had more of the latter), rags and bandages, each in its own place on one side; on the other, boxes of tea, coffee, soft crackers, tamarinds, cherry brandy, &c. Over the kitchen, and over this small supply tent, we women rather reigned, and filled up our wants by requisitions on the Commission's depot. By this time there had arrived a 'delegation' of just the right kind from Canandaigua, New York, with surgeon dressers and attendants, bringing a first-rate supply of necessaries and comforts for the wounded, which they handed over to the Commission.

"Twice a day the trains left for Baltimore or Harrisburg, and twice a day we fed all the wounded who arrived for them. Things were systematized now, and the men came down in long ambulance trains to the cars: baggage cars they were, fitted with straw for the wounded to lie on, and broken open at either end to let in the air. A government surgeon was always present to attend to the careful lifting of the soldiers from ambulance to car. Many of the men could get along very nicely, holding one foot up, and taking great jumps on their crutches. The latter were a great comfort: we had a nice supply at the lodge, and they travelled up and down from the tents to the cars daily. Only occasionally did we dare let a pair go on with some very lame soldier, who begged for them: we needed them to help the new arrivals each day, and trusted to the men being supplied at the hospitals at the journey's end. Pads and crutches are a standing want — pads particularly. We manufactured them out of the rags we had, stuffed with sawdust from brandy boxes; and with half a sheet, and some soft straw, Mrs. —— made a poor dying boy as easy as his sufferings would permit. Poor young fellow! he was so grateful to her for washing, and feeding, and comforting him! He was too ill to bear the journey, and went from our tent to the church hospital, and from the church to his grave, which would have been coffinless but for the care of ——, for the quartermaster's department was overtaxed, and for many days our dead were simply wrapped in their blankets and put into the earth. It is a soldierly way, after all — lying wrapped in the old war-worn blanket, the little dust returned to dust.

"When the surgeons had the wounded all placed, with as much comfort as seemed possible under the circumstances, on board the train, our detail of men would go from car to car, with soup made of beef-stock or fresh meat, full of potatoes, turnips, cabbage, and rice, with fresh bread and coffee, and, when stimulants were needed, with ale, milk punch, or brandy. Water pails were in great demand for use in the cars on the journey, and also empty bottles, to take the place of canteens. All our whiskey and brandy bottles were washed and filled up at the spring, and the boys went off, carefully hugging their extemporized canteens, from which they would wet their wounds, or refresh themselves, till the journey ended. I do not think that a man of the sixteen thousand, who were transported during our stay, went from Gettysburg without a good meal: rebels and Unionists together, they all had it, and were pleased and satisfied. 'Have you friends in the army, madam?' a rebel soldier, lying on the floor of the car, said to me, as I gave him some milk. 'Yes; my brother is on ——'s staff.' 'I thought so, ma'am. You can always tell; when people are good to soldiers they are sure to have friends in the army.' 'We are rebels, you know, ma'am,' another said; 'do you treat rebels so?' It was strange to see the good brotherly feeling come over the soldiers — our own and the rebel — when side by side they lay in our tents. 'Hallo, boys! this is the pleasantest way to meet — isn't it? We are better friends when we are as close as this, than a little farther off.' And then they would go over the battles together — 'We were here,' and 'You were there,' in the friendliest way.

"After each train of cars, daily, for the three weeks we were in Gettysburg, trains of ambulances arrived too late — men who must spend the day with us until the five P. M. cars went, and men too late for the five P. M. train, who must spend the night till the ten A. M. cars went. All the men who came, in this way, under our own immediate and particular attention, were given the best we had of care and food. The surgeon in charge of our camp, with his most faithful dresser and attendants, looked after all their wounds, which were often in a most shocking state, particularly among the rebels. Every evening and morning they were dressed. Often the men would say, 'That feels good. I haven't had my wound so well dressed since I was hurt.' Something cool to drink is the first thing asked for, after the long, dusty drive, and pailfuls of tamarinds and water — 'a beautiful drink,' the men used to say — disappeared rapidly among them.

"After the men's wounds were attended to, we went round giving them clean clothes; had basins, and soap, and towels; and followed these with socks, slippers, shirts, drawers, and those coveted dressing gowns. Such pride as they felt in them! — comparing colors, and smiling all over as they lay in clean and comfortable rows ready for supper 'on dress parade,' they used to say. And then the milk, particularly if it were boiled, and had a little whiskey and sugar, and the bread, with butter on it, and jelly on the butter — how good it all was, and how lucky we felt ourselves in having the immense satisfaction of distributing these things, which all of you, hard at work in villages and cities, were getting ready and sending off, in faith!

"Canandaigua sent cologne, with its other supplies, which went right to the noses and hearts of the men. 'That is good, now;' 'I'll take some of that;' 'worth a penny a sniff;' 'that kinder gives one life;' and so on, all round the tents, as we tipped the bottles up on the clean handkerchiefs some one had sent, and when they were gone, over squares of cotton, on which the perfume took the place of hem, — 'just as good, ma'am.' We varied our dinners with custard and baked rice puddings, scrambled eggs, codfish hash, corn starch, and always as much soft bread, tea, coffee, or milk as they wanted. Two Massachusetts boys I especially remember, for the satisfaction with which they ate their pudding. I carried a second plateful up to the cars, after they had been put in, and fed one of them till he was sure he had had enough. Young fellows they were, lying side by side, one with a right and one with a left arm gone.

"The Gettysburg women were kind and faithful to the wounded and their friends, and the town was full to overflowing of both. The first day, when Mrs. —— and I reached the place, we literally begged our bread from door to door; but the kind woman who at last gave us dinner, would take no pay for it. 'No, ma'am, I shouldn't wish to have that sin on my soul when the war is over.' She, as well as others, had fed the strangers flocking into town daily; sometimes over fifty of them for each meal, and all for love, and nothing for reward; and one night we forced a reluctant confession from our hostess that she was meaning to sleep on the floor that we might have a bed — her whole house being full. Of course we couldn't allow this self-sacrifice, and hunted up some other place to stay in. We did her no good, however, for we afterwards found that the bed was given up that night to some other stranger who arrived late and tired: 'An old lady, you know, and I couldn't let an old lady sleep on the floor.' Such acts of kindness and self-denial were almost entirely confined to the women.

"Few good things can be said of the Gettysburg farmers, and I only use Scripture language in calling them 'evil beasts.' One of this kind came creeping into our camp three weeks after the battle. He lived five miles only from the town, and had 'never seen a rebel.' He heard we had some of them, and came down to see them. 'Boys,' we said, marching him into the tent, which happened to be full of rebels that day waiting for the train, — 'boys, here's a man who never saw a rebel in his life, and wants to look at you;' and there he stood with his mouth wide open, and there they lay in rows, laughing at him, stupid old Dutchman. 'And why haven't you seen a rebel?' Mrs. —— said; 'why didn't you take your gun and help to drive them out of your town?' 'A feller might'er got hit;' — which reply was quite too much for the rebels; they roared with laughter at him, up and down the tent. One woman we saw, who was by no means Dutch, and whose pluck helped to redeem the other sex. She lived in a little house close up by the field where the hardest fighting was done — a red-cheeked, strong, country girl. 'Were you frightened when the shells began flying?' 'Well, no; you see we was all a baking bread round here for the soldiers, and had our dough a-rising. The neighbors they ran into their cellars, but I couldn't leave my bread. When the first shell came in at the window, and crashed through the room, an officer came and said, "You had better get out of this;" but I told him I could not leave my bread, and I stood working it till the third shell came through; and then I went down cellar, but (triumphantly) I left my bread in the oven.' 'And why didn't you go before?' 'O, you see, if I had, the rebels would have come in and daubed the dough all over the place.' And here she had stood, at the risk of unwelcome plums in her loaves, while great holes, which we saw, were made by shot and shell through and through the room in which she was working.

"The streets of Gettysburg were filled with the battle. People thought and talked of nothing else; even the children showed their little spites, by calling to each other, 'Here, you rebel!' and mere scraps of boys amused themselves with percussion caps and hammers. Hundreds of old muskets were piled on the pavements, the men who shouldered them a week before lying under ground now, or helping to fill the long trains of ambulances on their way from the field. The private houses of the town were, many of them, hospitals; the little red flags hung from the upper windows.

"Besides our own men at the lodge, we all had soldiers scattered about whom we could help from our supplies; and nice little puddings and jellies, or an occasional chicken, were a great treat to men condemned by their wounds to stay in Gettysburg, and obliged to live on what the empty town could provide. There was a colonel in a shoe shop, a captain just up the street, and a private round the corner (whose young sister had possessed herself of him, overcoming the military rules in some way, and carrying him off to a little room, all by himself, where I found her doing her best with very little). She came afterwards to our tent, and got for him clean clothes and good food, and all he wanted, and was perfectly happy in being his cook, washerwoman, medical cadet, and nurse. Besides such as these, we occasionally carried from our supplies something to the churches, which were filled with sick and wounded, and where men were dying, — men whose strong patience it was very hard to bear, — dying with thoughts of the old home far away, saying, as last words for the woman watching there, and waiting with a patience equal in its strength, 'Tell her I love her!'

"Late one afternoon — too late for the cars — a train of ambulances arrived at our lodge with over one hundred wounded rebels to be cared for through the night. Only one among them seemed too weak and faint to take anything. He was badly hurt and failing. I went to him after his wound was dressed, and found him lying on his blanket, stretched over the straw — a fair-haired, blue-eyed young lieutenant — a face innocent enough for one of our own New England boys. I could not think of him as a rebel. He was too near heaven for that. He wanted nothing — had not been willing to eat for days, his comrades said; but I coaxed him to try a little milk gruel, flavored nicely with lemon and brandy; and one of the satisfactions of our three weeks is the remembrance of the empty cup I took away afterwards, and his perfect enjoyment of that supper. 'It was so good — the best thing he had had since he was wounded;' and he thanked me so much, and talked about his 'good supper' for hours. Poor creature! he had had no care, and it was a surprise and pleasure to find himself thought of; so, in a pleased, child-like way, he talked about it till midnight, the attendant told me, — as long as he spoke of anything; for at midnight the change came, and from that time he only thought of the old days before he was a soldier, when he sang hymns in his father's church. He sang them now again, in a clear, sweet voice: 'Lord, have mercy upon me;' and then songs without words — a sort of low intoning. His father was a Lutheran clergyman in South Carolina, one of the rebels told us in the morning, when we went into the tent to find him sliding out of our care. All day long we watched him — sometimes fighting his battles over — oftener singing his Lutheran chants; till in at the tent door, close to which he lay, looked a rebel soldier, just arrived with other prisoners. He started when he saw the lieutenant, and, quickly kneeling down by him, called, 'Henry! Henry!' but Henry was looking at some one a great way off, and could not hear him.

"'Do you know this soldier?' we said.

"'O, yes, ma'am! and his brother is wounded, and a prisoner, too, in the cars now.'

"Two or three men started after him, found him, and half carried him from the cars to our tent. 'Henry' did not know him, though, and he threw himself down by his side on the straw, and for the rest of the day lay in a sort of apathy, without speaking, except to assure himself that he could stay with his brother without the risk of being separated from his fellow-prisoners.

"And there the brothers lay, and there we, strangers, sat watching, and listening to the strong, clear voice, singing, 'Lord, have mercy upon me.' The Lord had mercy; and at sunset I put my hand on the lieutenant's heart to find it still!

"All night the brother lay close against the coffin, and in the morning he went with his comrades, leaving us to bury Henry, having 'confidence,' but first thanking us for what we had done, and giving us all that he had to show his gratitude — the palmetto ornament from his brother's cap, and a button from his coat.

"Dr. W—— read the burial service that morning at the grave, and —— wrote his name on the little head-board: 'Lieutenant Rauch, Fourteenth Regiment South Carolina Volunteers.'

"In the field where we buried him, a number of colored freedmen, working for government on the railroad, had their camp; and every night they took their recreation, after the heavy work of the day was over, in prayer meetings. Such an 'inferior race,' you know! We went over one night and listened for an hour, while they sang, collected under the fly of a tent, a table in the middle, where the leader sat, and benches all round the sides for the congregation, — men only, — all very black and very earnest. They prayed with all their souls, as only black men and slaves can, for themselves and for the dear white people, who had come over to the meeting, and for 'Massa Lincoln,' for whom they seemed to have a reverential affection, some of them a sort of worship, which confused Father Abraham and Massa Abraham in one general call for blessings. Whatever else they asked for, they must have strength and comfort, and blessing for 'Massa Lincoln.' Very little care was taken of these poor men. Those who were ill during our stay were looked after by one of the officers of the Commission. They were grateful for every little thing. Mrs. —— went into the town and hunted up several dozen bright handkerchiefs, hemmed them, and sent them over to be distributed the next night after meeting. They were put on the table in the tent, and one by one the men came up to get them. Purple, and blue, and yellow, the handkerchiefs were, and the desire of every man's heart fastened itself on a yellow one: they politely made way for each other, though, one man standing back to let another pass up first, although he ran the risk of seeing the particular pumpkin color that riveted his eyes taken from before them. When the distribution was over, each man tied his head up in his handkerchief, and sang one more hymn, keeping time all round, with blue, and purple, and yellow nods, and thanking and blessing the white people, in 'their basket and in their store,' as much as if the cotton handkerchiefs had all been gold leaf. One man came over to our tent next day to say, 'Missus, was it you who sent me that present? I never had anything so beautiful in all my life before;' and he only had a blue one, too.

"Among our wounded soldiers, one night, came an elderly man, sick, wounded, and crazy, singing and talking about home. We did what we could for him, and pleased him greatly with a present of a red flannel shirt, drawers, and red calico dressing gown, all of which he needed, and in which he dressed himself up, and then wrote a letter to his wife, made it into a little book with gingham covers, and gave it to one of the gentlemen to mail for him. The next morning he was sent on with the company from the Lodge, and that evening two tired women came into our camp — his wife and sister, who hurried on from their home to meet him, arriving just too late. Fortunately we had the queer little gingham book to identify him by, and when some one said, 'It is the man, you know, who screamed so,' the poor wife was certain about him. He had been crazy before the war, but not for two years, now, she said. He had been fretting for home since he was hurt, and when the doctor told him there was no chance of being sent there, he lost heart, and wrote to his wife to come and carry him away. It seemed almost hopeless for two lone women, who had never been out of their own little town, to succeed in finding a soldier among so many, sent in so many different directions; but we helped them as we could, and started them on their journey the next morning, back on their track, to use their common sense and Yankee privilege of questioning.

"A week after, Mrs. —— had a letter, full of gratitude, and saying that the husband was found and secured for home. That same night we had in our tents two fathers, with their wounded sons, and a nice old German mother with her boy. She had come in from Wisconsin, and brought with her a patch-work bed-quilt for her son, thinking he might have lost his blanket; and there he lay, all covered up in his quilt, looking so home-like, and feeling so too, no doubt, with his good old mother close at his side. She seemed bright and happy — had three sons in the army — one had been killed, this one wounded — yet she was so pleased with the tents, and the care she saw taken there of the soldiers, that while taking her tea from a barrel-head as table, she said, 'Indeed, if she was a man, she'd be a soldier too, right off.'

"For this temporary sheltering and feeding of all these wounded men government could make no provision. There was nothing for them, if too late for the cars, except the open field and hunger, in preparation for their fatiguing journey. It is expected, when the cars are ready, that the men will be promptly sent to meet them; and government cannot provide for mistakes and delays; so that, but for the Sanitary Commission's Lodge and comfortable supplies, for which the wounded are indebted to the hard workers at home, men badly hurt must have suffered night and day while waiting for the 'next train.' We had, on an average, sixty of such men each night, for three weeks, under our care; sometimes one hundred, sometimes only thirty; and with the 'delegation,' and the help of other gentlemen volunteers, who all worked devotedly for the men, the whole thing was a great success; and you, and all of us, can't help being thankful that we had a share, however small, in making it so. Sixteen thousand good meals were given, hundreds of men kept through the day, and twelve hundred sheltered at night, their wounds dressed, their supper and breakfast secured, rebels and all. You will not, I am sure, regret that these most wretched men, these 'enemies,' 'sick and in prison,' were helped and cared for through your supplies, though certainly they were not in your minds when you packed your barrels and boxes. The clothing we reserved for our own men, except, now and then, when a shivering rebel needed it; but in feeding them, we could make no distinction. It was curious to see, among our workers at the Lodge, the disgust and horror felt for rebels giving place to the kindest feeling for wounded men.

"Our three weeks were coming to an end; the work of transporting the wounded was nearly over; twice daily we had filled and emptied our tents, and twice fed the trains before the long journey. The men came in slowly at the last, a lieutenant, all the way from Oregon, being among the very latest. He came down from the corps hospitals (now greatly improved), having lost one foot, poor fellow, dressed in a full suit of the Commission's cotton clothes, just as bright and as cheerful as the first man, and all the men that we received, had been. We never heard a complaint. 'Would he like a little nice soup?' 'Well, no, thank you, ma'am;' hesitating and polite. 'You have a long ride before you, and had better take a little; I'll just bring it, and you can try.' So the good thick soup came. He took a very little in the spoon to please me, and afterwards the whole cupful to please himself. He 'did not think it was this kind of soup I meant. He had some in camp, and did not think he cared for any more; his "cook" was a very small boy, though, who just put some meat in a little water, and stirred it round.' 'Would you like a handkerchief?' and I produced our last one, with a hem and cologne too.

'O, yes; that is what I need; I have lost mine, and was just borrowing this gentleman's.' So the lieutenant, the last man, was made comfortable, thanks to all of you, though he had but one foot to carry him on his long journey home.

"Four thousand soldiers, too badly hurt to be moved, were still left in Gettysburg, cared for kindly and well at the large, new government hospital, with a Sanitary Commission attachment. Our work was over, our tents were struck, and we came away, after a flourish of trumpets from two military bands, who filed down to our door, and gave us a farewell—'Red, white, and blue.'"

MRS. MARY W. LEE.

THIS name will recall to the minds of ten thousands of our brave soldiers who fought in the army of the Potomac the face and the figure of a cheerful, active, efficient, yet tender-hearted woman, herself the mother of a soldier boy, who for month after month, and year after year, while the war continued, moved about the hospitals of the army a blessing, a comfort, and a hope to thousands of weary sufferers.

She came to America from Great Britain when a mere child, and grew up with intense national pride and loyalty to the government which has given an asylum and opportunity to so many millions.

Her first efforts in behalf of the soldiers in our great war were in the hospital of the Union Refreshment Saloon, in Philadelphia. Here she labored with constancy and zeal during the greater part of the first year of hostilities; but when the conflict assumed the serious and bloody proportions that we saw in the summer of 1862, Mrs. Lee felt that she could do more good nearer the field of action. In August opportunity favored her, and she went down to Harrison's Landing on the Spaulding, a hospital transport, and there, with others, she found that enterprising and indefatigable army worker, Mrs. Harris, with whom she gladly coöperated in the arduous duties and melancholy scenes that attended the disastrous finale of the Peninsular campaign.

No sooner was the mutilated wreck of that grand army brought away from the sickly bottoms of James River, than all fit for service, and thousands of new recruits, were pushed forward in the relentless and deadly campaign which ended in disaster and repulse for the rebels at Antietam. In this great battle Mrs. Lee was one of the first on the field; and her labors, commencing among the first wounded, continued, without weariness or abatement, till the last poor, mutilated hero of the "crutch brigade" was moved from the general hospital late in December.

Although it was her first experience in a great battle, Mrs. Lee prepared for the awful scenes that were to follow with the coolness and judgment of a veteran. She had two large buckets filled with water, one for washing wounds, the other for quenching thirst. As the action grew hot, the first tub grew of a deeper and deeper crimson, till it seemed almost as red as blood itself; and the other was again and again replenished, as the men came in with faces black with powder, and clothes stiff with gore. The hunger, too, in many cases, was clamorous. Many of the men had eaten nothing for more than twenty-four hours. Mrs. Lee found a sutler, who, with enterprise that would have been becoming in anything less purely selfish, had urged his wagon well to the front, and was selling at exorbitant rates to the exhausted men. She took money from her private purse, and again and again bought his bread and soft crackers at his army rates. At last such repeated proofs of generosity touched the heart of the army Shylock, and he was determined not to be outdone so entirely by a woman. About the third or fourth time she pulled out her purse he exclaimed, "Great God, I can't stand this any longer. Give that woman the bread!" The ice was now broken, and from giving to her, he began to give away, himself, till his last cracker had gone down the throat of a half-famished hero, and he drove away with his wagon lighter and his heart softer for having met a noble-hearted woman.

While she was thus working just in the rear of the awful thunder, Sedgwick was brought to the rear, with his severe wound, and then Hooker, with his bleeding limb.

Mrs. Lee was probably nearer the front than any other woman on the day of the battle, and certainly much nearer than the commander-in-chief himself.

Among the fatally wounded was one named Adams, from the Nineteenth Massachusetts, whose brother brought him to Mrs. Lee, and said, "My good lady, my brother here will die, I think; the regiment is ordered to Harper's Ferry. Will you promise to look after him, and when he dies, to see that he is decently buried, and mark the spot, so I can find his body and take it on to our home in Massachusetts?" Mrs. Lee promised the heavy-hearted soldier that all his wishes should be respected; and he buckled on his sword and marched back to the front. A few days after, he sought out Mrs. Lee, and she gave him a full account of the last hours of his brother and his dying words; and then taking him out among the thick and fresh-heaped mounds, pointed out a grave better rounded than the rest, and distinctly marked, and told him his brother was buried there; and so he found it. Such was her fidelity and perfect reliability at all times and in all trusts committed to her.

Immediately after the battle there was that confusion and delay in the supply trains inevitable in the best-conducted army at the time of a great action. At one of the field hospitals where Mrs. Lee was doing the best she could for the crowd of sufferers, there was found nothing in the way of commissary supplies but a barrel of flour, a barrel of apples, and a keg of lard. To a practical housekeeper, as she is, this combination seemed to point to apple dumplings as the dish in which they could all be employed to the best advantage; and the good-natured astonishment of the poor fellows, who looked for nothing but black coffee and hard-tack, was merged in admiration for the accomplished cook who could there, almost on the battle-field, serve them with hot dumplings.

While the battle was still raging, and orderlies were galloping past where Mrs. Lee was at work, she asked one of them if Sumner's corps were yet engaged. "Yes," was the reply; "they have just been double-quicked into the fight." For a few moments her heart sank within her, and she grew sick, for her son was in that corps, and all her acquaintances in the army. Her anguish found relief in prayer; after which she grew so calm and cheerful that a wounded boy, who lay there on the grass beside her, said, "Madam, I suppose you haven't any one in the battle, or you couldn't be so calm."

The night after the battle she went to Sedgwick's division

hospital, and while preparing some food for the sufferers, was greatly annoyed by some worthless camp-followers, who would not carry food to the wounded, and when she left to carry it, they stole everything she had cooked. She went up stairs, where most of the wounded were, and asked if any one was there who had sufficient authority to detail her a guard. A pleasant voice from one of the cots, where an officer lay bleeding, said, "I believe I have. Just take the first man you can find, and put a gun in his hand." It was General John Sedgwick; and she had no more annoyance from camp thieves.

In a day or two after the battle she went, with Mrs. General Barlow, in an ambulance, to see if some poor fellow had not been overlooked on the field. They found two boys in a deserted cabin, who had never had their wounds dressed, and had been living on a few crackers and water. They were, of course, brought in, and tenderly cared for. Mrs. Lee was very much interested in a very brave little fellow, from Company B, Seventy-second Pennsylvania volunteers, named Willie Morrow. He had fought all day with uncommon bravery, acting as a sharpshooter. He and his companion, at one time, came marching in six rebel prisoners, captured by only those two, and Willie was the smallest boy in the regiment. As he was going back to the front, a cannon ball hit him, and carried off both his legs. When brought to the rear, he asked the surgeon if there was any hope of his getting over it. "No, Willie, there is no hope," said the doctor. Turning to his companions, he said, "Tell them at home that I died happy, — that I was glad to give my life for my country." The blood continued to run from the severed arteries, and he grew weaker. "Tell them I died happy," were his last words; and in death his pale young face wore a smile.

Not long after the battle, all the field and regimental hospitals were merged into one general hospital at Smoketown; and here Mrs. Lee was aided by a noble and efficient corps of army workers — Miss Maria Hall, Mrs. Barlow, Mrs. Husband, Mrs. Harris, and others, most of whom labored through the war, and enjoyed the utmost confidence of the surgeons and all who observed the superior character and spirit of their work.

During the fall many touching instances of noble youths dying of their wounds, and making the last sacrifice for their country, occurred among those daily visited by Mrs. Lee. Among others was the case of Henry Cole, of the Nineteenth Massachusetts. He had been wounded in the leg, and strong hopes were entertained that he might recover. His mother came on from Massachusetts to nurse him. He was her only child. As she bent over his cot, and saw him gradually becoming weaker and more pallid, tears fell fast on the coverlet, and she would exclaim, "O, if money could restore you, I'd gladly give all I have in this world."

He was a Christian, and a well-educated young gentleman; everything that a mother's heart, in its pride and its unfathomable love could hope for in a son. "O Henry, my son," she would say, amid her tears, "when you are gone, my light is gone out. I've nothing to live for."

"Mother," he would answer, "I am only going a little while before you; we shall meet again." Then, just before he died, repeating these farewells, he added, "Tell all the boys good-by for me, and tell them never to give up our noble cause."

This hospital was blessed with the attendance and service of a superior surgeon-general in Dr. Vanderkieft, and a most excellent and praiseworthy chaplain in Rev. Mr. Sloan. Hardly a soldier in the Smoketown Hospital but loved him as a brother. Many a face tortured with pain grew smooth when his cheerful countenance entered the tent.

When the hospital was fully established, the tents were divided between Mrs. Husband, Miss Hall, and Mrs. Lee; and their labors, thus systematic and persistent, continued till some time in December, when the wounded at Fredericksburg demanded attention.

Among Mrs. Lee's patients was one poor fellow who was so weak and reduced that no food would remain in his stomach. She tried every dish for which the hospital supplies afforded materials, but without reaching his case. One day, in overhauling some stores, she discovered a bag of Indian meal. "O, I've found a prize!" she exclaimed. "What is it?" asked the little fellow, who had been detailed to act as her orderly. "Indian meal, to be sure." "Pshaw! I thought you had found a bag of dollars." "Better than dollars now," was her reply, as she hurried away to the tent where her poor patient lay.

"Sandburn," said she, "could you eat some mush?" "Don't know what that is — don't like any of your fancy dishes." A boy on the next cot said, "Why, it's pudding and milk."

"O, yes," said the starving soldier, "I could eat a bucketful of that!" She made him some, and brought it to him in a cup with milk, sweet milk, and it agreed with him. Then he ate it three times a day, and soon could take with it a little broiled squab, and began to gain strength very fast. The discovery of that little sack of corn meal had saved his life.

The religious exercises at this hospital were often deeply interesting. Mr. Sloan was as much respected for piety as he was beloved for his kindness. Miss Hall commonly led the singing; and many a touching, fervent, and whole-souled prayer for the Union and the army was offered by men who would hobble in on crutches. The more they suffered in the cause, the more they loved it.

While thus occupied at Antietam, Mrs. Lee heard with alarm of the great explosion of powder at Harper's Ferry, by which so many of the Seventy-second Pennsylvania were killed or wounded. Her son was in that regiment. She hurried up there, and labored some time among those sufferers, compounding for their burns a salve that was found very grateful and healing. Her boy was fortunately not injured in the explosion.

From Antietam the hospital workers next went to Falmouth, on the Rappahannock, where the army was encamped, after Burnside's unfortunate attack at Fredericksburg. Upon leaving Antietam, Dr. Vanderkieft expressed his opinion of the character and worth of Mrs. Lee, and her labors there, in the following terms: —

"It is with great pleasure that I bear witness to the invaluable services of Mrs. Lee in this hospital. She knew no rest while there were any who needed her assistance. Her unwearied activity was a subject of universal comment, among officers and men, and her untiring efforts in behalf of patriots have won the love and esteem of all to whom she has ministered. I commend Mrs. Lee to the highest position that a noble and Christian woman can fill."

Chaplain Sloan, also, in a letter from Antietam, in which he speaks of the workers there, says of Mrs. Lee: "None of the newspaper notices tell half the story of her good works. Many a poor boy, that suffered here, will long remember her kindness. She labored harder, and did more to alleviate the pains and sufferings of the wounded at Antietam than any three others."

This describes her labors at the Falmouth hospitals, and all the others with which she was connected during the three years of her army life. She was regular, persistent, thorough, and obedient to the surgeons in all she did, and all she gave to the soldiers. Her wards were always found in perfect order, and well supplied. For a great part of the time she was placed in charge of the light diet and special diet department, where her duties were laborious, and often vexatious.

The rickety old stove upon which she prepared her food for the sick was often in a wretched condition. When set up in a tent it generally smoked, and fuel was not always abundant, or of a good quality. Notwithstanding all these discouragements, her temper was always cheerful, her health perfect, and her duty performed with thoroughness and punctuality.

After a temporary absence from Falmouth, with her sick

son, in March, she returned, and was on duty among the wounded at Chancellorsville.

She was at the Lacey House Hospital, and had a full view of the storming of Mayre's Heights, by Sedgwick's corps, on the 2d of May.

When that fierce engagement was at its height, the men that had been wounded in the skirmishes of the days previous all dragged themselves to the galleries and terraces of the house, Mrs. Lee helping them, and watched the conflict with eager forgetfulness of their own sufferings. When at length Sedgwick, and the brave Sixth corps, after two repulses, made the final and triumphant charge, sweeping over the battlements from which Burnside had been so terribly repulsed in December, everybody that had a well arm raised it, with ringing cheers, over his head, and shouted, till their brave companions on the other side heard and answered back their triumph. Mrs. Lee stood by her little cooking tent, wiping dishes, and joined in the general delight by waving her towel, as a flag, and shouting with the rest. She did more than this. She fell upon her knees, and thanked God that those formidable lines, from which the Union forces had been so often repulsed with frightful carnage, were at last carried, and the national flag waved in triumph over them.

But the eight thousand wounded that came pouring across the Rappahannock soon engrossed the attention of every one who could do anything for their relief, and Mrs. Lee, with the other ladies, labored all day, and a considerable part of each night, striving to mitigate some of the accumulated suffering and pain.

Some of her patients at the "Lacey House" interested Mrs. Lee very deeply. One, Frederick Allen, from Kendall's Mills, was very sick with typhoid pneumonia, and the doctor ordered stimulants. Frederick refused to take anything containing alcohol, saying he had given his mother a solemn promise that he would not take any while in the army. No inducement could prevail, until his father came down, and told him his mother released him from his promise, as she knew it was to save his life. He recovered health, and was in all the battles with his regiment. At Bristow Station he was color guard, and the regiment captured several guns. In the battle of the Wilderness he was wounded slightly in the arm, and went to the rear, but returned very soon, and received a severe wound in the head, and was disabled for several weeks. Returning to his regiment, he fought around Petersburg, till again attacked by typhoid pneumonia, of which he died only a few days before Lee's surrender — a brave and noble youth as ever shouldered arms; a soldier of the Cross no less than of the starry flag.

Mr. Allen and his family became greatly attached to Mrs. Lee on account of her kindness to Frederick and other soldiers. Upon his return home, he begged of Miss Amanda Lee the photograph of her mother, and acknowledged the receipt of it in the following terms: —

"I can think of no better title than *friend* to address you by, for it seems to me that one having so good a mother as you have must be a friend to God and humanity.

"But to the question of your mother's picture: we received it the next day after it was mailed; it did not stop in

Massachusetts at all. The postmaster had written under Mass., 'Troy, Maine,' and it came right along; and a beautiful picture it is, too. We have got a nice oval frame for it, and then we had her name and residence printed at the bottom of the picture; and I tell you it is a splendid thing. Then we have hung it in the centre of the mantel piece, with a soldier boy on each side, and our own dear son, Fred, in the middle; and, as they are arranged, your mother seems to be watching over them, as I have seen her in the hospital, on the Rappahannock. I wish you could step in and see them thus arranged: you might well feel proud of your mother."

Mrs. Lee was at Gettysburg as soon as the cannon smoke had cleared away from the blood-stained hill-side, and labored in the Second corps hospital, and also at Letterman General Hospital, for three months following the great battle.

One of the patients who died here, on her hands, was Aaron Wills, color corporal in the Seventy-second Pennsylvania volunteers, the regiment in which her son was serving. A ball struck the flagstaff, and shattered it. Aaron wrapped the flag around his arm, and shouted, "Don't let the colors fall, boys!" The next moment a ball struck him in a vital part, and he fell, yet held the flag up so that it would not touch the ground, till it was taken from his faithful hands, and carried on at the head of the regiment.

A year after, on the anniversary of his son's death, the father of Aaron Wills wrote an affecting letter to Mrs. Lee. "To-day," he says, "I walked out to the cemetery, to look at the little mound that covers the remains of my beloved boy. As I looked, the words of his last letter, those blessed words, came into my mind: 'Father, do not worry at my being in a dangerous position. I believe, as you say, I can die in no nobler cause; and, to tell you the truth, I would as soon die on the battle-field as I would a natural death.' He need not have said, 'to tell you the truth,' for *he never told a lie.*"

One of her most valued reminiscences of Gettysburg is a letter of thanks, drawn up and numerously signed by the boys in whose ward she had acted as nurse. They say, —

MRS. LEE.

Dear Madam: We now hasten to express to you our thanks for the numerous luxuries and kind services we have received from you, as from the hands of our own kind mothers, for which we shall ever feel grateful to you.

While endeavoring to meet the urgent calls of our wronged country, we had the misfortune to be wounded far from home, and, as we thought, from friends. Here we have found your kind hand to care for us, and alleviate our wants as much as possible. We shall ever feel grateful to you for such motherly care as can never be forgotten; and besides the thousand thanks bestowed on you, the God of our country will ever bless you with a special blessing — if not now, surely you will receive it hereafter.

This testimonial was signed by a large number in Ward B, Sixth division, General Hospital, Gettysburg.

Sickness in the family of Mrs. Lee detained her at home during a part of the winter of 1863–64; but she went down to Brandy Station, which was the hospital centre of Meade's army, in January, February, and March, 1864.

Here she was connected with the hospital of the Second division, Second corps, where were the wounded at the action of Morton's Ford.

Here she found Dr. Sawyer and Dr. Aiken, two physicians, who, for kindness and self-sacrificing devotion to the health, cheerfulness, and comfort of the soldier, had no superiors in the army of the Potomac. With such efficient aid in the nursing department as was rendered by such ladies as Mrs. Husband and Mrs. Lee, this General Hospital soon became the model for all the army. For cleanliness, order, cheerfulness, and the home-like air which surrounded it, no corps hospital was equal to it.

One of the boys, under Mrs. Lee's care, received a letter from his mother, saying that she was coming to see him, and asking what supplies and luxuries she had better bring with her. "Bring nothing but yourself, mother," was his reply: "this is not a hospital; it is a home."

About the middle of April, just before Grant's advance, Mrs. Lee returned home for a few days. But no sooner had he moved in the first days of May, than he found obstinate resistance from the rebel leader, and the great battles of the Wilderness and Spottsylvania were fought. The engagement commenced on the 5th, and was continued till the 12th of May, Grant being "determined to fight it out on that line, if it took all summer."

There was, of course, a vast number of wounded, and the demand for hospital workers was never more urgent than during the months of May and June, 1864. Mrs.

Lee made her way to Fredericksburg, and found that war-battered old town one vast hospital. The first and great clamor was for food. Transportation from Belle Plain was slow, on account of the fearful condition of the roads; and though the enemy was crippled and falling slowly back to Richmond, and Fredericksburg is only a day's ride from Washington, thousands and thousands of our men suffered constantly from hunger. Upon Mrs. Lee's arrival, Dr. Bannister gave her the charge of the special diet of the Second corps. The kitchen furniture with which she was supplied consisted of one small tin cup, and there was no source from which the proper utensils could be obtained. Mrs. Lee remembered, however, that the year before, Mrs. Harris, at the Lacey House, on the other side of the Rappahannock, had left a cooking stove, which might be there yet. Obtaining an ambulance, and going over on the pontoon, she found the old stove, dilapidated, indeed, and rusty; but she could make gruel and panada on it. She found some old kettles, too, which she took over, and scoured up, so that in a few hours a kitchen had been extemporized. The boys broke up clapboards and pickets for fuel, and soon the buckets of gruel, tea, and coffee, and bowls of chicken soup, began to circulate among the famishing heroes. As long as she remained in Fredericksburg, and, in fact, all that summer, from daylight till long after the nine o'clock drum-taps, she did little but cook, cook, cook. Sometimes, just as the hospital had become composed for the night, and the old campaign stove had grown cool for the first time in eighteen hours, an immense train of ambulances would come rolling in from the front, all loaded down with men, sick, wounded, dusty, and famishing. There was no other way but to rise, and work, perhaps, till long past midnight. It was fortunate that with such willingness of heart and such skill, nay, such genius, as she displayed for cooking under all the disadvantages of camp life, Mrs. Lee had also a robust constitution and excellent health; otherwise she must have broken down under the long-continued labors and sleeplessness of that last grand campaign against Richmond.

From Fredericksburg she went, over land, to White House; and there Miss Cornelia Hancock, of New Jersey, and Mrs. Lee assisted Dr. Aiken to dress the wounds and give nourishment to a long train of the wounded that were placed on transports and carried to northern hospitals. Remaining here some days, she proceeded next to City Point, which Grant had now made his base of supplies and his hospital centre.

For some time the accumulation of wounded here was far greater than could in any small degree be made comfortable. Many a night Mrs. Lee stood by the fly of her little kitchen tent, and looked upon long rows of helpless and bleeding men lying on the ground, sometimes with a little straw beneath and a blanket over them, all waiting, in mute and touching patience, for their turn to come to be taken up and cared for. At night such rows of silent sufferers, lying there in the moonlight, looked so much like graves, and summoned up, in a heart as sympathetic as hers, such troops of melancholy thoughts, that she could not look at them without shedding tears.

At City Point, among the wounded from Petersburg, Mrs.

Lee had some noble-minded and heroic men as her hospital patients. One was Major William F. Smith, of the First Delaware. Wounded severely in the leg, he suffered amputation, and death followed. He had been severely wounded at Fredericksburg, and again at Gettysburg. When urged by his friends to expose his life less freely, "No," he would reply, "I am no better than any other soldier." They urged him to remember how much it would grieve his mother. "I know it," said he; "but I am no better than any other mother's son." When informed that he could not live, he thanked the doctors for the pains they had taken with his case: "You have done all that you could for me, but Providence has some wise end in view in overruling your efforts." His last words to his young brother were, "Kiss mother for me, Lee."

Another, who sealed his devotion with his blood, was Lieutenant-Colonel John A. Crosby, of the Sixty-first Pennsylvania volunteers. He had entered the service as orderly sergeant, was badly wounded in both hips at Fredericksburg, and afterwards lost an arm fighting before Washington, in Early's last invasion. When his friends remonstrated with him for keeping the field thus mutilated, he said, "My country has had my arm. She is welcome to my life." Before leaving home for the last time, he bade his wife and family good by, telling them he should never see them again on earth. Those who knew him best, say that no better man or braver soldier ever died for his country. He fell in the last great battle of the war before Petersburg, in April, 1865.

A poor German boy was killed at the same time, and his heart-broken mother went on from Baltimore to get his body. Mrs. Lee gave the poor woman all the assistance in her power, saw the dead soldier in his coffin, and sympathized with the mother.

Upon her return, and after the burial, Mrs. Lee received from the mother the following letter, which is all the more interesting for its honest simplicity as well as its broken English: —

BALTIMORE, *April* 19, 1865.

HONORABLE MRS. M. LEE:

After I left City Point for Baltimore wish my dear son, I arrifet safe home, only wish a broken hart, on the 11th in the morning. We cept him till the 12th in the evening, and took him up to Pansilvaniae, to hes broter and sisters. The 15th, in the morning, he arrifet saf at hes stat of rest. Rev. D. Izenbury atent the funerl, and Bregt, hes text John 11th and 11th, and a great many tears has being shatt for hem. I arrifet at My home the 17th in the morning. I am so troubelt in my Mint and Week that I could not rite, and ask for barten me and excus me for not ansern zuner. My humbel dank to your Virtues and faver which you showed to me. I would ask your Kindness, if you ples. I wase so trobelt to see to every ting, namely my Son hat a very good Watch, and I would lik to have that for Membery, ples, and ask Mr. Geo. W. Low, Company F. 190th Penn. Vols. Fifth Core Hospital City Point Va. My Love and best Respect to Mrs. Hart and Mrs. Polk and Mrs. Ashe.

My Love and best Respect to you

from your obedien servent,

PAULINE BUSH.

P. S. Ef et should be not mutch to your trobel and you can com tru here, gif me a call.

Among many such letters received by Mrs. Lee during her three years of army life, the following, from a bereaved mother in New Hampshire, cannot be read by any mother who lost a boy in the army without unsealing the fountains of old grief.

Forever precious are such letters — consecrated by the sacred baptism of tears that ooze like life-blood from broken hearts!

WINDHAM, *May* 8, 1864.

MY DEAR MRS. LEE:

I had not received the painful intelligence of my beloved son's death until Friday afternoon. My heart is filled with sorrow; my grief I cannot express. You have a beloved son in the army. Dear Thomas told me of you and of your son in one of his letters. He told me there was a woman in the hospital by the name of Mrs. Lee; he said you were as kind to the soldiers as a mother, and that they all loved you as a mother. He said you were an angel. I wrote to him that I was happy to hear him say that there was an angel in his tent; for I never ceased to pray to God, my heavenly Father, that he would send his holy angels into his tent, to guide him by day and guard him by night. He wrote me, the day he went into the hospital, that he had the rheumatism in his arms and legs, but thought he should be able to go back to his regiment. I did not feel much alarmed about him. He then wrote to me he had the measles very lightly, but the cough hung on, as it always does.

His last letter was written to me March 29. He said he thought he was about rid of the measles, but the lameness was no better. Dear Mrs. Lee, I beg you to write me, and give all the particulars about my darling son. Were you with him in his last sickness? I suppose he was a great sufferer. Will you write when he was first taken with the fever, and if he was conscious of the approach of death. Did he speak of his mother or sister, or father or brother? Lieutenant Milton wrote me that he died the 9th of April. You will please to tell me at what hour, and when he was buried. Tell me if he lost his flesh.

O, I shall never, never again see my darling boy in this world! never again hear his joyous laugh! O Mrs. Lee, can you sympathize with me? I am thinking of your own darling son. May be now the battle rages! May our heavenly Father protect your dear son, and return him safe to you.

Will you please to ascertain the place where Thomas K. Ripley is buried. We shall bring his body home as soon as we can have permission. I have sent three letters to my son; two the last week in March; one had a five-dollar bill in it. Do you know if he received the money?

I pray that you will write to me as soon as you can, and I will satisfy you for it. If there is a pocket-book or letters left behind, you will please save them for his poor, afflicted mother.

My dear friend, I hope you will write to me; it will be a great consolation to my bereaved heart. I am much afflicted, and can hardly write. This is terrible!

MRS. MARY D. RIPLEY,

(Wife of Nathaniel Ripley.)

Having thus sympathized in the sufferings and disasters of our soldiers, and in the agony that their death occasioned at so many firesides, it was fit that Mrs. Lee should be present at the happy consummation, and join in that grand pæan of victory, that, commencing at Richmond, in the first days of April, went swelling, in a glorious chorus, from the Atlantic to the Pacific shores.

In the hospital where Mrs. Lee then was, the exultations of the poor, languishing soldiers were full of almost frantic joy.

"Such a time!" she writes; "the people nearly went crazy. Hospital help, ladies, wounded and all, were beside themselves. Processions were formed, kettles improvised for drums; all kinds of noises were made to manifest our joy. Bells were rung, cannon fired, steam whistles blown; men cheered and shouted themselves hoarse. President Lincoln visited the hospital while I was there. He went round to every man, and said he wanted to shake the hand of every man who had helped to gain so glorious a victory; and he had a kind word for all."

In the hospitals of Petersburg and Richmond Mrs. Lee continued for a month after Lee's surrender; for, though the war was ended, there remained a great multitude of the sick, and those wounded in the last engagements.

Then, when there were no more homeless and suffering patriots; no more wounds to be stanched; no more long trains of ambulances, with their groaning and bleeding freightage; no more caldrons of gruel and mutton soup to be cooked for great wards full of half-famished boys, Mrs. Lee went home, and slipped back into the happy routine of domestic usefulness.

Into those womanly duties she carries the rich consciousness of having given herself up entirely, for three laborious but happy years, to the exercise of heavenly charities, and to the practice of that mercy that is twice blessed.

MISS MAJOR PAULINE CUSHMAN.

THIS brilliant and impulsive being, whose life, if it could be fully written, would sound like some tale of romance, is of French and Spanish descent, and was born in New Orleans, in 1833. As she grew to womanhood, the charms of her person and the impressiveness of her manners drew her irresistibly to the stage, where she has had a brilliant career.

When the war commenced, in 1861, she was playing an engagement in Cleveland, Ohio, and soon after went to Louisville, where her histrionic success continued, and was even greater than ever before. Early in the year 1863, while playing in Wood's Theatre, she received many attentions from paroled rebel officers, who were then in Louisville; and, with the desire of making that foolish and ill-timed parade of secession sentiment, which was so often considered true bravery among them, one of these officers proposed to her to offer, in the midst of one of her parts, a toast to Jeff Davis and the Southern Confederacy. She consented to do so; and, upon reflection, it occurred to Miss Cushman that here was afforded her an admirable opportunity of serving her country, and at the same time gratifying her own love of romance and wild adventure. She at once sought and obtained an interview with Colonel

Moore, the provost marshal, who, after serious consultation, and becoming convinced of her genuine loyalty, received her proposition to enter the secret service of the United States.

She took the formal and solemn oath administered before entering that hazardous branch of the service; and the following night, in the midst of her part, and while the crowded theatre had all eyes riveted upon her graceful acting, proposed this astounding toast: "Here's to Jeff Davis and the Southern Confederacy. May the South always maintain her honor and her rights."

The sentiment fell upon the audience like the explosion of a shell. All the loyal persons present were at once mortified and indignant, while the southern sympathizers were delighted. Very prompt action was taken. Miss Cushman was formally expelled from the theatrical corps, and sent south, in the direction of her "sympathies," to be lionized as a victim of Yankee tyranny. She went to Nashville, and sought an interview with Colonel Truesdale, the chief of army police, who gave her the most minute instructions and details as to the information which she must endeavor to obtain in the rebel lines. Thus equipped, and with full confidence in luck and her mimetic talent, she started out on the Hardin Pike, as the people there call the road which leads from Nashville in the direction of Shelbyville. Within a few days, and amid a variety of adventures, she was able to collect many important items of information, with which she was about to return to Nashville, when for a time the run of good fortune was changed; and one night, while stopping at the house of a quiet farmer, by the name of Baum, she found herself under arrest, and was ushered into the presence of that renowned guerrilla and marauder, Jack Morgan. Jack had too much chivalry to be anything but civil to a prisoner so fair, young, and fascinating, and was truly profuse in his generosity as he was conducting her to Forrest's headquarters, offering the beautiful Pauline all his friendship, a magnificent diamond ring, and a silver-mounted revolver, and urging her to accept a position as aid-de-camp on his staff, as soon as she should be released.

Forrest she found a rougher custodian, and much less susceptible, than "Johnnie," as she familiarly called the other freebooter. Her first interview with him was a fine piece of melodrama, and would have excited applause and admiration in any theatre in the country.

"Well," said the hero of the card-table and the bowie-knife, "I'm really glad to see you; I've been looking for you a long time; but I've got this last shuffle, and intend to hold you. You've been here before, I take it — know all the roads — don't you? and all the bridle paths, and even the hog paths — don't you?"

Our heroine, drawing herself to her full height, and flashing indignant scorn from her black eyes, exclaimed, —

"Sir, every word you utter is as false as your own traitorous heart! I've never been here before, and I should like to send a bullet through the man who is mean enough to make the charge."

The ruffian gazed on her a moment, and with the savage gleam of the eye that he afterwards wore at Fort Pillow, replied, "Yes, and I'd send one through you, if I could, if you dared to repeat the assertion." Then his admiration for pluck got the better of his temper, and he added: "Well, you've got good fighting stuff in you, if you are a woman."

In the sharp skirmish of cross-questioning which followed, her woman's wit enabled her to spring a doubt in the mind of the cautious desperado, and he turned her over to Provost Marshal General McKinstry, who, he assured her, was a humane and just man, and would investigate the charges made against her, and decide on them with fairness.

After a little more bandying of words, the fair Pauline was dispatched to the headquarters of General Bragg; and as she rode away, Johnnie Morgan bade her adieu in the following elegant vernacular: —

"Good-by; I hope we shall meet again, where we shall have something better than corn bread baked in ashes, and rot-gut whiskey at fifteen dollars a quart."

Some months after, she saw the great marauder under circumstances very different. He had been captured, in his famous raid north of the Ohio, and was confined, like any other felon, in the Penitentiary at Columbus, in prison stripe, and with hair dressed by the prison barber. Advancing to him, she held out her hand, and laughingly exclaimed, "How are you, Johnnie?" "Ah," replied the jolly rebel, "the boot is on the other foot now."

Bragg she found a different man from either of the cavalry chieftains; and her talk with him was not so spicy, nor so cheerful in its termination.

She saw before her a bony, angular, sharp-pointed man,

without kindness or humanity, or any of the milder parts of human nature in his composition; of blunt address, impatient gestures, and heartless physiognomy.

Her colloquy with this cast-iron rebel ran somewhat as follows: —

Bragg. Of what country are you?

Pauline. I am of French and Spanish descent.

Bragg. Where were you born?

Pauline. In New Orleans.

Bragg. Your speech savors of the Yankee twang.

Pauline. Well, as an actress, I've been playing Yankee parts so long that I suppose I've caught the "twang."

Bragg. But to the point: you have important papers in your possession, and if they prove you to be a spy, nothing can save you from a little hemp.

Pauline (carelessly). Well, go on; root the whole thing up, if you like.

Bragg (picking up a package of letters). Without sending out any spies, I know what goes on at the Yankee headquarters better than the clerks there know.

Pauline. Suppose I am found guilty; what will you do with me?

Bragg. Why, you'll be hanged; that's all.

Pauline. Come, now, general, I don't think I'll be either useful nor ornamental dangling at the end of a rope. Won't you let me choose my method of dying?

Bragg. Well, really, I couldn't, as you might choose to die in your bed, in the natural way.

Pauline. Come, now, won't shooting do just as well? It wouldn't hurt quite so bad, you know.

This interview had given our light-hearted heroine an idea. She was soon after taken very ill, and seemed in a fair way to cheat the general out of his pleasant little amusement of hanging a female, for she was tried (or was so informed, at least), found guilty, and condemned. The execution was delayed only by her continued sickness. At the eleventh hour her fortune changed. As our heroine was lying on her cot one fine morning in the last days of June, feeling that she would soon be well enough to be hung, there were signs at the headquarters of the rebel general of sudden commotion; and, before she was informed what it meant, the joyous sound of the Union bugles, playing the national airs, reached her sick room; and soon Rosecrans' advance guard was in town. Bragg had fled for the mountains, and she no longer felt the terrors of her unfortunate position.

General Garfield, in consideration of her long service, and suffering and danger, in the Union cause, and of two severe wounds, received while engaged in the secret service, conferred on the heroine the rank and title of major, by which she was afterwards commonly known.

MRS. JOHN HARRIS.

AT the very outset of the war, before the blood had commenced to flow in the long fratricidal strife, a group of ladies in Philadelphia met and organized a system of relief for the sufferings and privations which they knew must follow in the train of war.

They were mostly members of the church of Rev. Dr. Boardman, and had frequently coöperated in charitable labors for the destitute or ignorant of their own community or in pagan lands.

Mrs. Joel Jones was made the president of this association, and Mrs. Stephen Colwell was its treasurer. Its secretary was one of those delicate, fragile, and feeble-looking ladies who are apparently condemned to lives of patient suffering and inactivity by constitutional defect of physical vigor. She was known merely as a lady of warm personal piety, and excellent but mild and unobtrusive sense. Charitable and beneficent she had been in her quiet, daily life; but any aspirations that she may have had to wide, national, and laborious activity, were apparently quenched in the demands for passive endurance which almost constant illness made upon her. A heroine of Christian patience she might become, one would say; one of the uncounted sisterhood of silent pain, whose sighs are reckoned and whose chambers of suffering are visited by the angel who stood beside the mute Wrestler in Gethsemane. Yet she it was, this pallid and low-voiced lady, who, when the brazen trumpet of war rang across the continent, glided from her sick chamber, and entered upon a self-imposed and self-directed career of Christian and sanitary labors, more extended, more arduous, and more potent for good, than any other that can be found in American annals.

If there were any such vain decorations of human approbation as a crown, or a wreath, or a star for her, who in our late war has done the most, and labored the longest, who visited the greatest number of hospitals, prayed with the greatest number of suffering and dying soldiers, penetrated nearest to the front, and underwent the greatest amount of fatigue and exposure for the soldier, — that crown or that star would be rightfully given to Mrs. John Harris, of Philadelphia.

Yet not one in all the noble sisterhood is more indifferent than she to all human applause. What she did was not to be seen or praised of men. It was other than the crown that human fingers can weave her that she sought, —

"The perfect witness of all-judging Jove."

Very soon after the organization of the Ladies' Aid Society, Mrs. Harris saw that work at the front and in hospitals was imperatively demanded.

After the first battle of Manassas, hospitals were created in Washington and along the Potomac. These rapidly increased, both in the number of their patients and in the amount of suffering and want they contained, as the demands of the war at first far outran the sources of supply. Her first visits to the front were immediately after the first bloodshed, and though no heavy battles were fought in Virginia till the following summer, when we remember that over two hundred thousand men were suddenly transferred from civil to military life, it will not appear strange that there were full hospitals all along the Potomac for miles above and below Washington. At that time there was no one in America who could be said to have a full practical knowledge of military surgery and hygiene. The European systems needed important modifications before they could be successfully applied to our army and our people. In the mean time, as the ponderous machinery was becoming adjusted, Mrs. Harris devoted herself to alleviating suffering as she found it, and where she found it, bringing to the work the clear practical sense of a person perfectly familiar with housekeeping in all its details.

Before the army moved in the spring of 1862, Mrs. Harris had visited more than a hundred hospitals, making donations of such articles as she had received from the society at home, and suggesting various simple but effective arrangements for the preparation and distribution of food for the sick. When the army moved out to Manassas in March, and soon after was transferred to the Peninsula, her exertions and exposures were made to correspond with those of the men.

When she entered upon these labors she seems to have been inspired by twofold motives, both alike blessed. Her sympathies embraced all the wants of suffering, dying men;

and in the details that follow, the full, sad, and touching story of her labors by a thousand death-beds, on the field, in hospital tents, in shelter tents, in transports, or in lodges for the refugees, we are at a loss which most to admire in Mrs. Harris — the practical good sense with which she labored for the physical comfort of sufferers, or the abounding Christian zeal and love with which she always strove to make sacred impressions on the minds of those she met; the saintly spirit in which she knelt by the dying, and whispered words of celestial consolation into ears that were growing deaf to all human voices.

To how many she thus ministered, and with what blessed results, no human records can possibly inform us. Hundreds, if they ever testify of her kindness, and of the supreme consolations received from her lips, will speak of her in the upper kingdom, and on the peaceful shore.

And how many, if they could speak from the rude soldier graves where they were buried, would say the last they knew was the touch of her soft hand on their clammy forehead, her low voice at their ear whispering of the Lamb that was slain for them, the sacrifice that atones for all, the blood that washes away sin!

But her name is cherished and linked with the most sacred and touching memories, on many a far-off hill-side, and in many a lonely cottage; for from her pen came the last record that ever reached them of the hero boy who was wounded on the Chickahominy, or at Manassas or Antietam, and died in a hospital; of the dying patriot, who, with glazing eye and shortening breath, begged of her to take the ring from his finger when he was laid out, and to cut a lock of his hair, and send them to *her*.

Fortunately the records of these labors of patriotic zeal and Christian love are more numerous and in better preservation than those of many who were her fellow-laborers. As the secretary of the Ladies' Aid Society, she wrote constantly and very full letters to its president in Philadelphia; and, in compiling their semi-annual reports, these ladies very wisely published copious selections from Mrs. Harris' admirable productions, and thus imparted, to what would otherwise have been a mere business pamphlet, touching interest and lasting value.

The first that we hear of Mrs. Harris, in these reports, is at Fairfax Seminary, early in the spring of 1862, before the enemy had moved down to the Peninsula, and when a battle was supposed to be imminent at or near Manassas Junction. She took with her to the general hospitals, in and near Alexandria, a large number of boxes sent to the Ladies' Aid Society, and was engaged for some time in a careful and judicious distribution of their contents. At one place she found two hundred poor fellows, who had been thrown into an unfinished hospital, some of them lying around on piles of shavings, and some stretched on the work-benches. They made few complaints, however; but they did think some improvement might be made in their tea, and Mrs. Harris pushed her way to the cook-room, to see if she could make a useful suggestion. Talking the matter over with the cook, she found the plant was not in fault, nor the water; but all the pot he had for his two hundred men was a new cast-iron caldron, in which he boiled his soup, vegetables, meat, and tea in succession, each mess waiting its turn. Mrs. Harris at once went out, and without troubling anybody with a requisition, succeeded in getting, for three dollars, a very good boiler, which had originally cost ten. "You would all say I could not have used three dollars more wisely, could you have heard the poor fellows tell how much improved their tea was."

But the Potomac ceased, for a few months, to be the principal theatre of the strife; and we find Mrs. Harris, in May, laboring in the hospitals at Fortress Monroe, full of those who had sickened on the Peninsula, in the first month of picket and trench duty before Yorktown, and the wounded of both armies at Williamsburg. On the 21st of May, she writes, —

"Mrs. D. in the Chesapeake and Miss S. in the Hygeia Hospitals are noble women. I cannot speak of all their worth, nor can I describe the state of things here. No language can give the faintest idea of the scenes of suffering and deadly anguish through which we are passing. My dear friend, say to the ladies, that no sacrifice they can make would be felt as such could they look upon the pains, the groans, the dying strife, of hundreds of the brave fellows whom we saw embark but two months since at Alexandria, then full of buoyancy, and eager for the conflict which was to vindicate the honor of our flag, and cover their names with glory. Could you have visited with me, on Saturday, the largest ward of the Hygeia Hospital, your whole being would have thrilled with anguish. Friend and foe are crowded together without distinction — all suffering. The first one approached had been wounded in the thigh and arm. The leg had been amputated, and an extraction made of the broken bones in the arm. Surgeons had been probing the diseased portions, not heeding the shrieks of the sufferer, whom I found covered with cold sweat, and nearing the dark valley; indeed, the mists of the valley were settling over him. When the gracious words, 'Come unto me, all ye that are weary and heavy laden, and I will give you rest,' were spoken, the suffering one looked up, and exclaimed, 'Rest, rest! O, where, where?' 'In the bosom of Jesus, if you will but lay your sins on him, and your suffering, throbbing heart close to his, you will be filled with rest in all the fulness of its meaning.' He tried to stay his faith on the 'Rock;' but very soon the unseen closed him in, and left us vainly endeavoring to follow the departing soul.

"Next him sat a boy from Carolina, who had been shot through the body, and could not lie down. The poor fellow was soliloquizing, in low, tremulous tones, his eyes shut, thus: 'This poor boy was in the battle of Bull Run; left his mother on the 12th of April; she prayed for him, and almost broke her heart weeping. He wrote to his mother that he was safe and well. And then he got along, seeing a good many hard times, till the battle of Williamsburg. There a ball went through his body, and poor mother will never see her boy again. What a pity — yes, a mighty pity —.' I listened for a time with a bursting heart, and then took his hand, and said, 'Shall I be your mother, and comfort you?' 'Yes,' he said, in a childish way (he was only nineteen), 'I'll try and think she is here.' After a short talk, in which Jesus was held up to the dying boy as better even than a mother, he begged me to write to his mother 'a very long letter, sending a lock of my hair; but you needn't take the hair now; say everything to comfort her; but,' he added, 'I want her to know how her poor boy suffers; yes, I do that, she would feel so for me.' He lingered till Monday; and, after a painful operation, sank away most unexpectedly, and when I got there was in the dead-house. So I went into that dismal place, full of corpses, and cut a lock from the dead boy's head, and enclosed it to the mother, adding some words of comfort for the sorrow-stricken. He had received a religious training, and told me to tell his mother he would meet her in heaven.

"Next him was a young man from Massachusetts — a face full of gentleness, but wearing a painful, anxious expression. He was not quite certain that he was on the right foundation, and shrank from death."

Next him lay a young Alabamian. He was evidently past all surgical aid, and Mrs. Harris could only do as she had with his fellow-sufferer from Carolina — pray with him, and whisper consolatory words of Christ, and take a lock of his hair to send to his mother, with some account of how and where her boy had died. Her letters were often interrupted by calls to come to this dying man, or that suffering boy; yet all this time her practical labors were not suspended.

She had with her ten boxes, five of which she appropriated to the Chesapeake and five to the Williamsburg Hospital, and wrote very earnestly to Philadelphia for eggs, butter, port wine, crackers, green tea, bandages, lint, pickles, and shirts. "Pads and cushions, of every imaginable shape and form, are in demand. Oil silk greatly, very greatly needed."

A few days later, in June, about the time the battle of Fair Oaks was fought, we find Mrs. Harris on the Vanderbilt, which had just been loaded with seven hundred wounded from that field. Many of them had eaten nothing for three or four days, and the first cry that met her ears was for tea and bread. Making her way into the cook-room, she took hold with her own experienced hands; and she tells us how glad she felt when the great boiler was heating with three pounds of tea in it, and she had five or six gallons of gruel bubbling for the boys. Meantime she bought and cut up twenty-five loaves of bread, spreading jelly between the slices, and soon had tea passed around in buckets. Then she made her way into the hold, and gave the sick some pickles, which they said did them more good than all the medicine. Wine she added to the gruel, and it was relished "you cannot tell how much." One poor wounded boy she speaks of, exhausted with the loss of blood and long fasting, who looked up, after taking the first nourishment he could swallow since the battle of Saturday, then four days, and exclaimed, with face radiant with gratitude and pleasure, "O, that is life to me; I feel as if twenty years were given me to live."

Laboring thus all day, she was overtaken by a shower when going back to the Hygeia Hospital, and reached her room with every garment saturated, where she lay down "aching in every bone, with heart and head throbbing, unwilling to cease work while so much was to be done, but fell asleep at last, from sheer exhaustion," the latest sounds that fell upon her ear being groans from the operating room.

On the afternoon of the next day (or the next but one), she describes the scenes on board another vessel, in like manner freighted with suffering.

"The afternoon," she writes, "found us on board the Louisiana, where fearful sights met us. The whole day had been spent in operating. In one pile lay seventeen arms, hands, feet, and legs. A large proportion of the wounded had undergone mutilation in some important member. Many must die. Four lay with their faces covered, dying or dead. Many had not had their wounds dressed since the battle, and were in a sad state already. One brave fellow, from Maine, had lost both legs, and bore up with wonderful firmness. Upon my saying to him, 'You have suffered much for your country; we cannot thank you enough,' he replied, 'O, well, you 'hadn't ought to thank me. I went of my own accord, in a glorious cause. God bless McClellan.'

"And here let me say, the young lady, Miss B., whom I brought with me, spent the whole of Friday night on board the Louisiana, dressing and caring for the wounded. When I left the boat, at eleven o'clock at night, I was obliged to wash all my skirts, being drabbled in the mingled blood of Federal and Confederate soldiers, which covered many portions of the floor. I was obliged to kneel between them to wash their faces. This is war."

During the latter part of June Mrs. Harris continued these arduous labors nearer the front. Much of the time she was on Dudley Farm and at Savage's Station, so near the battle line that the balls and shells whizzed over where she was at work. The style of labor here was much the same as on the ships. At one time, as she was passing a house, the sentinel told her there was a captain of a Maine regiment very sick within.

She describes the scene thus: "We went in, no door obstructing, and there, upon a stretcher, in a corner of the room, opening directly upon the road, lay an elegant-looking youth, struggling with the last great enemy. His mind was wandering, and as we approached him, he exclaimed, 'Is it not cruel to keep me here, when my mother and sister, whom I have not seen for a year, are in the next room? They might let me go in.' Only for an instant did he seem to have a glimpse of the real, when he drew two rings from his finger, placed there by the loved ones, handed them to an attendant, saying, 'Carry them home.' Then he was amid battle scenes, shouting, 'Deploy to the left! keep out of that ambuscade! Now go, my braves! Double quick! Strike for the flag! On, on!' he shouted, tossing up both his arms; 'you'll win the day.' As we looked on the beautiful face and manly form, thus wrestling with the strong enemy, and thought of the mother and sister in their distant home, surrounded by every luxury wealth could purchase, worlds seemed too cheap to give to have him with them.

"Having fought through three battles, he was not willing to admit that he was sick till the vital currents ebbed out, and he was actually dying. To the last he talked of his men; and now was no time to speak of the spirit-land. When I whispered a verse of Scripture in his ear, he smiled and thanked me, but could not appreciate the sacred words. He was a graduate of Waterville College, and twenty of his company were graduates of the same college. An only son, his mother and sister doted on him; but the mandate had gone forth, and there he lay, unconscious, in the grasp of a monster that would never relax till he had done his work."

Mrs. Harris was at Savage's Station and Seven Pines while the fight was raging. Here, in the primary hospitals, and under the trees in the rear of the carnage, she took part in scenes, and assumed duties, which not often fall to her sex. Now she was soothing patients under the hands of the operator; now preparing the minds of "great, noble-looking men, officers and privates," to submit to the amputation of an arm or a leg. Her woman's heart was much moved for a captain from Massachusetts, who pleaded very hard for his leg. "O, my wife and children," he would say (and he had seven), "it will kill them to see me so mutilated." But it was of no avail. The ball had shattered his knee-joint, and amputation was unavoidable. So the chloroform was pressed to his mouth, and he was taken insensible to the operating table.

Her opinion of some army chaplains, notwithstanding her earnest piety, does not seem to have been very high. It was the night after the battle of Seven Pines; and she had just seated herself, after a most exhausting day, to a cup of tea, "when a great, healthy man, there to look after the sick and wounded, and a chaplain, too, came to me, saying, 'They have just brought in a soldier, with a leg blown off; he is in a horrible condition; can't you wash him?' I was about to reply, 'Can't you perform that sacred office yourself?' when the thought *the man that acts so would not be tender*, checked me, and soon the duty was over; but I knew I 'had done it for his burial.' So a grave was dug, and we gave him back to earth, but not till I had cut away a lock of his hair for his Massachusetts mother."

During the first days of July these labors continued, and grew more tragical, before it was known in how tolerable a condition the army was brought to Harrison's Landing. When she reached that place — carried from the Landing to a wagon on a sailor's back, through mud knee-deep — the welcome she received from the crowds of poor, war-worn soldiers, who crowded the banks, was a reward for all her hardships.

Among the sick and wounded at Harrison's Landing and the hospitals along James River and at Fortress Monroe, Mrs. Harris labored through the months of July and August, with the same earnest devotion, the same mixture of Christian zeal with practical and physical kindness, that characterized her service elsewhere.

In August, her attention was directed principally to raising the spirits and health of the great number of the partially sick, who needed only rest, cheerful words, and palatable food. Ovens were built, and bread for whole regiments mixed and moulded, and baked by her directions. Pickles and jellies were brought from Philadelphia in large quantities, and distributed with the daily ration. Shirts, handkerchiefs, and socks were given out.

On the 20th August, she wrote from Fortress Monroe that she had been busy as possible getting a new hospital under way, had six hundred patients to begin with, and nothing to feed them with but the stores of the Ladies' Aid Society. In two days this number was swelled to fourteen hundred, mostly convalescents. Very opportunely, as she observed, she received sixty packages from New York and Massachusetts.

During the last two weeks of August, she distributed one hundred baskets, seventy-two barrels, five bags, and five boxes of onions; eight barrels of apples, eight of potatoes, three of beets, three of squashes; eighteen bushels of tomatoes; five barrels of pickles, one of molasses; two kegs of butter, six of dried rusk and crackers; eighty pounds of cheese, and large quantities of clothing, towels, farina, wine, milk, and cocoa.

Early in September these sanitary labors were again, for nearly two months, suspended, and her time was almost wholly occupied in the care of the dying and wounded, in the swiftly-following and bloody engagements that commenced with Jackson's advance up the Shenandoah Valley, and ended with Lee's defeat at Antietam.

The following extract, from a letter written just after Antietam, is a picture of her labors, and the sights and sufferings through which she moved during that battle autumn: —

"Night was closing in upon us — the rain falling fast; the sharpshooters were threatening all who ventured near our wounded and dying on the battle-ground; a line of battle in view, artillery in motion, litters and ambulances going in all directions; wounded picking their way, now lying down to rest, some before they were out of the range of the enemy's guns, not a few of whom received their severest wounds in these places of imagined safety; add to this, marching and countermarching of troops; bearers of dispatches hurrying to and fro; eager, anxious inquirers after the killed and wounded; and the groans of the poor sufferers under the surgeons' hands,—and you may form some faint idea of our position on that eventful evening. Reaching a hospital but a few removes from the cornfield in which the deadliest of the strife was waged, I found the ground literally covered with the dead and wounded—barns, hayricks, outhouses of every description, all full. Here and there a knot of men, with a dim light near, told of amputations; whilst the shrieks and groans of the poor fellows, lying all around, made our hearts almost to stand still. The rain fell upon their upturned faces, but it was not noticed; bodily pain and mental anguish—for many were brought to meet the king of terrors face to face, and would have given worlds to evade his cold touch—rendered them indifferent to their surroundings. Most of the sufferers were from General Meagher's Irish brigade, and were louder in their demonstrations of feeling than are the Germans, or our own native born. We could do little that night but distribute wine and tea, and speak comforting words. We were called to pray with a dying Christian; and I feel the grasp of his hand yet, as we knelt around in the rain, in the dark night, with only the glimmering lights around the operating tables, and looked up to the Father of our Lord and Saviour for his mercy and grace to fall upon the dying man, and all his comrades clustering round us needing dying grace. Then we sang, 'There is rest for the weary,' Miss G.'s loud, clear voice leading. The sound stopped the shrieks and groans of the brave men. They listened. They all seemed comforted. It was then midnight, or near it. Before the next sun threw its rays in upon these twelve hundred wounded soldiers, the darkness of death had settled upon eleven sons, husbands, and fathers, whose hearts had throbbed healthfully with loving thoughts of home and country but a few hours before. We remained at this hospital until the evening of the 19th; we had slept a few hours on the straw upon which our soldiers had lain, and upon which their life-blood had been poured out. We prepared tea, bread and butter, milk punch, and egg-nog; furnished rags, lint, and bandages, as needed, and then came on to French's Division Hospital, where were one thousand of our wounded, and a number of Confederates. The first night we slept in our ambulance; no room in the small house, the only dwelling near, could be procured. The next day was the Sabbath. The sun shone brightly; the bees and the birds were joyous and busy; a beautiful landscape spread out before us, and we knew the Lord of the Sabbath looked down upon us. But, with all these above and around us, we could see only our suffering, uncomplaining soldiers, mutilated, bleeding, dying. Almost every hour I witnessed the going out of some young life. No words can describe the wonderful endurance: not a murmur, not a word of complaint or regret. Many such expressions as the following have been heard: 'Yes, I have struck my last blow for my country; whether I have served my country well others may judge. I know I love her more than life.' The lip quivered with emotion, and the face was full of meaning, as he added, 'I am done with all this, and must meet eternity. I have thought too little of the future. I had a praying mother. O that I might meet her!' Another, a mere youth, with full, round face and mild blue eyes, said, 'Hold my hand till I die. I am trying to think of my Saviour; but think of my mother and father; their hearts will break.' Another, in reply to the remark, 'Well, my brother, you have fought a good fight; we thank you for what you have done and suffered for us; and now we want to talk to you about One who suffered and died for you and for us, eighteen hundred and sixty-two years ago, and now lives to intercede for us. He is near us now, and knows all your wants. Shall we ask him to abide with you, for the day is closing?' Putting his hand (he had but one) to his eyes—'It is growing dark; can it be death?' For a time emotion was too big for utterance; but, recovering himself, he said, 'I came into the army to die if need be, but did not think it would come so soon — my first battle. O, my wife and children! O God, have mercy upon them!' As we left him, his earnest 'Mother, come soon again,' fell upon my heart. When next seen, I turned from him with sorrow inexpressible. The straightened, defined form, covered over with a blanket, told of three orphaned children and a stricken widow. The love of home, and thoughtful care of mothers, sisters, and fathers, are manifested most touchingly, especially by our New England soldiers: perhaps this may be true of all from rural districts, in the several states. The loss of a strong arm or leg is a mother's loss. 'Who will support her if I am disabled? Who will cut her wood and fetch her water?' I just recall an instance of filial devotion on the part of a young boy, who sickened and died on his way to Poolesville the last month. He was extremely delicate, almost childish in appearance and expression. When told that he must be very quiet, that his physician thought he should have rested at Washington, and not come on with his regiment, he replied, 'Yes, I thought I ought to stay there; I felt awful bad and weak like; but it seemed so much like giving up.' Then he burst into tears, and his delicate frame quivered with emotion, as he added, 'My mother is weakly, and is trying to educate my little brother and sister, and I helped her; and now that I must die, what will she do?' After a time he grew calm, and said, 'I will try and leave her where she said she left me all the time — in the arms of our heavenly Father. If I die, he can and will take care of her and her children.' All this was said with many interruptions, for he was very weak. He languished a few days, and slept in Jesus. This is not an uncommon experience.

"Passing over the battle-ground of the 9th, such sights as might cause the general pulse of life to stand still met our eyes.

"Stretched out in every direction, as far as the eye could reach, were the dead and dying. Much the larger proportion must have died instantly — their positions, some with ramrod in hand to load, others with gun in hand as if about to aim, others still having just discharged their murderous load. Some were struck in the act of eating. One poor fellow still held a potato in his grasp. Another clutched a piece of tobacco; others held their canteens as if to drink; one grasped a letter. Two were strangely poised upon a fence, having been killed in the act of leaping it. How my heart sickens at the recollection of the appearance of these men, who had left their homes in all the pride of manly beauty.

"When they kissed their loved ones, and bade farewell, a gush of pride, mixed with the sadness of the parting, may have swelled the hearts of mothers, wives, and sisters, as they gazed upon the manly forms, in their bright, new uniforms, and for a time the perils of the soldier may have been forgotten. Now, how changed! Begrimed with dust, heads and bodies bloated and blackened, a spectacle of sickening horror, objects of loathing, the worm already preying upon them!"

Other letters, written in October, give full accounts of the deaths of various soldiers, whose devotion and excellence of character had interested Mrs. Harris, whose sufferings were soothed by her gentle and Christian consolations, and who finally died in full faith, glad to have suffered so much for their country, and hopeful when the summons of release reached them.

These letters of Mrs. Harris from the Peninsula and the Potomac, in 1862, were published and extensively read in the loyal communities of the North, and had a great effect in increasing her usefulness, and that of the society of which she was secretary. She displayed remarkable fitness for hospital and sanitary labors. Her usefulness in the trying duties she fulfilled was abundantly evinced by the testimony of surgeons, officers, and soldiers, in the field and in the hospitals; and now very large supplies were sent directly to Mrs. Harris, at the front, without passing through the rooms of the Ladies' Aid Society of Philadelphia.

During the period from October, 1862, to May, 1863, although but one great battle took place in Virginia, Mrs. Harris continued her hospital labors with unabated zeal and devotion. At no time in the long struggle was sanitary service more needed; for the winter of 1862–3 was in this war what that of 1777–8 was to the Continental army under Washington. The troops had been worn down by the unexampled fatigues of the fall campaign, and when the cold weather set in, sickness multiplied at a rate so alarming, as to threaten, at one time, the very organization of the army.

Between thirty and forty thousand men were in the sick and convalescent camps, that extended from the Rappahannock to the Potomac. Thirty thousand more lay in the military hospitals in and around Washington. Mrs. Harris was laboring, during the month of November, to direct the attention of government to the destitution and suffering in these convalescent camps; and finally Congress was aroused to action, and some slow and inadequate remedies were applied. Writing on the subject, in December, she says, "I am at present exercised in mind and body to a fearful degree. Think of the cold weather of the past week, and of hundreds of our boys, many of whom we had nursed at Bolivar and Smoketown, who came here to join their regiments, being thrown into this camp to suffer and die. So it has been. Fifteen of those in whom I was interested have died — shall I write it? — of starvation and exposure, within three weeks, and that under the shadow of our Capitol."

Early in January the command of the army passed into the hands of General Hooker, and by degrees a better spirit was infused into the whole Union force. But there was much suffering during the winter from cold and sickness. Picket duty was very heavy, and the sick at all times abundant. Mrs. Harris was for many weeks established at the Lacey House, where her self-imposed duties were onerous and varied.

She procured a stove, some corn-meal and ground ginger, and with wine and crackers prepared, every day, and often twice in a day, a large supply of hot ginger panada for the pickets as they came in from the line of the Rappahannock. The boys were extremely fond of this preparation, and were drawn up in line in front of her headquarters, each receiving in his tin cup, from her own hands often, the wholesome and stimulating preparation. It will never be known how many a poor fellow, coming in from his post, where he had stood for the weary hours of an inclement night in the mud and sleet of a Virginia winter, was saved from pneumonia by this simple expedient.

The following picture of Sabbath morning life at the Lacey House will illustrate the manner in which her time was spent during that winter and spring: —

"Could you have looked in upon us at breakfast time this day of sacred rest, your eye would have fallen on scenes and groupings all out of harmony with its holy uses. One cooking-stove pushed to its utmost capacity, groaning beneath the weight of gruel, coffee, and tea, around it clustered soldiers, shivering, drenched to the skin, here and there a poor fellow coiled upon the floor, too full of pain and weariness to bear his own weight. Seated along the table, as closely as possible, were others, whose expressions of thanks told how grateful the simple repast was — bread, stewed fruit, and coffee. All alike were wet and cold, having been exposed throughout the night to the driving snow and rain, the most uncomfortable one of the season. Two poor boys groan under the pressure of pain; they are carried to the chamber, their wet stockings removed, feet bathed with camphor, spice tea given them, and an ambulance sent for. Now we return to our room of all-work. The vapor from the clothing of the soldiers, mingled with the steam from the coffee and gruel, condenses on my glasses; the eye waters, too, and the lungs are oppressed with the heavy atmosphere, and for a moment I am ready to give up; but only for a moment. Suddenly the word 'halt' is heard, and an instant after such a chorus of coughs smites upon our ears, and each one seems to say, 'What thy hand findeth to do, do it with all thy might.' Seventy-two of our defenders stood there in the raw March wind, in need of something to keep the powers of life in action. Thoroughly wet, icicles on their blankets after a sleepless night, a march of from three to five miles before them, sinking every step over shoe-top in mud and slush, — could you have seen the eager pressing forward, tin cup in hand, to secure the coveted portion, simple as it was, you would feel that God's own day was honored."

These labors were continued till late in April, when the advance across the river commenced. Sometimes Mrs. Harris acted as apothecary, sometimes as physician, constantly as nurse and Christian friend.

The preparation of the ginger panada, or "bully soup," as the soldiers called it, was kept up as long as the north bank of the river was picketed. She continued to visit those who were very sick, and especially all she heard of who could not recover, and labored, in her simple and direct way, to fit them, if possible, for the great change.

Letters, full and graphic, descriptive of all these scenes and labors, were constantly forwarded to the Ladies' Aid Society, and, when published and extensively circulated, aroused a wide-spread sympathy for the heroic sufferers, and admiration for the no less heroic laborers in the army hospitals and at the front.

Early in May came the battle of Chancellorsville, and for a few weeks the letters of Mrs. Harris were less frequent, so completely was her time absorbed by the constant and painful demands upon her to act as nurse and Christian comforter to the ten thousand wounded in that fearful series of engagements.

The extent and degree of that suffering is best understood from an extract from a letter of May 18.

"After seeing Mrs. B. and Mrs. L. off, we filled two ambulances with bread and butter, prepared stewed fruit, egg-nog, lemons, oranges, cheese, shirts, drawers, stockings, and handkerchiefs, and went out to meet a train of ambulances bearing the wounded from United States Ford. Reaching Stoneman's Station, where we expected to meet the train, we learned we were a half hour too late, but could overtake them; so we pressed forward, and found ourselves in the rear of a long procession of one hundred and two ambulances. The road being narrow, steep, and most difficult, we could not pass, and so were obliged to follow, feeling every jolt and jar for our poor suffering ones, whose wounds had just reached that point when the slightest motion is agony.

"When this sad procession halted near the hospital of the Sixth army corps, we prepared to minister to the sufferers. Some gentlemen of the Christian Commission were there to assist us. No pen can describe the scene. Most of these sufferers had been wounded on the 3d instant.

"Amputations and dressings had been hurriedly gone over, and then much neglected, necessarily so, for the rebel surgeons had more than enough to occupy them in the care of their own wounded. You know we left most of our wounded on the right in their hands.

"By day and by night I see their poor mutilated limbs, red with inflammation, bones protruding, worms rioting as they were held over the sides of the ambulance to catch the cooling breeze! Those anguished faces—what untold suffering they bespoke! Many a lip quivered, and eye filled with tears, when approached with words of sympathy; and not a few told how they had prayed for death to end their sufferings, as they were dashed from side to side, often rolling, in their helplessness, over each other, as they were driven those twenty weary miles. We came to one poor fellow with a ball in his breast. His companion, who was utterly helpless, having been wounded in both arms, had rolled on him, and was thrown off only by a lurch of the ambulance. When we carried him some egg-nog, he drank it eagerly, and asked to be raised up, stopping at intervals to recover breath; but before his turn came to be lifted from the ambulance, the mortal had put on immortality, and his wife and five children left to plead with God the promises made to the fatherless and widow.

"We have sent large amounts of hospital supplies to Mrs. Husband and Mrs. McKay, in the Third corps. Miss Dix asked me to attend to the distribution of a half barrel of eggs and some oranges, and they were divided between these ladies, who are both admirable women.

"For six mornings we have prepared five gallons of custard, using six dozen eggs, and about eight gallons of pudding. The surgeons tell us to give as much wholesome, nutritious food to the wounded as they will eat. You may judge how completely our time is filled up. Our evening meetings are now so largely attended that we have been obliged to resort to the main building. They are temporarily disturbed, at nine o'clock, by the cry, 'Fall in, third relief,' when the heavy tread of men, the clatter of swords, and the rustle of the old relief taking their places are heard. We find it difficult to close these services, so full of enjoyment are they to the soldiers."

These religious meetings were continued for three months, and were very numerously attended. Mrs. Harris assumed the whole responsibility, occasionally calling upon clergymen and others, whom she knew, to lead the devotions of the audience. Her hospital labors continued, as described above, after the battles of the Peninsula and Antietam, with occasional flying trips to Washington and other points in the vicinity, to look up and forward the boxes of the Ladies' Aid Society. Late in June and on the first days of July, we find her, now in Harrisburg and soon after in Washington, sharing the general uncertainty as to where the struggle, that all knew to be impending, must take place, yet ready, with her sanitary stores, to commence labors at once.

On the 3d of July she was in Washington, and besought of the government, with tears, permission to carry forward to Gettysburg a car-load of supplies, but was advised that it was unsafe to go to the front. Taking some chloroform and stimulants, she left Baltimore on the 4th, and penetrated as near as possible to the scene of the conflict, ministering as much as in her power to the stream of wounded that filled the cars, and was now rapidly swelling with each arrival from Gettysburg. Hundreds of the soldiers greeted her, she says, with the kindest expressions.

On the 9th she writes from Gettysburg these few hurried words:—

"Am full of work and sorrow. The appearance of things here beggars all description. Our dead lie unburied, and our wounded neglected. Numbers have been drowned by the sudden rising of the waters in the creek bottoms, and thousands of them are still naked and starving. God pity us! — pity us!"

On the day following she gives a fuller account, saying she has been on the field of blood since the 4th, and has seen suffering of the most fearful character.

On the 12th Mrs. Harris and another lady, finding supplies in great abundance at Gettysburg, and a large number of assistants arriving daily, concluded that they could do more good by following the advance of General Meade, and attending to the fresh cases of the wounded and sick.

With two ambulances, one loaded with medical stores and the other with food and clothing, they followed the army in its rapid marches for nearly a month. Severe skirmishing was in progress much of the time, and great numbers were taken sick. At Warrenton the inhabitants refused them their kitchens, and they prepared food for the sick soldiers in the street, feeding the hungry and clothing the naked in barns, by the wayside, in churches, in cars, wherever they could find the suffering soldiers.

Her letters, during this month of labor, were neither long nor frequent. Yet she says it was a real trial to her to be so summary when so many moving incidents pressed upon her mind, and tingled at the tips of her fingers.

In August we find her again at Warrenton, giving out supplies for four hospitals recently opened there, and instructing the doctors and surgeons in the homely science of preparing farina, corn starch, and panada for the sick.

She says there was hardly a family at Warrenton but mourned one dead at Gettysburg. The extreme heat, and long-protracted and heavy service, had produced great prostration in many who were not suffering from acute disease. The water, too, was in some places very impure. She sent to Philadelphia for a large number of empty phials, and filling these with such stimulants as the doctors advised, left them at the head of each of the suffering soldiers, thus saving many lives, and alleviating much misery.

Early in September she found herself one evening so exhausted by labor, travel, discomfort, and the extreme heat, that she was for a little time fixed in the determination to seek health and repose among the mountain breezes and cool streams of the Alleghanies. But the next morning being somewhat restored by sleep, she was actively forming plans for further labors of relief and comfort for "the brave boys." After breakfasting on a piece of army bread, and some jelly, eaten with a rusty knife and an old tin tea-spoon, she heard that some cavalrymen, the Sixth Michigan, were not far distant, and greatly in need of aid. After much difficulty and delay in crossing a swollen creek, she was hailed with joy by all who knew the humane nature of her errand. She found sixty sick men, wholly without attendance or food. The surgeon in charge had been prostrated with camp fever — the hospital steward and the cook were both sick. They had camped in a low, marshy place; and, as the men were exhausted by long marches, irregular meals, and sleepless nights, they yielded in great numbers to the miasm of the swamp, and the glare of the sun, unbroken by any friendly shade. They had eaten nothing for several days but a few mouldy pieces of hard-tack, and drank black coffee, boiled in their tin cups.

Mrs. Harris drives up to where a little camp kettle is hanging over a low fire, and finds the whole cooking equipment of these sixty or seventy sick men consists of a small sheet-iron stove, a small tea-kettle, two tin pans holding a gallon each, one small water-bucket, a few spoons, and a broken earthen dish.

She collects all the canteens belonging to the men, and sends them with the bucket to the spring, replenishes the fire, gets the bag of farina from the ambulance, as also the sugar, dried rusk, nutmegs, brandy, butter, milk, and flavoring extracts. When the water was brought she filled up the vessels and sent them for more.

Then the horse-bucket, from the ambulance, was cleaned, and partly filled with dried rusk, a few spoonfuls of butter, a half bottle of brandy, four nutmegs, and boiling water poured over the whole, and the panada was made.

While this was being distributed, and, as there were but a few tin cups, but few could be supplied at a time, the largest kettleful of farina was boiling.

Then she adds, "If you could have seen the tears and heard the thanks of these sick braves, you would not wonder that I remain here day after day."

Soon after this, Mrs. Harris returned home for a few days of rest; but on the 24th September we find her at Culpepper, spending her days in preparing food for the sick, of which she says there were not less than four hundred in the four hospitals. Remaining a few days at this post of duty, she returned to Philadelphia early in October; and, after advising with the officers of the society, it is decided that she is to go west of the mountains, and labor for the lives and comfort of the thousands and tens of thousands whose hopes, health, and happiness had been crushed under the iron wheel of war.

Two great armies had marched and countermarched, for nearly a year, through the counties of Tennessee that are adjacent to the Nashville and Chattanooga Railroad. Rosecrans, after his great battle of Stone River, had pressed upon his antagonist, and partly by force, but mainly by stratagem, had driven him out of Middle Tennessee, and thrown him across the river of that name, into Northern Georgia.

There, on the 19th and 20th of September, a long and

bloody contest had taken place on the slopes of Lookout Mountain, and in the valley of the Chickamauga below, for possession of the roads leading to Chattanooga. The Union force was overpowered, and driven back to Chattanooga, taking a considerable part of their wounded with them, but leaving many in the enemy's hands.

Communication with the rear was greatly interrupted. Supplies could not be forwarded, and horses and mules were dying by the hundred every day in the mountain passes, all the way from Tullahoma to Chattanooga.

Refugees, of all ages and both sexes, and every shade of color and degree of intelligence, were crowded into Nashville, and the various towns along the road to Chattanooga. Most of these wretched people were poor and destitute to the last degree.

The Ladies' Aid Society, of which Mrs. Harris was secretary, was not confined in its operations to one army, or one class of sufferers. A noiseless channel for the distribution of genuine charities, its principle of action from the time it was organized, in April, 1861, till the Proclamation of Peace, was to relieve any suffering, in any part of the land, that arose out of the state of war, and in this noble mission to "sow beside all waters." A signal of distress in any quarter, whether from a provost guard at a fort, the captive in his prison, the soldier on the field, the mutilated but patient hero in the hospital, the refugee from starvation and death, the Cherokee in his devastated fields, the freedman in his destitution, even the bleeding rebel solder, alike called forth the sympathies and shared the bounties of this association.

As transportation was slow and difficult, the Ladies' Aid Society could not forward to the sufferers in Tennessee those supplies which they had so freely sent to the Potomac army; and when Mrs. Harris left for Nashville, in the middle of October, she was supplied with money from the treasury of the society, and a few boxes of the most portable sanitary articles, to be used according to her discretion. In two days after her arrival she commenced her labors of love among the Union refugees — that large class of the miserably poor who had migrated from the pine barrens of North Carolina, and settled on the mountain sides and in the obscure caves of the Alleghany and Cumberland ranges. In the days of peace and comparative plenty, these people were poor. But when the whirlwind of war swept through their secluded valleys; when the once united and harmonious communities were divided into bitter factions; —

> "When the clarion's music thrills
> To the heart of the lone hills;
> When the spear in conflict shakes,
> And the strong lance, shivering, breaks;"

then want and famine overtook these people as an armed man, and their condition became truly pitiable.

"It is a very dark picture," writes Mrs. Harris, "made up of miserable looking women and old men, with naked children of all ages. Many come here to die, no provision being made for them other than the food and shelter afforded by government. After herding together indiscriminately in some dirty wareroom, or unfinished, unfurnished tenement, in ill-ventilated apartments, they become an easy prey to that foe of all the ill-clad and ill-fed — typhus fever. It comes in the form of a chill, followed by fever; and this is followed by jabbering idiocy, with no great suffering, except to sympathizers. The mind of the sick one is filled with old home scenes; ghastly smiles, more saddening by far than tears, play over wan and haggard faces; the patient sinks, in a few days fills a government coffin, and is carried to a nameless grave. Going into a long, dark room, on the ground floor, in an unfinished mammoth hotel, now used as barracks, we found in the foreground some half dozen women with a crowd of children, crouching around a smoking stove; the women in tattered, dirty garments, their vacant, listless expression seeming to say, 'We are only poor white trash.' The children, dressed in hospital shirts, — no other garments, — would have looked comical had their poor little faces been hid; these were so unlike careless childhood that we could only look and wonder if any that surrounded our Saviour when he took them in his arms and blessed them were like these. In the background were beds, so close as scarcely to admit a passage between them. On one of the beds lay a sick old man, moaning; still farther on, a young woman in the last stage of rapid consumption. Two of these homeless sick had that morning found homes from which they will never be driven. The wretched inmates told us they were 'right smart better off then than they had been.' They made no complaints."

Among these unhappy people Mrs. Harris labored for more than a month. She watched with the sick, and prayed with those about to die. She assembled them in some large room, or, when the weather would admit, in the open air, and engaged some Christian speaker to hold before them the model of Him who knows our sorrows, and is acquainted with all human griefs; who was himself homeless, and had not where to lay his head. Not confining her labors to the refugees, Mrs. Harris visited various hospitals in Nashville, and was able to do a great deal for the comfort of those who were about to be sent forward to Louisville, on their way homeward.

In November we find her in Louisville, communicating with the towns in the North-Western States, and collecting the materials for a general thanksgiving dinner in Nashville. Having obtained large supplies for this purpose, she did not stay to see the soldiers enjoy their luxuries, but pressed forward with relief to the suffering and starving in Bridgeport and Chattanooga. Two weeks later she wrote from Chattanooga, where her labors for the wounded were similar to those for the Potomac army, of which a full recital has been given; but she saw more horror, and agony, and death, during her three months here, than she had ever seen in her whole experience in the East.

"As I write, an ambulance passes, bearing the remains of four heroes of the late battles; all of them full of hope when I came here, and, though wounded, talking only of victory; one telling how vexed he felt when the bullet struck him, half way up the hill; another rejoicing that he got to the top; another, that he grasped the flag, and held it aloft nearly at the top—is sure the old 'Stars and Stripes' saw the top, if he didn't. And so they talked, for days, only of their country's triumph; but a change passed over them. Gangrene was commencing its ravages, and they were carried from their comrades, and put in tents, lest the poison might be communicated to their wounded fellow-sufferers. There, in the 'gangrene ward,' the glory of battle and victory faded away, as the fatal disease bore them nearer and nearer to the great eternity that shuts out all sounds of war.

"Then the fearful misgivings that took the place of the hopes of earthly glory were deeply engraven on their poor, wan faces, and began to be whispered in the ears of Christian sympathy. No words can describe the condition of our hospitals here, and of the whole country. Think of Golgotha, the Valley of Hinnom, and all the dark places of the earth, and you may arrive at some conception of it."

Just as Mrs. Harris was entering systematically into measures of sanitary relief similar to those she had so admirably conducted on the battle-fields of Virginia, the long series of labors, exposures, and anxieties worked their natural effect upon her constitution, and for two weeks she was very sick. For a time, even, her life was despaired of; but while so much was to be done for those crowded hospitals, she could not give up her hold on life, and God, in his mercy, restored her to health, and gave her back, to be an unspeakable blessing and comfort to those who suffered in hope, and to those who languished without hope. Early in January she resumed her labors and her correspondence with the society, saying, in reference to her sickness, only these words: "I feel almost ashamed to consume your time with any account of it, the suffering all around me is of such an intense character."

During the months of January and February, 1864, she labored incessantly in the great hospitals of Chattanooga, still crowded with the wounded of two terrific battles. In January she was rejoiced when the transportation was such as to allow all the well men to be comfortably clothed and fed. The railroad was not opened till the middle of the month. The battle of Chickamauga had been fought four months before. In recapitulating the events of that time, she writes, "My experiences, since I reached Chattanooga, have been among the most painful of the three past eventful years. In looking back, amazement seizes me, and the attempt to rehearse them seems futile. War, famine, and pestilence have made up the warp and woof of our soldier life. As I entered one of the hospitals, early in December, and asked, 'Well, friends, how are you getting along?' the response came from many a cot, 'We are starving.' A surgeon remarked to me, in a careless tone, 'A great many of our men have starved to death, but they did not know it.' He was mistaken."

As spring opened, active operations were about to be resumed at Chattanooga. It was the commencement of Sherman's last magnificent campaign. Mrs. Harris accordingly returned to Nashville in March, and for two months continued her labors among the unhappy class for whom she had done so much in the fall.

As the Union arms became victorious in Northern Georgia, a great number of refugees from these counties came pouring northward, and stopped at Nashville.

The following picture of sights and groups, among which Mrs. Harris's daily life at Nashville was passed, illustrates at once the misery of these refugees, and the Christian kindliness of her ministration: —

"As I entered a house on the Murfreesboro' Pike, a few miles out of Nashville, which showed signs of former elegance, but was now occupied by twelve refugee families, I was met by a ragged little child, who said, 'That's our room; my aunt is there. I reckon she's dying.' Upon a bed lay a woman whose breathing told of the death-struggle. Stooping over the fire were the mother and sisters, in silent grief. They had been driven from comfortable homes in Dade County, Georgia, because their husbands were loyal, and had months before entered the Union army. After untold sufferings, they found themselves among strangers, miserably lodged, and worse fed. All of them had been sick. Two children had died; and now the daughter, a mother, too, was dying. None of them could read. I stooped over the dying woman, and repeated a part of the fourteenth chapter of John. She turned her dying eyes on me, and with a look of glad surprise, exclaimed, 'That's my home; Jesus is there, and he is here. I have had a power of trouble, and been pestered mightily; but it was worth it all to feel how good Jesus is.'"

After her return from these protracted and depressing labors in the West, the health of Mrs. Harris was so utterly wasted, that not even the inspiration of an heroic purpose or the promptings of holy zeal could sustain her in labors equal to those she had undergone. But when the life-blood of the army of the Potomac was poured out at so fearful a rate in the great campaign of 1864, she went down to Fredericksburg, and soon after to White House and City Point, and labored with her customary earnestness and efficiency.

Early in the spring of 1865 she went into the department of Virginia and North Carolina, and was in the latter state when Sherman brought his veteran army around in that gigantic curve to the rear of the rebel stronghold, and the closing scenes of the long tragedy were rapidly hurried across the arena. Almost her last acts of kindness to soldiers were bestowed upon the wretched victims of malignity that had staggered alive out of the infamous prison pens at Andersonville and Salisbury.

It was not until the army corps were disbanded and the primary hospitals broken up, not until the bloody stretchers were rolled up and stowed away with the bandages and lint, to gather dust in dim corners of government storehouses, that Mrs. Harris could regard her mission ended and her occupation gone. With returning and established peace she has glided back to the life of quiet duty and patient endurance, from which, four years before, she had emerged, her health feebler than before, suffering constantly from the effects of a sunstroke, received while laboring on the field at Savage's Station. But if the approving testimony of conscience is any reward; if ever mercy is twice blessed, enriching the receiver and the giver alike; if the affectionate admiration of the thousands who saw her labors, and were benefited by them, is precious, — this admiration, this blessing, this reward, she has, to alleviate the weariness of her sick chamber, and to brighten the pathway along which she moves to the heavenly approval.

MISS MARY E. SHELTON.

THE various scenes, movements, and charities of our great civil struggle can be divided into two grand enterprises, each having a widely separated, yet equally important object. The moral objective of the war was the capture of Richmond; the physical objective was to obtain and secure possession of the magnificent valley and river that occupy the centre of the revolted region.

Of course a result so important as either was not to be accomplished without labors, and bloodshed, and sufferings, whose sum no human method can ever express.

Though Vicksburg and the towns on the Lower Mississippi were more remote from the centres of supply than the Virginia towns, yet the directness of water communication nearly compensated for the difference in miles; and the western armies, led by Grant and Sherman, were represented at home by a population as warm in its loyalty, and as generous in the spirit of sacrifice, as those who stood behind the forces of McClellan, and Hooker, and Meade.

In the summer of 1863 the labors of Mrs. Anne Wittenmeyer had become so extensive, the field of her operations so wide, and her letters so numerous, that she needed a secretary to relieve her, in a portion at least, of her self-imposed duties.

It was in this capacity of secretary to Mrs. Wittenmeyer, in the fall of 1863, soon after the surrender of Vicksburg, that Miss Mary E. Shelton commenced her hospital experience.

On the 10th of August she left Keokuk, and on the way to St. Louis her time was fully occupied in answering a large number of letters, which Mrs. Wittenmeyer, as president of the Ladies' Aid Society of Iowa, had received from various parts of that and the adjacent states. From the number and tenor of these letters Miss Shelton was made more fully alive to the extent and the bitter results of the great war then at its height. Here was one from a heart-broken father, saying, "one of his sons had recently died in a southern hospital, and the only one remaining was very low with fever; would Mrs. Wittenmeyer see him, and ascertain his wants, and let them know?" A wife, with a family of little ones, almost destitute, wrote that her husband had consumption, and begged that he might spend his last days at home. A widowed mother had not heard from her sick son for many weeks; "would Mrs. Wittenmeyer inquire about him, and relieve the terrible suspense that was wearing her life away?" No other employment could have given her so wide an acquaintance with the sorrows by which the land was burdened.

At St. Louis they stopped a day or two, and visited the rooms of the Western Sanitary Commission, where they were cordially received, and made ample arrangements with the president, Mr. Yeatman, for receiving future supplies for their mission to the suffering soldiers down the river. On the 16th of August, just at sunset, they reached Helena,

Arkansas, and reported immediately to the office of the medical director, whom they found in great perplexity on account of the lack of nurses and supplies for the sick and wounded. He greeted them with the utmost cordiality, telling Mrs. Wittenmeyer that he had not welcomed any one half so gladly since the war commenced as he did her, as he had never before been so sorely in need of help and supplies. A large number of regiments had been brought up from Vicksburg and the Yazoo River, and General Steele's division had moved on to Little Rock, leaving their sick men behind. So rapid had been the movement that the sick were left in the streets, with scarcely enough convalescents to erect tents to protect them from the heat of the day, or the damp, malarious air of the night. Thirteen had died the first night they were there, and unless something was done immediately the mortality would be very great. More than two thousand were destitute of both medical and sanitary supplies.

Mrs. Wittenmeyer immediately sent to St. Louis for the necessary supplies; and, early on Monday morning, she and Miss Shelton began their labors of love, visiting the hospitals, and ministering all in their power to the sufferers there. One poor soldier they found wasted almost to a skeleton, and wearing the same suit of clothes he had worn all through the siege of Vicksburg and the fever that had prostrated him. He seemed past all feeling, and said he was going to die with no one to care for or relieve him. But an allusion to his mother called the tears in streams to his eyes, and convulsed his whole frame with sobs. Before they left, the hospital steward had promised to clean every room, and held in his hand an order for every shirt and pair of drawers in the sanitary rooms. In the afternoon they visited the hospital tents, speaking words of sympathy and kindness to the brave sufferers, and from twilight to midnight they were both busy in writing letters to their friends at home.

The next day matters were materially improved. The rooms were thoroughly scrubbed, the men attired in new and fresh garments, and even the poor Vicksburg soldier, in his clean shirt and new suit of clothes, talked hopefully of health and home again. After leaving some lemons, and such other comforts as could be procured in Helena, they started for the convalescent camp, about a mile from Helena, the way thither leading directly across the battle-field where so many brave men sealed their devotion to the Union with their blood. As they neared the first tent they heard the soldiers within singing, —

> "So, let the cannon boom as it will,
> We will be gay and happy still."

Then followed something the import of which was that the northern girls wouldn't marry Copperheads or cowards, but would wait till the soldiers got home. Thinking they were doing very well, the two ladies passed on to another tent, where were four sick men — three on the ground, one, the sickest of the four, on a cot. There was a pan with ice water in it by the cot, but no one to apply it to the sick man's burning brow. Mrs. Wittenmeyer dipped the towel into the water, wrung it out, and placed it on his head. Slowly the tears rolled from the closed eyes, and in a feeble voice, the sufferer said, "O, how like my own mother it seemed when you put the cold cloth on my aching head!" That day they saw and talked with hundreds of men from Iowa and other states, and were received by them as angels of mercy. One man staggered from his cot to where his knapsack lay, to give them some peaches; another insisted on their sharing with him some ginger beer; and, as they left, they heard a soldier remark to his comrade, "It does my heart good to see that kind of ladies come to camp; they care something for the soldiers." In the evening they visited a hospital in a brick church, where were eighty men, most of them very sick, and not one bed in the building. But they were very patient, and praised their steward in the highest terms — a very humane and kind-hearted man, who neither by day nor night would allow them to suffer for the cooling drink, or such other attention as was in his power to bestow. They talked of him as they would of a mother, and seemed glad to tell some one how kind he was. Tenderly he went from one to another, ministering to their wants; and when a soldier introduced to them "Liberty Hix," the ladies recognized him as a genuine Samaritan, of the New Testament type. One of the soldiers called Miss Shelton to him, and said, "I have something to tell you, that I want you to repeat when you return to Iowa. You may have heard of our sufferings at Milliken's Bend. We were in a hospital tent, and as no supplies could reach us, we became more and more feeble. Men that might have grown strong and well with proper nourishment, were daily sinking into the grave, and in each one that was carried out we read our fate. You can have little idea how a sick man loathes the coarse army rations. The only thing we could eat was bean soup; and this we had morning, noon, and night, week in and week out. I have seen men refuse it, saying, 'I will die before I will ever eat it again.' But a day came when unusual depression reigned throughout the hospital. The nurse came through with the soup; but it was steadily refused. When he came to me I covered my head in the bedclothes and wept. I thought of my good wife, with an abundance about her, and how gladly she would share with me. When I looked up, other men were weeping too; and, though it may seem very foolish to you, hunger and sickness take all the fortitude out of a man. In my distress I cried to God, and scarcely had the prayer passed my lips, when our nurse entered, and taking his stand near the centre of the hospital, where every man could hear, called out, 'Mrs. Wittenmeyer is coming with two loads of sanitary goods!' Just then we heard the rattle of the wagons, and my heart gave such a bound of joy as it never had done before. The men wept aloud for joy. An hour afterwards, amid laughter and tears, we greeted Mrs. Wittenmeyer, bringing us chicken, fruit, and other sanitary supplies, without which we should have died in a few days."

The two days following were spent in the same way, going from hospital to hospital, ascertaining what was needed, and supplying it as far as possible. But one sad feature of their situation it was beyond the power of the ladies to mitigate. None of the men hoped for speedy recovery unless they could be moved from Helena. The town is situated in what was once a cypress swamp, and in low places the stumps of the trees were still standing. Unless the sick could be inspired with courage and hope, it was useless to anticipate recovery. The commander of the post said he had no authority to send them up the river, and the medical director could do nothing without orders. After thoroughly canvassing the whole affair, Mrs. Wittenmeyer decided to go to Memphis, see General Hurlbut, and have arrangements made to make them, at least, more comfortable. On the morning of the second day she returned, and as she passed from one hospital to another, every man that was able raised himself on his elbow, and watched her till she was out of sight. Some wept, others laughed, — all were in great agitation, for she had brought with her orders for the removal of every man to some northern hospital. That day supplies came from Memphis, which were distributed among the men, and which, together with the hope of a speedy removal to a more salubrious air, diffused great cheerfulness among them all.

Their labors at Helena thus pleasantly terminated, Miss Shelton accompanied Mrs. Wittenmeyer to Vicksburg. Leaving Helena on the morning of August 23, the next day, about noon, the bluffs of Vicksburg came in sight. They found that the city presented a much less dilapidated and more inviting appearance than they had anticipated there, where for weeks "Death held his carnival." The first hospital they visited was in the Prentiss mansion, a most beautiful place. Though the house was large, comparatively few of the patients could be accommodated in it, but were in tents, on the surrounding terraces, in the shade of the magnolia and cypress trees, hedged about with myrtle and beautiful flowers. The sick were all well cared for, and were never without sanitary supplies. The City Hospital they found in the best possible condition. Dr. Powell, of Chicago, chief surgeon, received them cordially, as messengers of mercy from the Sanitary Commission, and expressed himself as having more faith in the efficacy of nourishing food for the sick soldiers than in the most skilful practice, or the most potent medicines.

One of the most interesting places they found in the city was the Soldiers' Home — a fine three-story brick structure, surrounded by cool verandas, on one of the pleasantest sites in the city, built by Senator Gwin for his town residence. This situation was selected by Mrs. Wittenmeyer, and there the tired soldier could find food and lodging, free of expense, furnished by the Sanitary Commission.

A few days after their arrival at Vicksburg, Mrs. Wittenmeyer and Miss Shelton went out to Big Black River, midway between Vicksburg and Jackson, visiting a number of hospitals located there.

In the fall of the year, returning to Iowa with Mrs. Wittenmeyer, Miss Shelton labored, with her voice and pen, in vindicating the Sanitary Commission, and arousing the people of Iowa to renewed activity, and more abundant liberality towards the distant and often suffering soldier. During the year 1864, and all the early part of 1865, for some time after the war ended, Miss Shelton was constantly in the field, acting a portion of the time as secretary to Mrs. Wittenmeyer; at other times taking charge of special diet kitchens in the different hospitals.

The summer of 1864 was spent mostly in the Nashville hospitals. Afterwards she went to Wilmington, and remained for several months. Of fine sensibilities, and well cultivated intellect, to see such varied suffering was to sympathize with it. And she has not allowed these vivid and often tragic scenes to pass from her memory, and perish from the recollection of the world.

Many of the more touching incidents she has recorded in a series of hospital sketches, whose interest and pathos have not been surpassed by any of the journals of the numerous hospital nurses and lady superintendents who have made so noble a page in American history by their heroism and self-sacrifice. We quote from her journal some of the most interesting passages.

Little Willie.

One sultry day in June, 1865, as I was passing through the wards of the Berry House Hospital, in Wilmington, my attention was attracted by a pair of bright eyes, which followed me from cot to cot with a hungry eagerness. Supposing it was the lemonade, which I was distributing according to the direction of the nurses, which attracted him, I inquired of the man who had charge of him if he could have some. He replied in the affirmative, and I placed the glass to his burning lips. He was a mere boy, only fifteen. His dark eyes and curly brown hair contrasted fearfully with his pale cheeks, while the thin white hand, with which he clasped the glass, told sadly of wasting disease.

I longed to speak words of cheer to the poor boy, but

could not stop then, as there were many feverish men waiting for the icy draught I was carrying. The eyes haunted me; and, as I went from one to another, I could not help glancing back at Willie's cot; and every time I met the same entreating look which first attracted my attention.

My duties called me to another part of the hospital; and, as I was passing him to go out, he called out, in a faint voice, "Lady, dear lady, please give me a kiss — just one kiss before you go. My mother always kissed me." I kissed him, with tears in my eyes — for who could refuse such a request from a dying child, far away from every friend and relative. He closed his eyes, murmuring, "You are a good woman — thank you. If you will sit down and hold my hand I think I can sleep; I am so tired." The nurses were very kind, and the surgeons remarkably so; but disease had undermined the frail structure, and we daily watched our Willie sinking to the grave.

One day I entered the ward, and found that the nurse had placed a chair by his cot for me, as usual; but he was sleeping, and I requested the nurse not to awaken him. "O, miss," said the man, "he cries and takes on so dreadfully when he wakes and finds that you have passed through, that I have promised always to wake him." To do this was no easy matter: the eyes opened slowly, and shut again. I leaned down, and whispered, "Willie! Willie!" "Yes, yes," he replied, "I was afraid they would not wake me, and I should not see you." He then began to cry like a grieved child, and begged me not to go North until he was well enough to go with me. "Promise," said the nurse, "for he will not live many days more." "No, Willie, I will not go until you are better," I said, and with the kiss he never failed to ask for, left him. The next morning the doctor came to me and said, "Willie is gone."

The coffin was placed upon two chairs, in the dispensary, and we stood and gazed long upon the marble face and folded white hands — white as the Cape Jasmine blossoms which they clasped. Then I learned his history as he had told it. A man of wealth had been drafted, and had bought the boy as a substitute of a heartless step-father. He had never carried a gun. Once from under his mother's watchful care, the overgrown boy had sunk beneath the hardships of camp life, and the spirit, pure as when it first entered the clay casket, returned to God who gave it. O Willie! those were not tears to be despised which fell upon thy coffin — soldiers' tears for a comrade lost. And though upon the well-contested field you never fought in deadly combat, the good fight of faith has been yours; and now, while your example lives in our hearts below, you wear an undying wreath of victory in our Father's kingdom.

Our work in this hospital was more satisfactory than in any other with which I was connected. There were only three wards, and we visited and talked with each patient every afternoon. A surgeon or the ward-master went with us to assist in giving out the lemonade which we always took with us. We also carried a portfolio, and took from the men outlines of the letters they wished us to write. Some of these were very original and amusing, and I regret that I did not preserve them.

As we had no "diet lists," we took down on a slip of paper every afternoon what articles of food each man thought he could eat. There was very little grumbling, and *many* thanks. While at work, the convalescents would gather in the corners of the kitchen and at the windows, and relate amusing anecdotes of their journeyings and fights.

I regret to say that *sham* marriages of the soldiers with pretty girls belonging to the "poor white trash" were not uncommon.

Much has been said of the ignorance of these people; but such miserable, vile, filthy, cringing wretches I never saw. Half has not been told of them; and truly it would require the pens of many ready-writers to do it. The "swamp fever," which carried off many of our soldiers, was even more fatal among them. While in Wilmington, the death of Mrs. George, of Fort Wayne, Indiana, made us more careful of our health. The surgeon advised us to change every article of dress, and take a *thorough* bath, before resting after our visits to the wards. This we did; and although we were exposed to small pox, and fevers of all kinds, we returned to the North in as good health as when we went South.

Wilmington life is with the memories of the past, as is all our hospital work. But though we "rest from our labors," "our works do follow us" in occasional letters from a thankful one, to whom we administered when we and they were strangers in a strange land.

HOSPITAL NO. 1, NASHVILLE, *July* 14, 1864.

I have *read* of things terrible and heartrending, but never heard anything to equal the sounds which a rebel in the third story sends forth. I was sitting by my table, reading, when a sharp cry of pain startled me, followed by earnest pleadings for mercy from our divine Father. Then, in a few moments, shouts of praise, cursing, raving, shrieks, fiendish laughs, growls like an enraged animal, and every feeling it is possible to express with the voice, followed each other in quick succession.

Our room is just across the street, and while I write night is made terrible by the poor delirious wretch. I can hear the sick men in the wards below wishing him removed so they can sleep. There! at last he is quiet. A lady nurse came in, and told me that it was a very wicked man in the rebel ward, who was "frightened out of his senses" because two men, in the most fearful agonies of death, were lying beside him. Finding it impossible to quiet him, the surgeon in charge had him gagged. It is a revolting *necessity* to treat him so. A thousand sick, wounded, and dying would be annoyed all night by him if they did not.

Hospital No. 14, Nashville, *August* 2.

When I first went through the wards of this hospital, I found a German woman sitting by her husband in ward one. This ward contains all the worst cases, and the smell of the wounds made me sick and faint before I was half through. But I learned that this woman had been sitting in her chair there, beside her husband, for two weeks, *day and night*. For recreation, she would walk out into the city, and buy some crackers and cheese, upon which she subsisted. Her face was colorless, and her eyes had a sunken, sickly look. I was carrying a bottle of excellent

15

cologne and a basket of handkerchiefs. I saturated one with the cologne, and gave her husband, and left the bottle with her. She was very grateful, and told me that she was compelled to go out and vomit three or four times every day, so great was the nausea caused by the impure air. I arranged for her to sleep at the Commission Rooms, which are near here, on Spruce Street, and we gave her her meals from the kitchen. This is against the rules of the hospital; but the surgeon says he will shut his eyes and not know we are doing it, if we will not do it again. Until to-day we have had no doubt of his recovery; but to-night she came to me in great alarm, saying her husband had a chill. I have never yet known a person with an amputated limb to recover after having a chill. This man looks so strong and well, that I *hope* he may be an exception.

August 6, 1864.

The German in ward one is dead. On Wednesday morning I went down very early to see him, and found the cot *empty*. I asked for his wife, and they said she had gone out in town. At the door I met her. She threw up her arms, and cried in piteous tones, "He's gone! O, he's gone! and I'm alone — alone!" She supposed he would be buried that day, and walked out to the cemetery — more than a mile — and found he was not to be buried until the next day. She asked me if I would not go with her on Thursday. I complied, and accompanied her, with a delegate of the Commission and his wife. As the coffins were taken one by one from the ambulance, it was found that her husband's was not there. The chaplain kindly proposed to wait until the ambulance could return to town; and while waiting we went to a farm-house near by, and made a bouquet for each of us. As we stood, with bowed heads, looking into the graves while the chaplain read the funeral service, she grasped my hand convulsively, whispering, "It's *so* shallow! O, ask them to take him out, and make it deeper!" Our nostrils had evidence of the shallowness of the graves every time the breeze swept over them. The "escort" fired their farewell over the "sleeping braves," and as the smoke cleared away, the bereaved wife dropped her flowers upon the coffin, and we wearily returned, — she to take the next train for the North, and we to our sad work.

August 10, 1864.

This evening, while busy preparing supper, we were startled by hearing a heavy fall on the pavement, outside of the window. We rushed to it, and found that a man had jumped from the third story porch. He was sitting up, looking about him with a bewildered look, when we reached him. The doctor says he has broken open an old wound in his side, and will not recover. He says he had been thinking all day how long he would have to suffer if he got well, and then thought he might suffer for weeks and months, and then die, and he determined to end his misery at one leap. The nurse caught him just as he was going over, but was not strong enough to hold him. He talks very quietly about it, and wishes he had not done it, or had succeeded in ending life and physical pain at once. He died two days afterwards.

"I wish you would take bed sixty-four, ward two, under your especial care," said the surgeon in charge to me. "We have just amputated his leg, and nothing but the closest watchfulness and most nourishing food will save him, and I doubt if they do."

I went at once to my patient. He was a young man, with what had once been a very strong constitution. As he lay there, with his pale face, and lips quivering with agony, I could not help thinking how grand he must appear in the glory of healthy manhood. I could see that he clinched his nails into the palm of his hand to keep back the cry which he deemed unsoldierly. But it would not do; a groan burst forth in spite of him. He turned his fiercely-black eyes upon me, and asked, dropping the words slowly, one at a time, "Can't — you — do — something — for — me?" I felt powerless, but prepared a stimulating drink for him, and then left him to attend to others.

One day I was too busy to carry his dinner to him, and sent it to him by the nurse, postponing my visit to that ward until afternoon. Between three and four o'clock I went to see him, and found him weaker than usual, and his dinner on the stand beside him, untasted. I carried in my hand a pretty, delicate fan, which a friend had given me, and I noticed his eyes follow it backward and forward, up and down, as I fanned him. At last he asked to take it. He gave it a few feeble flourishes, and then asked me to exchange with him. "This palm-leaf is so heavy I can't lift it. When I get strong I will give it to you again." I gave it, and asked what he would have for supper. "Coffee! coffee, with cream in it! Nothing else!"

was his answer. "But we have no cream," said I. "No cream! Why, my mother has milk pans big enough to drown me in, and the cream is *that* thick" — indicating on his finger its thickness. "Mother! mother! mother!" he cried.

Wounds and suffering had weakened body and mind alike; and the strong man was a child again, crying helplessly for "mother."

A few mornings later a nurse brought my fan to me, saying, "'Sixty-four' died last night; and when he knew he was going, he told me to bring your fan to you, and thank you." The ambulance, bearing him in his coffin, had scarcely left the gate, when the mother for whom he had yearned came to the hospital.

Poor woman! She bowed her gray head, murmuring, beneath the chastening rod, "*Thy* will, not mine, be done, O Father."

Hospital Scenes.

The inconvenience, suffering, and unpleasant consequences of ignorance of military regulations, endured by women who went to take care of sons, husbands, or brothers, sick in southern hospitals, might form an interesting, though sad chapter in the history of our great war, and I give you some instances.

At the sunset of a sultry day, I sat by my window, writing to the "friends at home," when my door was thrown unceremoniously open, and a lady entered, exclaiming, "What *shall* I do?" I knew from her face that she was a quiet, respectable, though uncultivated woman, and that nothing but the desperateness of her situation could have forced her to this abrupt entrance and question.

I gave her a chair, and listened to her story. Her husband had been so severely wounded in the leg as to make amputation necessary; and she had left home with a hundred dollars, which she had borrowed from a friend, and had come all the way to Nashville.

She had never travelled before, and had been troubled so much in getting passes and transportation, that her nervous system seemed quite exhausted.

Boarding and lodging were so dear that she found it impossible to pay for them in the city, while hospital regulations would not allow her to stay there. The surgeon said it would be weeks before her husband would be able to go home. "I cannot stay—and if I go back, he will die! What shall I do? What *shall* I do?" she cried, wringing her hands, and sobbing bitterly.

I proposed to walk into the ward and see her husband, while I thought what I could do for her. To my surprise she took me to the cot of one of my "special cases." "Is it *your* wife that has come?" I exclaimed. "Yes, it's *my wife*," he replied, while his eyes filled with a happy, peaceful light. "O Hattie, I have dreamed so often of your coming, that I am afraid I shall wake and find— But no, you *are* here—ain't you, Hattie?"

"Yes, Charlie, yes;" and the tears fell fast upon the clasped hands. The surgeon in charge consented to let her occupy an empty cot next to her husband, and the nurses changed him from the centre to one corner of the ward. For her board she helped us in the "special diet kitchen."

Eternity only can reveal the good done by her in the month she was in that large ward, containing a hundred beds. She remembered that Christ had said, "Inasmuch as ye have done it unto one of the *least* of these, ye have done it unto *me;*" and day and night occupied her spare time in administering to her husband's fellow-sufferers.

One day of the fifth week of her stay, I saw a cloud on her sunny face, and inquired the cause. She said a man had died in the ward, and the nurses had carried him out head foremost, and that she and her husband deemed this a bad sign. She had tried to divert his attention from it, but he had replied, "It is no use, Hattie; I shall go next." And he did. I cannot calmly recall that parting scene. You who have laid a dear one under the sod, near your own home, while friends and relatives wept with you, can know a *part* of her grief. But you who have, like her, left the dear dust to mingle with that of strangers, can realize the depth of her woe. As the carriage was announced to take her to the depot, she shrank back, exclaiming, "How can I go home to my children! I promised I would not return without their father; and to leave him in the cold ground!" Hers was indeed a sad case. Her trip home would use up the last of the borrowed money, and she would have to take in washing to support her children and pay back the borrowed hundred dollars.

One day, a well-dressed, intelligent woman called at the door of the diet kitchen, and asked to see one of the "Christian Commission" ladies. The surgeon had sent her to me to help her find her husband, and the directions were, "Bed one hundred six, ward two." As we went up the steps, I noticed that she trembled with excitement. I inquired if she was tired, and she said, "No," though she had slept none since leaving her home. We entered the ward, and the nurse pointed out the bed, but it was empty. I looked at her, and saw she was deadly pale, and hastened to assure her that there was some mistake, as she would not have been sent from the office to look for her husband if he had been dead. While I had been talking to her, the ward-master had referred to his book, and told us her husband's leg had been amputated a few days before, and he was then moved to ward four. Again her face was in a glow, and I could hardly keep her from rushing in unannounced. We could see his face from the door, and I thought him asleep. As I was holding her by the arm, and beckoning to one of the men to come to us, he opened his eyes full upon her. Such a scream as he gave! She bounded from me, and in a moment had her arms around his neck, both crying and laughing at the same time. I am sure neither of them uttered a whole sentence for fifteen minutes, so overpowering was the joy of their meeting. His recovery was almost miraculous, and one month from the time she came, she started home with her husband. The wife remarked, as she bade us good-by, that she was not half so happy the morning she started on her bridal tour as she was now, taking her husband, though he left one leg in a southern grave.

Persons unaccustomed to hospital life can hardly imagine how absorbing it was. Nor can they conceive how we could find any enjoyment in life while surrounded by hundreds of those poor wrecks of humanity, from whom life had been well nigh driven by southern bullets. Surely God will forgive us, if — as the long months of untold suffering rise before us, when we went in and out among the sufferers, while they wore out life in the vain hope of returning health, and finally were carried to the grave under the folds of the dear old flag — a bitterness comes to us that no words can express, and we cannot help rejoicing that God has said, "Vengeance is mine, and I will repay."

Peace has come to us at last; and now, when almost a year has passed since we sat in front of the White House, and looked upon the great army, "with banners," marching through the streets of Washington, — and the tears came more freely than the smiles, as we gazed at the bronzed faces, torn banners, and thinned ranks, — still those scenes are too vivid for us to realize that the work of the war is over, and that the dear, blessed hospital days shall come back to us *no more forever*. We call them "blessed days," because the joy of ministering to the suffering filled our hearts with a melody before unknown. But, as "the darkest day has gleams of light," so our usually dark days were often illumed with gleams of brightness. One gleam, especially bright, came to us November 4, 1864. It was a dull, rainy day; such a day as, glancing at the hospital windows, you would not fail to see pale faces, full of weary longing, looking forth. We had been all the morning in the "diet kitchen," and the dinner for our large family of over three hundred, on special diet, was well under way. A rustle at the door, and looking up, we greeted Mrs. E.

P. Smith, the wife of the Christian Commission agent. She was always the bringer of good tidings, and this time especially so.

"We have eight boxes of grapes for you," she said; "the nicest Catawba, Isabella, &c.; and as it is a gloomy day, it will be pleasant to distribute them at once, and show the men that they are not forgotten by the friends at home."

We acted upon the suggestion immediately, and, accompanied by the officer of the day, to tell us who could have grapes, we were soon passing from cot to cot. It was wonderful how the men brightened up. They could scarcely have expressed more gratitude had we given them clusters of gold instead of grapes. One elderly man sat on the side of his cot, and seemed very impatient as we paused to say a word to others near him. He had been long prostrated with a fever, and we were surprised to find him sitting up; for only a few days before we had taken him a few grapes, and they were the first thing he had eaten for days. We knew nothing would cheer the old man more than a little pleasantry. So, as I came up, I said, with much solemnity, laying the grapes on his stand, "To thy shrine, O hero of the war, I bring my humble offering" — but stopped short at that, for I discovered that his eyes were full of tears. He then went on to tell me, that one week before he had felt sure he must die. He could eat nothing, and felt himself sinking slowly into the grave. Then the grapes were brought him. In all his life he had never tasted anything half so refreshing. The first thing he did was to pray God to bless the good women that sent them. He took no more medicine, and his recovery was rapid, dating from the first grape he ate. "There is a good wife up in Wisconsin, and a house full of little children, that will bless the Commission while life lasts," said the old man, with fervency; and I turned away, lest my own tears should mingle with the grateful soldier's.

In one corner of one of the wards lay a man thin and pale, and with eyes sufficiently glittering to represent the Ancient Mariner. As we came near, we saw he was looking almost fiercely at the dish piled high with grapes. As we laid an unusually generous amount on the stand, he smiled grimly, and began crowding them into his mouth. The officer of the day came up in haste, and said that man must not have any; they would injure him. He was not to be so treated, and clutched them in both hands. The doctor, finding remonstrance in vain, took the grapes from him by force, as he was too weak to cope with a strong man. A disappointed child could not have wept more bitterly than he did, to be deprived of the only thing he had wanted for months. My heart ached for him; but the doctor's word was law, and we could only tell him how sorry we were. We were very careful, afterwards, to have the doctor go ahead, and point out any that could not have grapes, so as to avoid such disappointments in future. Here and there we found a man that would look longingly at the grapes, but shake his head, and say there were others so much worse than he that they should have them. How glad we were to be able to say, we have enough for every man in the hospital!

We had one case of a soldier that had been wounded, — shot through the breast, — and were thinking how much he would enjoy the grapes. To the surprise of all, he shook his head, and then told us that the discharge from his wound produced such nausea that he had not been able to eat anything for some time. He would enjoy the grapes so much but for that! There came to me a bright thought — just arrived from the young ladies of Mount Pleasant, Iowa — one box hospital stores, handkerchiefs, slippers, pillow-cases, and a few bottles of perfumery. It took but a moment to go to our room, return, and the soldier found himself surrounded by far more savory odors than ever floated from

"Araby the Blest."

In a short time our soldier was enjoying the grapes, and that evening ate his supper.

Not a great while after, as we entered the hospital gates with a basket of flowers — the last of the season — to brighten for a few days the wards, we were surprised to see the same soldier walking slowly towards us. He bowed politely, and to our "What! you able to be out?" he replied, —

"Yes, miss, the grapes and cologne saved me."

But it would be impossible to write out one half of the interesting occurrences connected with that one day's distribution of grapes.

One bright day in July, as we passed through the wards, many of the men told us, that they thought if they could get out into the sunshine, and see the trees and flowers growing, it would almost cure them. They were worn out with staring at the bare walls of the Gun Factory Hospital, and would so like to see something green.

Accordingly there was a "council of war" held in the diet kitchen, and the result was, that two very demure-looking women, wearing the badge of the Christian Commission, started out to steal. With covered hand-baskets they went directly to the cemetery. But they surely could not intend making any depredations there, for every few steps were signs — "Five dollars fine for breaking, or in any way injuring, the shrubbery." They went all round the grounds, and soon ascertained that there was only one grave-digger in the inclosure, and he in a remote part of the grounds. Whether the Nashville people ever discovered that day's work this deponent saith not; but one thing is sure: a table in Number One Hospital was soon covered with flowers, from two well-filled baskets. The next question was, What would be done for vases? That question was soon answered. The cans from which the condensed milk had been taken for the pudding were just the thing. Soon every ward was bright and fragrant with flowers. If the perpetrators of the crime had had any compunctions of conscience before, they all vanished as the thanks of the men came to them from every ward.

While the summer lasted, the flowers did their good work, but no one could tell where they came from.

CARRIE SHEADS.

GETTYSBURG will be ranked in history as one of the few great, decisive battles of the world; and, in consequence, every hero who fell, and a great many of those who figured there, will enjoy a prominence not accorded to those who fought and bled on the other fields. So of those who were casually connected with those three momentous days, so big with the destiny of the republic.

The name of Carrie Sheads, besides its association with that great battle-field, will be remembered as of one who, being summoned, by the terrible boom of hostile cannon, from a life of quiet and scholastic seclusion, met the terrible demands of the hour with the calmness of a heroine, and, amid the roar and crash of battle, and the fierce hate of the fiery belligerents, acted with a discretion and genuine courage which entitle her name and her act to be held in perpetual remembrance by the daughters of America.

When Lee's army advanced to the invasion of Pennsylvania, Miss Sheads was principal of Oakridge Seminary, a short distance west of the village. As many idle and groundless rumors of the rebel advance had reached the village, she had at length dismissed anxiety, become indifferent to the reports, and kept on in the even tenor of her way; little dreaming how soon or how fiercely the storm would burst around her. The evening of the 30th of June came, and with it Buford's cavalry, the van of the army of the Potomac. The first brigade of this division camped on the Chambersburg Pike, not more than two hundred yards from the seminary.

Closing the usual routine of the day, she promised her scholars a holiday on the morrow, to enable them to visit the camp, and contribute to the comfort of the weary and hungry soldier boys.

The next morning was ushered in by the heavy boom of artillery, soon followed by sharp volleys of carbine and musket shots. So suddenly and unexpectedly had war unfurled its gorgeous but bloody panorama around her and the cluster of girls in her care, that no time was left to withdraw to a place of safety, and the battle was now actually raging a few hundred yards from her door.

So near the line of battle, and situated on the turnpike, the buildings of Oakridge Seminary were soon used as a hospital; and, with that amazing suddenness which can happen only in a time of active and invasive warfare, Miss Sheads found herself converted from the principal of a young ladies' seminary into the lady superintendent of an army hospital. The world is familiar with the story of this great battle, of which this cavalry engagement on the morning of the 1st of July was the opening; how Buford, with his handful of cavalry, checked the advance of the rebel masses, till Reynolds, with the First corps, came to their relief, and, by the assistance of the Eleventh and part of the Third, seized upon the key point of the position, — the Cemetery Ridge, — which was strengthened by the entire Union force as it came up, and which, at the end of three days of awful carnage, remained secure in the iron grasp of the Federal army. The issue of the first day's fight was the falling back of Howard — who commanded after Reynolds fell — from Seminary Ridge, where the action began, to Cemetery Ridge, on the other side of the town. Slowly and sadly the veterans of the First corps turned to obey the order. And, although the rebels pressed them hard, and sought by desperate charges and wild huzzas to rout them in confusion, still they maintained their discipline, and obstinately contested every inch of ground.

Reynolds had fallen, but the dead hero had left his own gallant and self-devoting spirit in the breasts of his men. They were fighting on their own soil, by their own hearthstones, on hills that had been familiar to many of them from boyhood; and this had made heroes of them all.

Among the last to leave the field were the Ninety-seventh New York infantry, commanded by Lieutenant-Colonel Charles Wheelock, who, after fighting hand-to-hand as long as there was a shadow of hope, undertook to lead his broken column through the only opening in the enemy's lines, which were fast closing around him.

Arriving on the grounds of Oakridge Seminary, the gallant colonel found his only avenue of escape effectually closed, and, standing in a vortex of fire, from front, rear, and both flanks, encouraged his men to fight with the naked bayonet, hoping to force a passage through the walls of steel which surrounded him. Finding all his efforts vain, he ascended the steps of the seminary, and waved a white pocket handkerchief in token of surrender. The rebels, not seeing it, or taking no notice of it, continued to pour their murderous volleys into the helpless ranks. The colonel then opened the door, and called for a large white cloth. Carrie Sheads stood there, and readily supplied him with one. When the rebels saw his token of surrender they ceased firing, and the colonel went into the basement to rest himself, for he was thoroughly exhausted.

Soon a rebel officer came in, with a detail of men, and, on entering, declared, with an oath, that he would show them "southern grit." He then began taking the officers' side arms. Seeing Colonel Wheelock vainly endeavoring to break his sword, which was of trusty metal, and resisted all his efforts, the rebel demanded the weapon; but the colonel was of the same temper as his sword, and turning to the rebel soldier, declared he would never surrender his sword to a *traitor* while he lived. The rebel then drew a revolver, and told him if he did not surrender his sword he would shoot him. But the colonel was a veteran, and had been in close places before. Drawing himself up proudly, he tore open his uniform, and still grasping his well-tried blade, bared his bosom, and bade the rebel "shoot," but he would guard his sword with his life. At this moment, Elias Sheads, Carrie's father, stepped between the two, and begged them not to be rash; but he was soon pushed aside, and the rebel repeated his threat. Seeing the danger to which the colonel was exposed, Miss Sheads, true to the instincts of her sex, rushed between them, and besought the rebel not to kill a man so completely in his power;

16

there was already enough blood shed, and why add another defenceless victim to the list? Then turning to the colonel, she pleaded with him not to be so rash, but to surrender his sword, and save his life; that by refusing he would lose both, and the government would lose a valuable officer. But the colonel still refused, saying, "This sword was given me by my friends for meritorious conduct, and I promised to guard it sacredly, and never surrender or disgrace it; and I never will while I live." Fortunately, at this moment the attention of the rebel officer was drawn away for the time by the entrance of other prisoners, and while he was thus occupied Miss Sheads, seizing the favorable opportunity, with admirable presence of mind unclasped the colonel's sword from his belt, and hid it in the folds of her dress. When the rebel officer returned, the colonel told him he was willing to surrender, and that one of his men had taken his sword and passed out. This artifice succeeded, and the colonel "fell in" with the other prisoners, who were drawn up in line to march to the rear, and thence to some one of the loathsome southern prison pens, many of them to meet a terrible death, and fill an unknown grave.

When the prisoners had all been collected, and were about starting, Miss Sheads, remembering the wounded men in the house, turned to the rebel officer, and told him that there were seventy-two wounded men in the building, and asked him if he would not leave some of the prisoners to help take care of them. The officer replied that he had already left three. "But," said Miss Sheads, "three are not sufficient." "Then keep five, and select those you want, except commissioned officers," was the rebel's unexpected reply. On the fifth day after the battle, Colonel Wheelock unexpectedly made his appearance, and received his sword from the hands of its noble guardian, with those profound emotions which only the soldier can feel and understand, and, with the sacred blade again in his possession, started at once to the front, where he won for himself new laurels, and was promoted to the rank of a brigadier-general. He had managed to effect his escape from the rebels while crossing South Mountain, and, after considerable difficulty and suffering, succeeded in reaching Gettysburg in safety. General Wheelock finally died of camp fever, in Washington City, near the close of the war, in January, 1865.

As the battle raged, Miss Sheads and her little flock continued unterrified in the midst of the awful cannonade, she soothing and cheering the girls, and they learning from her that noble calmness in danger which, under all circumstances, and in either sex, stamps the character with an air of true nobility, and indicates genuine heroism.

The seminary was hit in more than sixty places, and two shells passed entirely through it. At length Miss Sheads and her young ladies became accustomed, as it were, to the situation, and in the intervals of the uproar would walk out in the grounds, and watch the magnificent yet fearful sight, that the slopes of Cemetery Hill presented.

All devoted themselves to the great number of wounded with whom their halls and large rooms were crowded. For many days after the fighting ceased, and Lee had withdrawn his mutilated army south of the mountain, these poor fellows remained there, and were most kindly cared for, till all whose injuries were serious had been removed to the general hospitals that had been fitted up on the hills at the other side of the town.

The annoyance suffered by having the battle at their threshold was not the only trial which the war laid upon the family of Miss Sheads. There were four brothers, who, imbibing the spirit of patriotism which animated so many thousands in all the loyal states at the outbreak of the rebellion, thought

"The time had come when brothers must fight,
And sisters must pray at home."

The two eldest joined the army at the first call for troops, and by reënlistment remained in service until one was discharged for disability, and the other fell while bravely fighting at the battle of Monocacy.

The other two joined the army later; one of whom entered the hospital at City Point, while the other received, at White Oak Swamp, wounds which have made him an invalid for life. All four have proved their loyalty on the bloody field, and, while two of them

"Sleep their last sleep,
And have fought their last battle,"

another, by her exertions in providing for the sufferers and for the family, at the time of the great battle, has rendered herself a chronic invalid. Thus five of this interesting and deeply loyal family have laid the most precious of earthly gifts — life and health — as free-will offerings on the altar of their country.

MRS. STEPHEN BARKER.

SAYS an old Greek thinker, "War is the father of all things." For it is only in the strife of strong passions, and amid the sudden and pressing demands which arise in a state of war, that fine qualities and superior abilities find a theatre for their action, and come to the light of day and the admiration of men. In all former wars opportunity was given to man only. He could distinguish himself. He could assert his manhood, prove his courage, and win his laurels.

For woman it only remained to sit in solitary and anxious sadness, to follow her hero in thoughts and dreams, and to await the conflict that should bring him back, shattered and bleeding, to receive the ministries of domestic kindness.

Our war has changed all this. The history of our armies, and especially of our hospitals; the great number of those who recovered from fearful wounds and went back to their regiments; the still greater number of those who rose from the beds where they had languished with lingering and painful diseases, — all show that a wonderful advance has been made in the sanitary condition of armies in active service. And this advance is due mainly to the efficiency, the warmth of devotion, and the systematized sanitary and hospital labor of unsalaried lady superintendents and lady nurses. In the broad field thus opened for woman, in the day of national trial and disaster, there is scope and verge for every style of female character; there is employment for every sort of feminine skill; there is good to be done, pain to be soothed, life to be saved, and armies to be kept up in numbers and in morale, by every class of talent, by every gift and grace which decorate the character of the sex.

As, among the men, some can organize an army, but cannot plan a campaign; some can lead a gallant charge, who could not restore a broken line; some can animate the flagging courage of a brigade, who could not take the same brigade across a rapid river, or over a rugged mountain, — so, among the women, one was found exactly adapted to the management of a large diet kitchen; another could do most good by sitting beside the cots of the sufferers, and speaking pleasant words of cheer and sympathy, or singing old songs in a low tone, or suggesting divine consolations to those who were passing beyond the reach of all human medicine.

Others, again, were found to possess a genius for organization. They could select agents and committees with unerring sagacity and insight. They knew whom to send on this errand, and who could not discharge this or that office with success.

Others again — and this number was not large — were found specially useful as superintendents and occasional visitors, who should see that no neglect or abuse sprang up amid the general profusion of fine qualities and generous acts; that kindness should not be wasted on the unworthy, or charities lavished on those who were hopelessly depraved; that the machinery of beneficence should not be employed to serve base or unworthy ends; that funds raised for the benefit of the soldier should redound only to his good; that luxuries should not be consumed by nurses and ward-masters; and that the gifts of the people should not supersede, but only make more complete and effective, the provision that government makes for her suffering sons. It is in this latter class, of the kind, wise, and judicious hospital superintendents, that Mrs. Barker belongs.

The period of her active service was the whole time of the duration of hostilities. She began her work in the summer of 1861, and did not cease her labors for the soldier till the armies were disbanded, and the hospitals dismantled, in the summer of 1865.

Her husband was appointed chaplain of the Fourteenth Massachusetts infantry — afterwards the First heavy artillery — in July, 1861; and Mrs. Barker, having resolved to share the fortunes of this regiment, in the service of its sick and wounded, went to Washington in August, and commenced at once her hospital labors.

Few of the army workers seem to have brought to their self-imposed tasks such an earnest desire to ascertain the precise line of duty and the sphere of greatest usefulness for a nurse in a military hospital.

In speaking on this subject, Mrs. Barker uses the following language, whose clear good sense at once recommends itself to those who may desire to learn the best manner of making themselves effective among soldiers: —

"Of course no useful work can be accomplished without

the consent and confidence of the surgeons. These can be deserved and won only by strict and honorable obedience to orders. The first duty is to learn what government supplies can properly be expected in a hospital; next, to be sure that when they are wanting they are not withheld through the ignorance or carelessness of sub-officials; and lastly, that the soldier is sincere and reliable in the statement of his wants.

"The discretionary powers granted by the surgeons was more than I had even hoped for, and the generous confidence shown by the officers of the Sanitary Commission, in furnishing the supplies I asked for, soon gave me all the facilities I needed for an engrossing and useful work."

Mrs. Barker was a general though constant hospital visitor in Washington during the winter of 1861 and 1862.

In March, 1862, and from that time on for two years, till the spring of 1864, she was located at Fort Albany, one of the defences of the capital, where the First heavy artillery was stationed. Here she was mainly occupied as special nurse of the sick and wounded of this regiment. She depended on the Sanitary Commission for most of her hospital supplies, and became thoroughly identified with the regiment, so that she was frequently asked, in jest, what were her rank and pay. On Sundays, while the chaplain was about his regular duties, she read aloud in the hospital, generally a sermon of Henry Ward Beecher, to which she always found a ready and attentive audience. The hospital tents were very near the quarters occupied by Chaplain Barker and his wife, and they visited the patients at all hours of the day and night; and the poor fellows who lay suffering there were constantly on her mind. "Even when absent from them," she says, "and engaged in other duties, I still gave to them the warmest offerings of my heart."

Early in 1864, the United States Sanitary Commission had determined to employ "hospital visitors," in order to secure a more thorough and faithful distribution of articles intended for soldiers, and Mrs. Barker was the first lady detailed to this special and important branch of service.

The plan upon which she proceeded was to make daily an inspection tour, visit each bedside, note the wants of each individual, inquire into any cases of neglect, omission, or inattention on the part of ward-masters or hired nurses, provide reading matter, stationery, and other needed comforts.

She found a surprising misconception in the minds of a great number of the men as to the real source of their comforts. Many supposed it was simply good Uncle Sam who was looking so closely and so kindly after the wants of his wounded boys. Others, again, were lavish, and even touching, in their thanks to *her*, as though this profusion, of which she was the only appointed almoner, came from her own supplies, or was purchased with her private purse.

"In all this I found," she writes, "a wider range of action, more varied calls for sympathy, greater demands for aid to both mind and body, all of which were enough to keep one on the keenest strain of active life, so that there was no gift, or knowledge, or graceful accomplishment, which did not come in play to complete the circle of woman's work in hospitals."

The hospitals assigned to her for this kind of visitation were the Harewood, the Engineers' Corps, the East Capitol, the Sherburn and Clifton Barracks, the Circle, Camp Barry, and the Deserters' Hospital.

Harewood contained as many as all the other six, and she regularly began at the first ward of Harewood every Monday morning, doing all she thought needful as she went along, going through as many wards as possible before dinner at two o'clock. After dinner she took some one of the smaller hospitals, devoting the entire afternoon to its wards.

Next morning she began among the Harewood patients where she left off, proceeding as before till dinner time, and in the afternoon took another small hospital. Thus, by constant and systematic labor, she made the round of all the patients who were in this general way assigned to her supervision. It was not possible that she should visit and talk with every patient in so many thousands. But her powers and duties were soon well understood. She was known as "the hospital visitor," and every marked or peculiar case, instance of neglect, privation, or uncommon suffering or destitution, was at once called to her attention. An attendant accompanied her, who was loaded with a great variety of articles. He spoke most of the common German dialects, so that she could thus understand the wants of those who spoke poor or broken English, and particularly many from the interior counties of Pennsylvania.

Meantime the First heavy artillery had gone out with

Grant, and was plunged into one after another of those bloody battles, which were the hard conditions on which alone the stubborn rebel chief was forced back to the lines before Richmond. Every few days she would find one of her boys coming back, in bandages and bloody uniform, from Spottsylvania, or Cold Harbor, or Petersburg.

Certainly the partiality was venial if she lingered a little longer by their cots, or ordered a special disbursement from the supply basket, or gave an extra word of direction to the ward-master and the special nurse. In addition to this regular and daily round of visitation, her leisure moments and the evenings were almost wholly engrossed with the labors of a steadily increasing correspondence.

Sceptical as the soldier had become of army agents and post-office clerks, he felt certain that any matter intrusted to her care would be thoroughly and promptly attended to. Thus she became a special forwarding agent for the soldiers of money, and various mementos and keepsakes, sent from the front to her, to be forwarded to their friends in Massachusetts, and other northern states. A letter was mailed at the same time the package was expressed. Thus, within a few weeks, several thousand dollars passed through her hands in small sums, and all safely reached their proper destination.

These labors continued till the latter part of the year 1864, when the New York Woman's Central Relief Association sent for Mr. and Mrs. Barker to engage in a special home service. Its president, Louisa Lee Schuyler, — than whom the war developed no organizing and directing talent more admirable among all the daughters of America, — had planned a tour and marked out a programme for them. They were to go to the various aid societies in New York, Brooklyn, Astoria, Harlem, Hastings, Irvington, Rhinebeck, Albany, Troy, Syracuse, Auburn, and Buffalo; and, while he gave one or more public lectures, she mingled socially with the various members, talked of her hospital life, and narrated many scenes and incidents; thus assuring them that their labors were not underrated, misconceived, or lightly valued in the army, and that by far the greater part of their supplies was faithfully applied to promoting the soldier's comfort, and hastening his convalescence.

This service continued till the spring of 1865, when she returned to the hospitals. At the time of Lee's surrender there was a call for a special relief system, in preparing the armies of war-worn veterans, who had suffered so much and accomplished so much for the nation, to return home in clothes less ragged and soiled than those in which they had chased Lee. Many too, poor fellows! notwithstanding the universal joy of the hour, were sick and worn down with protracted fatigues, and needed peculiar, and deserved the most grateful, attention from the citizens of the republic which they had saved. Mrs. Barker was engaged directing and aiding in a rapid, generous, and thorough distribution of sanitary supplies for the benefit of these noble fellows. Hospital work was for a time suspended, and the whole sanitary force was applied to this field of labor, which in twenty days was so thoroughly accomplished, that even the scattered men on detached duty were all visited, and their wants supplied.

With this service culminated the hospital labors of Mrs. Barker. Now she sought again home and its sacred privacy, carrying with her the abundant consolation of having passed four years of laborious usefulness in the most active and wisely directed beneficence.

MRS. BELLE REYNOLDS.

THE tocsin of war, when it penetrates to the cottage where young married life and love are nestled in the happiness of secure enjoyment, starts questions as difficult and as painful in their solution as any that life presents. Where lies the path of duty? What shall I do? Which horn of this fearful dilemma shall I grasp? I have a duty to my country, and also a duty, most tender and sacred, to my wife. Which is paramount? In how many cases, during our great national crisis, has this question been met and decided in a spirit that gave the army another hero, hoping to live, having everything to live for, yet ready to die for his country when that sacrifice should be demanded! On the wife's part, too, how painful and embarrassing are the questions that arise! If she remains at home, there are the constant suspense, the ceaseless anxiety, the abiding apprehension of evil tidings which may reach her in every newspaper, or from the cries of news-boys on the streets. These fill every waking hour, and even in sleep her dreams are haunted with visions of terror and coming sorrow. If, free from ties that retain her at home, she accompanies him, she must share all the rudeness and all the hardships of camp life, and the delicacy and refinement of her sex must, for a time, be laid aside; the earth must be her

MRS BELLE REYNOLDS.

couch, an army wagon her carriage, her carpet the green-sward, and her boudoir the thin and often dirty expanse of a triangular tent; black coffee, hard-tack, and a slice of fat bacon, fried on the end of a ramrod, must frequently be her bill of fare; and with all these she cannot really accompany her husband. His duties will keep him by the side of his men, where she cannot go, unless she should don the uniform and shoulder the musket; and this would not be permitted. But it is possible for the devoted wife, without sacrificing the delicacy of her sex, to be, for a great part of the time, within short distance of her husband in active service. When the forces are in garrison, she can be with him constantly; and when he is wounded, she may be near enough to dress his wounds; and when he falls, she may secure for him a careful and Christian burial. This course of life was the one Mrs. Reynolds chose in the summer of 1861, when her husband enlisted in the Seventeenth regiment of Illinois volunteers. She is a native of Shelburne Falls, Massachusetts, and had been married to Lieutenant Reynolds, a resident of Peoria, Illinois, but a few months when the war broke out. The regiment to which her husband belonged was the most popular in the western army, being one of the earliest in the field, and during the whole war in active service.

On the night of August 10, 1861, she landed at Cairo, Illinois, and the next morning joined her husband at Bird's Point, Missouri, his regiment being encamped at that place. From this time till near the close of the war, Mrs. Reynolds kept a journal of her army life and adventures. Of her first experience in camp she writes as follows: —

"How could I stay in such a cheerless place? No floors, no chairs, the narrow cot my seat, my feet imbedded in the hot sand, the confusion of camp close around me, with but the thickness of cloth between me and the eyes of all, the scorching August sun streaming through the low-roofed covering, — it seemed almost too much to endure; but I resolved to make the trial. On the evening of the third day after my arrival, while visiting the ruins of the railroad, our attention was arrested by a shouting in camp, which, on our return, we found was caused by the receipt of 'marching orders.' The steamer Chancellor was to convey us to Herculaneum, Missouri. Tents were struck immediately, but day dawned before the steamer left the landing. My husband was anxious to have me accompany him, if the colonel's permission could be obtained; but I feared to make the request, lest it should be denied. Wrapped in my husband's military overcoat, I sat on my trunk to await events and witness the embarkation. The confusion and excitement of the scene were so novel, that the hours glided by unnoticed. The grotesque figures standing out in bold relief against the high-piled fires of barrels, boxes, and other accumulated property, — the effigies, that seemed writhing in agony as the curling flames reached them, — had, mingled with the shouts of the confused and surging throng, made me forgetful of the lapse of time, of my exposed condition, and even unconscious that a heavy fog, rising from the river, had saturated my thick wrappings, when I was aroused from my reveries by the voice of our colonel, who said, 'Are you here, Mrs. Reynolds? You will be more comfortable on the boat.'

My unexpressed wishes thus granted, I went as soon as my husband, who was then on duty, returned."

She remained with the regiment, following it in all its campaigning in Southern Missouri, and on the Mississippi River during the fall and winter of 1861 and 1862. Sometimes she rode in an army wagon, sometimes in an ambulance, and sometimes on a mule. At others she marched in the dust beside the soldiers, with a musketoon upon her shoulder. The command was in active, though not in dangerous service; and this period of her army life is crowded with many charming reminiscences of out-door life in the romantic wilderness through which they were moving. Sometimes, behind her tent, Iron Mountain was towering in its bald simplicity; sometimes they encamped in a charming deer park; and at others were wending their way along the banks of the Mississippi, where the giants of the aboriginal woods were festooned with a beautiful tracery of wild vines, and the notes of the bugle could be heard echoing through the dim aisles of the forest. There was one period of quite painful suspense at the time of the battle of Belmont. She did not know whether her husband had survived that bloody engagement. "I dared not look too closely," she writes, "lest some shall be missing; and while the regiment is closing up in line to receive the thanks and praise due them from our gallant colonel, I ventured to ask if all had returned. One replies, 'We have lost our lieutenant;' another, 'I helped to bury my messmate.' Brief words! but some mother's heart will be wrung with agony as she reads of the victory, followed by the list of killed and wounded."

The winter was passed in military reviews and in the gayeties of camp, the Seventeenth Illinois being stationed at Cape Girardeau. In the early part of February, General Grant, then commanding the active force in that region, commenced that brilliant and ever-memorable series of movements which terminated in the capture of Corinth and Memphis, and the opening of the upper part of the Mississippi Valley. Mrs. Reynolds was present amid all these rude scenes, and in some of them took quite an active and prominent part. Her journal during this period is rich in incident and description, and contains one of the truest accounts of the first day's action at Pittsburg Landing that has been written.

"On reaching Fort Henry," she writes, "I found that the regiment had that day left for Savannah, Tennessee. I had but to remain on board, and we should soon overtake them. The sight of that fleet, steaming up the Tennessee River, was one never to be forgotten, — the gunboats, with their dark, frowning sides, leading the way for nearly two hundred transports, with their freight of human life. The little stream was swollen to a mighty river, and the banks were clothed in the fresh garb of spring. The few towns on the river seemed deserted of all but women and children, and they showed little rejoicing at the sight of Uncle Sam's legions. On the second day out, Captain D. was ordered on board the Dunleith, a stern-wheeler, as despatch boat; and as Mrs. D. would accompany him, I should be left alone. So I concluded to go with them on board the Dunleith. While steaming along, noting the peculiar appearance of the dwellings, and contrasting our situation with what it was one year ago, we heard a splash, and the boat seemed turning round and going down the stream. Soon the trouble was explained: the wheel had dropped off, and gone to the bottom. After drifting about for a short time, another boat came alongside, and commenced towing us up the river; but the current was so strong another boat was required, and we were three days in reaching Savannah. A dreary town we found here,—a scene of perfect desolation,—and but for the lovely dress of spring, in which all nature was clothed, the sight would have been deplorable.

"*March* 21, 1862.—We embark to-night in steamer D. A. January for Pittsburg Landing. Ten miles above we disembark, and camp about three miles from the river, on a most romantic spot—high bluffs and deep ravines, little brooks carelessly creeping through the ferns, then rushing down over a rocky precipice, and bounding along to join the river. Blooming orchards meet the eye, and tiny flowers peep out from their green beds. Deserted cabins are scattered here and there, which seem to have been built for ages, and tenantless for years. Shiloh meeting-house and that cool spring are all that make the place look as if ever having been trodden by the foot of man.

"*April* 4.—The long roll has called the regiment out, and we know not what an hour may bring forth. Pickets have been driven in, and skirmishing is going on at the front. Distant musketry and the rumbling of artillery past my tent give the situation a look of reality which I had not dreamed of an hour ago. Although so near the enemy's lines, we feel no fear. Mrs. N. and myself are the only ladies in camp, and our tents are adjoining.

"*April* 17. — It seems years since I wrote the last lines in my diary, such have been the suspense and torture of mind, and the variety and horror of the scenes through which I have passed. On Sunday morning, two days after the last date of writing, at sunrise we heard the roll of distant musketry; but supposing it to be the pickets discharging their pieces, we paid no attention to it. In about an hour after, while preparing breakfast over the camp fire, which Mrs. N. and I used in common, we were startled by cannon balls howling over our heads. Immediately the long roll was beaten, and orders came from the commanding officer of the brigade to fall in. Knowing my husband must go, I kept my place before the fire, that he might have his breakfast before leaving; but there was no time for eating, and though shells were flying faster, and musketry coming nearer, compelling me involuntarily to dodge as the missiles shrieked through the air, I still fried my cakes, and rolling them in a napkin, placed them in his haversack, and gave it to him just as he was mounting his horse to assist in forming the regiment. His last words to me, as he rode away, were, 'What will you do, Belle?' I little knew then what I should do; but there was no time to hesitate, for shells were bursting in every direction about us. Tents were torn in shreds, and the enemy, in solid column, was seen coming over the hill in the distance. Mrs. N. and I, thinking we might have time to pack our trunks, were doing so, when the wagon-master told us we must run for our lives; so, snatching our travelling baskets, bonnets in hand, we left the now deserted camp. We passed the large parade ground, close by our camp, where the cavalry was forming. Balls were flying and shells bursting among the terrified horses and fearless riders. On reaching General Ross' headquarters, supposing ourselves at a perfectly safe distance from the rebels, we took possession of a deserted tent, and sat resting ourselves, when Lieutenant Williams, acting quartermaster, passing by, saw us sitting there, apparently regardless of the flying missiles. 'For God's sake,' exclaimed he, 'run for the river; the rebels are coming!' We were by this time convinced of their close proximity; for we had scarcely left when a shell exploded close by, the pieces tearing through the tent, and a solid shot passed through headquarters. The troops were now moving up from the river, pouring along by thousands, fresh and hopeful, and sanguine as to the result of the conflict in which they were hastening to engage. Others were going towards the river, many sick, and scarcely able to drag themselves along through the almost impassable roads; and we, while hurrying along, were constantly asked, 'What's the matter back here, ladies?' But soon enough they ascertained, for the enemy were pressing closer and closer, and the musketry coming nearer and nearer each moment. When within about half a mile from the river, we came upon a number of ambulances, from which the wounded were being taken and laid upon the ground for the surgeons' attention. We stopped, took off our bonnets, and prepared to assist in dressing their wounds; but in less than ten minutes an orderly came dashing up, with orders to move the wounded immediately to the river, as the rebels were pressing so closely, they were not safe where they were. The surgeon said we had better go to some of the boats, as we should find plenty to do. So we made our way to the steamer Emerald, Captain Norton's headquarters; and, just as we were going aboard, General Grant and staff came up from Savannah. Anxious faces they all wore, though they little knew what lay before them. We were rejoiced to find that Mrs. C., one of our nurses, had arrived from Illinois, with quite a large supply of hospital stores, for they came not an hour too soon. A few moments after our arrival (about ten o'clock A. M.), Sergeant Autcliff, company A, was brought on board, supported by two comrades. Both arms were broken. His greeting to Captain Norton was, 'Well, captain, they have winged me.' To see that strong man, now utterly helpless, and almost fainting from loss of blood, and exhausted from a walk of nearly two miles, was a piteous sight indeed.

"Soon the wounded came pouring in upon us, and for thirty-six hours we found no rest. At night we had three hundred and fifty wounded on board our boat. I dared not ask the boys if my husband was unharmed, and feared each moment to see him among the almost lifeless forms that were being brought on board the boat.

"Through the day the thunder of artillery had almost deafened us; the air seemed filled with leaden hail, and the spent balls would patter upon the deck like a summer shower. Solid shot, directed at the ammunition boat, which was close by us, would pass over our heads and drop into the water. As the sun went down our army was gradually nearing the river: resistance to the infuriated masses opposed to them had been impossible. The rebels now occupied all the camps of the Federal army, and the alternative to perish beneath the waves of the Tennessee, or surrender to the exultant foe, was before them. Never had the fate of an army been more desperate, or its ruin more inevitable. Panic seized the half-crazed men, and rushing down the steep declivity, they came pouring along by hundreds, each intent on securing his own safety, regardless of others. Many attempted to crowd upon the hospital boats; others swam to the opposite shore. Captain N. guarded the gang-plank with a revolver in each hand, and giving me another, I stationed myself upon the hurricane deck, prepared to execute any orders he might give me. But deliverance came to the disheartened army; the gunboats Lexington and Tyler arrived from below, and steaming up to the mouth of a little stream, called Licking Creek, they opened a deadly fire upon the rebel army. Broadside after broadside of sixty-four pounders was discharged into the midst of the now terrified foe. Fresh courage seemed infused into our dispirited ranks, for now across the river we could see the long-expected troops hurrying forward at double-quick to our rescue. How we cheered them! All the transports were put in requisition to ferry them across, that they might add to the waning strength of the almost defeated army. Every effort was made to inspire the panic-stricken hundreds with fresh courage, but without effect. At the Landing it was a scene of terror. Rations, forage, and ammunition were trampled into the mud by an excited and infuriated crowd. Officers were rushing around, vainly endeavoring to collect the stragglers from their commands, and lead them once more to the scene of conflict. Trains were huddled together on the brow of the hill and in sheltered places. Ambulances were conveying their bleeding loads to the different boats, and joined to form a Babel of confusion indescribable. None were calm, and free from distracting anxiety and pain, save the long ranks of dead, ranged for recognition or burial, at the hospital on the hill-side. Night closed the scene. The two armies rested for the morrow's conflict; ours sad and disheartened, theirs hopeful and almost victorious. The gunboats were doing a great work; one after the other would send a broadside; and we, watching from the deck, would listen until the explosion, and then shout for joy. They were tokens of remembrance sent to our beleaguered friends. Soon the rain came pouring down. What a blessing to the wounded on the battle-field! Hour after hour passed, and the storm increased; but above all was the solemn thunder of the gunboat cannon. Towards morning we dropped down to Savannah, and unloaded the wounded; and morning found us again at work, dressing the wounds of others, who had but just been brought from the field.

"In all this time I heard nothing of my husband. I dared not ask those who had come from the field. I would wait until I should hear that all was well with him, or see him face to face. The mud and rain made it impossible to extend our labors beyond the boat; and reports were continually coming to us that the rebels were retreating, and that our army, strengthened and encouraged by the arrival of Buell's command, would probably push them to Corinth. They had passed beyond our camps, and the way was strewn with dead and dying. Lieutenant-Colonel Smith came from the regiment about dark, with a message to me from my husband. He had passed through that terrible battle unharmed, though his horse had been shot under him. How thankful I was none can know but those who have endured like suspense and anxiety. There had been no preparation made for a two days' battle when the army left their comfortable quarters on Sunday morning, and no rations had been provided. I knew there was a large supply of bread on hand, and making arrangements with the cook for a dozen loaves, I supplied the colonel with some impromptu saddle-bags, and filling them to the brim, and tying each end, he threw them across his horse, and started off. Fortunately for him, darkness enveloped him, or he might not have arrived with his precious freight. That night we rested, though the storm was still raging. Wednesday morning the sun came forth upon a scene of blood and carnage such as our fair land had never known. The roads were almost impassable; yet we felt it our duty to go out, and do all we could for those who were in the hospital. At nine o'clock we left the boat — Mrs. C., Mrs. N., and myself. We climbed the steep hill opposite the Landing, picked our way through the corrals of horses, past the long lines of trenches which were to receive the dead, and came to an old cabin, where the wounded were being brought. Outside lay the bodies of more than a hundred, brought in for recognition and burial — a sight so ghastly that it haunts me now. We passed on, and entered the house, which contained three rooms. In one were some fifty wounded; in another (smaller) the surgeons were amputating. The ladies left me there, and went to the tents, which were also filled. The sight of a woman seemed to cheer the poor fellows, for many a 'God bless you!' greeted me before I had done them a single act of kindness. The first call was for water; and none could be obtained nearer than the river. I stepped to the door, and called for volunteers to go with me to the river for water. Fifteen offered their services. Captain Norton furnished each with a pail, which they filled, and supplied the wants of the poor sufferers. After bathing and bandaging their burning wounds, I gave each some jelly, and distributed among them the little bread we had brought with us; but the supply was small for hungry men, and I found a sutler's stand, and emptied the contents of my purse for gingerbread — singular food for sick men, but very acceptable. An Irishman, though badly wounded, did much to keep up the spirits of the disheartened, as he was still in possession of his native wit, and anxious to make the best of everything. I was well repaid for my exertions in seeing them all more comfortable. How thankful a soldier is for a little attention! One old man, whose last days should have been passed in a quiet home, lay dying; at every breath his life-blood gushed from the wound in his breast. At his side lay a rebel soldier, both of whose limbs had been taken off below the knee by a cannon ball; his hours were few. Here lay another; a musket ball had pierced his cheek near the eye, and reached the lower part of the brain. The surgeon had probed in vain to find the deadly missile; his face and the front parts of his clothing were covered with blood, and his breathing was of that horrible sort which once heard is never forgotten. He, too, was past all cure. Another had a ball lodged deep in the upper part of his thigh. The surgeons had been unable to afford him any relief. He was very calm, and said he did not suffer much; but something about his face, when I looked at it, showed that *he* would soon be 'mustered out.'

"And that operating table! These scenes come up before me now with all the vividness of reality. Sometimes I hope it is only a fever-dream that haunts me, but too well I know it was no dream; for, one by one, they would take from different parts of the hospital a poor fellow, lay him out on those bloody boards, and administer chloroform; but before insensibility, the operation would begin, and in the midst of shrieks, curses, and wild laughs, the surgeon would wield over his wretched victim the glittering knife and saw; and soon the severed and ghastly limb, white as snow and spattered with blood, would fall upon the floor — one more added to the terrible pile.

"Until three o'clock I had no idle moments; then, having done all in my power to minister to so much wretchedness, I found my long-taxed nerves could endure no more. One of the surgeons brought me a spoonful of brandy, which revived me. Feeling that my labors were at an end, I prepared to leave, and had just turned to go in the direction of the boat, when a hand was laid upon my shoulder. The shock was so sudden I nearly fainted. There stood my husband! I hardly knew him — blackened with powder, begrimed with dust, his clothes in disorder, and his face pale. We thought it must have been years since we parted. It was no time for many words; he told me I must go. There was a silent pressure of hands. I passed on to the boat. I found Mrs. N. and C. hard at work, and apparently as fresh as when the day commenced. At night I lived over the horrors of the field hospital and the amputating table. If I but closed my eyes, I saw such horrible sights that I would spring from my bed; and not until fairly awakened could I be convinced of my remoteness from the sickening scene. Those groans were in my ears; I saw again the quivering limbs, the spouting arteries, and the pinched and ghastly faces of the sufferers.

"The following day we visited the boats near us. On one the surgeon objected to our coming on board, as he 'wanted no women around.' But nothing daunted, we went in search of any who might belong to our regiment. We found some of the boys with their wounds undressed, many of them having been wounded on Sunday; and, though there were three or four hundred wounded men on the boat, there were but two or three surgeons, and they unwilling to have us relieve what suffering we could. No hospital stores were allowed us; so, drawing from the small supply on the Emerald, and from the boat of the United States Sanitary Commission, in charge of Dr. Warriner, we removed the heavy flannels, stiff with blood, bathed their burning wounds and powder-stained faces, gave them food, and they sank to sleep like weary children. Mrs. N., while passing through the cabin, noticed a cot on which lay a man, his face covered with the coarse woollen blanket. Supposing it to be one who had died, she went up to it, raised the blanket, and, to her horror, discovered a man in the last stages of small pox! She immediately found the surgeon in command, and asked him if he knew of such a case being on board; when he insultingly informed her that he would attend to his business, and she might leave if she were not pleased. The surgeon's name I have forgotten, but his disregard and inhumanity to the wounded under his care was reported at headquarters; and, though his name may not have been branded before the world, it lives in the memories of those who suffered through his neglect.

"On Saturday night, we were happily surprised at seeing Drs. Guth and Colburn, of Peoria, they being members of the delegation from Illinois. Sorely needing rest and change of scene, my husband obtained permission for my return to Peoria when the Black Hawk should be loaded. There were about twenty of our regiment who would go. Sunday night found all in readiness, and my husband left me in comfortable quarters on board the Black Hawk, he to resume his duties in camp, and I to go to my friends. Each parting seemed harder than the last, for I knew now the dangers and uncertainties to which he was exposed. But my health had been failing since my first month in camp, and I felt I must recruit now, or I might not be able to spend the summer with him. There were but two ladies on board, their husbands being of the party. The conversation naturally turning upon the battle, many questions were asked; and as I had been an eye-witness, all eyes were directed to me. The terrible scenes were still before and seemed to be a dreadful part of me, which I was glad to have removed, if relating them might have that effect. I told my story to quite an audience of ladies and gentlemen,

Governor Yates being of the number. As I was one of the very few ladies who were present at the battle, and had witnessed so large a portion of its scenes, the story seemed to interest all who heard, and some one suggested, 'She deserves a commission more than half the officers.' 'Let's make one,' said another. No sooner said, than a blank commission was brought, and the governor directed his secretary to fill it out, giving me the rank of a major. This was done: the name of the governor, of Adjutant Fuller, and the secretary of state were added, the seal of the State of Illinois was appended, and the parchment handed me, with many congratulations. I received it, not so much as an honor which I really deserved, but simply as an acknowledgment of merit for having done what I could. I regained my health slowly, making my round three times a day, to see if all our boys were cared for. On board I found an old friend, not seen for years, who has since died from the effects of his wound; another captain, whom we had met on the morning of the battle, was suffering from a severe wound.

"At Cairo we took Captain Swain, of Tiskilwa, Illinois. Arriving at St. Louis, the most severely wounded were taken to Quincy, Illinois; and some twenty, who were to go up the Illinois River, were transferred to a stern-wheel boat, Captain Swain among the number. The journey, under the most favorable circumstances, is a tedious one; but to the wounded sufferers it seemed more than they could endure. Time passed slowly indeed, and to Captain Swain, who was suffering intense agony, the motion of the boat was exquisite torture. One by one the boys were carried from the boat as we reached the little towns along the river, and I gave each his descriptive list, and bade them good-by, some of them forever. Captain Swain was failing rapidly, and the surgeons thought it impossible for him to reach Peoria alive. His faithful attendant was always by him, but his oft-repeated words were, 'My poor wife and little ones!' They held him to earth by strong bands, and he only prayed that he might live to see them once more, and then he was ready to die; 'for it was a glorious cause to give a life to.' But his prayer was not answered. Conscious that his last hour was at hand, he gave a word of encouragement to each soldier who stood by him, beseeching them to give their life, if need be, for their country's freedom; then thanking those who had ministered to his comfort, and imploring God's blessing upon them in their arduous duties, he closed his eyes, and died without a struggle, just as we landed at Peoria.

"The next week, having an opportunity to return to Pittsburg Landing, though my health was not much restored, I concluded to accompany them. At the appointed time we left Springfield, and, when we arrived at St. Louis a boat was chartered for us, and the nurses, — fifteen in number, — with the delegation of surgeons, embarked for the Tennessee River, which we reached in safety, and I once more rejoined my husband."

The months passed in the usual variety of soldier life. Now the regiment was in Jackson, Tennessee, and then removed to Bolivar, where they were encamped four months.

"In September orders were received for the regiment to move immediately to Corinth. We were to go by railroad, thus escaping the tediousness of a march. General Grant and staff occupied the car I was in, and then I observed the trait, so much commented upon, which distinguishes him from most other men. He must have been planning his fall campaign, for from the time we left Jackson until we arrived at Corinth, a lighted cigar was in his mouth, one serving as a match for its successor; yet if his reverie was broken by a question, he answered it pointedly, as though his thoughts were all centred on that question. We arrived at Corinth just before nightfall. The regiment was to camp about three miles from town. The road thither lay through swamps, and was mostly corduroy, very badly broken by the passage of heavy army wagons; but at last, rising from the swamp to a high bluff, we came upon the regiment preparing for the night. No tents had arrived, the clouds were threatening rain, and a cold wind was blowing over the bleak hill-side. I had but my travelling cloak for covering. No trees were near to afford us shelter, and we saw we should have to pass a dreary and comfortless night. My husband spread his poncho on the ground, and I lay down, *not* to pleasant dreams or sweet sleep, but to be pelted by cold rain until drenched through and through, and then to lie and long for morning to come. But never were hours so lengthened; and just at daylight, though the storm was at its height, orders came for the regiment to move to Iuka. Colonel N.'s tent had just come, and he insisted on my occupying it, as he was so soon to leave. With the greatest difficulty I made my way to the tent, and throwing myself on the cot, was soon insensible to all that was passing. When I awoke, all had left but my husband, who remained for a short time, to make provision for my removal to Corinth. At five o'clock he left me in as dreary a place as I ever found myself in; but I must not complain. It was my *determination to share* with him the dangers and privations of soldier life that had brought me to such a pass, and I must endure it or leave him. The pitiless rain was pouring in torrents from a leaden sky, and a cold wind driving under the tent, with little streams trickling through the thin covering, made my quarters anything but comfortable, though, in contrast with the night I had passed, they were luxurious. Many of the boys, on leaving, had put their knapsacks in my care, and taking from one a blanket, I wrapped myself in it, and sat down to meditate on my forlorn condition. The fates seemed all against me, for the wind increased, and I saw, to my dismay, that the tent was loosened on one side, and that before many minutes it must go over. Soon a gust came, flapping the loosened side, and tearing up the few remaining pegs, lifting the tent from the poles, and laying it upon the ground, leaving me sitting in the open air, pelted by the merciless rain. I took refuge in an adjoining tent, whose inmates were gone, and soon succeeded in sending some of the boys to the rescue of the capsized tent and its contents. They righted it, and brought me a pair of military boots, which had been left in my charge; and though it was too late to save my feet from becoming wet, I donned them, and made my way back to my quarters,—a dreary place,—and sitting down in my wet clothes, to wait, as resignedly as possible, the arrival of the ambulance which was to conduct me to more desirable accommodations, I was startled

by a knock at my tent door; and who should stand before me but my brother, whom I had not seen for two years? His lieutenant was with him. Being at Corinth, they had heard that our regiment was camped here, and notwithstanding the storm, had found their way to see me. My appearance was so ludicrous, that both laughed outright; boots and blanket being the chief features in my apparel. I was unable to move, and hardly able to sit up. There was nothing to offer them, as I had eaten nothing since my dinner the day previous. They saw the necessity of procuring better quarters, and returned at once to Corinth, to obtain a horse and saddle. At five o'clock I mounted my steed for Corinth, and thought my best friend would fail to recognize me in the ludicrous and forlorn appearance I presented; but while crossing a swamp, where every moment I expected to be thrown from my saddle, as my horse was plunging and leaping from one bog to another, I saw approaching a general and his staff, whom I had met many times. They immediately recognized me, and after a few moments' pleasant conversation we passed on."

A short time after, Lieutenant Reynolds received orders to report to Major-General McClernand as aid-de-camp on his staff, and Mrs. Reynolds, after some unavoidable delay, joined him in March, 1863. The house occupied by General McClernand as his headquarters at Milliken's Bend, near Vicksburg, had been deserted by its owner. "Our tent," she says, "was pitched under the trees on the lawn — a charming spot, with its long sweep of green, dotted with bowers of roses of every variety. There were climbing vines, with their gorgeous bloom, and stately magnolias, whose heavy perfume filled the morning air, and suggested all tropical luxuriance. But our stay in this charming spot was of brief duration, General McClernand receiving orders, on the 29th of March, to move with his corps to Hard Times Landing, below Vicksburg, Mrs. McClernand and I remaining behind, with the promise of joining them when headquarters should be established.

"In the mean time the gunboats and transports were preparing to run the blockade at Vicksburg, and we received invitations to witness, from the steamer Von Phul, this fiery trial. At first eight gunboats and three transports were to be sent, with large river steamers, their boilers well protected with cotton bales. The transports were laden with commissary stores, and the barges and flat-boats with forage and coal for the army below. The night was clear and calm. At eleven P. M. they left their moorings at the mouth of the Yazoo. All was intense excitement. The Von Phul was crowded with spectators, Mrs. Grant, Mrs. McClernand, and myself being the only ladies. Our boat was darkened, and with head up stream, we quietly floated down with the current, until I feared that we, too, were to join in the daring adventure. The smoke, in dense, black volumes, mounted high, clearly defining their course, though their dark sides were with difficulty distinguished from the foliage lining the banks. At last one approached the batteries, closely hugging the Louisiana shore; another, and yet another, and still no sound or lightning flash. All had passed the upper batteries, and come in range of the city's guns. Could it be possible they would pass by unnoticed? There was breathless silence, then a flash, another, and soon the heavy booming of the cannon reached us. Other batteries opened on them as they came in range. As time passed, the batteries lower down came into action, indicating to us that some, if not all, the boats had escaped destruction, and were passing on towards Warrenton. While anxiously noting their progress, as chronicled by the reports of the enemy's cannon, we were horrified by observing that the rebels had lighted an immense beacon-fire on one of the highest bluffs of the city, which threw a clear and brilliant light over the river, and brought into bold relief every object passing on its surface. Guided by the light, the gunners at the rebel batteries now redoubled their fire, and along the whole line there blazed a constant sheet of flame. The light had also revealed to the gunboats the exact position of the rebel batteries, and soon the fierce screech of the Parrott shells from our gunboats mingled with the din, and more than one carried destruction into the batteries on shore. The upper batteries finally slackened their fire, and it was evident that nearly all, if not the entire fleet, had passed the most dangerous part of their journey; when suddenly a new light creeps up the sky, and soon we saw that one of the transports was on fire, and the dense white smoke arising was from burning cotton. General Grant, with field-glass in hand, stationed himself upon the hurricane deck, to watch the progress of his daring venture. He alone was calm. The whole city was now aroused, for lights were gleaming in every quarter. The transport burned was the Henry Clay, the cotton taking fire from the explosion of shells. Nothing more would be known that night, and we reluctantly returned to Milliken's Bend as daylight was breaking in the east."

After the fall of Vicksburg, Mrs. Reynolds remained with her husband at headquarters, near the city, for a number of months, her time passing very pleasantly in the customary gayeties of the camp, and in visits to neighboring places of interest or beauty. She broke off a bough of the famous "Truce Tree," under which Vicksburg was surrendered, which she preserves as an interesting memento of the great scene enacted there. The period for which Lieutenant Reynolds enlisted expired in the spring of 1864, and his military career and the long series of adventures in which "Major" Reynolds had figured came to a close, and they both turned again, with inexpressible relief and delight, to the blessings of privacy and the delights of home, grateful that God had seen fit to spare their lives through so many vicissitudes and amid such fearful dangers.

MRS. CHARLOTTE E. McKAY.

THE facts of personal history that led to the enlistment of the soldier were as various as the circumstances of human life; and the same variety and blending of motive were found among those who devoted their whole time to hospital service in the care of the sick and suffering.

A pure and mere desire to be useful to the country was the simple but powerful and all-sufficient motive with some. Others had sons, or husbands, or lovers in the army, and entered upon hospital life with a view of being near the objects of their love when sickness or wounds should overtake them in the line of duty.

Others, again, were impelled by religious zeal. They thought that among so many young men, homeless and suffering, in a life of constant change and perpetual danger, opportunities would be frequent for making moral and religious suggestions with happy effect; that when they saw Death in so many forms, and faced him every day, the propriety of being fitted for that change would be obvious to all. They hoped, too, amid so many dying, to do untold good by whispering the words of supreme hope and consolation in ears that were growing dull to all human sounds.

Others, again, sought the activity and self-forgetfulness of army life and army labor to soothe the pain of bitter bereavement, to give to the suffering patriot those attentions which had now no domestic object upon which they could be lavished. They might use the words of that Hebrew widow, who was also childless: "Call me not Naomi — call me Mara, for the Almighty hath dealt very bitterly with me."

"Death," writes Lord Bacon, "arrives gracious only to such as sit in darkness, to despairful widows, pensive prisoners, and deposed kings; to them whose fortune runs back, and whose spirits mutiny: unto such Death is a redeemer."

But the interval between the blasting of earthly hopes and the arrival of death can be passed in no activity so wholesome or congenial as in labors of public charity.

Thinking thus, in the spring of 1862, when her pleasant home in Massachusetts had been utterly desolated by the successive deaths of her husband and her only child, Mrs. McKay turned the key in the door of the house which was dear to her now only for the memory of what had been, and sought oblivion, and at the same time usefulness, in the army of the Potomac. Her army life began at Frederick City, in Maryland, on the 24th of March, 1862, where she arrived and commenced her labors just in time to assist in the care of a great number of wounded from the battle of Winchester, which had been fought between Banks and Stonewall Jackson the day before.

The hospital consisted of two old stone buildings, with some modern barracks attached, all quite unexceptionable in their external arrangements, and the inmates she found much the same as in army hospitals everywhere.

"I find," she writes, "much suffering, both physical and mental, depression, and discontent. In other cases there are patience, endurance, and gratitude, and the whole is often mingled and relieved by touches of the grotesque and ludicrous." The first care was to administer — sometimes before they were taken from the ambulances — food and some slightly stimulating drink. Then all those whose wounds were not very deep and painful, after they had been washed and combed, and their wounds dressed, their torn and bloody battle clothes replaced by those which were clean and wholesome, would sit up in their beds, or walk around the wards, cheerful, sometimes jolly, and always grateful that it was no worse with them.

The cases of many of these wounded soldiers became very interesting to Mrs. McKay, and the hospital diary which she kept, during the whole time of her labor in the army, is rich in incidents and recitals, which are written with uncommon taste and skill. One poor German boy she speaks of, who interested her as much by his misfortunes as by the noble spirit in which he bore his sufferings. His wound had not been dangerous originally. A ball had pierced his arm; but the hurt had been carefully attended to, and he was getting on admirably, when, as he was crossing the ward one day, his foot caught, and as he was large, he fell with the whole of his heavy weight upon the wounded arm. The consequence was a terrible fracture, which was found by the surgeons to be incurable, and the shattered arm was cut off. For eleven weeks he lingered, at first improving quite rapidly, but afterwards sinking, hopelessly. He received the most careful attention from both physicians and nurses, for he was a noble-looking fellow, a member of one of the Ohio regiments, and everything was done to save his life.

Mrs. McKay was his nurse, and her devotion was assiduous; but the care and skill were bestowed in vain. He was sinking into a soldier's grave, and as earthly scenes failed, he desired to have the supreme rites of his church performed over his dying pillow. He was always glad to hear portions of the Bible, or any good book, read to him. Just before he died she saw that he was making an effort to speak. She bent over him, to catch, if possible, his parting words. Slowly and with pain he whispered them, one by one, in her ear: "I want — I want — " said he. "What do you want, Russell?" "I want to tell you — what — what I will do — for you — when I get to — another place."

One Sunday, while Mrs. McKay was superintending the distribution of dinner in her ward, she heard footsteps at the farther end of the long ward, and, looking up, saw the chief medical director, and with him, a few steps in advance, a gentleman in civil dress, whose bearing at once riveted her attention.

There was nothing peculiar in his brown suit, white cravat, sallow complexion, heavy gray beard, and the anxious expression of his face. Yet in all combined there was something to arrest and fix the attention in the manner of the quiet and courteous, yet earnest stranger; and she stood looking at him, as he passed down the long row of hospital cots, his keen eye seeming to take in everything, and especially the amount and quality of the food that was being served out to the patients.

"Do you know who visited our hospital to-day?" asked Mrs. McKay of a lady friend, whom she met in the grounds soon after. "O, yes, he is a doctor; he was in the Crimean war, is very rich, lives in Louisiana, is a good Union man, and owns a large sugar plantation. He introduced himself to Dr. W., and asked to look through the hospital."

Not long after she asked the same question of a rebel soldier in the hospital, and he informed her that this man was Stonewall Jackson, and that he often penetrated the Union lines to acquaint himself with positions and movements, sometimes in one disguise, and sometimes in another.

The summer of 1862 passed without much novelty at the hospital in Frederick City, where Mrs. McKay was laboring. The wounded were mostly from Banks's force, who, during the greater part of that campaign, was pitted against Stonewall Jackson. But early in September came the astounding intelligence that the whole Union force had been engaged by the combined forces of Lee and Jackson, at Manassas, and driven in defeat across the Potomac into Washington City; and that the rebel army, victorious, but ragged and hungry, was advancing on Frederick City.

Mrs. McKay, notwithstanding the panic that prevailed in the neighborhood, determined to remain at her self-assigned post of duty, and take care of those who were too feeble to flee before the advancing foe. Meanwhile her pen was not idle, and she has preserved a connected and graphic account of the rebel occupation.

"As the town could not be defended," she writes, "the citizens prepared to give Lee as silent a reception as possible. The Home Guard was sent off, and every patient in the hospital who could walk hurried to the outskirts of the town, where teams were seized to carry them to a safe distance. Immense quantities of government clothing, blankets, and other stores, were heaped in piles and burned.

"Blinds were closed on the houses, and anon the streets became silent and deserted. We waited anxiously for their coming, quite ignorant as to what policy they might pursue, and uncertain to what fate they might consign us. At length, at about ten o'clock, on the morning of the 6th of September, the glitter of long rows of polished bayonets was flashing on the top of the hill east of the town, and soon after the long column began to pour rather lazily through Main Street. A miserable band, with a few cracked and battered instruments, attempted to play 'Maryland, my Maryland!' but the effort seemed soon to exhaust itself. Presently a squad of horsemen from the vanguard dashed into the hospital yard, and presenting drawn sabres to the few medical officers who stood leaning on the balcony of one of the old stone buildings, demanded, in the name of the Confederate States, the surrender of the post.

"The summons was immediately obeyed, and forthwith mounted guards were stationed at the door of every ward. 'Our men must have been asleep to let you come into Maryland,' said one of our hospital stewards to a stern-looking rebel. 'Yes,' replied the haughty Southron, 'a good many of them are sleeping at Bull Run.' Soon a brigade of Virginia troops marched up and encamped on the hospital ground. As they filed in, we could see that nearly every soldier had on his shoulder a watermelon, captured from the neighboring field. They quickly seated themselves in squads on the ground, and began to eat, throwing the refuse about our nicely-policed grounds. It was but the beginning of sorrows in that line; for, before the week was out, the place, which had been a model of neatness, was turned into a pen of filth. When I went to my quarters that night, just outside the hospital inclosure, I could enter the door only by stepping over the body of a rebel soldier, who was lying there insensible, either from fatigue or liquor. Another, in the same condition, was stowed along on the brick pavement under my window, in front of which a third stood guard. I passed the night without fear, though sleep was driven away by the continual tramp of troops passing along the streets, and the rumbling of artillery and baggage wagons. This continued, with little cessation, for the next two or three days, until the whole rebel army had passed through the town; and as I sat at my window, watching them hour after hour, I could almost imagine that all the beggars in the world had congregated in that mighty host, so ragged were they, so filthy and squalid in appearance. Yet these men were by no means ruffians. Seeing me at the window, they would sometimes stop, and ask politely for food; and when I gave whatever I had at hand, they received it with gratitude.

"When I went among them in the wards which they occupied, they promptly made way for me, and thanked me with fervor for whatever I could supply for the relief of hunger, sickness, or wounds. In my own ward, which was constantly thronged with them, we held long conversations on the origin, progress, and probable termination of the war; and many of them I found to be intelligent, thoughtful, even Christian men, having implicit faith in their cause, in God as its especial leader, and, next to him, in Stonewall Jackson.

"On parting with our soldiers, they shook hands cordially, and hoped it might never be their fortune to meet on the battle-field. Some of the officers manifested a more haughty temper. 'Are you tired, soldier, after your long march?' I asked of one. 'No; I shall not be tired till I get to Philadelphia.' 'But do you know that many of you poor fellows will find a grave before you get to Philadelphia?' 'We expected nothing else, madam, when we came out, and our homes and our little children are as dear to us as to any others.' 'But you are all caught in a nice trap, and we shall soon see you rushing out of this town much faster than you came in.' 'Perhaps you haven't heard, madam, how we fight the Yankees down in Virginia.' 'No. How is that?' 'We fight with our muskets till the powder is all gone; then we break our gunstocks over their heads; then we take the fence rails, and break them all up; and then fling rocks at them.' 'Very well,' I said; 'our soldiers can fight with fence rails and rocks as well as you, and by the time you get to Philadelphia, you'll have plenty of that sort of work.'"

A few days wrought an entire change. The rebel force vacated Frederick City. The Union army pressed forward to engage them, and then followed the great battles at South Mountain and Antietam, by which the hospitals at Frederick City, and all others in the vicinity, were crowded with the bleeding and mangled remnants of the great hosts who contended on those ever-memorable fields.

For many days the inmates of this hospital were surrounded by the roar and intense excitement of great military events.

Perched upon the highest point of the hospital buildings, Mrs. McKay, and the few who remained in the midst of scenes so rude, watched the swaying and changing lines. Now a party of skirmishers are making their way across a cornfield. "Soon they tear away the fence, and are in the hospital grounds. We rush to meet them, take them by the hand, lead them into the house, and set before them food, whatever we can find. They eat hastily, and hurry back to their places in the ranks, for there is no time or place for rest now."

Mrs. McKay remained on duty in this hospital for some time after Lee, with his decimated army, had fallen back into Virginia, and established his lines along the south bank of the Rappahannock.

At the time of Burnside's unfortunate advance and ill-planned attack at Fredericksburg, she went to Washington City, and in the hospitals there nursed many of those who had been brought directly from that disastrous field to Washington.

Early in January, 1863, she was, after much difficulty, furnished with a pass which admitted her within the army lines at Falmouth, where the army was encamped. She spent several days in visiting her brother and other friends in the Seventeenth Maine volunteers, and then sought active employment as a nurse in Third Corps Hospital, which had just been established. She was so fortunate as to find quarters in a house near by, and received permission from the surgeon in charge to work for the patients. There was need enough of work, and of hospital supplies for the poor fellows, many of whom, very sick, were lying in tents, on the cold, wet ground, with no other bed or covering than an army blanket, and no other diet than salt pork, navy beans, and hard-tack. For the establishment of a special diet kitchen there was literally nothing on hand. She had brought a few utensils from Washington, and with these and the cans in which preserved meats and fruits had been brought, and a little iron boiler, occasionally borrowed from an old negro woman, she was soon able to send out into the different wards puddings of corn starch and farina, beef tea, chocolate, tea, soup, and jelly, which, with good fresh bread and butter, were indeed luxurious fare for the poor fellows, as compared with army rations.

By degrees the hospital improved, and assumed a comfortable and even cheerful appearance. General Birney sent daily details of men to cut poles in the woods and make bunks, which, with the help of straw and blankets, made beds that were quite comfortable. And Mrs. Birney, who frequently visited the patients, encouraged and cheered them by her charming presence, and by the gifts of delicacies, with which she always came abundantly supplied. Other stores were drawn from the United States Sanitary

Commission, and various other sources, until the diet table showed quite an extensive variety.

About the middle of April the First division, Third corps, moved to Potomac Creek, about ten miles from Falmouth, and a new hospital was established there. A few days after, the whole army crossed the Rappahannock, and the long, bloody, yet indecisive battle of Chancellorsville ensued. Here Mrs. McKay's wish of being close in the rear of a great battle was fully realized. With an ambulance well loaded with supplies, she was able to follow the army across the pontoon bridge, and established herself at a large brick house, two or three miles from the front line of battle. In a few hours, this house, and all the surrounding grounds, were crowded with men wounded and dying, and there were exhibited all those various and ghastly spectacles which are the terrible, though inevitable, consequences of war. These scenes were soon made still more distressing for her by terrible reports that came from the front. She was told that her dear brother had fallen in the conflict, shot through the heart, and that many other friends had shared the same fate. After the army — baffled, though never fully engaged — was withdrawn to the north side of the river, immense trains of ambulances were busy, day and night, drawing their loads of wounded over roads indescribably wretched, while thousands were left suffering and dying on the field.

"We have lost too much to give up now; we have something to revenge," said Captain F., her brother's friend and tent-mate, as he stood one evening in front of her tent, just ready to mount his horse and ride away. He was very pale, and there was a gravity in his manner quite unnatural, for he was usually gay, and apparently light-hearted. A few weeks later, and he lay writhing in pain, and dying on the bloody field of Gettysburg.

When the Union army left its base at Falmouth and Acquia Creek, and moved forward to confront the haughty rebel force on northern soil, the hospitals were broken up, and the patients sent to Washington, where also Mrs. McKay went, to remain until it should be known where, along or within the border, the great blow had been struck.

On the 4th of July the Washington journals contained accounts of the great engagement on the 1st, 2d, and 3d, at Gettysburg. On the 6th Mrs. McKay went to Baltimore, and thence to the point nearest the field accessible by rail. After some delay and difficulty, travelling the last twenty-five miles in a huge army wagon, on a pile of forage, she reached the hospital of her division, about five miles from Gettysburg; and here, for the remainder of July and the greater part of August, her labors were such as the vast accumulation of suffering around her seemed to demand.

Her labors and annoyances in conducting the special diet department were greatly increased by the absurd and vexatious red tape-ism of some army officials, who not only objected to volunteer lady nurses, but threw all obstacles and impediments in their way.

For almost the whole time of her labor at Gettysburg she had no facilities for cooking for a thousand or fifteen hundred sick men but a row of camp kettles, suspended from a long pole. Her requisition for a stove was brought back disapproved by the medical director of the post, on the ground that he had stoves in Baltimore, which, when they came, were found entirely unfit for field use.

In the fall of 1863, when those who remained of the Gettysburg sufferers had been collected in one great hospital, Mrs. McKay again sought the front. Warrenton, in Virginia, was now headquarters, and there were much suffering and destitution in the numerous regimental hospitals. These, especially those of the Third division, she visited regularly, dispensing such comforts as she could draw from the Sanitary Commission and other sources.

Very late in that year came the fight at Mine Run, in which this division suffered severe losses; and soon after the Army of the Potomac went into winter quarters, and Brandy Station here became the hospital centre. The usual routine of well-organized hospital labor filled the time during that winter and spring, till the order of March 26th removed "all ladies connected with the various associations, commissions, and agencies, operating within the army lines."

Imposing as was the sound of this order, its effect was to banish good and faithful army nurses from the lines barely for a month. In the early days of May came the great battles of the Wilderness and Spottsylvania.

All the hospital workers agree that at no time during the war was there such an accumulation of suffering as during the months of May and June, 1864. Great battle followed great battle with appalling frequency. The contest seemed to have changed its principles. It was now a question which army could survive the most copious blood-letting. Hospital accommodations were large, yet sadly inadequate.

Transportation was at times so embarrassed and delayed that vast numbers suffered from hunger, and many of the sick and wounded perished for want of suitable and sufficient food.

In all these fearful scenes and constant labors, Mrs. McKay took an active and efficient part.

In the hospitals at Fredericksburg, White House, and City Point, she labored for the sick of the division with which she had been so long connected. But about the first of June the army organization was considerably changed. The old Third corps was so reduced by sickness and battle that it was now made the Third division of the Second corps. Most of the old surgeons were dead, or had left the service, and General Birney, who had long been her friend, was now transferred; and Mrs. McKay accepted an invitation from the surgeon-in-chief of the Cavalry Corps Hospital to attend there and take charge of the special diet department. Here she labored for nearly a year, till just before the fall of Richmond, and the close of the war.

Many incidents occurred during her stay which illustrate the swift vicissitudes and tragic scenery of war, as well as the kindness and fidelity of Mrs. McKay's labor. One evening, as she was sitting in her tent, the flap was drawn aside, and a pleasant-looking soldier boy inquired for Mrs. S. "She has gone out just now; can I do anything for you?" "I am her son," was the reply, full of repressed emotion. She directed him to the place whither his mother had gone, and soon after saw them united in a tearful embrace. Mrs. S. had given four sons to the Union army, and they had enlisted from the noblest and most patriotic motives. One, reduced to a skeleton by sickness following exposure, had gone home to die. Just a year from the day of his death a second son had died in the hospital. Hearing of his illness, in her home in the northern part of Maine, she had hastened to his bedside, to minister the last offices of maternal affection; but when she reached the Cavalry Corps Hospital he had been lying five days in the grave. Her grief was very great; but seeing so many suffering, whose kindred were far away, she restrained her emotion, and devoted herself to caring for the sick, becoming so much interested in the work that she begged to be put on permanent duty in the hospital. The men were always glad to see her in the wards, because, as they said to her, "you seem so much like my mother; your hand feels so much like my mother's hand." A third son was in service in Florida; and, after two years of separation, suffering much from hunger, weariness, and hardship, the fourth was for a few hours with her again. They speak tearfully of the past, and not without anxiety of the future. He tells her of comrades — some of them old playfellows from the same town — killed in battle; especially of one poor fellow who was shot on picket after his term of service had expired, and says of him, "Tell his mother he was a good soldier." They speak of him who has just passed away to his eternal home, and after a while go out to visit his grave. He lies in the little cemetery of the hospital, just in the edge of the woods, near the bank of the Appomattox. There sleep more than a hundred soldiers of the cavalry corps who have died in the hospital. They lie, each one with his little head-board, giving his name, regiment, and the date of his death, in rows as regular as those in which they lately stood on dress parade, or drawn out in line of battle. But time is precious, and they cannot stay long to weep at his grave, for the few hours of the son's furlough soon pass, and he bids his mother good-by, saying, "Do not fear for me, mother; if I die in battle or in camp I will surely meet you in heaven." He carries under his arm a little bundle, which it had been a pleasure to prepare for him: shirt, drawers, socks, handkerchief, towel, and some little dainties to tempt his appetite, tied in a large, colored handkerchief, which he will find it pleasant some cold night on picket to tie around his throat — little gifts, promptings of a mother's love, how invaluable to the soldier boy!

One afternoon one of the ward-masters came to Mrs. McKay, and said, "Jim is dead!" He was a man to whom her attention was called, when he came to the hospital, as a brave soldier, and worthy of special attention. It was hoped that something might be done for him; but all efforts for his restoration were unavailing, and he sank gradually away. On the morning before his death, he said, in reply to Mrs. McKay's inquiries concerning his health, that he felt quite well, and could eat anything; but his lips were then stiffening with the frosts of death, and his limbs nearly cold, and in a few hours he was gone. He was respectably connected, and the possessor of quite a large property. While absent in the three months' service, at the commencement of the war, the young girl to whom he was engaged to be married was lost to him through the treachery of one who had supplanted him in her affections. From the time he arrived home and learned the facts, his sole object in life had been to punish her seducer. The latter, being made aware of his intention, immediately left the place, and went to Washington. Thither he followed, and learning that he had enlisted in a Pennsylvania regiment, hesitated not to do the same. Before he could reach the regiment, intelligence came that the object of his pursuit had been captured while on picket. Whether this was true, or whether, learning that the avenger was at hand, he had deserted to the enemy, was never known; but it is certain that, after three years of baffled efforts, worn out with hard service and exposure in camp and field, added to the burden of mental anguish which he always bore, poor "Jim" came to the hospital to die, the wreck of a once noble and generous-hearted man. A few days before his death he transmitted to his friends a large sum of money, to be used for the poor girl's benefit, whom, with her child, he had maintained during his absence, though he had entirely relinquished the idea of marrying her.

The vigilance required to prevent sanitary stores in transit from falling into unprincipled hands is fully illustrated in a mishap which occurred to Mrs. McKay in the summer of 1863. At Washington she had packed a box containing a large number of articles, useful for her own mess and for preparing special diet, and some choice liquors. Having obtained transportation, it was put on the same train of cars on which she herself took passage. At the last station before reaching Sulphur Springs, Virginia, her destination, she inquired for her box, and was told that the baggage train had stopped several miles back, at Warrenton Junction; it had not come, but would be there the next day. She went on to General Birney's headquarters, at Sulphur Springs, nine miles from the station, that evening, in a mail wagon, and soon made herself acquainted with the wants of the sick in the division; but without her box — the contents of which would be a complete outfit for hospital operations — she could do nothing for them. The need was so great that one of the surgeons rode twelve miles for a paper of corn starch, and she herself rode sixteen to procure half a bottle of brandy. After repeated orders having been sent to have it brought up in a headquarters wagon, without effect, she started in her ambulance to hunt it up. She first went to Germantown, where were the headquarters of the army, thinking it might have gone to Dr. Letterman, it being consigned to his care. Not finding it there, she went to Bealton, thence to Warrenton Junction, and finally to Warrenton, where she had the satisfaction of finding her box, and bringing it back with her in the ambulance. After a laborious and vexatious trip of thirty-five miles, what was her dismay and chagrin, upon opening it next morning, to find it filled with old chains, halters, broken harness, and one old horse blanket! The teamsters at Warrenton, where she found it, had "confiscated" its contents, and filled it with old trash from their wagon boxes.

At the time of the battle of Hatcher's Run she was still engaged in this hospital, and speaks thus of the scenes that followed that action: —

"Hearing that several had been brought in dead, I went this morning to the tent used as a receptacle for such, to see if any of my acquaintances were among them. They were lying stiff and cold, in their uniforms, just as they fell in battle. As I drew aside the blue overcoat capes which had been turned over their faces, what was my surprise and pain to recognize among these frozen sleepers two young officers who were in the hospital with wounds only a few months ago! One had been a special friend, Captain Harper, of the fourth Pennsylvania cavalry. Only a few days ago he called at my quarters. He had just returned from a leave of absence, during which he had visited his home. Full of life and energy, in splendid uniform, and mounted on a powerful horse, he was the picture of a gallant soldier. Now, as I write, he lies stretched in his rough coffin, his manly features rigid in death, awaiting burial."

The labors of Mrs. McKay at the Cavalry Corps Hospital did not fail of being fully appreciated by the gallant men whose sufferings in wounds and sickness she was able to palliate. As a Christmas present, on the 25th December, 1864, they had given her a very handsome gold badge and chain, of exquisite manufacture, with the inscription, —

"Presented to Mrs. Charlotte E. McKay by the soldiers of the Cavalry Corps Hospital. Army of Potomac, in front of Petersburg. December 25, 1864."

So, also, a few months before, when nursing the wounded of the Seventeenth Maine volunteers, at Chancellorsville, she had received a magnificent Kearny Cross, with the front inscription, "*Dulce et decorum est pro patria mori;*" and on the reverse, "Presented to Mrs. C. E. McKay, by the officers of the Seventeenth regiment Maine volunteers. May, 1863."

Although her labors as nurse did not continue after March, 1865, she remained in Virginia for more than a year, engaged with the freedmen; nursing the sick, taking care of those who were unable to care for themselves, listening to many a weird tale of cruelty and injustice in the old days of bondage, and giving the rudiments of education to minds that were sitting in darkness.

Although as constant and laborious in hospital labors as any, she yet found time to record scenes, conversations, and incidents, many of which are of uncommon interest, and recited in graphic language, as the following, that are subjoined to this sketch of her labors, will show: —

The Soldier's Grave.

On the 28th day of October, 1863, the headquarters of the Army of the Potomac broke camp at Auburn, and moved to Colonel Murray's farm, about two miles from Warrenton Junction.

The headquarters moving, though not so grand or striking a spectacle as you will often see in military life, is still quite imposing, and by no means destitute of the "pomp and circumstance of war." Altogether it is about as long a procession as the eye can take in at once, consisting of the baggage wagons and private carriages of the generals and other officers filling the various departments of the army, accompanied by their battle-flags, a heavy escort of cavalry, a regiment of infantry, wagons belonging to the subsistence department, and at this time a large number of rebel prisoners marching under guard.

We moved along slowly over the hills, through the

wooded country, but soon emerged upon the plain of Bristow, where had recently been fought the battle which gave to Meade, instead of Lee, the coveted heights of Centreville, and to General Warren the laurels which have designated him "Hero of Bristow."

It is a desolate region, and, especially at this season of the year, affording little to attract or satisfy the eye. Yet, as we passed along, my attention was arrested by a little scene, which forms a picture in memory never to be effaced. Just off to the right, a short distance over the plain, was a soldier's grave, newly made; and ranged along, side by side, bowed on reversed muskets over the grave of their comrade, were four soldiers, apparently engaged in prayer. They had turned aside from the weary march, and there, unmindful of the gay procession passing by, with heads bowed low, and solemn countenances, gave a few moments to communion with Heaven, and a few tears to the sleeper below. Did they think, in those moments, of breaking hearts, far away, yearning with vain desire to kneel by that lonely grave? Were they recalling the many fearful engagements in which they and the fallen hero had fought, side by side, and crying out in their hearts, "Such is the price we pay for human freedom; so much it costs to secure to our children the blessings of a good government"? Or were they anticipating other battles speedily approaching, and wondering if they would be the next to fall, and who would be left to pray over their graves? I know not what were their thoughts; but these and many others rushed upon my mind, and I, too, gave a tear to the solitary grave. Yes, this was a solitary grave; but on many hill sides, and in many valleys of Virginia, you will find them strewn, "thick as autumn leaves in Vallambrosa's brooks." There sleep our brothers and our sons — the best we had to give; the costliest sacrifice we could offer on the altar of our country. Their last battle is fought, their last march ended; their last bivouac is made. They sleep well, in that deep slumber from which no bugle call, or sound of any kind, shall awake them, until the loud reveille, which shall "shake, not the earth only, but also heaven." But who can number the tears that flow, or the hearts that break with longing for the sight of those who shall return no more? What eye, save that which comprehends immensity, can measure a nation's grief, as, like the foot-worn soldier, she bows over the graves of her fallen sons, and from the depth of her anguish, cries out, "Such is the price we pay for human freedom"?

On a Stretcher.

When our colonel's wife came to camp last winter, she expected to have a good time of it. Our colonel had had his quarters arranged in the best camp style. A nice plank pavement all around, wherever she might choose to walk; trees planted so thickly about the tent that you would think you were entering a natural forest; a pretty archway, made of green boughs, at the entrance, with the red badge of the division in the centre, and everything about the premises quite *au fait*. Within all was cosy and comfortable; the walls splendidly illuminated with pictures from Harpers' Weekly and Frank Leslie's Magazine; good board floor; plenty of chairs and boxes, on which the colonel's numerous friends could sit around the capacious fireplace, and gaze upon the ever consuming, but never consumed secesh logs; or, if of an inquisitive turn, look into the little inner sanctuary, just big enough for a bed, and to turn around in. So we were all glad when the colonel's wife came among us, for the presence of a lady in camp is always welcome; and though we cannot all have our wives to winter with us, the sight of one seems to bring home nearer. Camp life is not always destitute of amusements, and last winter everybody said it was very gay. There were lots of balls and receptions, and visiting from one camp to another, riding on horseback or in ambulances, — for many other officers besides our colonel had their wives with them; and, although we were not within the charmed circle, we could see, as we paced our beat, or stood on guard, or lingered at the door of our hut, a good deal of what was going on. We knew when our colonel's wife got her new riding-dress and hat from Washington, and saw her when she first mounted her horse for a ride, and often afterwards watched the gay cavalcade, of which she was one, galloping over the hills, and vowed that if ever "this cruel war is over," our nice little wife should have just such a riding-dress and hat, and we would have a ride, if two horses were to be found in the country. So the winter was nearly over, and our colonel's wife had enjoyed her share of whatever amusement the Army of the Potomac had to offer. But there was one experience she little thought to encounter still in reserve for her, and that was, being carried "on a stretcher." It was brought about on this wise: she had taken several rather hard rides on horseback, to which she was not much accustomed, sometimes on cold, windy days, and on a fast horse; and being rather ambitious, and not willing to give up when prudence might have dictated rest, she all at once, and quite contrary to her plans, found herself on the sick list. Being sick in camp is no joke, and least like one to the lady in question; but pains in the back and head, and sleepless nights and days, and constant nausea, are stubborn facts, to which the stoutest heart must cry, "I surrender!" So, with all the colonel's good nursing, and the doctor's prescriptions, and visits from sympathizing friends, "she was nothing bettered, but rather grew worse." And right upon this, an order came for our division to move camp. Military orders make no exceptions; and hard as it might seem in this state of things, the cosy quarters must be evacuated, and new ones sought in a camp three miles distant. The lady's illness had reached a point where, indeed, it might be said, "the spider's most attenuated thread is cord, is cable, to the slender hold she had on life," and the slightest jar might snap the thread, and then all would be over. Riding in an ambulance over the rough roads and corduroy bridges was an experiment not in the least desirable, and the only resort which camp afforded was a stretcher. Our stretcher-bearers are sufficiently accustomed to bearing wounded and dead men from the field, or sick men to and from the hospital; but a lady on a stretcher is something quite unique. Eight men, making four reliefs, were detailed to accomplish the delicate task; and with infinite care and tenderness, our colonel's wife was laid on the ominous little vehicle, to commence her new method of transportation. The colonel accompanied the party on horseback, and six of the men took their turns in going ahead as pioneers, to select the smoothest places. "Is that a dead man?" "O, that is a woman. Is she dead, or what's the matter with her?" These questions being asked by stragglers, in the hearing of the lady, were not much calculated to raise her spirits and facilitate her convalescence.

The removal, however, was accomplished with much less disadvantage than was feared; and now that she is restored to health, she looks back upon it as rather a gay adventure, and declares that she outdoes the colonel in military experience, since he, in all his three years' term of service, has never been carried on a stretcher.

Life in the Tented Field.

"They have gone — they have all passed by." Nothing can be seen of them now but a long line of flashing bayonets, passing close under the brow of yonder hill. First went a few miles of cavalry (interspersed with batteries of artillery), the rattling of whose sabres always announces their approach before you hear the tramp of their horses. If you happen to be near them as they pass, you will hear them jesting in merry tones, or singing snatches of rollicking songs. They go out ready to do and die; and, whatever else happens, we may be pretty sure that the cavalry will not disgrace us.

Next to them went their ambulances, painfully suggestive of broken limbs, fearful sabre gashes, and bullet holes through the lungs; worse things than those sometimes, but we must not think of them now. Then their train of baggage and supply wagons, winding along for a mile or two, and this is the last we see of the cavalry.

A few hours pass on, and looking far away, over the hills, we see a long, dark line in motion; and experience tells us that it is a body of infantry. As they come out of the shadow of the hill, their bayonets begin to gleam, so that now, in the sunshine, they look like a line of blazing light, and come pouring on, officers riding at the head of their various commands, colors and battle-flags waving on the air, some of them pierced and torn in many places, but borne all the more proudly, and guarded the more sacredly, for that. Presently other columns, from other camps, and winding around other hills, come on; but they are all moving in one direction. Where they are going, or what for, nobody knows at present. As they come nearer, you see that many of them have attached to their knapsack straps tin cups, frying pans, tin pails, coffee pots, and also a loaf of bread on their bayonets. They seem in good spirits, and, like the cavalry, are amusing themselves with singing and joking.

"Glorious fellows!" exclaimed an officer of high rank, as a part of his command was marching by. He was thinking how gallantly they had behaved on many a hardly-contested field, and how well he might rely on them to follow wherever he should lead in future.

"Poor fellows!" said, in the same moment, a woman, in sympathizing tones. She was thinking of fearful sights in crowded hospitals, cruel wounds, amputated limbs, pale faces, and brave, faithful hearts, worn out with excess of anguish. So they pass along for many hours; and after them come their trains of ambulances, baggage and supply wagons, and lastly a drove of beeves, proportioned in numbers to the rations they are to serve. Now, at last, they are all gone. The camps are like deserted cities, for they have left their huts and tents standing, hoping to come back to them in a short time. A few soldiers, unfit for a march, are walking around, or lying in their tents; here and there you may see a smoke lazily ascending, but the atmosphere is relieved of that dense body of smoke which usually hangs over camp. The stillness is painful. We sit down mournfully, and wonder where our friends are going, and what is on the tapis now; for dear and noble souls have gone out to-day, and many such we have seen go out to return no more. In our hearts we pray for them, and then look out to see what signs of the weather, and hope it will not rain. At night we think of guerrillas. We know that our picket line is thin, and that a treacherous and unscrupulous foe is always going about like a roaring lion, seeking what he may "gobble." Our sleep — if we get any — is light, and often broken by anxiety. We dream of battle-fields, rebel cavalry, and journeys to Richmond. In the morning we hear a distant cannonading; but our ears have become accustomed to the sound, so that we are not startled by it: it may be fighting, or it may be only shelling the woods as they advance. We judge of its distance and direction by the sound. Sometimes it seems to come from the right, sometimes from the left, and sometimes from both directions at once. It continues, at intervals, through the day, though growing more distant. As the day wears on, a messenger comes in from the front, and reports our friends. We are relieved to know that they have had no fighting yet, and are doing better than we anticipated. But now a new cause of anxiety arises; for the weather, which was fine when they marched out, is changing, and ominous gusts of wind, and rain-bearing clouds, force themselves on our observation. We try to think we are mistaken, and look earnestly for patches of blue sky, and gleams of sunshine; but they are not there. Soon a starless, dismal night sets in, with drizzling rain. O, the pitiless storm! What can our friends do, with no shelter but their blankets, and no bed but the soft soil under them? The rain seems to beat on our naked hearts, and we abandon ourselves to fearful anxiety; for there is not only the exposure to the weather, but the danger that, the ground being softened into mud, their progress will be obstructed, and their plans defeated, or that the enemy will gain advantage of them. But all our fears, we know, cannot help them; so we strive to commit them to the care of that Providence which rules over all, and to hope for the best.

The next morning, going to the hospital, we observe a new patient, and are pained to see that it is a case of extreme suffering. The eyes are partly closed, an expression of mortal anguish is on his face, and the symptoms of dissolution already appear. "Whom have you here, nurse?" "He is a man of our division, ma'am, who went on the march, but fell out by the way, and they sent him back in an ambulance. He was very bad when he came in, and has been growing worse ever since."

The next day, the fourth since the march, is clear and fine. Our friends return without fighting, and we learn it was only a reconnoissance. The poor soldier in the hospital is dead, and we join the little escort that follows him to his long home, there on the hill-side, along with many who went before, and whose graves are marked by simple head-boards, bearing the inscription of their names and regiments. His grave is prepared, and the brown coffin lowered in. "I am the resurrection and the life" is read over it, a prayer is said, a salute fired, and he adds one more to the buried soldiers with whom the soil of Virginia is so thickly strewn. Poor fellow! he was a recruit, and this was his first and last march.

THE BLOODY FLAG OF FORT PILLOW.

DARK and damning was the act performed by the fierce partisan leader of rebels on the 14th of April, 1864. The names of Fort Pillow and Andersonville stand out in lurid relief from the stormy background of a great civil war, and stamp with perpetual infamy the authors of these great crimes against humanity.

Fort Pillow is a strong fieldwork, erected under the superintendence of Polk, and afterwards of Beauregard, on the east bank of the Mississippi River, about fifty miles above Memphis. It was designed as one of the defences of the Upper Mississippi Valley, and in the spring of 1862 was virtually evacuated by the rebels, in consequence of the Union victories at Donelson and Shiloh, the effect of which was to flank all the rebel positions north of the Memphis and Charleston Railroad, and concentrate all the forces of that department at Corinth, in front of Grant. For two years the fort had remained quietly in possession of the Union forces; but in the winter and spring of 1864 the rebel partisan leader and cavalry general, Forrest, led a force of some six or seven thousand into West Tennessee. For some time he had his headquarters at Jackson, recruiting and remounting his force. This was always with him a favorite ranging ground. Before the war he had lived at Memphis and on the river, following the cognate and equally infamous branches of business, negro-trading and river gambling. He was the last and most revolting specimen of that style of man which is the combined effect of a roving border life and of slavery—a man of powerful frame and unflinching nerve, insensible to fatigue, incapable alike of fear or of tenderness, an unequalled horseman, a fatal shot, a successful speculator, and a lucky gambler.

To such a man the opportunity afforded by the outbreak of the rebellion in 1861 was unlimited. A fierce champion of slavery, a desperado, and a ruffian, war had charms for him far beyond the milder horrors of the slave-yard and the smaller risks of the gaming-table. He plunged into the seething gulf of civil strife with a joy that only the bold and the depraved can know, and by a series of almost unbroken successes, rose from a private to the highest position which it was possible for a cavalry officer to hold.

The men he had drawn around him were similar to him in depravity, only not equal in strength and capacity for command.

Such was the general, and such the force, that, on the morning of the 14th of April, appeared before Fort Pillow. Soon after daylight the fight began. The garrison consisted of not quite six hundred, about two thirds of whom were negroes, and one half the balance were loyal southerners, or, as the rebels contemptuously called them, "home-made Yankees." Major Booth, of the Sixth United States heavy artillery, was in command.

About nine o'clock in the morning, while at the breastwork and directing the battle, Major Booth received a ball directly through the heart, and fell dead. There was continuous firing all day, but no charges, and the number of the garrison who fell was not over twenty.

About three in the afternoon Forrest sent a flag of truce, by which hostilities were suspended for near an hour. The demand which was sent with the truce was for unconditional surrender. Major Bradford, upon whom the command had devolved after Major Booth fell, replied that he could not surrender unconditionally. Forrest replied that he would give him twenty minutes to leave the fort or surrender.

Meantime the rebel force had been advanced furtively so as now to surround the works on three sides; and the lines awaiting the order for assault were but a few feet from the parapet when the twenty minutes last given by Forrest expired.

At this moment three thousand fierce ruffians sprang forward, and, raising the hideous cry of "No quarter," climbed over the parapet, and rushed upon the garrison.

There was no more fighting, properly speaking. On the river side there was a steep bluff, that rose directly from the water, and the whole garrison rushed down this hill towards the river, many plunging into the stream. Then followed a relentless and indiscriminate butchery of all ages, both sexes, and without reference to rank or color.

The heart sickens, and we turn away in loathing from the horrid recital. Of the negro troops hardly one escaped. They were shot down like hogs. They were stabbed and beaten when wounded. The sabre was often plunged into the hole made by the pistol ball. Some were pinned to the ground and burned. Some were buried alive.

Turn we now from this fearful scene of butchery to another that followed a few days after, by no means cheerful, but relieved by the play of nobler sentiments, and by the presence and heroic words of a brave, though heart-broken woman.

We enter Fort Pickering, situated on a high bluff, that for miles commands a view of the mighty river that rolls, broad, turbid, and swift, below. The ramparts all around bristle with heavy guns. A regiment of United States artillery is drawn up in perfect order. Every face is sober. A high and firm resolve is burning in many a dark eye. Six paces in front of the line are standing fourteen strong-built, hardy-looking, brave-hearted men. They have no commander. What wreck of war is this? What waif floating on the stormy ocean of civil strife? We shall see in a moment. A lady, clad in the deepest mourning, steps forward in front of these fourteen survivors. The silence is now full of solemnity and deep emotion. Many a brave face shows, by the quivering lip and the moistening eye, how the sight of that bereaved woman affects them; for she is the widow of Major Booth, and these fourteen are all that are left alive of the battalion he commanded at Fort Pillow.

In her hand she bears a regimental flag, torn with balls, stained with smoke, and clotted with human blood. Amid a silence that is broken only by the hoarse roar of the river chafing against the banks below, she commences to address them in a voice low and sometimes broken with the heavings of her mighty sorrow, but whose slightest cadence reaches their hearts.

"Boys," she says, "I have just come from a visit to the hospital at Mound City. There I saw your comrades wounded at the bloody struggle at Fort Pillow. There I found this flag — you recognize it. One of your comrades saved it from the insulting touch of traitors at Fort Pillow. I have given to my country all I had to give — my husband. Such a gift! Yet I have freely given him for freedom and my country. Next my husband's cold remains, the dearest object left me in the world is *this flag* — the flag that once waved in proud defiance over the works of Fort Pillow. Soldiers, this flag I give you, knowing that you will ever remember the last words of my noble husband — 'Never surrender the flag to traitors.'"

Colonel Jackson received from her hand the war-worn and blood-stained flag. He called upon the regiment to receive it as such a gift ought to be received. Then he and the whole line fell upon their knees, and solemnly appealing to the God of battles, each one swore to avenge their brave and fallen comrades, and never, "never to surrender the flag to traitors."

The scene was one the memory of which can never pass from before the eyes of those who witnessed it. It was no holiday presentation, no crowning of a May-queen. There stood the widow of their former commander, fresh from the grave of her hero-husband. Above them waved the old flag, enriched by a thousand memories, and now consecrated by the baptism of blood, while beside the spot where they stood rolled the grand continental river, whose waters a few days before had been reddened with the blood of their comrades.

While that river rolls thus grandly to the far-off ocean shall the deed of savage bloodshed that was enacted on its banks be perpetuated in the memory of men, and stamp infamy upon the name of the ruffian chief who thus dishonored our common nature.

MRS MARY MORRIS HUSBAND.

MRS. MARY MORRIS HUSBAND.

THE personal history and character of many, of both sexes, who distinguished themselves during our war, have proved that loyalty and unselfish patriotism are frequently hereditary. Devotion and loyalty to country are as often seen transmitted from sire to son as the height of the figure or the color of the hair. In a great number of instances the heroes and heroines of the war for the Union prove to be the direct descendants of those who distinguished themselves by their zeal, their courage, or their public spirit, in the war of the Revolution.

This remark applies with peculiar force to the person whose name stands at the head of this sketch. One of the many hundreds whom she nursed and blessed during her long career as a hospital matron and nurse, in speaking of the thorough and unostentatious heartiness of her work, said the soldiers could account for such unselfishness only from the fact that she is the granddaughter of Robert Morris, of revolutionary fame.

Many, like Mrs. Husband, have looked upon a noble lineage as only a circumstance that committed them to lives of uncommon labor for the public, and constant self-sacrifice, as proving that the blood of which they are justly proud has not grown ignoble while the republic has been rolling forward in its magnificent career of development.

In the noble group of patriotic nurses who moved about on their blessed errands among the great throng of bleeding heroes on the hills of Gettysburg, the granddaughter of Robert Morris and the granddaughter of President Dwight worked side by side.

Supplies collected by the descendants of General Philip Schuyler and of Benjamin Franklin were forwarded at the same time from different cities. When the little army of Washington had marked its path over the frozen roads to its winter quarters by blood from the naked feet of our revolutionary sires, the grandmother of Mrs. Husband labored untiringly in public for their relief.

Feeling that she was in a manner committed to a life of patriotic self-sacrifice by the example of her ancestors, and prompted by the natural kindness of her heart and the loyalty of her soul, Mrs. Husband was one of the earliest to devote herself to the good of the soldier.

In 1861 she was the librarian and a tri-weekly visitor of the hospital at the corner of Twenty-second and Wood Streets, in Philadelphia. The character and excellence of that work are fully described in the memoir of Mrs. Mary Brady, who at the same time was engaged in a similar work in the great hospital in West Philadelphia.

In the summer of 1862 our national affairs assumed a darker phase than ever before, and the demands of a bleeding and endangered country were brought home as earnestly to the self-sacrificing spirit of women as to the courage and patriotism of men. About the first of July, Dr. Hexon was sent on a hospital transport, from Philadelphia, to bring away a load of the sick from Harrison's Landing, and Mrs. Husband went with him. From this time till the close of the war, and the disbanding of the regiments, in June, 1865, —a period of three years, —Mrs. Husband was constantly in service, and, for a larger portion of the time, laboriously occupied in a great number of different hospitals, working very quietly, not for the praise of men, but for the love of God, and in earnest sympathy with suffering patriotism.

She made three trips to Harrison's Landing, and labored in the manner elsewhere fully described in an account of the hospital transport service. In the latter part of August she took temporary charge of the National Hospital at Baltimore, while the matron, who was sick, was recovering, and saw its wards filled and overflowing with the groaning and mutilated results of the second battle of Bull Run, and the fights of Chantilly and South Mountain. After two or three weeks thus spent in scenes of horror and agony, striving by constant labors to assuage a part of such immense suffering, and to rob the amputation-room of some of its terrors, the matron whose place she was filling resumed her former duties, and Mrs. Husband proceeded at once to Smoketown Hospital, where some of the sufferers from the great field of Antietam were collected. Here she remained two months, and labored, not in any position of command or superiority, but doing the very things that others had left undone, and given over to some utterly unselfish and truly noble character, like Mrs. Husband. The actual sufferers, who were in the wards which she mostly visited, who felt her soothing presence by their bedsides, and heard her voice speaking cheer to the desponding, or reading the words of the Saviour to those who had only his arm beneath them, all human skill having failed them, *they* can give the most appropriate and valuable testimonials as to the character and spirit of her work, and the deep impression it made on those who were so fortunate as to enjoy her attentions. The following is what a Massachusetts soldier says of her: —

"I arrived at the Smoketown General Hospital on the day the army moved into Virginia under McClellan for the last time. The larger part of the hospital was just established, and a great number of the sick of the army were sent there that day and night.

"When I saw Mrs. Husband for the first time, I was impressed by the very capable manner in which she labored. All the patients that could speak were loud in her praises, and those who were too sick to talk looked their gratitude and appreciation. For weeks and months she labored from an early hour in the morning till late at night, going from tent to tent, with always a cheerful word for all, never losing for a moment that perfect evenness of temper, and that admirable knowledge of the wants of the sick, with which only a woman is endowed. It was my good fortune to witness on her part several acts of heroism, one of which I will mention.

"A New York soldier, a mere boy, sick with fever, was discovered also to have diphtheria in its most malignant form. He was at once removed to a tent, put up for the purpose, in a distant part of the grove, away from all others, and a soldier detailed as nurse, who, however, fearing the disease, neglected him. Knowing this, Mrs. Husband took charge of the patient, staying every moment that could be spared from the rest of the sick, for several days and nights, tenderly caring for him like a saint, reading to him from the Testament, and taking his dying message for his mother, that 'she must not mourn for him, for he was willing and ready to die.'

"Hundreds of men, scattered all over the states, will always remember and revere her. In her labors she always sought such places as were farthest from ready help, and where they would be of the most use, never seeming to care for her own comfort, disregarding the requirements of her own health, never leaving her self-imposed duties till sickness and exhaustion drove her home for rest and quiet, and while so resting, preparing supplies to be taken to the army as soon as she was again able to resume her duties."

Another of the Antietam sufferers, who was so fortunate as to be under Mrs. Husband's care, expresses his admiration and gratitude in the lines transcribed below. What star or badge, given by a monarch to a subject, what order of nobility, is so true and rich a testimonial of personal worth as letters like these!

"I was sick with the typhoid fever in the fall of 1862. As soon as I could be moved I was taken to the Antietam Field Hospital, where I met Mrs. Husband. Before I was taken to the hospital I was insane for a week, so that when I arrived there I was so completely exhausted, so near my grave, that I have only an indistinct recollection of much that transpired. I was under her care for six weeks, when I was removed to another hospital. I was confined to my bed nearly all the time I was under her care, so that I had no opportunity of knowing much personally with regard to her, outside of my own tent. As I owe my recovery to her exertions, I am happy to be able to testify to her never-tiring zeal in the care of the sick and wounded soldiers, thousands of whom would, I know, gladly acknowledge the kindness they met while under her care. She always seemed to me to be happy only when engaged in alleviating the sufferings of the soldiers, over whom she watched with all the tenderness and love of a mother, many of whom called her by no other name. Her presence always seemed to bring sunshine even to the most disheartened. Her face always wore a smile so sweet that I forgot my pain when in her presence. She had ever a kind word for every one, and was always pleased to lend a listening ear and a sympathizing heart to the thousand and one little troubles and complaints which the sick man's brain continually conjures up. She seemed to consider the soldiers as her children, and I know not how a mother could watch over her own sons with more tender solicitude. She never appeared to think of herself — her thoughts all centred on the sick or wounded soldier. I have known her, on many a winter's night, when the storms were raging, to go around two or three times to the bedsides of those whose lives seemed hanging by a thread, to watch the progress of the disease, and see that no sleepy nurse had neglected to properly care for them. She has told me many times of sleepless nights she has passed, thinking of some sick one, whom she did not expect would live from hour to hour. She was only too happy to be of service to any one in trouble. When the army was encamped at Brandy Station, in the winter of 1863–'64, she was the matron of a division hospital, and when not engaged in the care of the sick, she used to visit the various guard-houses in the corps (the Third), and interest herself in the cases of those confined there, many of them unjustly, for the soldiers well know there is but little justice in a military court-martial. I visited her frequently, and on one of those occasions I learned the following. She found a soldier sentenced to be shot. Satisfied, from what she could learn concerning his case, that he was innocent of the charges brought against him, she set herself to work to save his life. Failing to make any impression at brigade, division, and corps headquarters, she, nothing daunted, carried her case to army headquarters, where she met only with a repulse, even from the kind-hearted Meade. Not yet discouraged, she resolved to make one more attempt, determined to save that young man's life. She went to Washington, and finally carried her point. This is but one instance of many similar acts; but I cannot recollect the facts of others with sufficient accuracy to mention them."

The winter of 1862–'63 was to our army what the winter at Valley Forge was to Washington's army. It was a time of uncertainty and disaster, of suffering and deep anxiety. Active operations were kept up by Burnside, though with no fortunate results, till January. So much exposure and hard service, and the bloody conflict of Fredericksburg, threw upon the hands of the nurses a large number of sick and wounded. The army lay at Falmouth, on the north side of the Rappahannock. Here Mrs. Husband went, and labored constantly all winter. She took charge, as matron or lady superintendent, of the General Hospital of the Third division in General Sykes's corps.

One very important use of such a person as Mrs. Husband at a field hospital is the moral cheer, the hopefulness and refinement, that her presence inspires. After the patient is able to leave his bed, a long interval occurs before his health is confirmed so as to render him fit for the field. During this time he is naturally low in spirits, unoccupied, and liable to fall a prey to melancholy, and become permanently demoralized. This is particularly the case in an army like ours, where every man thinks for himself, and the mistake or incompetence of a commanding general is understood and commented on over every camp fire, in every hospital, and by every soldier, from the major-general to the drummer boy. The great demand at such a time is for wholesome and suitable *amusement*. Mrs. Husband was unusually apt and skilful in meeting the want.

At all times, and in the whole of her hospital experience, she was attentive to her convalescents, as well as to the very sick, and to those who must die. She fitted up her tent or her office with books and pictures, so as to make it cheerful and home-like. She had facilities for innocent games, writing materials, and amusing books, so that the soldier forgot about himself and the home for which he had so constantly longed. In the enjoyment of the hour he gained strength, and was soon fit to take up his sword or musket.

Spring came at length, and Hooker moved across the river, while everybody connected with hospitals had enough to do in taking care of the eight thousand wounded at Chancellorsville. This labor continued throughout the month of May and for a part of June, and was very arduous. Nearly two thousand of our wounded had been left on the field, in the hands of the enemy, who, having eight or ten thousand himself to care for, neglected ours. When these poor fellows were brought in, under a flag of truce, from the 18th to the 21st of May, the accumulation of misery and suffering was such as was hardly equalled during the whole war. Some died in the ambulances. Others could be seen tearing off the dressing of their wounds, and holding the mutilated stumps over the side of the conveyance, to assuage the burning pain by the contact of fresh air. Mortification and gangrene were common. But medical and sanitary supplies were quite abundant. The organization was excellent, and before many weeks the groves on the hill-sides, above Potomac Creek, began to look cheerful, to resound with the familiar songs of the camp, and the talk of cheerful and hopeful convalescents. Her duties here were principally in the field hospital of the Third division, Third corps, where she labored with the constancy, devotion, and kindness which distinguished her service everywhere. By the middle of June these hospitals were all broken up, and the whole army was in eager pursuit of Lee, who was now in the full tide of his invasion, scouring the fields of Pennsylvania, and threatening the national capital and the border cities. For a few days Mrs. Husband lingered in the hospitals of Alexandria and

Washington, awaiting news from the front, where events were now culminating daily to the grand national tragedy, which, on the first days of July, made Gettysburg one of the great names in American history, one of the great names in the annals of the world.

On the 4th she was on the bloody field, and labored constantly till all the field hospitals were broken up, and the more serious cases were removed to the cities near by, or to the General Hospital, which was established near the town, and which was in operation till in December, when the last ambulance of mutilated men started for Pittsburg. She remained at home for a few weeks after all the worst cases were made comfortable, but returned to the General Hospital in response to numerous and urgent letters from "her boys" who were there, and longed for her kindly presence and cheerful voice.

In the fall of 1863 her attention was aroused by a very painful and alarming instance occurring in the circle of her most intimate associates, to the gross and terrible injustice that may be done by courts martial acting with undue haste, and having their mandates promptly executed.

From that time till the war ended, Mrs. Husband had no equal in the noble corps of volunteer army workers in that peculiar and difficult line of usefulness.

Of fine presence, accustomed from girlhood to the quiet, but polished and impressive manners of the best circles of Philadelphia, and with much practical familiarity with the forms and documents of legal proceeding, she had important advantages in her favor. Case after case came to her knowledge of young men who had been found guilty of desertion and sentenced to be shot, under circumstances that would have made their sentence, if executed, a palpable murder. She undertook these cases, one after another, going to the various brigade, division, corps, and department commanders, and, if unsuccessful here, seeking and gaining an interview with the Secretary of War, and finally, having the ear of that great, patient, kind-hearted president, who was never too tired, never too busy, and never too firmly resolved to be unable to give a full and thoughtful hearing to any woman begging him to spare life.

Once, and only once, she was met with a little coldness on the part of the executive. In her disinterested zeal, she had undertaken several cases at the same time, and having all the proofs and affidavits in file, awaited her turn to speak with Mr. Lincoln. She began by mentioning the first case on her docket. Mr. Lincoln glanced at the package in her hand, and asked if all those papers were suits for pardon. She said they were. He replied that it was too much of a good thing, and denied her a hearing. But, changing her tactics, and approaching him differently, she drew his attention to each case, and in most of them secured the exercise of his clemency.

Whenever she went to the army, one of the first places to which she sought access was the guard-house. The condition of many she found there awaiting sentence, or awaiting trial, was sometimes most pitiful. They had, perhaps, been arrested months before, when the weather was hot, and summer clothing appropriate; now they were shivering on the damp ground, without a fire, and clothed with perhaps a thin cotton shirt, under a ragged and threadbare coat. One poor youth she found thus wretched and shivering, whom she had known in Philadelphia. He was under sentence of death for desertion, and would have been taken out and shot upon his coffin within a few days, unless some one had become interested in his case. She at once sought an interview with the corps commander, and asked him, before that boy was executed, to talk with him for five minutes, and see whether he had any clear knowledge of the duty of a soldier, or what constitutes desertion. The general did so, and in three or four questions to the unfortunate youth found him of such mental capacity that execution would have been a judicial murder, and at once ordered his release.

By acts like this, repeated again and again during the three years of her army life, she did much to relieve the iron severity of martial law, and literally drew upon her head the blessings of many who were ready to perish.

In the month of December, 1863, about the time of Meade's campaign of Mine Run, Mrs. Husband went down to Brandy Station, where the principal hospitals were situated, and there labored, with untiring assiduity, until April, 1864, when, by General Grant's order, all females were removed from the army. Here she saw a great variety of service, some of which was exceedingly laborious, and connected with great hardships.

In her correspondence with the Ladies' Aid Society, from whom she received constant supplies, we find numerous interesting paragraphs.

February 15, 1864, she writes, "It is very difficult for me to write; my tent is most uncomfortable. For two days I could not have a fire in consequence of smoke. This morning early was very pleasant, but I had not more than commenced writing, when a wind springs up, my tent fills with smoke and ashes, and fairly drives me out. Wind increases. I venture back, and find my smoke-pipe down, and smoke unendurable. After vain efforts to keep it in place, I remove the fire, open and air the tent, and again essay to write; but it is a perfect hurricane: tin cups, nutmeg graters, clothing, and papers are driven about, and the tent threatens to follow suit; so I forsake it again, and go to take some tapioca jelly — which I made, fortunately, when my fire would burn — to a sick lieutenant, one of General Carr's staff, who is threatened with diphtheria. I had intended it for two regimental hospitals, but cannot reach them to-day."

Again, on February 18, she writes, "An hour since I was seated comfortably in my tent, writing you a full account of visits I have been paying regimental hospitals, when I heard a cry, and I saw through my tent a bright light. I rushed out to behold the adjoining one in flames. Mine was smoking as the ropes were cut, and it lowered, trunk, bed, &c., removed, and everything scattered. I believe that nothing is lost; but my papers, letters, journal, and memoranda were blowing about."

A few days later she writes, "I have been much interested in G. B., in the Fourteenth New Jersey Hospital. My attention was called to him by the surgeon, who told me he was sinking rapidly from chronic diarrhœa and depression of spirits, in consequence of his arrest for desertion. He was brought from the guard-house to the hospital. I visited there again last Saturday, and the surgeon and chaplain besought me to try for furlough or discharge for him, as nothing but the hope of reaching home could save him. They had been to some of the authorities unsuccessfully, and feared the immediate effect when he should be told that they could give him no hope. I formed my plans; visited him, and cheered him so much that there was a visible improvement next morning, when I walked a mile and a half to tell him all was going on well, and in train. The poor boy's eyes brightened. Said he, 'How can I ever pay you? How can I ever thank you?'"

March 3, she writes, "I will give you an account of to-day's work, and each day is much the same. Rise at six o'clock; make my fire; whilst dressing, boil chocolate, make tea. My toast for the patients is brought me from the kitchen; I butter and soften it; poach eggs for some, and stew potatoes for the rest; arrange on plates, and send to the wards. Make milk punch and egg-nog, a tapioca pudding, corn starch, and blanc-mange; visit each patient, the surgeon, and kitchen; give directions for beef tea, soup, &c.; stew tomatoes on my own stove; mash and prepare potatoes for dinner. Afternoon, go to the station to market; buy oysters, eggs, and butter; stop at head-quarters and see medical director of division about a cow which was promised us, — hope we may get it; returned and amused and entertained a couple of convalescents in my tent for an hour; then buttered toast, soaked crackers, and arranged the plates to suit the cases, with peaches, jelly, and corn starch; visited the wards; found R., our most dangerous case, suffering; heated whiskey, and applied flannels, also a bottle of hot water to his feet; wrote a letter for him to his family, and finish my day's work by writing to you, stopping now and then to stir fruit which I am stewing. Day before yesterday I visited the first division guard-house. Some new ones have been brought in—thirty-two there in all—most of them in want of stockings. I distributed some, and will see them again in a few days. How the poor fellows gathered around me, glad to receive a few words of sympathy!"

March 5. "Poor R. is gone to a better world. He was a Christian, and leaves neither wife nor parent to mourn him."

The heart that prompts such labor as this, day after day, for months, can have no common interest in the suffering soldier, and deserves all the aid she could have in her self-denying work, and all the praise that such large-hearted charity so abundantly merits.

The order of Grant expelling all females from the army lines was issued on the 15th of April, and Mrs. Husband enjoyed a brief visit to her home in Philadelphia.

Two weeks after, Grant advanced across the Rappahannock and the Rapidan, and from the 5th to the 12th of May had hard fighting every day on some part of his line, and most of the time what amounted to a general engagement. His force was large, but it suffered fearful losses. It was during those battles of the Wilderness that John Sedgwick, that soldier, true and brave, met his fate, and somewhere in those gloomy and intricate pine forests, that the noble old hero and patriot General Wadsworth fell, and was buried by stranger hands in an unknown grave.

Mrs. Husband was among the first to offer her services in behalf of the great number of wounded, that made the war-worn old town of Fredericksburg one great hospital. As she went forward to labor there, she met the funeral cortége that was bringing the body of Sedgwick to the rear. Remaining there till about the first of June, she went around to the Peninsula, where her army labors began two years before, and, touching at Port Royal, went on, and was actively engaged in the great hospitals established at White House and City Point.

At White House she had charge of the low diet for the whole of the Sixth corps, which had suffered very heavily in the battle of Cold Harbor. At City Point she was for some time in charge of the diet of the Second division of Hancock's corps, and made a visit to the front, to the Third Corps Hospital, where the boys, who had so many of them been under her care when sick, gave her a hearty welcome. At City Point she eventually resumed her old and favorite line of usefulness, and took wards to visit. At times, between three and four hundred patients lay, for hour after hour, on their narrow cots, awaiting, as the one bright event of each weary day, her arrival at their bedside, in her regular and blessed round of mercy. She modified her dress so as to move without inconvenience up the narrow alleys that divided the rows of cots, and made herself a great apron, with a row of deep pockets, which were several times each day filled as she made her round. Almost every patient received some little thing or other from those deep and roomy receptacles. For one she had an apple, for another a newspaper, for another a pair of stockings. At this cot she left a Testament, at the next a handkerchief, and smiles, pleasant words, and hopefulness everywhere.

One of the soldiers, who lay very sick, and felt his hopes rise whenever she approached his cot in her daily rounds, thus describes her service, and the effect of her visits: —

"I can never forget her kindness to me. Her untiring devotion to the sick and wounded soldier won the hearts of all. She was indeed a mother to us. Night and day she was always at her post, ever ready to relieve the sufferings of our brave boys.

"I have no doubt she saved the lives of many by her skill in dressing wounds, and her unceasing attention. No wife or mother could have been more devoted. The daily visit of that good woman to our tent was the one pleasant feature of my hospital life. She was always cheerful, and had a kind word for us all. Few women sacrificed so much for the good cause as Mrs. Husband did in leaving her family and home, and undergoing all the hardships of a camp life."

This life in the hospitals was continued till May, 1865, when, Richmond having been evacuated, and Lee captured, the hospitals grew thin, and began to be dismantled, and the heroines as well as the heroes of the war could receive honorable discharges.

In the early part of May, as the army came through Richmond, on its way to Washington and home, Mrs. Husband went up from City Point with a quantity of supplies which had been sent to hospitals, but which fortunately were no longer needed there. Stopping at Manchester, on the opposite side of the river from Richmond, she had the pleasure of distributing, with her own hands, the bounties which a generous people had sent her, to the foot-sore, weary, and voracious boys of Hancock's corps.

On the 6th, in Richmond, she had the supreme satisfaction of seeing almost the whole army, with whom she had labored so constantly from its organization, march in triumph through the rebel capital.

Nor was she an obscure witness of the grand pageant. The soldiers of the Second, Third, and Sixth army corps were almost as familiar with her face and figure as they were with Hancock or Sickles, or Meade himself. As the regiments passed the window where she stood, the boys would pass the word down the line, "There's Mother Husband!" And cheer after cheer, and shout after shout, ascended from the ranks of stalwart and brawny fellows, beside whose hospital cots her form had so often stood. It was an ovation in which she might justly feel a genuine and honest pride.

That popularity was not the reflection of another's fame. It was an outburst of unfeigned gratitude and real admiration, which so many of them had long felt for a noble and accomplished woman, whose patriotism and humanity alone had impelled her, for year after year, to follow up the march of our armies, on her ministry of love; to devote herself to the welfare of suffering patriots with as much tenderness as though they had been in fact all her boys; to know nothing of home and its sacred comforts as long as one lonely or desponding soldier was languishing in a hospital ward.

Touched with this involuntary tribute, and full of generous admiration for those who had suffered so much and accomplished so much, she was determined that they should not disperse and be disbanded without having had, in health and in victory, some taste of luxuries which had been long richly deserved. Going home to Philadelphia, she sent word to her friends, — those same friends who had kept a cornucopia of comforts for soldiers at her side all through the war, — and she soon had abundant supplies of all kinds prepared. Mrs. Husband took them to Washington, and found her soldier boys at Bailey's Cross-Roads. Six successive days she took an ambulance, loaded with bounties and comforts of every sort, over to the encampment, and gave them out to the returning heroes. These closing acts of rejoicing, and of generous appreciation, consumed the greater part of the month of May, and were the last that she could do for soldiers in the field.

The warm personal relations that grew up between the soldiers and their benefactress, and the frequency with which her acts and virtues were mentioned over the camp fires of the army of the Potomac, have caused her to be extensively known and honored as the soldier's friend. Her cabinet abounds in trophies, rings, bullets, shells, guns, swords, pistols, mementos, pictures, photographs, and keepsakes, presented by her grateful army patients; and now, if any of the boys in blue fall sick, or in any way become helpless or distressed in the city of her home, she is at once thought of and referred to. No case of real merit and genuine distress ever comes to her in vain. Judicious, as well as generous, her friends rely upon her opinion, and when she says, "Give," a hundred purses are opened.

But, above all, she has the supreme and all-sufficient approval of her own spirit; the rich memories of those years crowded with great events in which she took a part; great battles which she witnessed, and great crowds of suffering men to whom she brought relief and comfort, when she was the almoner of the generous gifts of the large circle of home workers, who ever followed her with their prayers and their sympathies; when she constantly delighted in relieving the wants of her fellow-creatures, and cultivated that divine pleasure by the most liberal and unpretending methods, and daily thanked her Creator for being permitted to do good.

MRS. E. E. GEORGE.

WHILE there were none of the loyal states that did not furnish nurses and heroines who displayed an enthusiasm as genuine as any of the volunteers, and a devotion as deep as any who fell in battle, some were conspicuous, and deserve honorable mention in history, for the thoroughness and energy with which all their sanitary enterprises were conducted.

In the East, Maine seems to have done more for her soldiers than any other state. There was in Portland a regular and well-conducted organization of army nurses, to which those ladies made application who desired to make themselves useful in the hospitals. In the West, Indiana seems to have been the most active, the most systematic and profuse, in her labors for the comfort and health of the volunteers. The Military Agency at Indianapolis, among its various duties, assumed the general direction of the volunteer lady nurses who went out from that state. By an active correspondence with various medical directors, and with the general agents of the Sanitary and Christian Commissions, the Agency was constantly informed in regard to the positions of great destitution, where the largest number of suffering soldiers were assembled, where the wounded of a bloody battle were principally concentrated, and at what point a particular nurse or corps of Christian women could be of the most effective service. During the last three years of the war this Military Agency sent out from Indianapolis two hundred and fifty ladies as nurses. They were in all parts of the field, and ministered to the sufferers in every great battle from Fort Donelson to the Five Forks. They were at Memphis, at Helena, at Young's Point, at Vicksburg, and at New Orleans. They went with Rosecrans through Tennessee, and with Sherman through Georgia. They dressed wounds that were received in the charge over the rugged heights of Lookout Mountain, they nursed patients that were languishing with malarious fever caught in the Yazoo Swamp, they bound bleeding limbs at Gettysburg, and after all the battles of the war were fought, they received the skeleton wrecks of the armies that came out alive from Salisbury and Andersonville, and endeavored to restore life and cheerfulness to eyes that had so long been familiar with famine and death in their most hideous aspects.

Some account of one of the most earnest and laborious of these Sisters of Charity, one who engaged in the service from the purest motives, and sealed her loyal zeal by death at the post of duty, may serve as a type of the heroism and sacrifices of all.

Some time in January, 1863, Mr. Hannaman, the general military agent for the State of Indiana, received a note from correspondents at Fort Wayne, recommending Mrs. E. E. George, of their city, as a lady well qualified to serve as hospital nurse. A few days after, Mrs. George addressed him in person, and tendered her services. He could not at that moment assign her to a field of labor, and she went to Chicago, hoping to find her services required by the Sanitary Commission. While there, Mr. Hannaman received advices from Memphis, stating that a great demand had suddenly arisen there for attentions to the wounded at the first assault on the northern defences of Vicksburg. They had been brought to Memphis on hospital transports, and a large number of nurses could find immediate employment among them. He telegraphed at once to Mrs. George, and she presented herself at the sanitary rooms. Her age seemed against her, for she had reached that period of life which suggests the quiet of the fireside and the comforts of home, rather than a rude, changeful, and wearing succession of exhausting toils and midnight vigils. This objection was suggested to her. "True," she replied, "I am old; but my health is good, and I am very desirous to do something for those who are every day exposing their lives for our country. If unable to go through as much as some, I will engage never to be at all troublesome or in the way." The mainspring of her zeal was as much Christian devotion as patriotic sacrifice. To do good was the law of her life. To assuage suffering was her greatest pleasure.

With other ladies she arrived in Memphis early in the spring of 1863, and commenced her work. The physicians, who know how much depends upon nursing, and how useless are all drugs without skill and judgment at the bedside, soon saw the value of Mrs. George, and she had full permission to visit every ward of all the hospitals in Memphis. Governor Morton, of Indiana, also sent her a special commission to inquire for and dispense to all the sick and wounded of the Indiana regiments. With these credentials her means of sanitary usefulness were greatly increased. Her excellent practical sense, and the Christian meekness of her character, made her a suitable person to be invested with unusual authority, while her age and the elevation of her motives won involuntary respect and admiration from all with whom she was connected. During the spring and summer of 1863 her labors in the Memphis hospitals were unceasing. Early in the fall of that year she gave herself a short respite, visiting her friends in Fort Wayne, and in October she returned to Memphis, soon after proceeding to Corinth. She made frequent trips between those places, with various hospital supplies and sanitary comforts for the men; and although the cars were often fired into by guerrillas and squads of Confederate cavalry, she acted as though fear of death, while in the line of duty, was a passion that had no place in her calm and well-regulated mind.

When General Sherman's army left Corinth, and moved up the Tennessee to reënforce Grant at Chattanooga, Mrs. George returned to Memphis, and went around to Nashville. Thence she went southward to Pulaski, where she assisted in opening a hospital. There was no mode of reaching this place by railroad, as the cars were not running south of Columbia. The intervening distance of forty miles she travelled in a rough army wagon. At Pulaski she remained several months, and during the time made several trips to Indiana, where she collected hospital supplies, and took them forward to Pulaski. The stores intrusted to her hands were always carefully guarded, and distributed with fidelity and discretion. When the spring campaign of 1864 opened by the advance of Sherman from Chattanooga into the heart of Georgia, Mrs. George, with several other ladies, accompanied the army. She and they shared in the dangers, the hardships, and the glory of that ever-memorable campaign. There were few, if any, general hospitals south of Chattanooga, and at Kingston, Resaca, Kenesaw Mountain, and the other battles of that summer, she labored in the field — sometimes at the front, often all night as well as all day, after the battles, binding up wounds, and giving water to cool inflammations and allay thirst. Labors of this sort were sometimes continued till the powers of endurance were quite exhausted, and she wrapped an army blanket around her, and fell asleep under a tree or a wagon, to be awakened in a few hours by the moans of the wounded, and to resume her labors till nature was again overcome. Upon the investment of Atlanta, Mrs. George became connected with the Fifteenth Army Corps Hospital. When this corps marched to Jonesboro she had an ambulance assigned her, and, at the earnest request of the men, went with them. During the battle of Jonesboro, she was dressing the wounded in a tent so near the front as to be in range of the enemy's guns. A shell from one of their batteries pierced the tent, and, exploding within a few feet of where she was standing, killed two wounded men. When asked if the circumstance did not somewhat alarm her, she replied, "No, I was not alarmed, for I looked upon it as simply the intention of Providence to test my courage."

In the fall of 1864, when General Sherman's army returned from Jonesboro to Atlanta, Mrs. George went home for a brief period of rest. Returning shortly after to Nashville, she found that Sherman's army had taken up their march directly for Savannah, and as all communications with his rear were impossible, she was unable to rejoin the Fifteenth corps. The winter of 1864 and 1865 was therefore passed at Nashville. During the siege of that city by Hood, and the subsequent battle, by which the enemy was driven across the Tennessee River, Mrs. George and two other ladies opened a hospital, and were very useful and unwearied in their attentions to the wounded. As soon as she ascertained that Sherman's army had reached Savannah, she reported to the state agent of Indiana at Indianapolis, and prepared to rejoin the corps to which she had attached herself. While passing a few days at Fort Wayne, she learned that some of the agents of the Indiana Sanitary Commission were about to leave New York for Savannah, and went immediately to that city, with a view of joining them. By some oversight, transportation and a pass were not provided, and the agents sailed without her. She was then compelled to go to Washington, to procure the necessary pass; and while waiting for her papers to be made out at the war department, she called on Miss Dix, who urged her to go to Wilmington, North Carolina, which had just passed into possession of the Union force, and where there was a large amount of suffering. Fearing that with Miss Dix her character as a representative of Indiana would be lost, she hesitated, and would not go except upon the condition that she should devote herself especially to such Indiana volunteers as she might find at Wilmington. Miss Dix assented. Hardly had the noble woman arrived at Wilmington before there reached that point eleven thousand Union prisoners, who had just been released from the stockade at Salisbury. Their condition was in the last degree pitiable and wretched. Two thousand of them had not a whole garment upon their bodies; two hundred had lost their feet by frost. To these sufferers, and with very inadequate hospital supplies, Mrs. George devoted herself, day and night, in labors to relieve, as far as possible, the most acute and pressing of their wants.

Here it was that this excellent lady finished her toils, and crowned her long and active career of beneficence by deliberate self-martyrdom. She literally worked herself to death. By day she was constantly occupied in superintending the manufacture of clothing for the naked; at night she went into the hospitals, and, depriving herself of sleep, passed many of the hours of darkness in nursing the greatest sufferers. Exertions such as these could not, from the nature of things, last long. For more than two years, she had taken only brief periods of rest: she was advanced in years, and the peculiar form of typhoid fever which attacked the released prisoners for whom she so heroically labored, was in a high degree contagious. Suddenly her system gave way, and she was pronounced severely ill with typhoid fever. As soon as this was known to the Indiana Sanitary Commission, who had always regarded her as one of the most faithful and efficient of their representatives in the field, they sent Dr. William H. Wishard to her relief. When he arrived she appeared considerably better, and expressed herself as though she might be permitted to reach home, and see the faces of her daughters once more. All the preparations were made for her removal. As she felt a little faint, Dr. Wishard ordered a stimulating drink, and went out into the city, to attend to some final business before starting. Upon his return, what was his astonishment to find his patient a corpse! The grasp of the disease had been deeper than he supposed, and after the fatigue and excitement of preparing to return home, she sank into a relapse which nothing could arrest, and passed directly from the scene of her last and greatest labors to the immediate fruition of her abundant and heavenly reward.

ANNA MARIA ROSS.

NO war was ever so sustained by the persistent devotion and zeal of the home population as was the great civil contest from which we have just emerged. Aside from the regular and enormous expenditures of government, nearly eighty millions of money were raised and expended by the loyal citizens in providing for the soldier, and the widows and orphans of those who perished in the strife. The great cities near the border vied with each other in the effort to do most for the columns of war-worn soldiers, who, from time to' time, filed through their streets, or were hurried forward to the field. Philadelphia, situated as it is in the direct line of travel, — a point through which nearly every man who at any time belonged to the army of the Potomac must pass, — was noted throughout the war for the devotion of its citizens, and especially of its ladies, to the comfort and welfare of the soldier.

Several of its wives and mothers gave up the comfort of happy homes, and, while the war raged, applied themselves, with a constancy and a spirit of self-sacrifice that were never surpassed, for the relief of those who were suffering in the camp or languishing in the hospital. Among the home laborers, no daughter of that City of Brotherly Love was more abundant in her works, or more earnest and untiring in her zeal, than she whose name is written above.

The Cooper's Shop Saloon, inaugurated mainly by her exertions, and in a large measure sustained by her untiring labors, became at once her grave and her monument. The devotedness and the love she there manifested were witnessed and will be remembered by thousands who will never know the benefactress to whom they were indebted till they meet her on the shining shore. And she passed directly from these toils and anxieties, when the hoarse voices of the war were loudest and most threatening, to the crown of the just, to the kingdom of perpetual rest.

The blessed destiny of this saintly woman can be spoken of with great certainty, for the life of beneficence in the midst of which her days were cut short did not begin with the demands of our civil war. By fifty years of active usefulness, by the example and the blood of noble ancestors, some of whom had moulded bullets for the army of Washington, and fought under the eye of that great chieftain, her character had been confirmed in excellence long before the sullen roar from Charleston harbor went jarring across the continent.

In a city famous for its public and its private charities, in a community originally made up of philanthropists, she had long been most favorably and widely known for the rare kindness of her heart, the activity of her sympathies, and her Christ-like consecration to good works.

When the war assumed its colossal proportions, and brought its demands to the door of every cottage in the land, the good ladies of Philadelphia, under the lead and inspiring example of Miss Ross, determined to do all in their power for the soldiers who were temporarily brought within their reach. By their exertions the Cooper's Shop Saloon was opened and sustained — a plain but spacious building, where every soldier that passed through the city was welcome, where he would find prepared for him an abundance of wholesome food, and where, if sick or exhausted, he could remain and receive medical advice, nursing, and necessary articles of clothing, all the free gift of the citizens of Philadelphia. As early as November, 1861, there is recorded a vote of thanks from the Cooper Shop committee to Miss Ross and her lady friends for the able and effective manner in which they had fitted up the new hospital attached to the eating saloon, and for their indefatigable exertions in providing all the necessary comforts for sick and wounded soldiers.

From that time, for two years, when the curtain of death fell upon her career of philanthropic devotion, she shrank from no toil, avoided no exposure, withheld neither time, nor money, nor life itself, from the cause in which she had enlisted. Yet the work grew upon her hands, and its demands increased, rather than diminished, as the war deepened. As McClellan's campaign progressed to its disastrous close; as Pope fell back to Washington, and the Union force again advanced, and met the flushed enemy on the hills of Antietam; as Fredericksburg, and Chancellorsville, and Gettysburg followed, with their great host of wounded, — the hospital of the Cooper's Shop Saloon was kept constantly full of soldiers, who had come, on their way home, or to general hospitals in the North, and were obliged to remain, sometimes to gather strength for the remainder of their journey, sometimes on one of these well-kept hospital cots to receive final discharge from all earthly service.

In this hospital, with its various demands, Miss Ross worked from the hour of its establishment, till those hands that labored so faithfully, and were willing to do so much more, were stiffened by the frosts of death.

In the summer and fall of 1863 these labors were uncommonly severe and earnest. It was as though her self-forgetting heart had received some premonition of the change that awaited her; as though some voice in her dreams had uttered those words of solemn incitement, "What thou doest do quickly." The sick and wounded in the hospital demanded her care. Tenderly and wakefully, while others sleep, she passes from couch to couch, soothing the feverish fancy, moistening the fever-cracked lips, giving medicine here and cordial there. At the same time, a great fair is in progress, and the substantial and permanent interests of the hospital and the soldier can be secured as effectually by labor there as among the sufferers. And thus she takes upon herself double duty, and burns the candle at each end. She canvasses through the city, pleading the soldiers' cause from street to street, and from door to door. Then her exertions take a wider range, and she travels through many of the cities and towns of Pennsylvania on the same noble errand. Restless and anxious, regardless of fatigue and nervous exhaustion, forgetting herself, and imbued with the one high aim of accomplishing a great and a noble work for the soldier, she makes deep inroads on the fund of her own life, and almost literally "coins her very blood," that the pecuniary returns of the fair may be abundant.

Private sorrows, at the same time, make their demands upon the large sympathies of her heart. She watches the dying hours of an aged and saintly clergyman, and after his death remains to condole with the bereaved family. The fair, in the mean time, is held, and the returns are large, equal to her fondest hopes; and the "Soldier's Home," the object to which these labors had been aimed, is accomplished.

But her disposition was that which the old historian applies to the nation of the Greeks—she thought nothing accomplished so long as anything remained undone. The pleasing task of furnishing and fitting up the Home is now hers, and abundant funds are at her disposal. In making these purchases, and effecting the necessary arrangements, she continued her labors one night till past twelve o'clock, retiring cold and benumbed, and thoroughly exhausted by a succession of great exertions. She thought rest would restore her; but in the morning the numbness is colder and more alarming. Medical skill is summoned, and the practised eye and hand soon pronounce the case hopeless. . . . In the month of December, 1863, on the very day that her pure spirit was released from its toil-worn frame, the Home, for which she had lived, and for which she had also died, was dedicated, and entered upon its mission of blessing, and restoration, and cheer to the soldier.

The memory of one who was so truly noble, alike in her life and in her death, was justly honored. The funeral train was immense; the eulogies were eloquent; yet none could say too much of such a life and such a work. Resolutions were passed by the committees of the Saloon and the Home, that had been the principal theatre of her sacrifices and benevolence.

The incitement of so rich an example was not lost. Others arose and labored in the same cause, with a devotion only less entire than that which had cost her life. The Saloon and the Home continued to flourish and bless thousands upon thousands of weary and war-sick men, for months and years after her hands were mouldering in the long rest of the grave.

As truly as the hero who fell, pierced with his death shot just as his regimental flag was carried by the storming column over the battlements of the routed foe, so she, as true a heroine as any, fell at her post, in the heat and depth of the conflict, just before the blessed dawnlight and the joyful shouts of victory.

Eng^d by G. E. Perine & Co. N. Y.

MRS. A. H. HOGE.

MRS. A. H. HOGE.

AS among the men who enlisted in the war there was every grade of natural ability, so with the women, who in their way enlisted also as hospital nurses and sanitary laborers, every rank in life, and all stations in society, sent their representatives into the field.

There were many rude and uncultivated, yet kind-hearted and pure-minded camp followers, like Bridget Divers, who took naturally to the rough life of the soldier, and followed the men in camp and on the march, with a saddle or an ambulance cushion for a pillow, and no covering from the dews of heaven but a brown army blanket.

Others became hospital nurses, and, for month after month, and year following year, could be found bending over the same cots, though their occupants constantly changed, wiping clammy foreheads, soothing feverish fancies, moistening parched lips, writing messages of love and hope to distant homes, singing hymns of Christian cheer, and closing the lids over glazing eyes.

Others, again, there were, — and that number is not large, — who brought to the altar of their country rare gifts, splendid social powers, the fascination of a noble or a winning presence, and all the qualities that combine to make a woman widely known, profoundly respected, and deeply loved.

Of the great number of persons who saw Mrs. Hoge, of Chicago, and heard her pleading the cause of the suffering volunteer, before so many gatherings of her own sex, who met her in her long and frequent journeyings, the soldiers who saw her in hospital wards, or in the trenches before Vicksburg, and especially those who saw those generous, unwearied, multiform, and most successful labors at the great Sanitary Fair of Chicago, there are none who would not assign her a high position among the queens of American society. And those of her own sex, who saw her moving thus brilliantly in that noble career of public usefulness, would be the first to apply to her that culminating eulogy of Solomon, "Many daughters have done virtuously, but thou excellest them all."

The native city of Mrs. Hoge is Philadelphia. Whether anything is due to the spirit of William Penn, and the mild flavor of peace on earth and good will to men which has ever breathed from the religion of the Quakers, need not here be discussed. Certain it is that many of those of the gentler sex who, in our great war, have distinguished themselves by the consecration of the finest social genius to the most extensive philanthropic labors, came from the City of Brotherly Love.

After her marriage, Mrs. Hoge, whose family name was Blackie, removed with her husband to Pittsburg, and not long after, in 1848, to Chicago, a city which then hardly numbered twenty-five thousand inhabitants. Living thus in the most vigorous and enterprising community on the continent, in a city that doubles its population once in four years, and seeing the vast regions of the north-west, for which Chicago is the commercial emporium, expanding with imperial strides under the system of free labor, and beneath the common flag and the matchless constitution, it was not strange that she became, in a manner, inspired by the irresistible flood of enthusiasm which swept over that community, when it became an assured fact that eleven great states had inaugurated a civil war, in violation of the constitution, in derision of the flag, and to make human bondage perpetual in the nation. Her first act was freely and promptly to give up her sons to the service. One of these boys began in the ranks, and commanded a company when the war closed. The other rose from captain to the rank of brevet brigadier-general.

While the conviction was general that the war would not be protracted, Mrs. Hoge remained in Chicago, and occupied herself in the usual and happy routine of home duties, and in sewing for the soldiers. But in the winter and spring of 1862, it became apparent to most thinking persons that the American States were committed to a long and deadly struggle, whose duration and whose stages no mortal could anticipate, and whose issue could be known no further than that the right must eventually prevail.

At this period of the conflict, Mrs. Hoge assumed, as it were, a new character, and commenced a life wholly in contrast with the domestic seclusion in which her days had hitherto passed. In company with her friend and co-laborer, Mrs. Livermore, she entered upon a series of patriotic and philanthropic labors, on a plan commensurate with the vastness of the scale on which the war began to be conducted, and with an earnestness and zeal not unworthy the priceless interests which it involved.

Their operations were in connection with the Chicago branch of the United States Sanitary Commission. They had worked with this organization from its inception in that city, and now, in January, 1862, these two ladies took upon themselves the herculean enterprise of keeping the shelves and the treasury of the Commission filled, notwithstanding the constant and enormous demands made upon it by over two hundred thousand soldiers in active service.

Without asserting that the liberality of the people might not have been developed through other agencies, the brilliant success of these admirable women appears in the fact, that with their labors the funds increased from eighteen thousand dollars to more than two hundred and fifty thousand dollars, and the boxes of sanitary and hospital supplies from five thousand to fifty thousand, during the two years and a half that war raged west of the Alleghanies.

Their plan was to go from city to city, and from town to town, throughout the North-west, and assemble the ladies of each community. Mrs. Hoge often read them a narrative of the experience she had enjoyed among the soldiers, and aided in the formation of a Soldier's Aid Society. In many, and, towards the close of the war, in all the places they visited, some organization of the kind was in existence. Here their object was to stimulate to fresh industry and incite to larger generosity.

These travels and organizing labors in the loyal towns

and cities were interrupted by a number of visits made by Mrs. Hoge to the front, where she remained many days, and sometimes weeks, at a time, dispensing, with her own hands, the supplies that she had collected from the home communities. So numerous were these trips, and so incessant were her hospital labors when at the front, that during the war she stood at the bedside of more than a hundred thousand sick or wounded patriot soldiers.

To Mrs. Hoge also belongs the honor of originating, and carrying through to a brilliant success, the first great Sanitary Fair at Chicago. In the spring of the cardinal year of the war, the year that saw the Mississippi running free within Union lines from Lake Itasca to the sea, Mrs. Hoge, and those associated with her in Chicago, commenced their operations on a larger plan than anything before attempted in the country. A few hundreds, or three or four thousands, of dollars had been the utmost that had been realized by any previous enterprise for the soldier. It was now proposed to inaugurate a scheme of charity on a national scale, aiming at large financial results. By it Mrs. Hoge proposed to add at least twenty-five thousand dollars to the treasury of the Sanitary Commission.

Her travels and lectures had made her the most widely known of any lady in Chicago among all those communities that look to that city as their emporium. Circulars were issued, and vice-presidents appointed in a great number of towns, extending westward across Wisconsin to the city of Iowa, and northward to St. Paul, and the vigorous and deeply loyal communities of the Upper Mississippi Valley.

There were not wanting those who pronounced the plan chimerical, and predicted its failure; but the result showed how much more correctly Mrs. Hoge and her associates had estimated the strength of the general sympathy with the suffering soldier. The sum originally proposed sinks almost into insignificance when compared with the splendid result, and is well nigh lost when contrasted with the millions that were afterwards poured into the same treasury from those similar enterprises that took their rise and found their model in the Chicago Fair.*

It had proposed twenty-five thousand dollars. It realized eighty thousand. From other fairs, held in other cities, after the plan of this at Chicago, not less than ten million dollars were contributed towards the sanitary well-being of the Union armies.

After this noble enterprise had been carried to success so triumphant, Mrs. Hoge resumed her visits to the hospitals. She also visited various other cities as an experienced adviser in all matters connected with sanitary labor. Several times, in eastern cities, she recounted her experience among the soldiers, with the happiest effects in the communities where the influence of her example and of her eloquence were alike made to bear upon the cause.

In the spring of 1865, just before the war was ended, she read an address at a meeting of ladies held at Packer Institute, in Brooklyn, which was greatly admired, and immediately published by the Sanitary Commission, as one

* For a sketch of the fair, and an account of its plan, management, and success, see North American Review, January, 1864; also the History of the Philadelphia Sanitary Fair.

of its regular documents. As a narrative of sanitary labor and experience in hospitals and at the front, nothing could be more interesting or satisfactory. It is a graphic and touching compendium of the field labors of Mrs. Hoge, from the commencement of active hostilities in the West, till the surrender of Vicksburg. After this time she was chiefly absorbed in home labors, in connection with the Chicago and other great sanitary fairs.

"The first great hospital I visited," said Mrs. Hoge to the Brooklyn ladies, "was Mound City, twelve miles from Cairo. It contained twelve hundred beds, furnished with dainty sheets and pillows, and shirts from the Sanitary Commission, and ornamented with boughs of fresh apple blossoms, placed there by tender female nurses, to refresh the languid frames of their mangled inmates. As I took my slow and solemn walk through this congregation of suffering humanity, I was arrested by the bright blue eyes, and pale, but dimpled cheeks, of a boy of nineteen summers. I perceived he was bandaged like a mummy, and could not move a limb; yet still he smiled. The nurse who accompanied me said, 'We call this boy our miracle. Five weeks ago, he was shot down at Donelson; both legs and arms where shattered. To-day, with great care, he has been turned for the first time; and never a murmur has escaped his lips, but grateful words and pleasant looks have cheered us.' Said I to the smiling boy, — some absent mother's pride, — 'How long did you lie on the field after being shot?' 'From Saturday morning till Sunday evening,' he replied; 'and then I was chopped out, for I had frozen feet.' 'How did it happen that you were left so long?' 'Why, you see,' said he, 'they couldn't stop to bother with us, *because they had to take the fort.*' 'But,' said I, 'did you not feel 'twas cruel to leave you to suffer so long?' 'Of course not! How could they help it? *They had to take the fort;* and when they did, we forgot our sufferings, and all over the battle-field went up cheers from the wounded, even from the dying. Men that had but one arm raised that, and voices so weak, that they sounded like children's, helped to swell the sound.' 'Did you suffer much?' His brow contracted as he said, 'I don't like to think of that; but never mind; the doctor tells me I won't lose an arm or a leg, and I'm going back to have another chance at them. There's one thing I can't forget, though,' said he, as his sunny brow grew dark; 'Jem and I — nodding at the boy in the adjoining cot — lived on our fathers' neighboring farms in Illinois; we stood beside each other, and fell together. As he knows, we saw fearful sights that day. We saw poor, wounded boys stripped of their clothing. They cut ours off, when every movement was torture. When some resisted, they were pinned to the earth with bayonets, and left writhing like worms, to die by inches. I can't forgive the devils for that.' 'I fear you've got more than you bargained for.' 'Not a bit of it; we went in for better or worse, and if we got worse, we must not complain.' Thus talked the beardless boy, nine months only from his mother's wing. As I spoke, a moan — a rare sound in a hospital — fell on my ear. I turned, and saw a French boy, quivering with agony, and crying for help. Alas! he had been wounded, driven several miles in an ambulance with his feet projecting, had them frightfully frozen, and the surgeon had just decided that the discolored, useless members must be amputated, and the poor boy was begging for the operation. Beside him lay a stalwart man, with a fine face, the fresh blood staining his bandages, his dark, damp hair clustering round his marble forehead. He extended his hand feebly, and essayed to speak, as I bent over him, but speech had failed him. He was just brought in from a gunboat, where he had been struck by a piece of shell, and was slipping silently, but surely, into eternity.

"Two days afterwards I visited Jefferson Barracks Hospital. In passing through the wards, I noticed a woman seated beside the cot of a youth apparently dying. He was insensible to all around; she seemed no less so. Her face was bronzed, and deeply lined with care and suffering. Her eyes were bent on the ground, her arms folded, her features rigid as marble. I stood beside her, but she did not notice me. I laid my hand upon her shoulder, but she heeded me not. I said, 'Is this young man a relative of yours?' No answer came. 'Can't I help you?' With a sudden impulse, that electrified me, her dry eyes almost starting from the sockets, and her voice husky with agony, she said, pointing her attenuated finger at the senseless boy, 'He is the last of seven sons: six have died in the army, and the doctor says he must die to-night.' The flash of life passed from her face as suddenly as it came; her arms folded over her breast; she sank in her chair, and became, as before, the rigid impersonation of agony.

"As I passed through another hospital ward, I noticed a man whose dejected figure said plainly, 'he had turned his face to the wall to die.' His limb had been amputated, and he had just been told his doom. Human nature rebelled. He cried out, 'I am willing to die, if I could but see my wife and children once more.' In the silence that followed this burst of agony, the low voice of a noble woman, who gave her time and abundant means to the sick and wounded soldiers, was heard in prayer for him. The divine influence overcame his struggling heart, and as she concluded, he said, 'Thy will, O God, be done! 'Tis a privilege, even thus, to die for one's country.' Before the midnight hour he was at rest. The vacant bed told the story on the next morning.

"At one time I spent six weeks with the army on the move, having in charge a large amount of hospital stores, and having the privilege of personally dispensing them to those who so greatly needed them. As the steamer on which we had our headquarters was tied up for the night, I was sent for by the colonel of a Wisconsin regiment, in great haste, to see a young man who was very ill on board the steamer Express. As we entered the boat we were met by the colonel, who said, 'Ladies, I am in great distress; I have in my regiment a young man who had graduated, studied law, and was about to enter into partnership with his father, when my regiment was forming. He was an *only child*, and a young man of rare promise. He enlisted in my regiment. The day we left Wisconsin his father and mother were with us. The mother, forgetting all but her only child, threw her arms around me, and said, 'O, colonel, for God's sake, guard my treasure, for it is my all; and now I'm afraid he's going to die.' We threaded our way through the long cabin, on which lay rows of sick soldiers, with no pillow but a hard knapsack, no bed but the bare floor, and no clothing but that in which they had marched and picketed for many weary weeks. The young man referred to had been placed in a state-room. As we entered, he drew the soiled blanket over his once neat collar and neck-tie, that had not been removed, and said, 'Ladies, don't come in; I'm too filthy to be seen.' As he lay there, I thought I had seldom seen a finer face; a broad forehead, clearly-cut features, and dark, expressive eyes, betokened intellect and refinement. We talked with him cheerfully, told him the colonel had granted him a furlough, to be removed to our boat, to be carefully nursed till we could place him in his mother's care. He looked so bright, and spoke so cheerfully, that we cherished hopes of his early recovery. We promised to send a stretcher for him early in the morning, and after making all arrangements for his comfort, and giving him a cup of tea, we left him. After leaving the room, I thought, What if he should die? Who will receive his last words, or know his last thoughts? I turned back, and said, 'We shall send for you in the morning, if we live; but life is *so* uncertain, especially in the army on the move! Suppose we never meet on earth again, — what would you say?' Looking serenely up, he said, 'I understand you. Should I die, tell my mother, as I have lain here these weary days, all her early teachings have come back, and I trust have done their work. My Sabbath school lessons, that she struggled to teach me, are now remembered and prized. Tell her I hope to meet her in that heaven where she is sure to go; and tell her I never regretted the step I have taken. She must not mourn for me as without hope, for if I die 'twill be in a glorious cause, and our separation will be short.' I said, 'Thank God! I hope you may be spared long to comfort your parents and serve your country and your Maker.' He thanked me earnestly for returning, and, as I was told, talked cheerfully for an hour about going home. The next morning we sent a stretcher, but the answer came back, that William had gone home, not to his mother, but to his Father's arms. Three weeks later, on my route to Vicksburg, I met a friend of the family in search of William's body. He said the parents were longing for the precious casket of their jewel to lay it to rest, under the old willow tree at the homestead. They had well nigh sunk under the crushing blow, but were upheld by his parting words of love, and faith, and heroism, which I had transmitted to them.

"After the first repulse of our army from Vicksburg, sad stories of sickness and suffering reached the ears of the Sanitary Commission. I was intrusted by the Commission with a choice supply of stores, and, accompanied by two gentlemen, started for Vicksburg. The river was high, the weather miserably rainy and depressing; guerrillas constantly threatening our boat — everything portentous and gloomy. After a painful but rapid journey, we reached Young's Point, when I was immediately transferred, with my stores, to the Silver Wave, the Sanitary boat of the United States Sanitary Commission. For ten days I stood in the little storehouse of the Commission, dealing out life, and health, and happiness to our emaciated soldiers. As I stood at the rude counter, I had beside me a barrel of soft crackers, a bag of onions, a sack of potatoes, a box of herring, a box of pepper, and a box of home-made gingerbread. Green tea, lemons, codfish, and white sugar completed the assortment. The news spread quickly that a lady was on the Sanitary boat with comforts for the sick. Requisitions poured in rapidly, for, alas! the need was great. The number of the hospital, the exact number of sick men, the character of supplies needed, were carefully designated, signed by the surgeon, as well as a solemn pledge given that not one jot or tittle should be used but for the sick soldiers. I believe, with rare exceptions, it was kept. Careful subsequent examinations of all the hospitals supplied proved it. As I stood at my post, convalescent soldiers, that we should call skeletons at home, by dint of canes and crutches, and friendly hands, came in solemn procession to receive for themselves these treasures. I rejoice to be able to say I did not turn one away empty-handed; and also to remark, to the honor of the brave soldiers, that not one applied whose appearance was not a complete certificate of his necessity. I said to one of these emaciated men, 'Will you have a few soft crackers?' The only answer was an outstretched hand and a tearful eye. 'Shall I give you an onion?' 'O, how I've longed for that, and wished I had ten cents to buy one from the sutler!' To another I said, 'Perhaps you would like a lemon.' 'A lemon! just let me look at and smell one; I believe 'twould cure me.' 'How about some home-made gingerbread?' That always brought the gushing tears, and was, without fail, just like wife's or mother's. One poor fellow, who was obliged to seize both railings to support himself up the narrow stairway, opened his battered haversack, and drew forth a small paper of coffee. Said he, 'I know you don't sell anything here; but I thought, if I could change this coffee I've saved from my rations for a little green tea, I'd get an appetite. If I could only get a cup of tea like mother made, I believe I should get well.' I motioned back the parcel, for I could not speak, and gave him a little package containing white sugar, and a lemon, some green tea, two herrings, two onions, and some pepper. He looked at the parcel a moment, and said, 'Is that *all* for me?' I bowed assent. He covered his pinched face with his thin hands, and burst into a low, sobbing cry. I laid my hand upon his shoulder, and said, 'Why do you weep?' 'God bless the women!' he sobbed out; 'what should we do but for them? I came from father's farm, where all knew plenty; I've lain sick these three months; I've seen no woman's face, nor heard her voice, nor felt her warm hand till to-day, and it unmans me; but don't think I rue my bargain, for I don't. I've suffered much and long, but don't let them know at home. May be I'll never have a chance to tell them how much; but I'd go through it all for the old flag.' 'Who knows,' I said, 'but the very luxuries I've given you have been sent from the Aid Society to which your mother belongs?' 'I shouldn't wonder,' he replied, 'for my mother writes me she never lets anything keep her away from the meetings. I'm glad of it, for I don't know what would become of us poor fellows but for the Sanitary Commission.' He wiped away his tears with the back of his hand, gave me his 'Good-by! God bless you!' and said, 'I *feel* that I've turned the corner; I haven't felt as strong for months as I am now.' With the help of *one* railing he descended the stairs, and called out from the landing, 'Farewell! God bless you!'

"In one of my frequent trips to the army, I was detained for some time at Columbus, Kentucky, on the Mississippi River, and improved the time in moving about among the waiting regiments, and talking with the different soldiers. I passed from group to group, and said a cheering word, and told how we loved, and honored, and labored for them at home. It required but a moment to gather large audiences; and O, what listeners! The words *home*, *wife*, *mother*, always brought cheers and tears, worshipful reverence, and grateful thanks. I believe there does not exist, nor ever has existed on this earth, a more noble, brave, honorable, tender, patient, and enduring race of men than our Union soldiers. As I turned from the last group to walk up the fortifications, I heard a quick step, and, turning, saw a fine young man, in the uniform of an orderly sergeant. He touched his cap, and said, 'Madam, excuse me; but if you will not consider it impertinent, I would ask the favor of accompanying you. I've always been accustomed to female society, and during the nine months I have been in the army, you are the first lady I have spoken to.' Said I, 'I consider it a great honor to be escorted by a soldier, and as you are about the age of one of my sons, I should be glad to have your strong arm to lean upon, as I ascend the hill; and you can tell me something of your history.' 'I am the last of my mother's eight children,' he said, solemnly, 'and she is a widow. I had a fine position, was postmaster in a flourishing town in Iowa, and could not ask for brighter prospects than I had when the war broke out. At the first call I felt that I must go, and said so to my mother. She faltered, saying, 'John, not yet; so many mothers have more than one child, *and some that have but one are not widows!* I felt 'twas true, especially as father had left her to my care. The second call came. As it happened, 'twas harder than ever to go, for I had another's consent to ask beside my mother's then. Next door to us lived an orphan girl, whom I had known and loved from childhood — I never knew how much, till it appeared possible I might have to leave her. Before I knew it, I had told her all, and found she loved me also. We were engaged to be married; nevertheless, I felt I must go now, and at once told mother. She turned pale, but said, 'John, I'll be as good as my word; go, and God bless you! but what of Mary?' I'll see her at once, I said; and in five minutes I was beside her in the porch, where she stood every evening, waiting for me, on the very spot where we first pledged our troth. In the dim twilight her quick woman's eye read something. She said, quickly, 'What's the matter, John? Are you ill?' 'Not ill, but sad, Mary. The president has called for three hundred thousand more, and I must be going. Mother says yes; what says my darling?' The color had faded from her cheek, but her eye brightened as she said, 'God forbid I should stand in your way; as your mother said, I say, Go, and God bless you! I've been fearing and hoping for this. I love you better than ever, and should have felt ashamed had you held back. But, John, one thing must be done; I never expected to say this; but we must be married: if you are sick or wounded I must go to you, and when you leave I must live with your mother;' and as she laid her head upon my shoulder, she whispered, 'and, John, I would rather be your widow than another man's bride.' Next day we were married, I enlisted, and before nightfall was on my way to my regiment. Strange as it may seem, I have never regretted the step. Mother and Mary live together, and write such cheerful letters twice a week that I could not be despondent if I would. They say, 'Keep up your courage, John. God takes care of us, and will of you. We expect you home at the end of the war, loaded with honors; and O, what a welcome we'll give you!' I brought my wedding coat with me, and looked at it, with smiles and tears, night and morning, as it hung up in my tent. Some villain stole it last night, and the gold of California could not have bought it. No matter; I have their daguerrotypes. I wish it were not too dark for you to see them.' Just at this point we had reached the brow of the hill, crowned with its frowning battlements. The golden purple had faded from the clouds; the dimly-defined battle-field of Belmont lay across the stream; the heavy moan of the Father of Waters mingled with the distant hum of moving squadrons, as they filed into the boats; the heavy tread of the sentinels, and the booming of the evening gun, completed the warlike character of this strange but fascinating scene. We stood in silence; our hearts were too full for utterance. My young friend passed his hand across his eyes hastily, as he said, 'Don't think I would have things otherwise; I counted the cost, and am willing to pay the price, be it what it may.' I said, 'A moment since I pitied you, but now I envy you;

you are happy in your choice; are sustained by wife and mother; know what self-sacrificing patriotism means, and trust in God implicitly.' 'You are right,' he said, 'I will write your words to mother and Mary, for I am proud of them both.' We walked down the hill rapidly, and were soon at John's camp. As we parted he said, 'I believe God sent you here, madam; for the first time in nine months I had a touch of home-sickness just before I met you; it is all gone now — farewell! God bless and keep you.' He vaulted lightly over the ditch around the camp, and was soon lost among the white tents of the encampment. I know not whether John still lives to honor his regiment, or whether he lives in a hospital, or sleeps in a southern grave; one thing I know, living or dying, he is one of the Lord's own, and will shine among his jewels. In a few days after this interview I entered the Gayoso Block Hospital, at Memphis, under the care of Mother Bickerdyke, of great renown. My visit was unexpected, and happened at supper time. As I entered the door I met Mother Bickerdyke in the convalescent dining hall, where everything on the table was nutritious and appetizing. As she was on her way to the hospital wards, I accompanied her. There lay six hundred freshly-wounded men from the battle of Arkansas Post. Each man was eating such food as we would have given them at home. The air was perfectly pure, and the snowy sheets, and shirts, and soft pillows were refreshing.

"Mrs. Bickerdyke knew every man by name, as by intuition, and, as she passed, spoke to one and another. When we reached the centre of the room, she said, 'Boys, this is

Mrs. Hoge, from Chicago, from the North-west Sanitary Commission. Look at your shirts, sheets, and pillows; they are all marked with the name of the Sanitary Commission; your good suppers to-night all came from there, and what you get every day comes from the same place.' As from one voice arose the cry, 'Three cheers for the Sanitary Commission! God bless the women at home!' As we passed from cot to cot, Mrs. Bickerdyke would ask, 'William, how does your egg suit you?' 'Exactly right, mother.' 'Well, John, how goes the milk toast?' 'Bully, mother — tastes like the old cow's milk at home.' Said a gray-headed man, with a shattered arm, 'Mother, I don't believe my wife could beat that cup of green tea you made me, with white sugar in it; it has about cured me; I feel as chirk as a robin.'

"At one cot knelt a bright, bronzed-faced, motherly woman, feeding her husband cautiously. His jaw had been shot away, the splintered fragments removed, and he lay a woful spectacle, not able to speak intelligibly. 'How do you feel to-night, James?' said Mother Bickerdyke. 'All right, now, since she's come,' said he, laying his hand fondly on her head. The constant woman's face beamed with joy as she said, 'I believe I can take him home next week.'

"As I was about to leave, I stood in their midst, and said, 'Boys, you look so bright and happy, and seem so cheerful, I think you must be shamming: you are all heroes; but are you badly wounded?' 'Why shouldn't we be happy?' cried out a brave, manly voice; 'we left all to fight for the old flag, and put it where it belongs, and we left it flying at Arkansas Post, if we did get hit.' Another cried out, cheerfully, 'Madam, what do you call this?' and drew aside the sheet, to show the stump of a leg. Another pointed to where the strong right arm had been, and another to his bandaged head, from which a piece of shell had been extracted. A Wisconsin battery boy, beside me, called out, 'What do you say of me? One of my arms was taken off nine months ago, and the doctor says the other must go to-morrow. I've been in nine battles, and been wounded every time; but 'the Post' has used me up. What am I to do in the world, not twenty years old, and no arms?' 'My grand fellow,' said I, 'the women will take care of you. God never spared your life but for some great purpose, and I believe you will live to bless and be blessed.' Tears burst from his eyes, as the boys cheered, and he said, fervently, 'Thank you for that.'

"The long and weary siege of Vicksburg had continued many months previous to the terrific assaults of our brave army on the fortifications in the rear of that rebel stronghold. On the 19th and 22d of May were made those furious attacks, up the steep acclivities, in the teeth of bristling fortifications, long lines of rifle-pits, and sharpshooters, who fringed the hill-tops, and poured their murderous fire into our advancing ranks. It would seem impossible that men could stand, much less advance, under such a galling fire. They were mowed down as wheat before the sickle; but they faltered not. The vacant places of the fallen were instantly filled, and inch by inch they gained the heights of Vicksburg. When the precipice was too steep for the horses to draw up the artillery, our brave boys did the work themselves; and then fought, and conquered. When they had gained the topmost line of rifle-pits, they entered in and took possession; and when I made my last visit to the Army of the Mississippi, there they were, ensconced as conies in the rock, enduring the heat of a vertical sun, and crouching like beasts of prey, to escape the rebel bullets from the earthworks, almost within touching distance. The fierce and bloody struggle had filled long lines of field hospitals with mangled victims, whose sufferings were soothed and relieved beyond what I could have conceived possible; and it rejoiced my heart to see there the comforts and luxuries of the Sanitary Commission. The main body of the army lay encamped in the valleys, at the foot of the rifle-pits, and spread its lines in a semicircle, to a distance of fourteen miles. The health of the army was perfect, and its spirit jubilant. They talked of the rebels as prisoners; as though they were guarding them; and answered questions implying doubt of success with a scornful laugh, saying, 'Why, the boys in the rear could whip Johnston, and we know it; and we could take Vicksburg if we chose, and not disturb them.' Each regiment, if not each man, felt competent for the work.

"One glorious day in June, accompanied by an officer of the Eighth Missouri, I set out for the rifle-pits. When I reached them, I found the heat stifling; and as I bent to avoid the whizzing minies, and the falling branches of the trees, cut off by an occasional shell, I felt that war was a terrible reality. The intense excitement of the scene; the manly, cheerful bearing of the veterans; the booming of the cannon from the battlements, and the heavy mortars that were ever and anon throwing their huge iron balls into Vicksburg, and the picturesque panorama of the army encamped below, obliterated all sense of personal danger or fatigue. After a friendly talk with the men in the extreme front, and a peep again and again through the loopholes, watched and fired upon continually by the wary foe, I descended to the second ledge, where the sound of music reached us. We followed it quickly, and in a few minutes stood behind a rude litter of boughs, on which lay a gray-haired soldier, face downward, with a comrade on either side. They did not perceive us, but sang on the closing line of the verse, —

'Come, humble sinner, in whose breast
A thousand thoughts revolve,
Come with your guilt and fear oppressed,
And make this last resolve.'

I joined in the second verse, —

'I'll go to Jesus, though my sin
Hath like a mountain rose;
I know his courts; I'll enter in,
Whatever may oppose.'

In an instant, each man turned, and would have stopped; but I sang on, with moistened eyes, and they continued. At the close one burst out, 'Why, madam, where did you come from? Did you drop from heaven into these rifle-pits? You are the first lady we have seen here;' and then the voice was choked with tears. I said, 'I have come from your friends at home, and bring messages of love and honor. I have come to bring you the comforts we owe you, and love to give. I've come to see if you receive what they send you.' 'Do they think as much of us as that? Why, boys, we can fight another year on that — can't we?' 'Yes! yes!' they cried; and almost every hand was raised to brush away the tears. 'Why, boys,' said I, 'the women at home don't think of much besides the soldiers. If they meet to sew, 'tis for you; if they have a good time, 'tis to gather money for the Sanitary Commission; if they pray, 'tis for the soldiers; and even the little children, as they kneel at their mothers' knees, to lisp their good-night prayers, say, "God bless the soldiers."' A crowd of eager listeners had gathered from their hiding-places, as birds from the rocks. Instead of cheers, as usual, I could only hear an occasional sob, and feel solemn silence. The gray-haired veteran drew from his breast pocket a daguerrotype, and said, 'Here are my wife and daughters. I think any man might be proud of them; and they all work for the soldiers.' And then each man drew forth the irresistible daguerrotype, and held it for me to look at, with pride and affection. There were aged mothers and sober matrons, bright-eyed maidens and laughing cherubs, all carried next these brave hearts, and cherished as life itself. Blessed art! it seemed as though it were part of God's preparation work for this long and cruel war. These mute memorials of home and its loved ones have proved the talisman of many a tempted heart, and the solace of thousands of suffering, weary veterans. I had much to do, and prepared to leave. I said, 'Brave men, farewell! When I go home I'll tell them that men who never flinch before a foe sing hymns of praise in the rifle-pits of

Vicksburg. I'll tell them that eyes that never weep for their own suffering, overflow at the name of home, and the sight of the pictures of their wives and children. They'll feel, more than ever, that such men cannot be conquered, and that enough cannot be done for them.' Three cheers for the women at home, and a grasp of multitudes of hard, honest hands, and I turned away to visit other regiments. The officer who was with me grasped my hand. 'Madam,' said he, 'promise me you'll visit my regiment to-morrow — 'twould be worth a victory to them. You don't know what good a lady's visit to the army does. These men, whom you have seen to-day, will talk of your visit for six months to come. Around the fires, in the rifle-pits, in the dark night, or on the march, they will repeat your words, describe your looks, voice, size, and dress; and all agree in one respect, that you look like an angel, and exactly like each man's wife or mother.' Such reverence have our soldiers for upright, tender-hearted women.

"In the valley beneath, just having escaped the front line of rifle-pits, with the regiment now occupying it, encamped my son's regiment. Its ranks had been fearfully thinned by the terrible assaults of the 19th and 21st of May, as they had formed the right wing of the line of battle on that fearful day. I knew most of them personally, and as they gathered round me, and inquired for home and friends, I could but look in sadness for many familiar faces, to be seen no more on earth. I said, 'Boys, I was present when your colors were presented to you by the Board of Trade. I heard your colonel pledge himself that you would bring those colors home, or cover them with your blood as well as glory. I want to see them, if you have them still, after your many battles.' With great alacrity, the man in charge of them ran into an adjoining tent, and brought them forth, carefully wrapped in an oil-silk covering. He drew it off, and flung the folds to the breeze. 'What does this mean?' I said. 'How soiled, and tattered, and rent, and faded they look! I should not know them.' The man who held them said, 'Why, ma'am, 'twas the smoke and balls did that.' 'Ah! so it must have been,' I said. 'Well, you have covered them with glory, but how about the blood?' A silence of a minute followed, and then a low voice said, 'Four were shot down holding them: two are dead, and two in the hospital.' 'Verily, you have redeemed your pledge,' I said, solemnly. 'Now, boys, sing "Rally round the Flag, Boys!" And they did sing it. As it echoed through the valley, as we stood withih sight of the green-sward that had been reddened with the blood of those who had fought for and upheld it, methought the angels might have paused to hear it, for it was a sacred song — the song of freedom to the captive, of hope to the oppressed of all nations. Since then, it seems almost profane to sing it with thoughtlessness or frivolity. After a touching farewell, I stepped into the ambulance, surrounded by a crowd of the brave fellows.

"The last sound that reached my ears was cheers for the Sanitary Commission and the women at home. I soon reached the regimental hospital, where lay the wounded color-bearers. As I entered the tent, the surgeon met me, and said, 'I'm so glad you've come! for R. has been calling for you all day.' As I took his parched, feverish hand, he said, 'O, take me home to my wife and little ones, to die!' There he lay, as noble a specimen of vigorous manhood as I had ever looked upon. His great, broad chest heaved with emotion; his dark eyes were brilliant with fever; his cheeks flushed with almost the hue of health; his rich brown hair clustering in soft curls over his massive forehead, — it was difficult to realize that he was entering the portals of eternity. I walked across the tent to the doctor, and asked if he could go with me. He shook his head, and said before midnight he would be at rest. I shrunk from his eager gaze as I approached him. 'What does he say?' he asked, quickly. 'You can't be moved.' The broad chest rose and fell; his whole frame quivered. There was a pause of a few moments. He spoke first, and said, 'Will you take my message to her?' 'I will,' I said, 'if I go five hundred miles to do it.' 'Take her picture from under my pillow, and my children's also. Let me see it once more.' As I held them for him, he looked earnestly, and then said, 'Tell her not to fret about me, for we shall meet in heaven. Tell her 'twas all right that I came. I don't regret it, and she must not. Tell her to train these two little boys, that we loved so well, to go to heaven to us; and tell her to bear my loss like a soldier's wife and a Christian.' He was exhausted by the effort. I sat beside him till his consciousness was gone, repeating God's precious promises. As the sun went to rest that night, he slept in his Father's bosom."

MISS EMILY W. DANA.

PROBABLY there were none of the military hospitals that had concentrated within their walls a greater number of the elements of deep and touching interest than the General Hospital established in the buildings and on the grounds of the Naval Academy at Annapolis, Maryland. Others were nearer the front, and contained a greater proportion of surgical and very serious cases. The amputating table, with its terrible array of glittering apparatus, was little used at Annapolis. The soldiers who came there were those whose constitutions had been shattered to the foundation by long sickness, fearful hardships, or deep and torturing wounds. The sufferings of many were hopeless. They would never again shoulder arms or draw a ramrod. And, what was a far keener thought, the bent and wasted figure that a few months before had stepped across the threshold full of the vigor and hope of young manhood, would never enter again the far-off mountain or prairie home. The only hope of the doctor and the nurse was to alleviate the sufferings of the patient, and make his slow march to the grave less gloomy and appalling.

During the last year of the war this hospital became the general rendezvous of the hundreds and thousands of starving prisoners just released from Belle Isle, Libby, Salisbury, and Andersonville. No language can be too graphic to depict the appearance of those miserable groups that every few days came in special trains from Washington, or in boats from Fortress Monroe, fresh from the long tortures of those infamous prison pens. Moving skeletons they were, or shrivelled mummies they seemed, half restored to the world of breathing, hopeful existence, the minds of many stupefied by the dreary and hopeless monotony of suffering through which they had passed. Others, again, were goaded almost to madness by the thought that these enormous cruelties, and the countless deaths they had witnessed, and which they had expected to suffer, were the result of a system of slow torture, deliberately adopted by the rebel authorities, or of a reckless indifference to the lives of captured enemies and the usages of civilized warfare, equally barbarous and criminal.

None of the sufferers by war appealed more directly or more feelingly to the sympathizing heart and the Christian charity of woman than the inmates of the Naval School Hospital. And nobly was that appeal met by the corps of nurses who devoted themselves to these hundreds and thousands of patients. The surgeon in charge at the Naval School was Dr. Vanderkieft. The lady superintendent in charge of the nursing and special diet of the whole establishment was, for a time, Miss Tyler, of Baltimore; and afterwards, that model of what is most excellent in character, and most admirable in practical efficiency, Miss Maria M. C. Hall, of Washington City.

At different times there were associated with Miss Hall,

in these labors, more than twenty ladies, from various loyal states. The most of those who occupied this interesting field were from Maine and Massachusetts. So numerous was the deputation from the former state that they were sometimes called the "Maine stay" of the Annapolis Hospital.

In the fall of 1863 a large number of ladies came out from Portland and its vicinity, and labored for different periods in the various wards of the hospital. The work was so systematized that each person had a particular number of patients assigned to her. The hospital was divided into sections, and each section into wards. Miss Emily W. Dana came, with several others, in August, 1863, and was assigned to wards B and C of section three. The most of these patients were prisoners just released from Belle Isle and Libby Prisons. Medicines were of little avail to reach their cases. Suitable food, in proper quantities, seasoned with cheerful talk, sometimes a song or a story, and, more than all, the presence of a graceful woman, reminding them of the homes and delights they had so long been absent from, and suggesting the hopes and joys of social and refined existence, were more potent for their recovery than any drug, or balsam, or sulphate.

During the eight months that Miss Dana was ministering to the succession of sufferers who filled the cots and chairs of these wards, she saw many cases of the most profound and touching interest.

It was never an easy matter to obey the instructions of the physician, who ordered a special and carefully regulated diet for those whose systems had become thoroughly impaired by slow starvation. Every day, and many times each day, she was obliged to say to some of these poor fellows, "You must not have this or that," while their longing eyes were watching each mouthful, and devouring every morsel of a heartier neighbor's food. So bitterly had they suffered the pangs of hunger, that often their latest breath was expended in the most pitiful supplications for something to eat.

One day Miss Dana found a new patient in one of the cots that she was accustomed to visit. He was a beautiful boy from Kentucky, and his name was Thomas Munday. Not even the terrible ordeal through which he had passed had dimmed the sunny lustre of his chestnut curls, or blurred the brightness of his eye. She asked him what she could do for him — the usual question upon approaching a new patient. "Write to Kentucky, immediately, for my father to come." She wondered, somewhat, at the earnestness of the request, for there was nothing threatening about his symptoms; but a day or two proved that the poor boy knew best. The suffering from hunger had gone too far, and though he had "gotten back" — as he called it — "to God's country," and the ample resources of the Sanitary and Christian Commissions afforded abundant variety of the most delicate and tempting dishes, nothing that was brought could, for a moment, satisfy or nourish him. Day after day, for a week, his strength wasted, until all likelihood of recovery was abandoned; and Miss Dana could only hope to keep the vital spark alive, so that the father might arrive from the distant state in time to see his bright-haired boy before he died. He never complained, but occasionally asked, beseechingly, "Can't you do something for me?" his great blue eyes, with their dilated pupils, pleading even more earnestly than words. But suddenly she saw them charged with an expression entirely new and fearful. One morning, as she approached his cot, the boy that had been so patient and passive cast upon her a wistful, greedy look, as of a hungry animal. She was bringing him a little brandy. He raised himself with a painful and nervous energy, and clinched the glass, exclaiming, "I'm glad you've come! I'm so hungry! Is that all the breakfast you've brought me? I'm starving! O," said he, in tones inexpressibly plaintive, "I'm *so* hungry!" He drew one deep sigh, that seemed loaded with the agony of the long months of pain which he had suffered, and fell back upon his cot. The wildness died out instantly from his eyes; they became dim and stony. The slow torture was ended. It was not until the next day that the old Kentucky farmer came, and looked down at the pinched features, and heard from his nurse, with a heart whose heaviness none can tell, the story of his death.

One beautiful Sunday morning in September, Miss Dana entered ward C with a handful of flowers for one of her patients. In the cot beside his she saw a fresh arrival, a noble-looking soldier, with evidences of a high order of intellectual and spiritual manhood stamped upon his fine features. The patient to whom she brought the flowers introduced him as Sergeant Martin Armstrong, and he seemed proud to claim him as a friend, and a member of the regiment to which he belonged. The little hospital cot seemed too small for his manly proportions, as he lay half bolstered up, his grave and penetrating but kindly eyes following every look and motion of those about him, silently measuring and fathoming all. Though his brow was knit from the exquisite pain he constantly suffered, no one thought of offering to him, that august and self-contained spirit, the sympathy which he quietly bestowed on others. Tortured by his wound, and steadily sinking to his grave, there was yet a something about this man that changed the atmosphere of the whole ward; and all the men in it were lifted above their every-day selves by the magnetism of his noble patience, and the elevated fortitude with which he faced death. The more she saw of him, the more deeply was she impressed with the rare qualities of this dying patriot. It was evident that he had entered the army fresh from the fine and pure enthusiasms of classic culture, and communion with the most elevated authors of antiquity. His studies had been religious, as well as literary. Homer and David, Moses and Tacitus, Solomon and Seneca, had been his chosen authors before the gown of the scholar was exchanged for the sword of the dragoon, and they had been his companions at many a solitary picket stand, and his consolation at the camp fire. On the little table by his side lay his books — an uncommon collection, surely, for a soldier's knapsack. They were all well worn, and had been collected, since he took the field, from miscellaneous sources. There were the campaigns of that "laurelled scholar" of Rome, and all adown the margin were notes and criticisms, that indicated how carefully he had studied, and how thoroughly he comprehended the matchless military genius of Cæsar. Beside it was a *Viri Romæ;* and all the passages where the peculiar fortitude of the Roman character was delineated were approvingly marked and commented upon. His books would have indicated the scholar and the moral enthusiast, even if his manner had not already betrayed it.

His sickness was caused by an old wound in the left thigh, which, from a forced march to Richmond, after being taken prisoner at Gettysburg, a distance of a hundred and eighty-two miles, opened afresh, and with fatal symptoms. Two weeks he suffered from the wound, and from a slow typhoid fever. At last gangrene set in, and ended the chapter. Once only he wondered what he had ever done that he should suffer so; and then not in a spirit of complaint, but rather as a religious philosopher. Adams, the nurse in the ward, was from the same place, Pittsburg, a member of the same company, and a personal friend of Armstrong. It was touching to see the tenderness with which the strong, bearded soldier nursed his dying friend. His love was like the love of Jonathan; it passed the love of woman. He had neither eye nor ear for others, but sat, night and day, with a Roman patience, watching, in painful solicitude, the long, hard struggle between such fine physical powers and the relentless grasp of the disease. The poor body was fearfully racked and emaciated. At length, after two weeks of great agony, his reason gave way. Wild snatches of old songs, fine passages from classic orators and poets, were mingled with cries of distress and incoherent mutterings. Even in its chaos, and in the extremity of death, those around him could not but say, with Ophelia, —

> "O, what a noble mind is here o'erthrown!
> The courtier's, soldier's, scholar's eye, tongue, sword."

Death at length ended the melancholy scene. Early one Sunday morning, Miss Dana, at the first bugle-call, hastened to the ward, and found the officer of the day closing his eyes, and fitting the chin-cloth under his marble features. Close beside the manly but now rigid figure sat poor Adams, his head bowed upon his hands, and his strong frame convulsed by the grief that would have way. Never afterwards could Armstrong's name be mentioned that quick tears did not start in his eyes. From him she learned that Armstrong was nearly fitted for the pulpit when the war broke out; that he had enlisted in the Sixth United States cavalry, and was noted in the regiment for his soldierly qualities, and the grave and elevated spirit of patriotism and manliness with which he was ever actuated. The presence and the death of this man in the ward had a marked effect upon the patients. They recognized in him a strength of moral character, and a power in his reliant, yet self-sacrificing example, that made them proud to suffer in a cause that was consecrated by the death of victims so noble.

During the whole of her period of attendance, from August till the following May, Miss Dana was impressed with the uncomplaining endurance with which all the sufferings she witnessed were borne. "No matter," she says, "what the case or cause, — I rarely heard a word of repining or regret; so rarely, indeed, that such a word was noted, and the unfortunate complainant marked, and almost scorned, by those of stronger will."

The whole of her experience there, though in the midst of agony, and under the shadow of frequent deaths, was so full of instances of what is most admirable and praiseworthy in human character and the manly virtues, that she regards it by far the richest and most satisfactory in life.

MRS. S. BURGER STEARNS.

WHEN the great organized charities that did so much to bless the soldier were first instituted, the people were, for the most part, ignorant of the system upon which they operated, and the precise method in which they accomplished their benign results. There was, moreover, much scepticism as to the genuineness of their charity. Many could not be convinced that the active agents of the Sanitary Commission were not instigated by some selfish motive, and were, in fact, seeking wealth or promotion under a saintly guise.

What becomes of all the magnificent sums of money that are received from our Sanitary Fairs? Who are benefited by these tons upon tons of delicacies and luxuries which are constantly forwarded to the poor wounded soldier? Does he receive them? Is the condition of our disabled men as much above that of armies in all previous wars as the unexampled generosity of our people would imply?

To answer questions like these; to explain the objects, the origin, and the working of the Sanitary and Christian Commissions; to illustrate the manner in which they reached the soldier on the battle-field or in remote hospitals; to show the utility of lady nurses in military hospitals, and the good accomplished by them; to give individual instances of courage, fidelity, and self-sacrifice, thus proving the value of past contributions, and affording warrant for new sacrifices and larger generosity, — in order to secure all these ends there was demanded a new and peculiar class of self-sacrificing laborers. The Commissions were too much occupied with their duties in the field to undertake a home enterprise like this. Those ladies whose hearts were wholly enlisted in the work could find in the hospital and on the battle-field a life more engrossing, whose romance would in a manner compensate for its hardships.

A few could be named, as Mrs. Hoge in the West, and Mrs. Harris in the East, whose fine natural gifts and social position enabled them to be singularly effective and useful in both lines of service. They were indefatigable at the front, and at the same time, with their pens or in oral addresses, stimulated fresh largesses from their friends at home.

Mrs. Stearns's mission was somewhat different. As her husband was a colonel in active service, she held it her duty to be in readiness to go to attend upon him the moment he should become disabled. She accordingly devoted herself earnestly to home labor in explaining, illustrating, and recommending those magnificent systems of sanitary usefulness. Her mission and her work were, during the war, to relieve, cheer, and strengthen the brave soldier in the field, and the anxious patriot at home, by eloquent words. While she fully appreciated the value of all unselfish workers in all parts of the harvest-field, she felt that the example of that noble corps of co-laborers ought to be made a power to incite to blessed acts of charity those who were taking no share in the work; and therefore she took upon herself the task of rousing the indifferent, and employing the inactive, through the influence of lectures upon "Our Soldiers' Aid Societies," and upon the "United States Sanitary and Christian Commissions." In Michigan, where these lectures commenced, and in most of the large towns of that state where they were delivered, Mrs. Stearns was known as a highly accomplished and earnest young woman, who had made special efforts to secure for herself and others of her sex the advantages of a complete classical course of studies in the State University of Michigan.

When the war broke out, and her husband went into active service, though prompted to accompany him to the field, she was sure she could engage in a more important line of activity at home. She accordingly visited Washington, and the hospitals in its vicinity; and becoming familiar with the system of the Commissions and the wants of the soldier, she came before the people full of arguments and incidents illustrative of the untold good that had been done by Soldiers' Aid Societies and their public representatives and almoners, the two Commissions. Her own example was rich in the virtue of self-sacrifice. Without pecuniary recompense were her labors, but not without rich reward. She so fully appreciated the soldier's brave devotion, that it was ever a joy to her to offer him her tribute of praise, and a double joy to find her zealous and loyal words inciting others to generous gifts and abundant labors in his behalf.

Aside from the direct aid to the soldier thus secured,

Mrs. Stearns' success in these lectures was incidentally beneficial in showing how much good can be effected by any accomplished and true-hearted woman, without transcending the proprieties of her sex, or violating the decorum of society. Referring to her lecture before a large audience in the Representatives' Hall, an editor says, "Her discourse was listened to for an hour, with profound attention, by as many persons as could find seats in the hall. Some of the audience came to hear Mrs. Stearns partly out of curiosity; but all went away with the conviction that it is possible for a lady to speak effectively to a promiscuous audience in behalf of suffering humanity without stepping out of her true sphere, or compromising her modesty and dignity as a woman."

The Hon. Schuyler Colfax, in an address at Washington, alluding to the example of Mrs. Stearns and some others who were equally zealous and earnest, says, "We have on record the example of the prophetess Deborah, who, in her rejoicing song before the children of Israel, poured out her praises upon those who, as she declares so strikingly, 'jeoparded their lives unto the death in the high places of the field,' and her curses upon the inhabitants of Meroz, 'because they came not to the help of the Lord — to the help of the Lord against the mighty;' and I have not found in that sacred record that she was regarded as unsexing herself by public comments on the patriotism of her fellow-citizens."

In other cities, notices equally kind and complimentary appeared after the lectures of Mrs. Stearns; and her example now remains before the American public a proof of how much good may be effected by one loyal, accomplished, and fearless woman, whose time and whose talents are devoted, without reserve, in a holy cause.

The advantage to their sex from such instances as Mrs. Hoge and Mrs. Stearns is very great. The boundaries which public opinion had placed on the legitimate activities and the proper sphere of woman have been enlarged. They have shown that a wife, a mother, or a sister is never more truly lovely than when she pleads, even before a large and promiscuous assembly, the sacred cause of humanity, presenting reasons that flow from the fountains of charity, and descend from the celestial heights of religion.

MRS. HARRIET W. F. HAWLEY.

AMONG the many thousands of patriotic women of the North, who earnestly desired, from the first moment of the great struggle, to take such part in it as a woman might, whose whole soul was in the issues of the conflict, was Mrs. Harriet W. F. Hawley, a native of Guilford, Connecticut. When Sumter was fired on, her husband, Joseph R. Hawley, was the editor of the Hartford Evening Press. He at once laid down his pen, and enlisted for the war, — the first one enrolled in the first volunteer company that was accepted by the state, and became its captain before it was on its way to Washington.

During the first campaign no opportunity was afforded Mrs. Hawley to participate directly in the glorious work going forward, other than that given to every woman at home, who labored in the work of equipping the soldiers for the field, and forwarding to them such comforts as were indispensable to the sick and wounded. Indeed, it was not supposed by Mrs. Hawley's friends that she would ever be able to do anything more than home work in the war. With a slight frame, a constitution not strong, health never firm, an organization delicate and nervous, she seemed entirely unfitted to endure hardships. But an indomitable spirit continually urged, and in the fall of 1862 her long-hoped-for opportunity came. Her husband was in the Department of the South, and in November she obtained permission to go to Beaufort, South Carolina, with the intention of teaching the colored people, whose first cry in freedom was for the primer. But circumstances, and the necessities of the sick and wounded soldiers, directed her into another field of labor, in which she continued, with little intermission, until the war ended. She became a regular visitor at the hospitals in Beaufort. Of her services here and the like at other places, it is not necessary to speak in detail; the pages of this volume sufficiently show the nature of the duties of the noble women who devoted themselves to hospital work.

In January, 1863, she went to Fernandina, Florida, where her husband — then colonel, afterwards brevet major-general, and since governor of Connecticut — was placed in command. Here, and afterwards at St. Augustine, she was a regular visitor of the post and regimental hospitals, remaining until November, when she rejoined her husband on St. Helena Island, South Carolina, to which he had returned from the siege of Charleston. During the winter, frequently, and as often as her strength would permit, she visited the post hospital at St. Helena, and the general hospitals at Beaufort and Hilton Head, especially exerting herself when the ship-loads of wounded men arrived, after the battle of Olustee, in February.

In April, 1864, when the Tenth army corps went north to join Butler's expedition up the James, greatly desirous to be near the regiment and brigade of her husband, in the individual welfare of the men composing which her sympathies were strongly enlisted, she endeavored to procure a situation as attendant or nurse at Chesapeake Hospital, to which the wounded of that expedition were likely to be sent. Failing to do so, she went to Washington, and was placed in charge of a ward in Armory Square Hospital. This hospital was at that time one of the most arduous places of labor in the country, besides being, from its low situation, subject to malarious diseases. Standing near the Potomac, it usually received the most severely wounded, who arrived by boats from below and could not be moved far.

Mrs. Hawley reached there the morning after the wounded began to arrive from the battles of the Wilderness. Her ward was in the armory itself; it was always large, and for a time contained more patients than any other — ninety-seven during those dreadful April days. To add to the horrors of her ward, it had no separate operating room, and surgical operations were necessarily performed within it. The poor fellows who arrived there, the mutilated wrecks of that fierce campaign, were so exhausted by their marching before, and by the long journey after they were wounded, that they died very rapidly. One day forty-eight were carried out of the hospital, dying, with singular regularity, about one in every half hour. The entire hospital was calculated to accommodate about nine hundred, but it was made to take in over fourteen hundred for a time.

Surrounded by such scenes, a daily witness of the results of the terrible Virginia campaign of 1864, Mrs. Hawley lived in this hospital, in charge of the ward assigned her, for four months; months of the severest labor, taxing her utmost strength, and drawing upon her deepest sympathies, and that, too, in a climate peculiarly trying to a Northerner. In September her overtaxed energies gave way, and she was forced, by illness, to relinquish her charge. She returned, however, to the same ward in November, and remained in the hospital until March, 1865. The writer visited this hospital in the May following, and found Mrs. Hawley's name a cherished one there, many a poor fellow, lying on his weary bed, speaking of her kindness and devotion with beaming face and tears in his eyes.

After the capture of Wilmington, Brigadier-General Hawley was assigned to the command of the south-west portion of North Carolina, headquarters at that city. Thither Mrs. Hawley followed him shortly, and there encountered new horrors of the war of which she had already so much sad experience. When Wilmington surrendered, it was in a shockingly filthy condition, destitute of supplies, of medicines, of comforts for the sick. The conquering army which entered it was stripped for marching and fighting, and poorly supplied with what the city so shortly needed— hospital stores and clothing for the destitute. When Mrs. Hawley arrived, nine thousand Union prisoners had just been delivered there, recently released from Andersonville and Florence. The North remembers in what sorry plight they were, all of them in immediate need of food and clothing, and three thousand of them subjects of hospital treatment. As if this were not enough, there came also a motley crowd of refugees, which had hung upon the skirts of Sherman's march — old men, women, and children, white and black, dirty, ragged, hungry, helpless. Such a conglomeration crowded into the little city — never a healthy place — soon bred a pestilence, a sort of jail or typhus fever.

The medical officers exerted themselves to the utmost; the Union citizens and all good people contributed liberally such clothing as they could spare, and what delicacies they had for the sick. But what could they do to alleviate the suffering of so many thousands? The fever increased in virulence, and those attacked died rapidly. At one time there were four thousand sick soldiers, including a few wounded from Sherman's army, in the extemporized hospitals of the city, the large dwellings and the churches. Supplies could not be obtained, and it was some time before even one clean garment could be given to each released prisoner; and meantime disease increased, and deaths multiplied. The chief of the medical staff died, and others were seriously sick: of five professional lady nurses from the North, three sickened, and two died. One of the chaplains died, and another was severely ill; and among the detailed soldier nurses the pestilence was decidedly worse than any battle — they died by scores. It is needless to say that Mrs. Hawley exerted herself to the utmost to mitigate the sufferings by which she was surrounded. She organized the efforts of the women who would lend their aid, superintended the making of garments, went among the refugees and sought out the most distressed, visited the hospitals, shunning no danger, not even the small pox. Some idea of the condition of the town, and of the labors thrown upon the few there who were competent to improve it, may be gained from the following extract from a private letter, written about this time by Mrs. Hawley, in the freedom of friendly correspondence, with no thought of its publication. She wrote: —

"You know that over nine thousand of our prisoners were delivered to us here; and no human tongue or pen can describe the horrible condition which they were in. *Starving to death*, covered with vermin, with no clothing but the filthy rags they had worn during their whole imprisonment — a period of from five to twenty months; cramped by long sitting in one position, so that they could not straighten their limbs; their feet rotted off! O God! I cannot even now endure to speak of it.

"Of course they brought the jail fever with them — it could not be otherwise; yet they must be fed, and cleansed, and clothed, and cared for. There were no hospital accommodations here worth mentioning. There were not doctors enough, and those here overworked themselves, and caught the fever and died. Buildings of all sorts were converted into temporary hospitals, and the nurses (enlisted men) fell sick at the rate of fifty a day. The chaplains worked as only Christian men can work; and they sickened too. Chaplain Eaton (Seventh Connecticut volunteers) died, a real martyr. Mr. Tiffany (Sixth Connecticut) has barely struggled through a most terrible attack of the fever, and is slowly recovering. Another, whose name I cannot recall, is still very low, and can hardly be expected to live. Three out of the five lady nurses sent by Mrs. Dix have been very ill, and one, Miss Kimball, died this morning, resigned and happy, as such a woman could not fail to be, yet leaving many friends to mourn for her, and a place here that no one can fill.

"Dr. Buzzell, the general medical officer, and one who cannot be too highly spoken of, both as a man and a physician, died of the fever last week. Dr. Palmer has since followed him; but the terrible list of those dead and still sick of the fever is too long for me to try to write it. It is only within the last five days that they have received any hospital supplies: previous to that time many of the sick men were lying on straw spread on the floor, although the Union citizens have given and done all in their power. What could a few families do, from their private supplies, towards furnishing three thousand nine hundred men with beds and bedding? Besides these, there were the convalescent ones to be clothed. Thank God! the vessel that the Sanitary Commission sent came soon, with nine thousand shirts and drawers, so that when I first saw them, they had at least so much in the way of clothing.

"We got possession of twelve hundred yards of cotton cloth and a bale of cotton. I called a meeting of the benevolent ladies of the place. The Sanitary Commission gave us thread, and in a week's time the materials were made up: one hundred and thirty-eight pillow-cases, one hundred and fifty-three pillows, eighty-four bed sacks, and as many sheets. And now the hospitals are all tolerably well supplied.

"Of course many have been sent North, — all who were able to go, — and many have died on the road; yet there are still many here. And, as if this were not misery enough for one poor little city, Sherman sent here six thousand refugees — black and white, old men, women, children, and babies, with nothing but what they could carry on their backs, or, as in a few cases, drag in a little old mule cart.

"And these poor wretches must be housed and fed, with the city already crowded, and the fever spreading among the citizens. It is impossible for you to imagine the misery which has stared me in the face at every step since I have been here. I can find no words to describe it. Why, this very afternoon I carried food and wine to a woman who had been lying sick, for *three days*, on a little straw in an old wagon, in an open shed, discovered accidentally by one of our officers. Of course this is not an every-day case, but it is a wonder that it is not. Many of these refugees have been sent North, and many more will be; but the mere fact of their being thus transported involves a vast amount of labor, which must mostly fall upon the soldiers; and the garrison here is small, as small as it can be kept, and do the necessary work and guard duty. And, besides all this, the city has been shamefully neglected for many months, and it is fearfully dirty, and there is but a small number of teams and wagons to do so great an amount of scavenger work.

"It did, and still does, sometimes, look very hopeless here, on all sides. You at the North will never be able to conceive or believe the true condition of our prisoners. You may see all the pictures, and read all the accounts, and believe, or think you believe, every word of them, and then you will have but a faint idea. Men have lain on the ground here dying, with the vermin literally swarming, in steady paths, up and down their bodies, as ants go in lines about their ant-hills. One poor fellow, a sergeant, died in the house of a kind lady here, whose limbs were so cramped by long sitting, through weakness, that they could not be straightened, even when he died, so that his coffin had to be made with the cover shaped like a tent, or house roof, to accommodate his knees. Women were afraid to walk over the plank sidewalks where some of the prisoners had been congregated for a little time, through fear of vermin. Men who had once been educated and cultivated, with fine minds, were reduced to idiocy — to utter and hopeless imbecility.

"More than forty men, whose feet, or portions of them, had rotted off, left on the steamer yesterday. I do not know how many more such cases there had been among them; but these men I saw. Think of it! feet so rotted away that the surgeons cut them off, with the *scissors* above the ankle! Has God any retribution for those who inflicted such suffering? Has their country any rewards for the men who suffered thus, month after month, rather than turn traitor — rather than deny the old flag?

"To-day we have been firing salutes and ringing the bells for the capture of Richmond. You should have heard the hoarse voices of the boys in the hospitals, as they tried to cheer when they heard the bells this noon. I stood still in the street, and cried like a child when I heard them; and it all rushed over my mind at once how much it meant to *them!*"

By the arrival of supplies and aid from the North, the exertions of the military authorities in cleaning the city, and the shipment North of the prisoners, and many of the sick and wounded, the disease was at length subdued, and by the latter part of June, though the town was unhealthy, the worst was over.

In July Mrs. Hawley accompanied her husband to Richmond, the latter being appointed chief of staff to Major-General Terry, and, quartered in the spacious and comfortably furnished mansion of the fugitive chief of the rebellion, she enjoyed a most needed rest from the labors and turmoil of the camp and the hospital. Thus the summer passed, and she looked forward to a speedy return home. But the full price of her presence among the exciting scenes of the war was not yet paid. In October, while returning from the battle-ground at Five Forks, whither she had gone, with an uncle, to find the grave of his son (Captain Parmelee, of the First Connecticut cavalry), the ambulance in which she rode was overturned, and she received an injury on her head, which for a long time made her life doubtful. Her whole nervous system sustained an almost irreparable shock, and she continues an invalid.

Such is a brief sketch of one of the many noble women of the country who have fought the good fight, sustained by a pure patriotism, the story of whose sacrifices will always be sweet and sacred in our annals.

MISS MARIA M. C. HALL.

AT no time since civilization commenced on this continent, has so loud a call been made on the patriotism of the people as in the spring and summer of 1861. The government was assailed by dangers new, vast, and undefined. The people of eleven states, with a unanimity that seemed appalling, had discarded the old love of national union in which Americans had been educated; and this languid fealty to the constitution was by no means confined to the seceding states.

No community was more agitated by diverse sympathies, and distracted by fierce partisanship, than the society of the national capital. Many there were, of both sexes, a number amounting almost to a majority at one time, whose southern sympathies were neither moderate nor disguised. Others, again, felt their whole natures stirred with a pure and holy zeal to do all things, and suffer all things, to sustain the government just as it was bequeathed to us, and our national ensign, "with not a stripe erased or polluted, nor a single star obscured."

Born in Washington, and reared amid the stirring and historic associations of that political metropolis, Miss Hall approved, with her whole soul, the efforts that the government was disposed to make for the preservation of everything most dear and sacred in American nationality. This patriotic sentiment took the form of an earnest desire to make a personal consecration of herself on the altar of country.

Her father was too far advanced in years to take the field as a soldier. Brother she had none of an age to shoulder a musket. She had read of Florence Nightingale, and the noble work she did in the Crimean war; and, in the enthusiasm of a spirit naturally strong, and capable of intense devotion to an object large enough to call out all its powers, she planned for herself a course of action, and a career of usefulness, that would in effect be reproducing the Crimean heroine under our flag, and in the hospitals of our great civil conflict.

Who shall say how many noble aspirations and unselfish plans have been inspired by the golden record of that English girl? By her it was proved that youth and grace, education and gentleness, charming manners and winning person, so far from unfitting woman for a life of effective beneficence among homeless and suffering men, only render her presence and attentions all the more powerful for good, by the union of loveliness with efficiency, and by combining the graces of girlhood with the dignity of the matron.

> "Day unto day her dainty hands
> Make Life's soiled temples clean,
> And there's a wake of glory where
> Her spirit pure hath been.
>
> "At midnight, through that shadow land,
> Her living face doth gleam;
> The dying kiss her shadow, and
> The dead smile in their dream."

Thus wrote one of England's sweetest poets of the noblest of British heroines; and the lines might have been written with equal justice and propriety of Miss Hall's labors, from the time she washed the blood and dust from the faces of those who fought at Manassas, till the last of the long procession of famished wretches from the Andersonville stockade had filed through the wards of the Annapolis Hospital.

From the summer of 1861 till the summer of 1865 — four long, stern years — Miss Hall thought of nothing, and cared for nothing, but how she could be most useful to the suffering defenders of the national Union. No patriot who shouldered his musket at the successive calls of our president, felt himself more thoroughly committed to the cause, or was more determined to march and fight, so long as marching and fighting remained to be done. While there were wounded soldiers to be nursed, or famished prisoners to be fed, — while there remained a hospital that could be made home-like by the ministry of woman, or cheered by her song, or illuminated by her smile, — there might be found for her noble work, happy usefulness, and a blessed mission.

To her, with as great force as to any who thus devoted themselves to lives of loyal charity, can be applied the words which an old English author has written of women in general: "To the honor, to the eternal honor, of the sex be it recorded, that in the path of duty no sacrifice is to them too high or too dear. Nothing is with them impossible but to shrink from love, honor, innocence, and religion. The voice of pleasure or of power may pass by unheeded; but the voice of affliction, *never!* The chamber of the sick, the pillow of the dying, the vigils of the dead, the altars of religion, never missed the presence or the sympathies of woman. Timid though she be, and so delicate that the winds of heaven may not too roughly visit her, on *such* occasions she loses all sense of danger, and assumes a preternatural courage, which knows not and fears not consequences."

In the summer of 1861, when those who were wounded at Bethel and Manassas were first thrown upon the hands of the medical department, there was a disposition very much to disparage, and practically to exclude from army labor, all females who were not very plain, very practical, and at least thirty years of age. Miss Dix, whose long humanitarian labors had entitled her opinion to much weight, was clear that army nurses should be simply kind-hearted and efficient. If they were sufficiently advanced in years to have sons or grandsons in the army, that circumstance was an advantage in their favor whenever application was made to be permitted to labor for the soldier.

Miss Hall found all these views as to the proper character of hospital nurses adverse to her own employment. She was young, cultivated, and enthusiastic; but she was resolute in her intention.

Mrs. Fales, of Washington city, was a lady who, during the long struggle, interested herself in the soldier, and to her Miss Hall applied for permission to visit the sick and wounded. The first request was denied. Mrs. Fales shared the views of Miss Dix, that youth, grace, and talent were poor recommendations for a hospital nurse. She tried to discourage the warm-hearted girl by telling her that the work to be done was very plain, very practical, and sometimes repulsive; that the men were dirty, and needed washing; and their hair was all in tangles, and must be combed out and brushed; that they were very hungry, and cared for nothing but to get something good to eat. But all these representations served rather to stimulate than to abate her desire to go and work among them. It was only more clear, from Mrs. Fales's account, that these poor fellows needed nursing; and the kind-hearted woman at length yielded to the earnest wishes of the noble girl, and took her to the Indiana Hospital, which was established in an unfinished wing of the Patent Office. "Now, girls," said she to Miss Hall and her sister, as she opened the door of one of the wards, "here they are, and everything to be done for them. You will find work in plenty."

The discouragements and annoyances of hospital labor, as Miss Hall found it, had not been overstated by Mrs. Fales. The surgeons afforded few or no facilities for the successful discharge of her duties; and for some time she was rather tolerated as a young lady who had a whim to be indulged, than appreciated as a true and earnest worker. She labored for nearly a year at the Indiana Hospital, being much of the time a solitary visitor, and all the year the only regular and persistent worker. For a part of the time, rather than be turned out of the hospital as a volunteer, after the general order to that effect, she was enrolled as "nurse," and drew army pay. This service at the Indiana Hospital lasted for a year, from July, 1861, to July, 1862. It was never pleasant, nor in any respect flattering.

She had no position of command. She was not, as afterwards, the head and centre of a platoon of hospital nurses, all acting under her advice, and subject to her direction. But the duties were assumed in a spirit of genuine loyalty and self-sacrifice, and they were carried through with uncomplaining fidelity and patience to the end.

In the summer of 1862, Miss Hall, with many other ladies, bore a part in the fatigues and disappointments that attended the close of the Peninsula campaign. She went to Harrison's Landing on the hospital transport Daniel Webster No. 2, and at one time remained there for two weeks. In that position she met and coöperated with that indefatigable and most admirable army worker, Mrs. Harris, and conceived the highest admiration for a character where the zeal of the Christian missionary seemed to be united with the keenest insight and the most practical sense.

For a week or two after her return from Harrison's Landing, Miss Hall was at her home in Washington, having made an arrangement to go out with Mrs. Harris as soon as there should be an urgent call from the field.

In a few days the battle at Antietam Creek was fought; and almost before the result of that long and bloody struggle was known, she received the telegram from Mrs. Harris, "Meet me at McClellan's headquarters." In prompt obedience to the call, she hurried to the front, finding much difficulty, unattended as she was, in penetrating the lines, and was unsuccessful in reaching either the commanding general or her friend and fellow-laborer. As night was closing over the confused and bloody field, she found herself at a hospital where most of the wounded were rebels, whom the rude fortunes of war had thrown helpless upon the hands of the Federal surgeons. The surgeon in charge, who very much needed assistance, begged Miss Hall to remain and aid him. This she was reluctant to do, both on account of her desire to find Mrs. Harris, and because she preferred to work for the loyal sufferers. But these objections were soon overcome, and she entered upon her work.

One of her first experiences in this hospital was quite touching. It was on the morning after her arrival. As she entered one of the wards the usual sight met her eye. A long row of narrow cots, with only space enough between to admit the passage of an attendant and surgeon; men lying very quietly, and nothing in their dress, manner, or language to indicate which side they had taken in the recent bloody struggle. She talked a little while to a wounded Union boy, and gave him some writing materials. She then spoke to another sufferer, and served him in a similar manner. On the next cot was lying, very quietly, a man of a settled and resolute countenance. "Would you like to have writing materials also?" said Miss Hall to him. "It wouldn't be of any use, ma'am," was his quiet reply. "Why not?" said she; "are you wounded in the arm?" "Yes," said he, "in the right shoulder; but that's not the only reason." "Perhaps I can write for you; tell me what to say, and I will write it down." "It would be of no use," was his reply. "Why not? Isn't there some one that would like very much to hear from you?" "Yes, indeed; I have an old mother, who would be very glad to hear from me; but no letter would reach her now." "Yes, I think it would," she replied. "Uncle Sam can take letters anywhere, and he gives special attention to the letters that his boys write." His face now grew more sober than before, and the eyes were fixed directly on the ceiling. "Uncle Sam isn't likely to do much for me," said he, slowly; and then, unwilling for a girl to see a tear upon the cheek of a soldier, he drew the sheet over his face, and added, in a half-smothered voice, "my mother lives in South Carolina." She went at once to the surgeon in charge, and asked if letters could not be sent to South Carolina by flag of truce? "Certainly, Miss Hall," said he; "there is no difficulty at all about it, and I will send as many as you are willing to write." There was, after that, no discrimination made by her. A wounded soldier was a suffering man, no matter whether he had fought under Lee or McClellan. Miss Hall remained at this hospital more than a week, and then went to the hospital of French's corps, where Mrs. Harris was at work. Here she continued another week.

In the early part of October, all the field hospitals that had been established in and around Antietam were broken up, and the wounded conveyed to the General Hospital at Smoketown, then in charge of Dr. Vanderkieft. To this place Miss Hall went, and labored for nearly nine months. The special diet department had been commenced and systematized, in a very thorough and admirable manner, by Miss Tyson, of Baltimore, who, however, on account of failing health, was obliged to retire from the field. Not long after Miss Hall's arrival there, two very excellent and efficient ladies came to her aid from Philadelphia — Mrs. Lee and Mrs. Husband. Between these three ladies the hospital was divided into sections, each having from two to three hundred patients under her charge. Miss Hall's duties here were at once arduous and monotonous; but as they were noble and beneficent, she was more than contented. In the midwinter Mrs. Lee and Mrs. Husband went down to the front, at Falmouth; and from January till May, 1863, when this hospital was discontinued, Miss Hall was, for the greater part of the time, the only lady in regular attendance. For a few weeks, in the summer of 1863, she was at home. When Gettysburg was fought she was very solicitous to reach the front, and engage in field service; but not meeting with any encouragement, she yielded to the earnest solicitations of Dr. Vanderkieft, who, having become thoroughly impressed with the excellence of her service, and her fine administrative talent at Antietam, begged her to come to Annapolis, where he was in charge of a General Hospital, and coöperate with him in his labors there. Although much preferring service at the front, she went to Annapolis, and for two years — from midsummer of 1863 till midsummer of 1865 — her labors there were incessant, her vigilance unceasing, and the executive ability which she displayed was such as to command the admiration of every person in the corps of hospital workers, and of all who visited the establishment. Much of this success is to be attributed to the entire appreciation and hearty approval which she always enjoyed of Dr. Vanderkieft, the surgeon in charge. Upon her first going there, the doctor gave her, as he called it, a separate command, making her superintendent of section number five, embracing all the hospital tents in the parade ground.

Her immediate assistant here was Miss Helen M. Noye, of Buffalo, N. Y. Miss Noye was a person who fell far short of Miss Dix's idea of a hospital nurse, being very much under thirty years of age, enthusiastic, graceful in person, and winning in manners. But Miss Hall found her a hearty worker and cheerful assistant.

During the time that she was in charge of section number five, Mrs. Tyler, of Baltimore, was lady superintendent of the wards in the building. A very earnest laborer, thinking nothing done while anything remained undone, her duties wore upon her health to such an extent that in the spring of 1864 she was obliged to resign her position and retire. Miss Hall then became lady superintendent of the entire hospital. At times there were more than four thousand persons under her care, and although she had from ten to twenty assistants, to whom separate wards were assigned, her labors of visitation were as unremitting as ever. Her mind seemed to be in all parts of the hospital, and she recollected the peculiarities of almost every case. Her judgment as to the fitness of her assistants was unerring, assigning to each such duties or such wards as she was best fitted for. During the latter part of the time, a great number of the patients were those wretched victims of rebel malignity who had come out alive from that forever infamous concentration of horrors, the Andersonville stockade.

Miss Hall describes the condition of these unhappy men, when they were first received at Annapolis, as in the last degree pitiable and appalling. Sometimes, in looking at them, she would find herself involuntarily carrying her hand to her cheek, to see if it were possible that their flesh was like hers, human and vitalized. The combined effect of starvation, cold, sickness, and filth, had, in many cases, parched the skin and flesh, so that they looked like mummies, that by some strange witchery had been evoked from the catacombs. "They seemed," she says, "to have come from some strange outer world, some horrible land of dimness and groans; 'a land of darkness, where no light is;' a world where the comforts, the sympathies, and the hopes of common life are utterly excluded." The minds of many of these poor creatures had been temporarily, at least, crushed by the fearful ordeal. They seemed like persons awaking from some long and horrible nightmare, and would say, in their plain, but touching way, "Boys, does 'pear strange — don't it? — to see folks moving 'bout that are white and clean?" "I declare, boys, it's like a streak of daylight to see a woman moving about here." "Boys," said she, one day, to a group of them, "how did you live through it? I would have supposed that the last one of you would have died in such a place." Instantly there was a chorus of answering voices, "Because we were *right*, Miss Hall — because we were right, and knew we were; that's what kept us alive." Then a grim old Tennesseean, with a shaggy, weather-beaten mat of yellow beard, added, "'Twas the flag that kept us up; if we'd been rebels, we should all have perished to death."

The effect of this life upon the bad was to make them worse. A returned prisoner was cursing one day in the hospital, and the surgeon reproved him, saying such language was not permitted there. "I don't care," said he,

"But I should suppose that you would respect God if you didn't respect men." "I'm not afraid of God, nor of hell," said he; "I have lived through that stockade, and I can live through hell."

Others, again, were brought to reformation by their sufferings. Miss Hall was one day passing by a cot of a poor, little, famished-looking boy, who turned a bright, fine eye upon her, and seemed to wish she would speak to him. "I think it has done me good," said he; "I think that I shall be a better boy now that I've got out." "This is a very good time to begin," said she. "I have begun already," he replied, pulling a little Testament from under the edge of his mattress; "I promised my God, that if ever I *did* get out from that horrible place, I'd never forget him any more, and I read this every day."

MRS. GOVERNOR HARVEY.

IT will be a long time before the people of Wisconsin will forget the thrill of horror which pervaded the entire state when the sad news was flashed over the wires that their honored and beloved governor, Lewis P. Harvey, was drowned at Savannah, Tennessee, just after having completed his noble labors in behalf of the Wisconsin soldiers who had been wounded at the battle of Pittsburg Landing, on the 6th and 7th of April, 1862. Just in the prime of a life much of which had been spent in honorable public positions, trusted and honored as few men in the state were, with a bright future before him, and without a blemish on his past career, it seemed an inexplicable and bitter providence that removed him, by a sudden casualty, just as he was returning with the blessings, heartfelt and feelingly expressed, of the sick and wounded soldiers, to whom he had been a very angel of consolation.

Deep as the affliction was to the state, and universally as it was expressed, there was one to whom it was almost beyond endurance — his devoted wife, thus suddenly and cruelly bereft. What her trial was no one can tell; but its result showed that she bore it as few women would, and proved her worthy of the husband she had lost. As he had fallen a martyr through his devotion to the welfare of our soldiers, so she would devote her energies to the same noble cause.

Within a short time after the loss of her husband, she asked and received the appointment of state agent, to visit Wisconsin soldiers in the field and in the hospitals. The state had but a few of these agents, but they were generally very faithful laborers, and accomplished an immense amount of good. None of them, however, were able to do as much as Mrs. Harvey. Among all the higher officers of the western armies her position and the story of her terrible affliction were known, and to her favors were granted and privileges given which no others could obtain. Besides her ability, her experience in public life, her manners, and her determined energy added to the influence she otherwise possessed.

To us there is hardly a more beautiful or romantic episode of the war than the army career of this noble woman, thus waiving her widow's right of pious mourning, leaving all the comforts of home, and devoting herself for years to the care of our sick and wounded defenders. Her purpose once made, there was no faltering till the end, and out of the depths of her own great sorrow she gathered strength to console thousands of afflicted ones, to whom she was mother, guardian, and protector. Of the details of her work we are, unfortunately, unable to speak. We can only write from what we have heard and read, and that without anything more distinct than a general knowledge and recollection.

The story of her army life has, throughout, the same general features. It was a constant succession of labors involving no ordinary endurance, risks, unpleasantness, and care. During the last three years of the war, wherever there was the greatest need for her services, — whether up the Tennessee or the Cumberland, at Vicksburg, Memphis, or Helena, on the White River or the Arkansas, in the field or in the hospitals, — there Mrs. Harvey was to be found, energetically working with her whole might for our suffering soldiers. A friend who knew her long before the war, and watched her labors in the army with the greatest interest, has told us something of the manner in which she worked.

He says that he never saw man or woman in the army who was more entirely inwrapped in the noble work she had undertaken. Her earnestness was something extraordinary, and made everything yield before it. Were there difficulties in the way of providing necessaries or comforts for the men in hospital, she would insist on them in such a way that every one either became imbued with her spirit or for the time yielded as before an irresistible force. They *must* be had, even if red-tape were cut a hundred times. Was a boat needed to remove the sick from an unhealthy place, the military authorities were asked for it, in the name of humanity, in such a manner that a refusal was well nigh—impossible.

Officers of the better class so confided in her judgment, and so honored her philanthropic heroism, that they cheerfully gave her what to others would have been denied. Those who were disposed to deny her requests soon came to learn her persistence and determination, and, as well, that she could and would appeal to the powers above them, generally with success. Our informant has heard of more than one case where the sick and wounded soldiers were rescued from the bad management of subordinate officers in charge of hospitals through her strenuous efforts. The same qualities which gave her such power for good in the army were of the greatest service to the soldiers in another way. Her representations to the governor — a noble and worthy successor to her husband's office — were always heeded, and the action of the executive was based on them, as all the Wisconsin officers well knew.

By the bedside of hundreds of dying soldiers she was a minister of Christian consolation, her very life a most eloquent proof of the reality of the faith she would have them accept. She was preacher and mother in one, and the two sacred characters were beautifully blended. It was her rare combination of womanly refinement and softness, of an earnest and loving Christian spirit, and of unusual business and administrative qualities that enabled her to perform a work such as we believe was accomplished by no one else in similar circumstances in the army. Others were equally devoted, earnest, and enduring; but in none was such a variety of qualifications so united.

The close of the war brought no change in her purpose. Its close did not terminate the countless sufferings that grew out of it, nor the need of philanthropic effort for the sufferers. Of all these, the class that were most innocent, most helpless, and most needing help, were "the orphans of the war;" and in their behalf Mrs. Harvey began a new work of love, as soon as the fighting had virtually ceased. A friend, who was an officer in our army, and long an intimate acquaintance of Mrs. Harvey, met her in May, 1865, at Memphis, as she was about beginning this work, and gives us a few interesting facts.

He writes, "I met Mrs. Harvey on board the steamer Luminary, at Memphis, in the latter part of May, 1865. I had not seen her since her husband's death, and was at first sadly struck by the great change in her appearance. I had known her as a leader of the best society at the state capital, accomplished, full of buoyant life and spirits; not at all gay, but always cheerful; interested in, and thoroughly understanding, the state and national politics; fresh, vigorous, and in the enjoyment of life's best gift. She had, in the few years of her affliction and unceasing labors, become almost entirely changed, as it first seemed to me. There was much more than the mourning suit to show how her great loss had borne upon her. Subdued, yet with no loss of latent energy, and altogether indifferent to aught but the work to which she had devoted herself, she appeared at least a dozen years older than when I had seen her last, in 1862; and well she might, for in the interval she had compressed the work of a lifetime. She had with her a half dozen young children—'orphans of the war'—whom she had brought with her from Vicksburg, not knowing how she would provide for them, but trusting that provision would in some way be made. They had fallen into her care, and had no one else in the wide world to look out for them. That was sufficient to establish their claim on her protection. They were to be the first inmates of her Home for like helpless ones, which she had then determined to found at the state capital. There was something very beautiful to me in the sight of this woman, so bereaved by the war, taking home with her these little sufferers by its calamities, from the once stronghold of those who brought it on. She went to Wisconsin, and appealed, through the press and personally in behalf of her project, with such effect, that the purpose and prayer of her heart have become a visible and beneficent fact. The Home has been established. Mrs. Harvey is its efficient superintendent, and is to-day as assiduous in her labors as she was in the field. She could not be more so."

MISS AMY M. BRADLEY.

MISS BRADLEY'S work of charity and self-sacrifice commenced on the 1st of September, 1861, a few weeks after the first battle on Manassas Plains. The sufferings of our sick and wounded had not then sent their strong appeal to the hearts of the noble and the charitable all over the land. She went out to seek as well as to save. Her first position in the army was as nurse in the Third Maine volunteers. She left East Cambridge, in Massachusetts, on the 28th of August, and entered upon that long series of labors for the soldiers — labors that varied with the demands of the hour, and with the shifting scenes of war; labors which took in the whole welfare of our suffering patriots, and met their calls for aid in every form.

Her early experience in the army was by no means repulsive. She was fortunate in her associations, for the colonel of the Third Maine was at that time O. O. Howard, that Christian gentleman and Christian soldier, the Havelock of the war. She found the journey over the road, where so many of our brave men had so recently passed, pleasant and full of interest. Arriving in Washington, she started at four in the afternoon for the scene of her duty.

"Very pleasant," she writes, "did I find the ride along

the banks of the beautiful Potomac, now studded with the white tents of our army, and protected by forts Runyon, Jackson, and Ellsworth, the latter being near our encampment. Twilight found me safe with the regiment, and surrounded by old familiar faces.

"It was tea time, and the band was playing a lively national air. I was ushered into the tent by our worthy surgeon, and introduced to Colonel Howard, the lieutenant-colonel, the adjutant, Mrs. Sampson the matron, and Miss Graves, who, like myself, is a nurse in the hospital.

"When we were seated at the table Colonel Howard meekly bowed his head and asked our Father's blessing upon the food before us. What, thought I, is this the rough life of the camp, which has so often been pictured to me? It reminds me more of a camp-meeting, only more quiet."

Her work commenced almost immediately upon her arrival, on the 1st of September. "I shall not soon forget that day," she has written in her hospital journal. "Dr. Palmer called at my tent in the morning, — a bright, sunshiny Sabbath morning, — and asked me if I would like to accompany him through the hospital tents. My hat was quickly donned, and we started. He was intending to select some of the sickest ones, that morning, to be sent to the General Hospital at Alexandria.

"There were four large hospital tents, filled with fever cases, resulting from exposure at the long-to-be-remembered battle of Bull Run. They were lying on mattresses placed on the ground. How sick they looked! No comfortable beds or soft pillows. It was terrible to see! We passed through the first tent, the doctor prescribing for each in turn. In the second were sufferers very delirious. These the surgeon proposed sending to Alexandria. As we stood by the side of one poor fellow, I spoke to him. He looked up with a lost expression, as though he never heard that voice before. 'Would you like to have anything?' said I. He looked up wildly, as before, and supposing that he was to start on some journey, said, 'I would like to see my mother and my sisters before I go home.' I burst into tears, and said, 'Please, doctor, do not send him away, but let *me* take care of him for his mother and sisters until he *goes home!*' for I knew by his looks he could live but a few days. So it was decided that he should remain, the doctor saying, 'If *that* is what you came for, we will give you plenty of work. I have another boy in a similar condition in another tent. I will have him brought in here, and you may take care of him for his mother. If he lives, you shall have the credit of saving him.'

"Thus I commenced my work. William (whom I had known when a boy, in Gardiner, Maine) lived; but my first patient, young Campbell, died a few days after.

"All the worst cases of fever were brought to me; and, from the first drum-beat in the morning till the last at night, I was busy enough, and very happy to know that I was able to alleviate the sufferings of many.

"At the end of September Colonel Howard was promoted to brigadier-general, and Dr. Palmer to a brigade surgeon. Dr. Brickett was made surgeon of the Fifth Maine volunteers, and I was transferred with him. I had been two weeks with the regiment, and had got the hospital in a fine condition, the Maine people having sent us some two or three dozen of bed-cots; and I, availing myself of an offer in a note Mr. F. N. Knapp wrote me soon after I arrived in the Third Maine, had drawn bedding, pillows, dressing-gowns, jellies, &c., from the Sanitary Commission, when General Slocum came to visit the hospital. 'How is this, Dr. Brickett,' said he, 'that your boys are so much more comfortable than those of the other regiments in the brigade?' 'O,' said the doctor, 'we have got a Maine woman here who understands how to take care of the sick. She has drawn these things from the Sanitary Commission, and has arranged the whole with some of the nurses' assistance.' 'I can't have any partiality in my brigade,' said the general. 'Give my compliments to Miss Bradley, doctor, and tell her I should be happy to have her take charge of the sick of the brigade. I will take the Powell House and the Octagon House, that are empty, a short distance from here, where we will move them all; and tell her I would like to have her go there and make a home for my boys.'

"Of course I accepted. Did it not widen my sphere of usefulness? How grateful I was to our kind-hearted general for allowing me the privilege of caring for his boys! The surgeons immediately made requisitions for iron bedsteads, straw bed-ticks, — about seventy-five, the number our two houses would hold, — and I made another requisition, on the United States Sanitary Commission, for quilts, blankets, sheets, pillow-cases, shirts, drawers, towels, &c. As the government had made no arrangements for brigade hospitals, supposing the sick from the various regiments would be sent to general hospitals, these things could not be obtained in sufficient quantities to supply a hospital like ours; and here I learned, as early as November, 1861, that a Commission like this was necessary as an auxiliary to government, and could be the means of mitigating a vast amount of suffering, and saving very many valuable lives."

On the 15th October the sick from the various regiments were conveyed to the places designated by the commander of the brigade, and there Miss Bradley established her head-quarters, taking with her two boys from the Fifth Maine — one to act as orderly, and the other to cook. She found a negro family living in a cabin in the rear, and old Aunt Hagar agreed to furnish milk, and do the washing for the hospital. The boys from the different regiments, detailed to carry out her wishes, commenced their work in earnest, and soon this "Home," the first established in any part of the army, assumed an appearance of comfort and cheerfulness.

The Powell House was just across the road from the first encampment of the Third Maine, and there commenced Miss Bradley's experience as hospital nurse. A peculiarity of her service from the first was the deep personal interest she felt in her patients. Her feeling towards a sick soldier was not that, here is suffering that I can alleviate, or, here is one of our brave defenders to be made well as soon as possible and sent to the front again; but, this is my boy Charley; I think I can save him; he over there is George ——; he is very sick, but if nursing can save him, he shall not die.

Of the patients in the first little hospital at the Powell House she speaks thus: —

"In the room at my right are six very ill. Do you see their pale faces? Three have typhoid fever: the two so emaciated have passed the crisis, and he with the large blue eyes has congestion of the lungs. How my heart aches for them! In the room opposite are four, three from the Mozart regiment; and that shadowy form, the fourth, has been my patient since my arrival, one month ago. He is rapidly recovering, after having been reduced very low with typhoid fever. Sometimes I am a little sad that I am left behind, and surrounded by strange regiments; but it is only momentary, for I note the light which beams in the faces of the sick ones as I enter the room."

This hospital was in operation all winter till the 15th of March, when the brigade was ordered to move on to Centreville, that place having been evacuated by the rebels. During this time Miss Bradley kept a private record of all the patients, and particularly of each death that occurred, and she seems to have taken a personal and vivid interest in a great number of the sick.

The first death that occurred was in November. Of the circumstances that attended the decease she speaks thus feelingly: —

"My first patient, Charles G. Nichols, died of diphtheria. I feel very sad. I did not count on losing any of my boys; but alas! the best of nursing cannot save them. His disease was too far advanced before he came into the hospital. He suffered very much, and was loath to have me leave him for a moment. He could not lie down at all. The night he died I talked with him about his coming dissolution. He seemed willing to depart. He had been a professor of religion for some years. On inquiring for his friends, I found his mother was own cousin to my brother-in-law, and that I visited her, with my sister and her husband, the year before I came out. How strange that I should be the one to minister to him, and to be able to care for him, and make his last hours as happy as possible! They have voted in our regiment to raise money enough to send home the body of every one who dies. We have had our Charley nicely packed in salt and saltpetre. There is a hot-house near by; so I have purchased some delicate flowers, and placed them around his pale face. How beautiful he looks asleep in death! We shall meet again. I have telegraphed to his friends in Damariscotta, Maine, as I found letters from them among his effects."

A few days after she makes the following entry in her journal, which throws a flood of light upon the character and the motives of the writer: —

"Many are the letters I write for the dear soldiers under my care, to their friends; and deep, earnest, heart-letters do I receive in return, filled with thankfulness that I am permitted to watch over them. But methinks there is not one among them who feels more thankful than does Amy herself. How happy I am in the performance of my duties! Although I suffer fearfully in losing a patient, still I am glad that my Father gives me strength from day to day to administer to their wants, and cheer them in the absence of nearer friends. I lost several dear boys the month I was in the Third regiment of Maine volunteers."

One of these "dear boys," whose life she labored to save with as much assiduity as if he had been an only brother, was Walter H. Davis. The account of his sickness and death is so touching, and so admirably illustrates the character of Miss Bradley, that we give the affecting story entire, as she wrote it in her journal at the time. He belonged to company C of the Fifth Maine regiment. "He was sick several weeks; disease, typhoid-pneumonia. He was a darling boy, so patient when he suffered so much! How his great blue eyes would brighten when I opened the door to enter his room! Once, I remember, I had been gone all day to the Octagon House (where a large number from the Sixteenth New York are sick). When I returned it was evening; I immediately went to see my sickest patients. When I asked him 'if they had taken good care of him in my absence,' he answered, 'Yes, but not as good care as you do.' And when I said, 'Why not?' he answered, while a faint smile irradiated his heavenly countenance, 'They don't love me as well as you do.' True, too true is it, that after having watched and cared for them so long, *I love them as if they were my own children.* Poor fellows! why shouldn't I love them? Away from every fond heart, how they do yearn for sympathy and kind words! A soldier's life is a hard one, and woe be unto me if I do not strive to alleviate their sufferings, and make them feel that one heart is full of pity and love towards them. I am almost sick from the loss of this dear child; I felt that I could not give him up. For fifteen days after the surgeons said he could not live the day out, I kept him alive by giving him nourishment and stimulants, or, as Dr. Burr called it, '*giving him doses of stick-to-him.*' That day he was in great distress, so that his groans could be heard all over the house; the blood was settling under the finger-nails, and the doctors said mortification was taking place in the bowels. I cried bitterly, and said I could not have him die. When he would look up with his great eyes and say, 'Don't cry for me, don't cry!' I was almost distracted. I prepared mustard, and covered his bowels, wrist, and feet, and gave him brandy frequently, when, to the surprise of all, the pain subsided, his feet and hands became warm again, and the doctors, when they came next morning, were astonished to find him alive and apparently better. Fifteen days after that he lived; but vain were my efforts! Dr. Brickett said his lungs were entirely broken down. Human skill or kindness could not save him. He died! — and another link bound me to the spirit world. Beautiful in life, in death his countenance was almost seraphic. A more finely moulded face I have never seen; a broad, high forehead, nose purely Grecian, with an exquisite mouth and chin. Flowers the most rare were thickly strewn around the body. He looked too beautiful to lay away in the dust; but such is the decree. The funeral ceremony was most affecting. The entire company, with the band, attended the corpse to the express, and my beautiful adopted boy was sent to his own mother. Did she feel worse than Amy did?"

On the 10th of March the brigade was ordered to Centreville. Five days after, the hospital was broken up and the patients moved, some to Alexandria and some to Fairfax Seminary.

Early in April Miss Bradley went forward with the division to Warrenton Junction. After various adventures, —

some of a rather exciting character, in crossing Bull Run,—she remained about a week at Manassas, and on the 13th the order came to return to Alexandria and proceed to Yorktown.

During the two weeks that followed, "long, dreary weeks," she calls them, she was awaiting orders to proceed with the command to Yorktown, at the end of which time she offered her services to the Sanitary Commission. On the 2d of May she went to Washington, and found Mr. F. L. Olmstead, of the Commission, had gone to Yorktown. She saw Dr. Jenkins, and hoped her offer would be accepted. The doctor telegraphed at once, and on the afternoon of Sunday, the 4th of May, the message came: "Send her to Yorktown immediately." On the day following she took the cars for Baltimore, stopped at the Eutaw House, and embarked for Fortress Monroe, in company with a party of surgeons and dressers. Miss Dix was on the same boat. The day following they were at Fortress Monroe, and the next day after Miss Bradley was made lady superintendent of the floating hospital Ocean Queen, which had been assigned to the use of the Commission. She took on board about a thousand patients. Several ladies were designated to assist her in the labor of nursing and care for so many sufferers on their way to New York, among whom, as very efficient workers, Miss Bradley mentions Mrs. Hyde and her lovely daughter Estelle. This cargo of suffering humanity was taken to New York; from thence the sickest were transferred to Bedlow Island, and the others to the General Hospital.

On the 21st of May she had returned to White House, and

was assigned to the Elm City, where she found several ladies, among whom were Miss Gardner, Miss Wheddon, Mrs. Strong, and Mrs. Balustier, engaged in the work of relief. Here commenced the most strenuous and the most painful service she had as yet seen. For the crowded and tragic days that followed, when the magnificent army of McClellan was being trailed through the mire of the Chickahominy, and pounded to pieces in the seven days' battles, the journal of Miss Bradley is very full, and gives an excellent picture of her labors, and the spirit in which they were performed.

"For several days," she writes, "we had been working admirably on the Elm City, when, about nine o'clock of the 26th of May, we received orders to transfer all our patients and stores to the steamboats L. R. Spaulding and Knickerbocker, as the quartermaster must have our boat immediately. The night was dark, but orders must be obeyed: the majority of the sick were conveyed to the Spaulding, some twenty of the feeblest to the Knickerbocker, and the next day the Spaulding started with her freight of human souls for New York, taking some of our best nurses with her. Mrs. Balustier, Miss Gardner, and myself were transferred to the Knickerbocker. Here we found Mr. Olmstead, Mr. Knapp, Mrs. Howland, Miss Woolsey, Miss Wormley, Miss Gilson, from Chelsea, Massachusetts, and others. Mrs. Balustier and I had a consultation, and concluded our services would not be needed there: so we decided to ask permission to go ashore, and work among the thousands left by the army as it advances. Mr. Knapp approved the plan, and agreed to pitch a tent, and make arrangements for us to work for the sickest ones.

"Wednesday, May 28, was ashore all day; carried some canned chicken, some crackers, some brandy, cologne, &c., and distributed them amongst the sickest. Returned to the boat towards evening, when, as I went aboard, I met Mr. Olmstead, who told me he wished me to take charge of the Knickerbocker, and put her in order to receive wounded men from the battle of Fair Oaks. I objected; he insisted, and, of course, carried his point, as he was to decide all things, being at the head of this enterprise.

"The next morning, the 29th, Mr. Olmstead and his party returned to the Wilson Small. The Knickerbocker was in a very filthy condition, and there were several state-rooms filled with soiled clothes, that were exceedingly offensive. The surgeon in charge, Dr. Swan, requested me to arrange matters to suit myself, furnishing me with all aid necessary. First, then, these clothes must be counted and sent ashore to be washed; four girls (colored) to be hired to wash on board the boat, so that no more should accumulate. Done. Second, see the captain of the boat, and have the crew, with the assistance of attendants, clean the boat. *They went to work with a will.* Mr. Knapp promised me bed-cots to fill the saloon on the main deck and lower one; promptly they were sent. There was a large quantity of clothing on board: this I arranged myself, so that I could know where to find each article needed. Meantime Mrs. Balustier left for home, sick, and Mrs. Annie Etheridge, of the Third Michigan, reported for duty. How faithfully she labored! We divided a little saloon at the forward part of the boat, leaving six berths on one side, and six on the other, making two rooms, the one occupied by the surgeon and his staff, the other by us.

"Sunday, June 1, found us nearly ready, our boat clean, our beds set up, and clothing arranged in order. About four P. M. the wounded began to arrive. I shall never forget my feelings, as, one by one, those mutilated forms were brought in on stretchers, and carefully placed on those comfortable cots. 'What,' said I, 'must I see human beings thus mangled? O, my God, why is it? why is it?' For nearly an hour I could not control my feelings. But when the surgeon said, 'Miss Bradley, you must not do so, but prepare to assist these poor fellows,' I realized that tears must be choked back, and the heart only know its own suffering! *Action* was the watchword of the hour. Then Amy was herself again. We received more than three hundred, some very badly wounded. One poor fellow, shot through the bowels, suffered the most excruciating torture, calling constantly for water: his thirst seemed insatiable. He died before morning.

"It was past midnight before they were all fed and composed for rest. Weary and sick at heart, I sought my pillow. Sunrise found us up, however, and ready to wash and dress the wounds of the sufferers, and change their battle-stained garments for clean hospital clothing. One solitary rebel was among the number of our wounded. He lay on the floor at the side of the boat; we were obliged to place many along the side, the boat was so crowded. As I was distributing the breakfast that morning, — my table was but a few feet from where he was lying, — my attention was attracted by a number of the attendants, who were collected there, talking to him, and by their language, I found their feelings were none of the kindest. About eleven o'clock A. M. I took a turn through the boat, to see if all had been properly attended to, and if there was anything more they needed for the present to make them comfortable. All seemed satisfied, and exceedingly grateful for the attention they had received from the surgeons, dressers, and nurses. The upper saloon had been divided into two wards, with Miss Gilson and Mrs. Etheridge in charge; the lower, under Miss Gardner and her attendant, Ellen, — a noble-hearted Irish girl, who never wearied in her labor of love, — with Mrs. Reading, assistant dresser.

"When I came to the 'rebel,' I stopped as I had to others, and bade him good morning. He was shot through the left wrist; the arm and hand were fearfully swollen and inflamed: his face was flushed; his breakfast lay untouched by his side. He said, in answer to my inquiry, 'My arm pains me very badly.' 'Can't you eat your breakfast?' 'I have no appetite.' 'Has your wound been dressed?' 'The doctor has not been along yet.' I called a colored boy (who assisted me), and bade him pull off the wounded man's boots, and bathe his feet. I brought a basin of cool water, washed his face and hands, and poured some upon the wound, telling him that the doctor would soon be there. He thanked me more with his countenance than with the words he uttered, though they expressed pain relieved and a grateful heart. His name was William A. Seawall, company H, Eighth Alabama regiment; his home in Mobile, Alabama. In the afternoon the surgeon in charge called me aside, and said, 'Miss Bradley, are you aware that you are subjecting yourself to severe criticism?' I started, surprised: 'Why, what have I done, doctor?' 'Don't be alarmed,' said he, smiling to see me so excited; 'it is your attention to that reb over there. I think you had better not do anything more for him, for many are criticising you very severely, and I am afraid it will do you harm, holding the position you do.' 'Doctor,' said I, 'I profess to be a Christian, and my Bible teaches me, if my enemy hungers, to feed him; if he is thirsty, to gave him drink: that poor boy is wounded, and suffering intensely; he was my enemy, but now he needs my aid. If I obey not the teachings of the Saviour, I am not a true disciple. I shall certainly see that he is cared for with the rest.' 'Very well,' said he, 'you have my advice, and can do as you please.' 'If you wish to criticise and blame me, I cannot help it; I shall do my duty, and take care of my enemy,' I replied. So I attended to my Secesh boy. Once, while talking with him, I found that, though wounded and a prisoner, his feelings were very bitter towards the North; still I saw that his wants were supplied with the rest, for the attendants had neglected him from the beginning.

"Tuesday morning, the 3d, we were ordered to take our wounded to Newport News. As I was passing where Seawall lay, he called to me — 'Mother, come here a minute.' I approached him: he put out his hand, which I took, and said, while tears welled up to his eyes, 'Mother, you have conquered me!' 'What?' said I. 'You have conquered me,' he replied: 'if I get well, I will never raise my hand against the North again; for, if I should, I should raise it against you; and that I could never do, after your kindness to me.' I blessed him for the good tidings, with tears running down my cheeks, for joy that I was able to do my duty amidst reproach, and reap the reward, not only in the consciousness of divine approval, but in winning one rebel by gospel measures to the side of truth and right. I related my interview to the surgeon, and told him they might talk on; it would do no harm; I had conquered the rebel by obeying the golden rule."

These labors upon the hospital transports continued till the termination of the Peninsula campaign and the removal of the army to Acquia Creek. During this time Miss Bradley was lady superintendent on the Knickerbocker and on the Louisiana, though sometimes engaged temporarily on the Daniel Webster and other transports.

On several occasions she was on board the truce boat which went up to receive the wounded who had fallen into the hands of the enemy; and we find several touching incidents in her journal, none perhaps more affecting than the following: —

"Our third trip to City Point was successful; we filled our boat with the poor sufferers. How glad they were to see once more the old flag, and meet kind friends! Several died soon after they were brought on board. Our surgeon performed a number of amputations, which I witnessed; one, in particular, I shall not soon forget. The subject was a lad of some nineteen years, a delicate-looking boy, who had been shot in the upper part of the right arm, near the shoulder. He was very patient, and could not bear the thought of losing the arm. His appetite was poor, and it was evident that he failed daily. The doctor said he must examine the wound. He talked with the little fellow, and finally obtained his consent to be put under the influence of chloroform, though not with the intention of amputating the arm, for he was not sure that it would be necessary to do that. But the cause of the daily decline of boy's health was quickly made evident. The bone near the shoulder-joint was badly fractured, and mortification was commencing. The arm must come off, or he could not live long; but the little fellow had not expected that. Should we arouse him and tell him, or should it be done at once, as it would have to be done anyhow? All said, 'Do it now; it will be better for the lad in the end.' A few minutes and the shoulder-joint had been unlocked, the arm taken off, the skin neatly closed over the bone, every sign of blood removed, and our hero, all unconscious of the operation, restored to consciousness again. I wish you could have heard our noble surgeon as he prepared him for the loss of that good right arm. He told him that he had examined it, and found the bone sadly fractured; he explained the necessity for amputation, — that he must die if it was not done, — talking so gently, and with the sympathy of a noble heart, till at last he said, 'Yes, you may take it off.' The doctor asked him if it pained him as badly as ever, and began to call his attention to the arm; told him what had been our consultation, and at last our decision. The effect for a moment was most distressing; he turned as pale as if he were dead. We thought for an instant he would die; but the soothing words and voice of the doctor brought the color again to his lips, and the brightness to his eye;

and, thanks to that gray-haired, whole-hearted surgeon, our pet rallied from that moment. In a few days there was a visible improvement; and when we transferred him he was in a fair way to recover.

"Many were very feeble, and I found that milk punch worked wonders with them. I told the boys, when their faces would brighten as I approached their bedside, that it was no doubt the 'snifters' which I brought. Those were days of labor and happiness! We had excellent officers and attendants, and all enjoyed life as much as possible."

After three trips in truce boats, Miss Bradley was on the steamer which took the sick from Harrison's Landing to Philadelphia. This was in the early part of August. Here she lost the aid of one of the most efficient of her co-workers, Mrs. Etheridge, who returned to the regiment in which her husband was enlisted. While the boat was coaling in Philadelphia, she met her whole-souled friend, Philip Eastwick, whom she had known as a noble laborer in the early part of the campaign, went with him to see some of her patients that had been removed some weeks before, and writes in her journal, "How glad they were to see me again!"

Returning now on the final trip, about the middle of August, she saw, with melancholy, the evacuation of the last strip of territory on the James which had been gained at a cost of fifty thousand men. When this last ship-load of the sick from the Peninsula was discharged, Miss Bradley was for a few days unoccupied, and recruited her health, that had been much worn by labors so strenuous and protracted.

But, early in September, her rest was over, and we find her transferred to another branch of the sanitary service, not quite so painful as had been her experience on the Peninsula, yet requiring more administrative talent and firmer executive and business qualities. To this service she brought the same warm heart and the same clear head that had made her so admirable in the hospitals and on the transports.

The Commission had found a great and growing demand for a Soldiers' Home in Washington — a house where the private soldier, often moneyless and always homeless, could go and remain a few days while awaiting orders; where the slightly sick and the convalescent could find the care and comfort they needed; where old, soiled clothing could be exchanged for new, and the old be washed; a place with books, and newspapers, and music, and cheerful looks and words, sanctified by the presence of woman, and not unworthy of the sacred name which was applied to it. Mr. Knapp requested Miss Bradley to take charge of the Home, put it in good order, act as its matron or lady superintendent, and administer its hospitalities. She accepted the invitation, and in a letter to her sister gives the following account of the institution and the manner in which she organized and conducted it.

"The Home is for all soldiers discharged from the service and awaiting the settlement of their accounts with government; for those who fall sick on their marches, and those of the new regiments who are taken sick while passing through the city. A great number of those admitted must remain each a few days, and we can accommodate about one hundred and twenty comfortably. When these poor veterans come in, weary and ragged, shirtless and with soiled raiment, Amy has the privilege of giving them clean, warm clothing for theirs, so torn and dirty; of feeding them, and sending them on their way. Mrs. Murray has the charge of the culinary department, and occupies, with her help, the first floor. I have charge of the rest. Mr. J. B. Abbott, a very efficient and just man, is the superintendent. I have two colored girls, who do the chamber-work, and an Irish girl for the washing and ironing. I find leisure to visit other hospitals, and do a great deal of good, I hope."

In one of these trips of hospital visitation she found a collection of sick and convalescent soldiers at the "Rest," and reporting their condition to Mr. Knapp, a reprimand from the medical director to some careless subordinate was the result. The person thus censured said "they would move them over the river, where these women couldn't get to them, and they wouldn't have the privilege of reporting on them again." Miss Bradley remembered this speech, and a few days after, armed with a pass from General Wadsworth, she made her way out to "Camp Misery," near Fort Ellsworth, and found there suffering and discomfort such as she had not seen before. During September, October, and December, 1862, besides her duties at the Home, which were always admirably discharged, she made frequent visits to this camp, and drew stores from the Sanitary Commission, and distributed them there with her own hands.

The energy and discretion she thus displayed, and the interest she manifested in the soldiers there, directed the attention of the Sanitary Commission to her as the most proper person to be made their special relief agent at Camp Distribution.

This was located near Alexandria, and about nine miles from Washington. Frequent inspections and reports had failed to reform its sanitary and social condition. From the nature of things it was eminently a place of discomfort. Here was sent the soldier who had been discharged from hospital, but was not quite able to shoulder his musket and march to his regiment; the soldier whose health and spirit were broken, and who was awaiting his discharge papers. Others were here who had received their papers, with the word "Deserter" branded in red ink across the back, yet who were conscious of having discharged the duty of a soldier, and who deserved well of their country. Some were very poorly supplied with clothing, having but a single cotton shirt in the cold nights of late November.

In the note from Mr. Knapp, releasing Miss Bradley from the superintendency of the Home, in order that she might devote herself to the alleviation of Camp Distribution, he says, "Will you please to show Mrs. E. all your methods by which you have made, and continue to keep, the Home so neat and well ordered?"

Miss Bradley's labors at Camp Distribution as special relief agent of the Sanitary Commission were more difficult, and required a better order of ability, than any to which she had yet been called; but whatever the talent or ability required, it was not found wanting when the demand was made. During this period of twelve months, one hundred and eleven thousand eight hundred and twenty-five soldiers entered the camp in passing from the military hospitals to their respective regiments, or to their homes, on certificates of permanent disability. To these soldiers Miss Bradley distributed a vast amount of commissary stores, yet with judgment, and after ascertaining, by personal knowledge, the wants of each.

She arrived on the 17th of December. On the 21st, when the soldiers were all assembled in line for inspection, she passed around with the officers, and supplied seventy-five men with woollen shirts, working on the principle of supplying only the very needy. She soon had a hospital, and began to nurse such poor fellows as she had gathered from those whom the doctors had pronounced well men. Others she found, whose discharge papers had been lying in the office for some time. But the men were too feeble to stand in the cold and wet and wait their turn. She carried them to her hospital, and warmed and clothed them, applied for their papers, and sent them into Washington, on their way home.

From May 1 to December 31, 1863, nearly all the soldiers discharged from service in the camp were conveyed by her to the Commission Lodges at Washington. The number thus kindly aided was over two thousand. When it is remembered that the majority of these men were suffering from incurable disease, prostrated in strength, and rendered highly sensitive to all the trials and exposures of transportation, the value of Miss Bradley's labors may be, to some extent, appreciated; but a few passages from her journal at Camp Distribution will illustrate the character of this uncommon and most admirable service.

"*December* 31, 1862. — Since the establishment of my

hospital, forty have been admitted. These have been washed (we have a nice bath-tub, which I bought with some money a lady gave me to buy crutches), and have received clean clothes in place of the soiled ones which they wore. I have a wash-house, and a man detailed, who washes the clothes as fast as they come out of the hospital. My whole establishment — my office, one cook tent, two hospital tents, bath-room (a wedge tent), wash-room (a wall tent) — is all in good working order. The officers have been very kind, and I feel with the new year I may begin a work which will be a blessing to the suffering in this camp, and a credit to the United States Sanitary Commission.

"*Tuesday, January* 20, 1863. — After attending to my patients in hospital, started, with my three discharged boys in my ambulance, for Washington. At Long Bridge overtook another poor fellow. Took him in, and proceeded to the Lodge. Mr. Abbott there took charge of the two feeblest ones, and I started for Major Pomeroy's office and Major Holman's with the others. One received his pay. The other was charged with desertion, and concluded to return to his regiment, to clear himself of the charge. Poor fellow! how I pitied him! I then took them in my ambulance, and carried them to the Home, where I bade them good by; thence to the medical director, Dr. Abbott, to ascertain what a soldier must do when he loses his discharge papers. He was very kind, and gave me the information. Returned, and wrote to Mrs. Jacob B. S., N. Oyster Bay, Long Island, whose husband had lost his papers.

"22*d*. — This morning made an appeal to the president of one of the Examining Boards in behalf of the sick boys in my hospital. It touched his heart, and notwithstanding the regular labors of the day pressed upon him, he agreed to come after examination hours. He came, and discharged several. God bless Dr. Hunt! I had seen him before, and worked with him among the wounded in the Peninsula."

From December 23, 1862, to April 1, 1863, the names of those who entered her little sanitary hospital, with their company, regiment, state, character of disease, and remarks on each case, were carefully recorded by her, and it appears that in that time she took care of one hundred and thirty patients, of whom only fifteen died.

In some of these sufferers she took a deep and touching interest. One fine boy, from Massachusetts, interested her very much, and she did all that care and skill could to save his life; but it was in vain.

On the 21st of February she writes thus affectingly about him: —

"My darling boy, Greenwood, died at four P. M. His father arrived about two hours prior to his death. He was perfectly sensible, and on being told he could live but a few hours longer, replied, "If I must die, I die in the cause of God and my country." He was wounded in the left cheek by a minie ball, during the battle of Antietam, and was in hospital in Newark, New Jersey, nearly four months, when, instead of discharging him, as was the surgeon's duty, he was cruelly sent to this camp. Came from Washington, in a tough snow-storm, January 28; stood with a squad at the receiving office till he was thoroughly chilled, before his name was recorded. His discharge papers were made out the next day after he arrived; but the cold he took coming through that storm settled on his lungs, and in three weeks after his arrival the noble boy passed to the spirit-land. The discharge papers came the day before he died. Too late! Only the lifeless body was his aged father permitted to carry to his home in Hubbardston, Massachusetts."

Labors and experiences like these consumed the whole of that memorable year 1863. Miss Bradley had her hospital full of the sick. Almost every day she took soldiers in her ambulance, and with them went to the different offices in Washington, aiding each one to obtain or correct his papers, as each case differed; and, when these arduous and vexatious labors were concluded, she passed her evenings mostly in writing to the friends of the sick and of the dead the most complete and satisfactory account of their sickness and all its symptoms, and the circumstances and last words of the death-beds.

When it is remembered that such labors were wholly gratuitous, and bestowed upon those who had no claim upon her sympathy and love, more than being soldiers in the cause of our common country, and bestowed in the name and for the sake of the loved ones they had left in their distant village homes, truly we may say of devotion so uncommon, —

"Earth has angels, though their forms are moulded,
Fashioned of clay, like all things here below;
Though harps are wanted, and bright pinions folded,
We know them by the love-light on their brow."

On the last day of the year, Miss Bradley, in a report to the special relief agent of the Sanitary Commission, gives a review and summary of these labors, which, aside from its intrinsic interest as an illustration of her character, is valuable as a guide to the zeal of those who aspire to a similar distinction in the walks of beneficence.

"The changes in this camp," she writes, "have been numerous and extensive since my establishment here. We have hardly a single officer, surgeon or soldier, now, that was present on my arrival. To labor systematically and with effect, where such important changes are constantly taking place, is difficult. How have I succeeded? Let us see.

"First, then: What was I to do? I had devoted myself to the general duty of alleviating the sufferings of the soldiers of the Union. To accomplish this most effectually, I must work upon a system. Now, what shall this system be? Can rules be established at once? I found, after a few days of effort and embarrassment, that they could not. You will ask, 'Why not?' Briefly I answer, Because any plan of mine which proposed an established routine, would operate, or attempt to operate, in the midst of a general anarchy. System there was none, in any department, military, commissary, quartermaster, or medical. State agents came with their stores of clothing, and gave them out profusely, without any investigation as to whether the recipient was needy or otherwise. The Commission had sent agents who had poured down their stores by the wagon-load, and these articles of clothing had been used once, and when soiled, thrown upon the ground, and left to rot by the thousands.

"I entered upon my duties as soon as the camp was moved to its present location, on the 17th of December, 1862. The soldiers were in tents; no barracks had been erected. Many I found sick, and stretched on the almost frozen ground in midwinter, with only a suit of ragged and fever-soiled clothes and one army blanket, with no nourishment that they could take, or that was suitable for sick men. What did I do? Did I, as some others have, sit down and prepare a fearful communication to the New York Tribune, making bitter complaints of the Sanitary Commission, and accusing the commanding officers of neglect and incompetency, — that the quartermaster did not furnish clothing, and the surgeons left their patients to languish, and finally to die on the bare ground? This was not my plan. Did I give indiscriminately from the abundant supplies of clothing to every man that asked? Not so.

"Making out a requisition in form, I drew a quantity of woollen shirts, and on Sunday morning, at inspection, I went with the officer, and found in the line of men, on that damp and chilling day, on the banks of the Potomac, in midwinter, seventy-five with only thin cotton shirts. To these I gave warm flannels at once; and ever since the really needy have been supplied. Then I went through the sick tents, and immediately after sought an interview with the commanding officer, told him my plan, and asked for hospital tents. These were at once pitched and floored. Stoves were placed in them, and the sick collected and made as comfortable as possible. A squad of men was detailed to assist me, and every facility placed in my power.

"Another wretched class I found, of those who had proved incapable of service on account of chronic ailments, or feeble constitutions, but who had not as yet received honorable discharges, or their arrears of pay. Their papers had been lying for three or four weeks in the surgeon's office, while they were too weak and ill-clad to go out in the cold and stand till their turn came. These I brought to my hospital; warmed, fed, and clothed them; applied for their papers; obtained their transportation orders, and sent them to Washington, in my ambulance, to the stations where they could take the proper train, go home, and die among friends.

"In January, 1863, Lieutenant-Colonel Samuel McKelvy took command, and the organization of the divisions became more perfect.

"At first I placed my cards, authorizing the bearer to draw clothing, in the hands of the surgeons, as there were two in each division. I found, however, they did not have leisure, or take time, to learn the actual wants of their patients as to clothing; so I had a soldier detailed in each division, whose sole business it should be to ascertain who wanted clothing. Now, when a soldier brings me a clothing card, I refer him to the agent of his division, who first examines his knapsack, to learn the actual condition of his wardrobe, then ascertains from the quartermaster whether he can draw, and, if not, gives him a written order on me, which I fill at once.

"Since the 1st of May I have gone over to Washington with nearly every discharged soldier, taken him to the Lodge, and assisted the majority of them in obtaining a prompt and satisfactory settlement of their account with the government.

"I have preserved, in a book kept for the purpose, the names, company, regiment, and state of nearly two thousand soldiers who have for the past seven months been thus aided by me. I took them first to the Lodge, No. 389 H Street, where they deposited their knapsacks for safe keeping; thence to the paymaster-general's office; thence to their regimental paymaster's, when any doubt or difficulty arose. Finally, they went with me to the office of Major Taylor, the paymaster for discharged soldiers, where they settled their final account, and I then took them back to the Lodge, where they resumed their knapsacks, found lodging and meals free, and obtained tickets to return to their homes at reduced rates.

"Within the past two months I have obtained certificates for the arrears of pay for some one hundred and fifty soldiers, several of whose names were 'dropped from the rolls.' These I have had reinstated by proper authority, and they then drew their pay. In nearly every case I have preserved in a book, kept for the purpose, the names, company, regiment, and state of all these cases, and a memorandum of the amount of their claim, and the time and manner of final adjustment. The sum total of the moneys thus paid in settlement to soldiers whose accounts were placed in my hands during the year, is between seven and eight thousand dollars.

"In conclusion, I will add, that I have always tried to accomplish my work by peaceful measures. Though I have made many suggestions, not one failed of being adopted;

but I carried none of them by storm. Opposed at times by state agents and by ambulance women, the Commission officers have always sustained me against their jealousies. For a time the agents of the Christian Commission failed to trust me with some articles of clothing, but afterwards 'concluded to leave all that to Miss Bradley.' Two assistant surgeons tried to injure my usefulness in the camp. The result was their dismissal from the service. I speak it not as a boast, but to show that my peace method has been successful."

A warm and appreciative friend of Miss Bradley has given the author a graphic and somewhat amusing description of the appearance of our heroine when she came over, day after day, from "Camp Misery," as the boys would call it, with a forlorn-looking escort of broken-down soldiers, and took them from one office to another till their papers and accounts were all made entirely satisfactory.

A small figure, erect, and made for activity and endurance, sitting composedly in the ambulance — a soldier driving, and two or three cripples riding; the rest moving in single file, as a right wing, — poor, sick soldiers, but trying to look as trim as they can, — marching up the avenues of the national capital, all in silence, moving after that little woman as though she were their brigadier-general! Now the procession comes to the door of a government office. She lifts one white finger of her little hand, and they obey as quickly as though General Hancock had roared out his "Column, halt!" She points towards the door. That means "file right," and is just as effectual as the drawn sword of General Grant.

Soon the file comes out again, as obedient to the movement of that one woman's fingers as the Great Eastern to her helm. It is shorter than when it went in. Two or three of the boys start off with more elastic step, their papers, "all right," in the side pocket of the old blue blowse, and a wad of new greenbacks in their vest pocket. They don't know what to say to Miss Bradley. Their sensations are a mixture of gratitude, admiration, and reverence. There was no tedious waiting at a circumlocution office. One cut of her scissors severed the red-tape with which their hopes and rights had been tied up for weeks and months. And so the little procession moves on from one office to another, till she takes them back to the Lodge, when the heavy and greasy old knapsack, all stained with Virginia mud, is lashed on for the last time, and they start off, in little irregular squads of two or three, with buoyant feelings and bright eyes, for the station of the railroad that goes north, for now

"Johnny comes marching *home.*"

Throughout the year 1864 Miss Bradley continued the same persistent and systematic labors for the soldiers which she has herself so well described in her report for 1863.

In January and February seven hundred and fifty were discharged, and sent in ambulances to the Lodge, where they were assisted by Mr. Neal, of the Commission, in the regulation of their papers, Miss Bradley being prevented by sickness from going with them.

About this time a radical change was made. Camp Distribution was broken up, but the same locality was named "Rendezvous of Distribution," and orders were that none should be sent there but deserters and men fit for field service. During these changes Miss Bradley was sick for some time from excitement and over-exertion. When her health was partially restored (about the 17th of February), she assumed the editorial chair of the Soldier's Journal, "published every Wednesday, at the Rendezvous of Distribution, at the subscription price of two dollars per annum, payable always in advance; single copies, five cents."

The objects of this Journal were declared to be, to give instructions how to procure pay and clothing when entitled to such; what are the requisites exacted by government when furloughs are granted; how discharged soldiers can be put in the way of securing prompt settlement of their accounts with government, without the interference of claim agents. Aside from this, it contained interesting original and selected reading matter. Its prospectus was dated the 17th of February, 1864, and it gave its valedictory eighteen months after, when the "cruel war was over," on the 22d of August, 1865. It began with a debt of five hundred and fifty dollars, and wound up with a profit of twenty-one hundred and fifty-five dollars and seventy-five cents, besides the press and type, all of which was devoted to the relief of orphans of soldiers.

Besides these editorial duties, Miss Bradley was, during a large part of the year, the superintendent of the special diet at the Augur General Hospital; and, by records carefully preserved by herself, it appears that during the two years ending December 31, 1864, she received from soldiers, and delivered to J. B. Abbott, the chief assistant of the general relief department of the Sanitary Commission, four thousand one hundred and forty-six dollars and fifty cents, to be forwarded to their friends, and in the same manner, during January and February, 1865, received and forwarded seven hundred and seventy-nine dollars.

The plan and system of her work were organized under ten heads, which she followed, from the beginning of her connection with this camp, in the winter of 1862, till the war ended. They were as follows:—

1. Distributing clothing among the needy.
2. Procuring dainties for the sick, and administering to their comfort, by furnishing gruel, stimulants, &c.
3. Accompanying discharged soldiers to Washington, and assisting them in obtaining their pay.
4. Distributing note paper and envelopes, and writing letters for the sick.
5. Receiving and forwarding money for soldiers to their friends at home.
6. Obtaining certificates of arrears of pay for soldiers, and getting unjust charges of desertion removed.
7. Answering letters of inquiry to hospital directory.
8. Distributing reading matter in camp.
9. Telegraphing to friends of very sick soldiers.
10. Giving meals to feeble soldiers in the barracks.

Little credit would be reflected on our brave soldiers and officers if it should appear that services such as these failed of due appreciation and the meed of just praise. By all she was looked upon as the friend of the soldier, and by him she was received with the kindest regard and gratitude. On the 22d of February, 1864, she was presented with an elegant gold watch and chain by the officers and private soldiers of Camp Convalescent, with which she had so long been connected. "It was about two P. M., on the 22d," she says, "that, on answering a rap at my door, I was met by a little army of soldiers, headed by Lieutenant-Colonel Samuel McKelvy commanding, and Surgeon Sanford B. Hunt, accompanied by the chaplain, William J. Potter, and the other officers of both camp and hospital. As I opened the door, Mr. Potter stepped forward and said, —

"'Miss Bradley: Be not alarmed at the coming of this army to your door. We are not hostile, but come on a friendly mission; and here I have the *countersign* that will show that we are friends. In this box you will find a watch and chain, which, in behalf of the officers and soldiers of this camp and hospital, I have the honor to present to you.

"'I present it to you in behalf of the officers, some one of whom, who has been longer acquainted with your work here than I have been, I would have preferred to speak on this occasion; but I know that I speak for them, for I but repeat what I have heard from the commanding officer and from the surgeon in charge of camp and hospital, and also from others, when I say that they recognize the importance of the work you are doing here, and the remarkable ability, faithfulness, and entire self-devotion with which you have performed it; and they recognize this work not only for its beneficence to the soldiers, who from time to time have been gathered here, but as an important aid towards the good order and discipline of the camp; and by their share in this gift they mean to testify this recognition of the value of your services.

"'But I present this gift also in behalf of the private soldiers; full half of its value belongs to them. They in various ways have felt your sympathy, and had your kind assistance. No words of mine can tell in how high regard they hold your work for them.

"'By their share in this gift they have tried to tell you a part of their gratitude; and those who have not been able to add their mite to increase the value of the gift, give you their blessings and their prayers.

"'Let me add, also, that we welcome you back to health, and to the work you love so well. And now, in behalf of these your friends, and many others who are not here, allow me to put into your hands this token of their appreciation and friendly regard — a gift from soldiers to the Soldiers' Friend.'"

In some form or other nearly every officer who saw her works has given his opinion of them, sometimes in terms that do all that can be done by words to show the deep impression she made on the minds of those with whom she came in contact during those four years of her conspicuous and splendid beneficence.

Colonel Taylor, of the paymaster's department at Washington, under date of August 17, 1864, writes, "Since March 4, 1863, I have been in charge of this office, and from that date Miss Bradley has assisted more than two thousand discharged soldiers in adjusting and collecting the amounts due them. To the sick and wounded she has ministered faithfully. Her services have been valuable to the Commission, to the country, to the soldier, and honorable to herself."

Mr. E. H. Brooks, chief clerk in the office of the paymaster-general, and ten of his associates, unite in presenting to Miss Bradley a testimonial of their esteem and their valuation of her service, in which they say, "We desire to bear testimony to the deep interest which you have always manifested in the welfare of the sick and wounded soldier, and the valuable services you have rendered in procuring arrears of pay, and in removing erroneous charges of desertion, for hundreds of those who stood in need of a friend. While we regret that the poor soldier is to be deprived of your valuable services, we trust that in your retirement from the busy scenes in which you have so long been engaged, you may enjoy health and prosperity, and all the blessings that flow from a well-spent life."

Dr. G. L. Sutton, surgeon in charge of the Rendezvous of Distribution, referring to her labors there as he saw them during the year 1864, says, "Her notoriety as 'the soldier's friend' is wide spread, and needs no comment. If he needs a counsellor, her advice is ever ready. If his case needs an advocate at the heads of the departments, she is prompt and discreet in presenting his case. The sick she has nursed as a mother, and the well she has incited to deeds of valor. Possessed of superior executive ability, associated with a generous heart and honesty of purpose, she is peculiarly well qualified to fill the position of special relief agent of the United States Sanitary Commission. I would in the most earnest manner recommend her to all who appreciate true worth, and would reward true merit."

After the close of the war, in August, 1865, the officers

of the Commission noticed with pain how deeply these long and arduous charitable labors of Miss Bradley had intrenched upon her health; and the organization, acting through their general secretary, John S. Blatchford, Esq., addressed her the following letter: —

"Your impaired health, incurred in the performance of your self-imposed and most arduous labors for the welfare of our soldiers, is observed by your friends with solicitude and regret.

"The service which you have rendered in the cause of humanity, and the influence you have exerted, resulting in untold alleviation and comfort to those to whom you have ministered in many ways beyond the ordinary experience of women, are such as to secure to you the lasting regard and love of all who have known you in your work. That work has been characterized by rare judgment, great efficiency, untiring zeal and devotion. It is above praise.

"It will afford me, on behalf of the Commission, especial satisfaction if I can in any manner promote your personal comfort during the period of relaxation and rest which you now allow yourself; and I will thank you if you will indicate any wish in this connection, and permit me the pleasure of serving you."

In reply, Miss Bradley thanked the secretary for the terms in which he had seen fit to speak of her services, and suggested that, as she greatly needed rest and a change of scene, and her limited means did not allow her to take a trip to visit her friends in Maine, the Commission should give her a salary for that part of the current year then passed.

On the following day she received a note from the central office, enclosing a draft for four hundred and fifty-five dollars; and the treasurer remarks that, "in his judgment, the Commission had never expended a dollar more worthily, or with more perfect returns to the good cause."

He closes his communication with a sentiment which every reader of this sketch will heartily indorse: "Your course as related to the soldier, Miss Bradley, is beyond any words of mine. It has illustrated to me, more perfectly than any other instance I have ever seen, the nobility of woman's sacrifice to truth and right."

MISS REBECCA R. USHER.

VERY early in the struggle the people of Maine entered warmly into the plans and labors of the Sanitary and Christian Commissions. But in addition to these national organizations it was generally felt that some more special and direct system was required for reaching all the Maine boys in the army, and making sure that the bountiful supplies given by the people at home did not fail of their purpose.

More effectually to accomplish this object, a society was formed in Portland, in the fall of 1862, called the "Maine Camp and Hospital Association," the various members of which held themselves in readiness to respond to any call for hospital nurses that might reach them from the front. Aside from Mrs. Fogg and Mrs. Eaton, who were the pioneers from the state in sanitary labor, Miss Usher was among the first to enter upon the work of humanity, and devote herself to the alleviation of the untold and unmeasured sufferings produced by the great war.

Her first experience was at the General Hospital at Chester, in Pennsylvania. This had been opened early in the spring of 1862, at the time of the Peninsular campaign, and was for some weeks supplied with nurses by the ladies from the village. As some disagreement arose between these occasional laborers and the surgeon in charge, he sought to change the system of hospital service, and secured Mrs. Tyler, of Baltimore, as lady superintendent, requesting her to call to her aid a suitable corps of skilful and permanent assistants.

Mrs. Tyler sought volunteers exclusively as being more intelligent, more refined, and more devoted to the welfare of the soldier than those whose labor was salaried.

The little band she secured as aids was composed of Miss Sarah Tucker and Miss Kendall, from Boston; Miss Dequindre, from Michigan; Miss Hattie Southgate, daughter of Bishop Southgate, of New York; Miss Ellis, of Bridgewater; Miss Titcomb and Miss Newhall, from Portland; and Miss Usher, from Hollis, Maine.

The large building erected for a normal school was appropriated to the use of the surgeons and the ladies of the hospital. Most of the amputations were performed here, and the building was also used as a special ward for such patients as were so ill as to be disturbed by the noise of the crowded wards, and whose recovery depended on the most watchful attention. They had under their care nine hundred patients in the fall, and during a considerable part of the winter of 1862 and 1863. These were distributed in barracks, each barrack being divided into wards, with from sixty to seventy men in each; every lady having a ward in her special charge, except Mrs. Tyler, who was lady superintendent, and visited all. The immediate and constant nursing was performed by soldiers detailed for the purpose. Government supplied the ladies with a daily ration costing fifteen cents, and a free pass on the cars; and this was all they sought or desired, as remuneration, beyond the consciousness of doing good, and a conviction that their labors directly promoted the final success of the Union arms.

Among the severely wounded, requiring special attention, was a Confederate officer from South Carolina, who had been captured in one of the great battles on the Chickahominy. The bone of his shoulder had been terribly crushed by a fragment of a shell, so that his right arm was lashed to his side for eight months. He was in Miss Newhall's ward; but Miss Usher often called to see that all his wants were supplied, and became quite interested in him as the first specimen of a genuine and full-blooded Southerner that had come under her notice in the hospital. At times he would grow strong enough to walk up and down the halls every day for a week or two; and then, his wound opening afresh, he would sink almost to the verge of the grave. He was but twenty-one years of age, and as his wound became worse, his suffering depressed his spirits to the lowest point. At such times the ladies used every method to cheer him. They found him well educated, and intelligent, gentlemanly and refined in his language, and polished in his manners. He was graceful, yet abundant, in his expressions of gratitude for the kind treatment he received. One day, when Mrs. Tyler's name was mentioned, he exclaimed, "She's a noble woman, and ought to live forever!"

He spoke freely of the conflict going on between the sections, and seemed to regret it very much, saying, if the southern and northern people could have been brought together, and exchanged their real sentiments on the value of the Union to all the states, there would have been no secession and no war, and added that, if he ever lived to get home, he should do all in his power for the Union prisoners.

One day, in the spring of 1863, he asked Miss Usher if the North considered their currency worth anything. "O, yes," was the reply. "If I had money to invest, I should put it into United States bonds in preference to anything else." He looked surprised, and added, "Well, we know ours is worthless." In another conversation that took place soon after, the young South Carolinian gave a chapter from his plantation reminiscences that seemed strangely in contrast with the refinement he had hitherto manifested.

"He was telling me about his father," says Miss Usher; "what a careless and indulgent master he was, and that he wanted him to take charge of the plantation. 'This,' he went on to say, 'I agreed to do on one condition — that I should have entire control of the negroes. After some hesitation, father consented, and I went to work and laid down the rules for them. They early found out that I would as soon flog father's favorite negroes as any others, and they began to be afraid of me.

"'One day I sent a boy to the grist-mill with a load of corn. He was absent the greater part of a day, and, when he came back, said the miller wouldn't grind it. I took him right into the wagon and drove back to the mill, ascertained that he had been spending the day with the free negroes in the village, had given out the better part of the corn among them, and reached the mill too late to have the grinding done that day. I turned to the boy, and said, 'Jerry, you deserve a good threshing for this, and you shall have it too!' He started to run. 'Run,' said I, 'if you dare!' But when he thought about it he concluded to stop and take the whipping. He was afraid I would fire. I had no idea of that, but if he had taken to the woods I would have had my hounds after him, and pulled him down in five minutes!'" "His story shocked me," says Miss Usher; "yet I did not argue the case, but left him to be instructed by the logic of events. He ran through his narrative with as much frankness and *sang-froid* as a northern man might speak of dismissing a servant that did not suit him. It had never occurred to him that setting bloodhounds after an escaping slave was improper treatment *for negroes*. Yet towards white people no person could be more considerate or polite. At another time he said, 'I don't see how you northern people can stand it to have negroes brushing by you on the sidewalk. I should knock them down.'" In May, 1863, this polished champion of southern institutions was so far recovered as to leave the hospital. He was taken to Baltimore and exchanged, so that Miss Usher heard no more of him and his views of plantation discipline.

The next incident that Miss Usher relates is entirely different.

"One evening," she writes, "Miss Titcomb and I were sitting in Mrs. Tyler's reception-room when we were startled by the sound of loud weeping in the hall. It seemed like the voice of an old man; and we went out to witness one of those touching reunions that can occur only amid the desolations and fearful uncertainties of a great war.

"An old gentleman had just arrived from Iowa to see his

son, who had been very ill. This son was nineteen years of age, and the youngest of five brothers, all of whom were marching and fighting under the same flag. This one, while on a visit to his older brother's family, in Illinois, enlisted in the army of the Mississippi, while his four brothers were in the Missouri division. The father had managed with much difficulty to carry on the large farm alone, as it was found impossible to hire labor. After various experiences in the West, the youngest of these five soldier boys had been transferred to the army of the Potomac, and marched under Burnside to those awful and hopeless charges on the intrenched lines at Fredericksburg. A minie ball pierced his breast, wounding the left lung, and coming out near the spine. Though apparently a mortal wound, the vigor of his constitution had carried him past the point of greatest danger, and he was nearly well when he went out to the water-side to see a monitor launched. The exposure was too great; a cold fastened upon the injured lung, and his life was despaired of. When lowest he had sent a message to his father from ward A to come on at once. But before his father reached Chester his boy had been removed to ward D. When the old man arrived, having travelled night and day fifteen hundred miles, hoping and praying that it might not be too late, he saw some soldiers, and asked them if they were from ward A. They said they were. He then asked if his son was there, describing him and giving his name. 'No; there was no such man in ward A.' Presently he met another squad from the same ward, who gave the same report. Then the old man's heart sank within him. But he came up to the hospital, and inquired of several surgeons for such a patient in ward A. They knew nothing of any such man. Finally, a surgeon from ward D happened to be present as the father was repeating the description, and without saying anything, sent for the young man to come to the office. Summoned thus peremptorily, the poor boy crept off his cot, and came slowly forward through the hall, supposing that a false charge had been made against him, and he would have to march off to the guard-house. In a moment he found himself clasped in his father's arms. It was their first meeting for two years. The father said it seemed to him as though he had him back from the grave, and, like another Jacob, he lifted up his voice and wept.

"He was so pleased with the hospital and satisfied with the attention his boy received, that after much debate he concluded to leave him there; and yet he would add, his eye growing moist again, 'I don't know but it will kill his mother, when she sees me coming back without him!'"

In the early part of the summer of 1863 the Chester hospital was broken up, and for about eighteen months Miss Usher was not engaged in army work. Early in the winter of 1864 and 1865 we find her again at the front, near Petersburg, actively laboring for the Maine boys. The hut in which she lived and the life of excitement and hardship which she, with Mrs. Mayhew and Mrs. Eaton, led, are described in a series of letters addressed to her friends at home. The following by Mrs. Eaton, dated City Point, December 8, 1864, gives an account of their establishment there, and the way in which their log hut was built: —

"For a week we have been very busy. The First Maine

heavy artillery detailed men to cut our timber for the stockade. The second and third batteries sent teams to haul it; the second battery and first battalion of Maine sharpshooters have sent their men to put it up. We are under great obligations to them for their kindness, as it is against military regulations to detail men from these grounds for such a purpose.

"Our stockade is now all up and chinked, but we have no door or fireplace. Our roof is of canvas, and we use rubber blankets, quilts, and bed-sacks for doors. A nice little army stove was given me for our use on yesterday. To-morrow we expect to build the chimney; and all this is being done while we live within. You may imagine the confusion, with our pile of stores in the centre, to give room to set up the logs, and a long procession of our boys continually coming for what is frequently at the bottom of the pile. The stockade is forty feet by fifteen, and contains three apartments: at the entrance is a reading-room, which we mean to make literally a 'Soldier's Home,' then our own dormitory and store-room, and in the rear the cook-house. We wish to keep our reading-room supplied with late Maine papers, and with stationery, that the boys may have facilities for writing here. Sacks, boxes, and barrels are piled six feet high on every side."

Here these ladies staid, and devoted themselves to the work for which they left home, for six months, until Richmond fell, Lee capitulated, and the war was over.

On the 8th of February Miss Usher writes home as follows: —

"Our vegetables, twenty-eight barrels, came on Monday,

via Baltimore, and yesterday the boys opened them and picked them over, throwing away those that had been frozen on the passage. There were twenty barrels of good potatoes to distribute. All day the soldiers roasted them in the ashes of the reading-room fire; and some would ask us for a strip of salt fish, and thus made out, as they said, a luxurious meal. Could you see how glad the men are of them, you would feel that it pays to send them, even though a fourth are lost by freezing. The soldiers come in and ask for a potato, as if it were the most delicious peach, or a bunch of Hamburg grapes. A Pennsylvania boy, sick in one of the wards, heard Mrs. Mayhew say our potatoes had come; but she supposed they were all frozen, they had been so long on the way. The next day she received a note from him, asking if she would be so kind as to let him have a few of those frozen potatoes. Of course we sent the poor fellow some nice ones."

On the 7th of April, just after the great closing battles of the war, Miss Usher writes home as follows: —

"Dear E.: The wards are filled with the wounded. It is estimated that there are ten thousand patients in the hospitals here, and our Maine regiments have suffered severely. We are very busy, doing all in our power to alleviate suffering. Eleven hundred badly wounded were brought in on one day. In the evening the wards are dismal enough — long and narrow, without floors, dimly lighted with lanterns, and resounding with the groans of the sick and dying. Mrs. Mayhew and Mrs. Sampson go to the front to-morrow. One of us will work there all the time now.

"A few days ago I saw Bridget, who came out with the

First Michigan cavalry, and has been with the regiment ever since. She had just come in with the body of a captain who was killed in a cavalry skirmish. She had the body lashed to her horse, and carried him fifteen miles, where she procured a coffin, and sent him home. She says this is the hardest battle they have had, and the ground was covered with the wounded. She had not slept for forty-eight hours, having worked incessantly with the wounded. She is brave, heroic, and a perfect enthusiast in her work. Bridget said to me, in her earnest way, 'Why don't you ladies go up there, and take care of those wounded men? Why, it's the worst sight you ever saw. The ground is covered with them.' 'We should like to go,' I said, 'but they won't let us.' 'Well, they can't hinder *me*,' she said; 'Sheridan won't let them.'"

Mrs. Mayhew, in speaking of her life before Petersburg, during the winter and spring of 1865, refers to Miss Usher in the following language: "My labors here were shared by Miss Rebecca R. Usher, of Hollis, Maine. By her warm interest in the cause, and her highly cultivated mind, she added much to my happiness, and lightened those days of toil."

In a letter home, dated the 28th of May, and written from Alexandria, Miss Usher gives the following incidents of her hospital experiences there and at City Point: —

"One of our patients — a young man, twenty-two years old — had an amputation of the thigh bone, near the body, and we nursed him very anxiously, hoping he might recover, yet fearing the worst; but in a few days he was seized with one of those slight chills which do not seem an alarming symptom, but to the eye of an experienced surgeon indicate great danger. As he was gradually sinking, I wrote daily to his mother, informing her of every change. One morning, as I was standing at his bedside, he took a package of letters from under his pillow, and handing them to me, said, 'I want you to keep these for me.' Then he gave me a lady's ring, saying, feebly, 'If I die — you — will answer these letters — won't you? — and return — the ring.' Waiting some time, to gain a little strength, he said, suddenly, 'Bend your ear close down to my lips.' I bent over him, and he said, in an earnest tone, as if his whole heart was in the words, '*Tell her I loved her all the while!*' 'I will,' I said; when he looked into my face with a satisfied expression, and soon fell asleep. Shortly after I found it my duty to open the package and perform the sad work to which the dying lover had commissioned me.

"Mrs. C., a widow lady, living in Houlton, Maine, had lost one son in the war, and came to our hospital in search of her youngest boy, from whom she had received a letter, stating that in battle before Richmond, he had lost one leg, was wounded in the other, and was on his way to City Point. After waiting a fortnight, and hearing nothing more from him, she set out for Washington, and wrote to us for information. The state agent, Mr. Hayes, searched the hospital records through, but could find no account of him. Then she came down to City Point, but we could give her little encouragement. The supposition was, that he had died on the way from one hospital to another, and was buried as 'unknown.' Mr. Hayes, however, offered to go up to the front, and hunt for him. Next evening he returned with the cheering report that he was alive and doing very well in one of the hospitals. 'Now,' said I, 'Mrs. C., you'll sleep to-night—won't you?' 'O, no,' she replied; 'I'm too happy. I can't sleep now till I'm at his side.' And the next day she joined her boy."

MRS BYCKERDYKE.

Engraved Expressly for the Women of the War.

MOTHER BYCKERDYKE.

AMONG the many noble women whose names will be forever enshrined with those of the brave defenders of their country, that of Mrs. Byckerdyke, of Illinois, will be held in especial honor. From no merely romantic impulse, but acting from the dictates of her mature sense of duty, she entered the service of the country as a volunteer nurse for its soldiers early in the war, and continued her work of patriotic charity until the war closed. By all those who remain of the armies who conquered their way down the Mississippi, Mrs. Byckerdyke is affectionately and gratefully remembered, as one of the most constant, earnest, determined, and efficient laborers for their health and comfort in the hospital and in the field.

Mrs. Byckerdyke, who is a woman of middle age, commenced her labors for the soldiers in August, 1861, when—at her own solicitation, and because her judgment was confided in—she was sent from Galesburg, Illinois, to Cairo, to ascertain what was needed by the troops stationed there. After ascertaining the condition of affairs there and reporting, her Galesburg friends advised her to remain, which she did, exerting all her energies to remedy the many miseries attending the establishment of a large camp of soldiers, nearly all of whose officers were as ignorant of camp discipline as themselves. When the battle of Belmont sent a large number of the wounded to the Brigade Hospital at Mound City, she went there, and remained until the most of them were sent to their homes.

Returning herself to her home, she barely continued long enough to put her household in order for a more prolonged absence. She had enlisted for the war. At the bloody field of Donelson — where the sufferings of our wounded were most distressing, from the lack of medical attendance and the severity of the weather — she was untiring in her efforts for the poor fellows. She took a prominent part in shipping five boat-loads of wounded men, her kind and motherly care doing more than aught else to save the soldiers from neglect. Hardly through with this severe labor of love, she was in a few days called to Pittsburg Landing, to assist in the care of the immense numbers of wounded men for whom the provisions of the medical department were not half adequate. She stationed herself at Savannah, ten miles below Pittsburg Landing, where the most of our wounded were brought. An incident of her experience while there will illustrate her character better than anything we can say. It was told us by an officer who was at Savannah at the time.

Governor Harvey, of Wisconsin, had been visiting the field of battle, and the hospitals there and at Savannah, to learn what was the condition and what were the wants of the soldiers from his state. He had a small but excellent staff of volunteer surgeons, and ten tons of the best sanitary supplies. He saw every sick and wounded Wisconsin soldier individually, and gave to all the medical attendance and sanitary supplies they needed. Our informant could not restrain the tears as he recalled the kind acts, the cordial and sympathetic greetings of this noble-hearted governor, whose life was so suddenly ended in its prime by a distressing casualty. After his work was through, Governor Harvey met our friend at the Savannah levee, perfectly satisfied that he had done all in his power, and happy that he had been permitted to do so much good. He had still five tons of sanitary stores left, and had been in great doubt as to what to do with them. He distrusted the surgeons in charge at Savannah, and finally concluded to turn over the stores to Mrs. Byckerdyke. He had known nothing of her antecedents, and had only seen her while at Savannah. Still, as he told our friend, he observed how efficient she was, with how much business-like regularity she was performing her work, and that honesty, decision, and judgment seemed written on her plain, but good-looking face. He would trust her, and no one else.

After the governor's death, Mrs. Byckerdyke began to suspect that her supplies were diverted to the private uses of a certain surgeon's mess. She resolved to stop that, and did, in a very summary manner. Going into the tent of this surgeon just before dinner, she discovered on the table a great variety of the jellies, wines, and other comforts belonging to her stores. She at once made a clean sweep of these articles, went straight down to the levee, took a boat to Pittsburg Landing, saw General Grant, and within twenty-four hours had the guilty surgeon under arrest. The surgeons had little disposition to interfere with her or her stores after this example, and the sick and wounded men rejoiced to find that their faithful friend had won so complete a victory.

Occupied all the time of the Corinth campaign with the wounded in the rear of General Halleck's army, she was put in charge of the Main Hospital at Corinth, when our force entered that place. While there her indomitable force and determination to serve the soldiers had another trial and another victory. Learning that a brigade was to march through the hospital grounds, and knowing that the soldiers would be nearly exhausted from their long march under a burning sun, she got out her barrels of water which had been brought for the men in hospital, had a corps of her assistants ready with pails and dippers, and gave the soldiers water as they passed through. When the commanding officer came up, Mrs. Byckerdyke asked that the men be halted; but he refused, and, going ahead, ordered his men to march along. At the same time a voice in the rear — that of Mrs. Byckerdyke — was heard giving the reverse order, "Halt!" in very clear tones. The woman's order was obeyed, and the "Tin Cup Brigade" worked energetically for a few minutes, rejoicing in the triumph of *their* commander.

At the siege of Vicksburg Mrs. Byckerdyke undertook the difficult task of correcting abuses in the use and distribution of sanitary supplies. The lasting gratitude of the sick and wounded, and the approval of the higher officers in command, attest the fidelity and efficiency with which she executed this trust. She was not at all times a welcome guest to the agents and officers having in charge sanitary supplies. One of these latter applied to headquarters to have a woman removed from his hospital, on the complaint of improper influence. "Who is she?" inquired the general. "A Mrs. Byckerdyke," replied the major. "O, well," said the general, "she ranks me; you must apply to President Lincoln."

After the battles of Mission Ridge and Lookout Mountain she remained in the field thirty days, till the last of the wounded were removed to northern hospitals, working with all her remarkable energy, and with her untiring determination, that the soldiers should be well cared for. On the Atlantic campaign she followed the army with a laundry, and had daily from fifteen hundred to two thousand pieces wsahed, besides the bandages and rags used in dressing wounds. In addition to this work, which was more than enough for one woman to perform, she superintended the cooking for the field hospitals, and, when the commissary stores failed, supplied the tables from those of the Christian and Sanitary Commissions. To meet emergencies, she has been known to take passage in an afternoon train, ride fifteen miles, get her supplies to the hospital, and have the bread baked and distributed to over a thousand patients the same day, and in proper season.

Perhaps a good idea of the nature and value of the labors of Mrs. Byckerdyke can best be given from an extract of a letter, written from Chattanooga by Mrs. Porter,—another noble laborer for the soldiers,—soon after the battle there. Mrs. Porter says,—

"I reached this place on New Year's Eve, making the trip of the few miles from Bridgeport to Chattanooga in twenty-four hours. New Year's morning was very cold.

I went immediately to the field hospital, about two miles out of town, where I found Mrs. Byckerdyke hard at work, as usual, endeavoring to comfort the cold and suffering sick and wounded. The work done on that day told most happily on the comfort of the poor wounded men.

"The wind came sweeping around Lookout Mountain, and uniting with currents from the valleys of Missionary Ridge, pressed in upon the hospital tents, overturning some, and making the inmates of all tremble with cold and anxious fear. The cold had been preceded by a great rain, which added to the general discomfort. Mrs. Byckerdyke went from tent to tent in the gale, carrying hot bricks and hot drinks, to warm and to cheer the poor fellows. 'She is a power of good,' said one soldier. 'We fared mighty poor till she come here,' said another. 'God bless the Sanitary Commission,' said a third, 'for sending women among us!' The soldiers fully appreciate 'Mother Byckerdyke,' — as they call her, — and her work.

"Mrs. Byckerdyke left Vicksburg at the request of General Sherman and other officers of his corps, as they wished to secure her services for the then approaching battle. The field hospital of the Fifteenth (Sherman's) army corps was situated on the north bank of the Genesee River, on a slope at the base of Missionary Ridge, where, after the battle was over, seventeen hundred of our wounded and exhausted soldiers were brought. Mrs. Byckerdyke reached there before the din and smoke of battle were well over, and before all were brought from the field of blood and carnage. There she remained the only female attendant for four weeks. Never has she rendered more valuable service.

Dr. Newberry arrived in Chattanooga with sanitary goods, which Mrs. Byckerdyke had the pleasure of using, as she says, 'just when and where needed;' and never were sanitary goods more deeply felt to be *good goods*. 'What could we do without them?' is a question I often hear raised, and answered with a hearty 'God bless the Sanitary Commission,' which is now everywhere acknowledged as 'a great power for good.'

"The field hospital was in a forest, about five miles from Chattanooga ; wood was abundant, and the camp was warmed by immense burning 'log heaps,' which were the only fireplaces or cooking-stoves of the camp or hospitals. Men were detailed to fell the trees and pile the logs to heat the air, which was very wintry; and beside them Mrs. Byckerdyke made soup and toast, tea and coffee, and broiled mutton, without a gridiron, often blistering her fingers in the process. A house in due time was demolished to make bunks for the worst cases, and the brick from the chimney was converted into an oven, when Mrs. Byckerdyke made bread, yeast having been found in the Chicago boxes, and flour at a neighboring mill, which had furnished flour to secessionists through the war until now. Great multitudes were fed from these rude kitchens. Companies of hungry soldiers were refreshed before those open fireplaces and those ovens."

We will merely add a few words in conclusion. Mrs. Byckerdyke not only performed a great work in the field, but several times visited the leading cities of the North-west, and by her judicious advice did much to direct aright the enthusiastic patriotism and noble charity of the ladies of that region. They needed no stimulus to effort. Distinguished from the outset of her efforts by her practical good sense, firmness in maintaining the rights of the soldiers, and an unceasing energy, she was soon known among all the western soldiers as one of their best and most faithful friends. In addition to the consciousness of having performed her whole duty, Mrs. Byckerdyke has another reward in the undying gratitude of the thousands of gallant fellows who have received or witnessed her motherly ministrations. May she live long to enjoy both of these rewards for her good deeds.

MRS. ANN HITZ.

IN all the large cities along the border there were a number of ladies whose age or whose family cares did not allow them to leave home for sanitary enterprises, who, notwithstanding these circumstances, performed a large amount of very valuable hospital service. Washington city, especially, furnished many of these local visitors, and among them none, perhaps, was more active, or impelled by higher motives, than the wife of the resident Swiss consul, Mr. John Hitz.

The circumstance that Mrs. Hitz is a foreign lady makes her conduct the more praiseworthy. Many of the ladies were drawn towards the army by the strongest ties. They had sons, brothers, husbands, and old neighbors in the various regiments. In hospitals they often met those they had known all their lifetime, and when bathing a fevered head, or bandaging a shattered arm, the thought would often arise, "Perhaps some other woman is at this moment doing this very kindness to my brother." But the charity of Mrs. Hitz could have no such incentives. The union of the American states was a political question in which she could not be expected to feel a direct interest. The number of Swiss enlisted in the Union ranks was small; but the fact that she spoke the languages of Central Europe, and could appreciate the feelings of the Germans, and address them in their mother tongue, made her presence in the Washington hospitals peculiarly grateful to that large class of recruits who could speak but little English.

"My labors among the soldiers," says Mrs. Hitz, "began with the first arrival of volunteers in Washington. The weary, travel-worn men, thankful for a kind word, a cup of coffee, a piece of bread, were always made welcome by my husband and myself. It was some time before I saw the necessity of the Aid Societies, and other organizations, which we afterwards found so useful.

"Among the arrivals of troops just before the first battle at Bull Run were the Twelfth and Twenty-fifth New York. They were quartered on Capitol Hill, near the Gasparis House. Wet and weary when they arrived, no preparation had been made to receive them, no refreshments were at hand, and the commissary arrangements were imperfect. Our house was near the camp, and my husband threw open our doors, and we went to work with a will.

"All the boilers we could find were filled with coffee, and we collected all the bread we could either buy or beg. Among these volunteers we found some little German drummer boys, one of them so homesick for his mother! 'O, madame,' he would exclaim, 'may I come and see you every day? You are so like my mother!' Poor boy! In a day or two marching orders came, and they went out to that first, disastrous battle. When he came to bid me good-by, he said, 'Please pray for me and my comrade; 
he has no mother.' The tears fell as I asked God to bless

them both. They were in the engagement the next day; one was killed and the other taken prisoner, but managed to make his escape.

"My husband, as Swiss consul, and a member of the German Aid Society, visited the hospitals almost daily, and becoming well known, whenever a patient was brought in whose language could not be understood, we were sent for. One poor man from New York City, whose mind was much affected by his sufferings, could not be induced to take any food except such as I cooked and carried him. In his delirium he imagined that I was indeed his mother, and that the nurse was trying to poison him.

"On his return to the North, as he passed through Baltimore, he recognized the place where the regiment to which he belonged had been attacked by the mob, and recovered his wandering senses. From his brother I afterwards received a letter of grateful acknowledgments for what I had been able to do for him in his suffering and helpless condition.

"One of the nurses at Armory Square Hospital sent me word that there was a patient there whose language no one of them could understand. On going down I found a poor German, suffering sadly from a wounded limb, unable to make his wants known, and apparently about to die.

"As soon as I spoke to him, the effect of a few words of his mother tongue operated like magic. For some time I attended him daily, and all seemed well, till one day a sudden change came upon him. He sent a special message to me, and I took with me a priest to his bedside, as he was a Catholic. We saw him die in peace.

"After the great battle of Antietam, when even the Capitol was crowded with the wounded, Dr. Campbell came to me one morning, and wished me to visit one of his patients in the old House of Representatives. I found there a poor fellow from Pennsylvania refusing to take either food or medicine, but begging for some one to pray for him. I knelt by his cot, and when I arose he was calm, and willing to do anything I advised him. He recovered, and always insisted that it was that prayer that saved his life.

"At Mount Pleasant Hospital there was another patient who had not found any one who could understand a word he said, till they sent for me.

"He was delirious, and believed the nurses, and even his own wife, who had now come to attend him, were trying to poison him, and he would not take a mouthful of food. After praying with him and dressing his wounds, he grew calm, and consented to do everything I wished of him.

"Several cases like this came under my care, and I found no difficulty in managing them. My only secret was, that I never lost patience with them, listened quietly to all their complaints, sympathized with their hardships, and gradually led them to do what was for the best."

Miss Hall, Mrs. Fowle, and all who were active in the Washington hospitals, unite in their praises of Mrs. Hitz. Hundreds of sick and dying Germans made her their mother confessor, and she could be seen almost every day sitting by the cot of some sufferer, and reading blessed words of heavenly consolation in tones that recalled the fatherland and the home from which they were so far away. She was beloved and honored by a great number of

American soldiers, whose names she never knew, and whose faces she has forgotten.

"When travelling in the East," she writes, "I have been at many places unexpectedly recognized by fine-looking young men, who came forward with, 'Mother Hitz, don't you remember me?' My experience," she adds, "among the American soldiers has been altogether a most pleasant one. Certainly more patient, God-fearing men could not be found in any army; and it is but a just tribute to the young men of this country for me to say, that in all my visits among them in camps and hospitals, as long as the war continued, I never heard a word improper for the ear of a lady."

"AUNT LIZZIE" AND "MOTHER."

AMONG a great number of unostentatious, but effective and noble-hearted hospital nurses, who labored with the sick of Grant's and Sherman's armies in the West, two, who went from Peoria, Illinois, deserve special mention.

Neither matrons nor lady superintendents, they have left a record of love, admiration, and gratitude on the hearts of thousands whom they saw and nursed in the hospitals.

They were Miss Lizzie Aiken and Mrs. Sturgis, or, as the soldiers always called them, "Aunt Lizzie" and "Mother."

Although they labored at other points, it is for their work in the Memphis Hospitals that they are principally known and most affectionately remembered.

Their appearance, language, service, and the extent of their usefulness will best be understood from the letters of soldiers who were under their care, and saw most of their life at Memphis.

Charles M. Kendall, a Wisconsin soldier, writes, "On the 2d of February, 1863, I was sent to the Adams Hospital, in Memphis, having met with a serious accident in breaking one of my shoulders, so as to disable me for field service. The first word of consolation that I received was from 'Aunt Lizzie.' She came to me with these words: 'My dear boy, what can I do for you?'

"I felt sure from that moment, that, as long as she staid in the hospital, I should not want for anything. After I was able to do duty, I was put in charge of one of the wards. There I had an opportunity of seeing what the ladies were doing to alleviate the sufferings of our brave boys. About this time I also became acquainted with 'Mother.' Every one called her by that name; and for me, it was easy to follow their example, for she seemed to have the feelings of a mother for all of us. I do not suppose any soldier ever asked for anything he ought to have, that she did not procure it. If she could not get it of the Commissions, she would buy it for him with her own money. I saw her in the wards by night and by day for months, preparing and giving suitable food to the sickest of the men.

"A careful observation of over two years has taught me that nursing is fully as important as medicine. In the wards where there was the best nursing, there were always the fewest deaths.

"When the sanitary stores were nearly expended, these ladies hit upon the idea of getting up a Soldiers' Fair, from which they realized quite a large sum of money. Whenever they could find time, they would go from house to house asking for donations.

"Though spurned from some doors, and insulted at other houses, they never faltered, but kept on till they were successful. The money thus obtained was judiciously expended, and the amount of good accomplished cannot be estimated.

"Towards the close of the war, when some of the Andersonville prisoners were brought up the Mississippi River, the boat on which they came remained several hours at Memphis. These ladies were soon on board, working with a will; and many a poor, starving soldier was feelingly refreshed in body and mind by the visit of these angels of mercy. Often did I hear the exclamation, 'God bless that woman! Why, she talks just like mother; and who is she, that she takes so much interest in my welfare?'

"Then, again, when that terrible disaster took place, the explosion of the Sultana, as usual they were on hand, doing all in their power for the sufferers. I have known a great many men in their dying moments send for some lady to come and talk with them. How often have I seen 'Mother' sit by their cots and point them to the Lamb of God! Doubtless many a soul is happy in heaven to-day, saved through the influence of that Christian woman in the dying hours of life.

"These ladies can never receive their full reward till they hear the welcome plaudits in the blessed kingdom. Many other ladies there were, who, for their noble course, deserve all the praise that words can bestow. Some of them are dead, and their names will never appear in human histories; but the good they accomplished will never be forgotten by us private soldiers."

Another soldier, Charles P. Hopkins, of Indiana, furnishes the following charming sketch of 'Aunt Lizzie' in the hospital, and the reputation these ladies enjoyed among the western soldiers: —

"I entered the United States army," says he, "Company

K, 7th Kansas cavalry, John Brown, Jr., my captain, in September, 1861. Nothing worth record occurred till October, 1862, when we were at Rienzi, Mississippi, and took part in the ever-memorable battle of Corinth. There I first saw the true heroism of our noble northern ladies, flitting from one to another of the wounded, speaking words of comfort, cheering the depressed, binding up wounds, moistening the lips of those from the front who came nearly perishing with thirst and loss of blood.

"Soon after this battle I was taken sick, and sent to Paducah, where I heard boundless praises of 'Aunt Lizzie' and 'Mother Sturgis.'

"So often did I hear them mentioned, and in terms so warm, that I came to look upon them as angels in disguise.

"In March, 1863, I was discharged, but during the following summer regained my health, and reënlisted in the 7th Indiana cavalry. The winter following, was very severe. Many of our boys fell a prey to disease, myself among the number. On the 1st of March, 1864, I was sent to the Adams Hospital, in Memphis.

"Hear I first saw 'Aunt Lizzie,' of whom I had heard the boys speak in such exalted terms. I was very sick at the time. Three of my comrades had been numbered with the dead, and I had given up all hopes of again

'Mounting barbèd steeds to fright the souls of fearful adversaries,'

but lay calmly waiting for what might come, when 'Aunt Lizzie' came through our ward. How well do I remember that evening! Let me describe her as I saw her then. A little old lady, dressed in brown, with a red sontag over her shoulders; black hair, interlaced with silver, and neatly brushed. She carried a pair of silver-bowed spectacles in her left hand, and with the right, which looked smooth and soft, she grasped the hand or stroked the forehead of every patient as she came to his bedside, all the while speaking words of comfort, and throwing out her sympathies broadcast, with smiles so winning and motherly, that tears would moisten our eyes, and great unspoken words of love and gratitude well up from the hearts of us poor sufferers as she passed.

"When she came to my cot with that kindly touch on my forehead and the stereotyped inquiry, in a tone so sympathetic that it could never grow old, 'Well, my boy, how do you do to-day? Are you better?' it was too much for me. I cried, and could have fallen down and done homage to a spirit so saintly. From that hour I began to get well, and was soon strong enough to do light service around the hospital. So they made me baggage master, and I had charge of all the boys' knapsacks as they were brought in. I often visited 'Aunt Lizzie' and 'Mother Sturgis' in their room, and found that they gave, not only the whole day, but a part of the night, to these labors of charity. The day was spent chiefly in the different wards in nursing the sickest patients. After the gas was lighted, there they sat, 'Mother' on one side of a table, 'Aunt Lizzie' on the other, mending the blue regulation pants or the frock of some neglected soldier boy, or darning a pile of socks, and singing, 'Home, sweet home,' or, 'We are coming, Father Abraham.'

"It was a treat to go through 'Aunt Lizzie's' ward with

her. She knew the state from which every one of them enlisted, and would say, 'How are you now, Wisconsin?' or, 'How does my Michigan boy feel this morning?' and, 'Indiana, how is he?' and so on all through the ward. They would smile in all their pain when she was talking with them. Did they ask for anything, she did all in her power to procure it for them, frequently taking from her own scanty allowance to purchase an article if it was not among the stores. Never weary, always ready; no matter at what hour, if help was wanting, she was there.

"And 'Mother'—no day was too long or night too dreary for her. Often I found her at midnight beside the cot of some poor boy about to enter the vast Unknown; the tear of sympathy in her eye, putting to his lips some cooling draught, or trying to stay the fast-ebbing sands of his life with some carefully-mixed punch or egg-nog, the materials for which she had bought from her own slender purse. There were others in this hospital who performed excellent service—Mrs. Brake and Jenny Matheson in wards B and C. Letty Covell was to be found from early dawn till late at night in the diet kitchen of ward B, and Mrs. Webb in the kitchen of ward A, while our two noble 'Maggies,' as we called them, Miss Miller and Miss Staffer, had charge of the linen-room."

No correct estimate can ever be had of the good accomplished by these quiet, earnest, Christian nurses during the four years of their unceasing devotion.

When the war was almost over, "Aunt Lizzie" stated to a friend that she had kept count of nearly all, and it was then about three thousand soldiers to whom she had read passages of the Bible, with whom she had prayed, and whose eyes she had then closed in death. In how many cases these dying exercises were of unspeakable importance to the parting soul, is known only to the recording angel. But in reflecting upon such opportunities of Christian usefulness so admirably improved, we are permitted to suppose that they will not fail to win for her at last the golden sentence, "They that turn many to righteousness shall shine as the stars forever and ever."

MISS MARY E. DUPEE.

MISS DUPEE, of Portland, Maine, for about a year acted as a nurse at the Naval School Hospital, in Annapolis, and afterwards went to the Union lines before Richmond, as an agent of the Maine Camp and Hospital Association, where she remained till the war ended.

She went to Annapolis, in company with Miss Susan Newhall, of Portland, on the 3d of August, 1863. These young ladies here found a broad and most interesting field of labors, engaging at once the activities of the hands and the deepest sympathies of the heart.

Miss Dupee had thirteen wards assigned to her for regular visitation, each ward containing from six to eight cots; and much of the time every cot was occupied.

The majority of the patients at this hospital were Union soldiers, just released from the horrible and infamous rebel prison pens at Andersonville, Salisbury, Belle Isle, and the Libby. Here they came, in all their rags and squalor, to be clothed, fed, nursed, and cheered; to be consoled into forgetfulness of the atrocious scenes they had so long witnessed; to be reassured of the gratitude and sympathy of their friends at home; many of them, alas! only to have their eyes closed by Christian hands, and their skeleton frames laid to rest in Christian graves.

They dropped the filthy rags that hardly covered their wasted forms outside the doors of the building, and after being thoroughly washed and dressed in clean shirts and drawers, were laid in comfortable beds. Then the ladies could commence their ministries of sympathy and kindness. At first the poor fellows, starved as they were, did not think much about food. They were content to lie perfectly still, and wonder if it was really so, that they were alive and dressed in clean clothes, and if these were real women who came to their bedsides with cambric handkerchiefs fragrant with cologne, giving them words of the tenderest pity, more refreshing than their perfume.

As soon as they were in some degree comfortable, the first request was for paper and pen and ink, that they might write home. Many were too weak to do this for themselves, and the ladies in those cases acted as secretaries. Nothing seemed to give more satisfaction than to have a lady pass some time at their bedside and listen to the fearful story of their life in the stockade — the horrors, the sickness, the slow starvation, the uncounted deaths.

In two or three days, those whose constitutions were not entirely sapped would commence to rally; and then such hunger! Their diet was regulated by the surgeons, but considerable discretion was allowed Miss Dupee and her associates in adding to the regular fare such harmless delicacies as custards, eggs, jellies, with which they were liberally supplied by the different Commissions. Miss Hall, the lady superintendent, says that many of them, when recovering, had apparently no other aim or thought beyond getting enough to eat. Yet so deep had been the inroads of the long succession of hardships upon those constitutions, which a few months before were vigorous, that it was a long time before the most generous diet seemed to restore health. Many would rally, and mend for some weeks, and then in some unaccountable way be found dead in their cots in the morning. Some believed that rebel malignity had added a slow and subtile poison to the little food they had to eat in the stockade.

The ladies visited each patient once a day, and the very sick as much oftener as possible; reading to some, writing for others, talking with all.

"We are not used to this sort of treatment," they would say, "but rather to being spit upon, like dogs!"

The soldiers called the ladies "sunbeams," and they were justly proud of the title. One would slowly turn his head to find among the cots the bearded face of a fellow-sufferer, and then call out, "I say, partner, don't it seem like a streak of daylight to see these girls walking around our beds here?"

Among the Belle Isle prisoners Miss Dupee found a very interesting boy, from Durham, Maine, only eighteen years old. When she first saw him he was lying on his cot looking so happy and contented that she could hardly think he had a trouble. He showed some bad-looking sores on his feet and hands which were quite painful. His head and eyes were so weary and weak, that he could not read; and she made it a special duty to pass an hour every day with him, reading to him and talking. Nothing appeared to give him so much pleasure as her visits. He seemed in a fair way to recover, and could sit up occasionally, and go out on the walk a little while when it was pleasant. The surgeon said he would never be fit for line service again, as his sight was dimmed, and he told him he would try and get him a discharge. This delighted him very much; and as she entered the ward he exclaimed, "O, Miss Dupee, the doctor has promised my discharge to-morrow. Are not you glad?" She congratulated him, and assured him of her heartfelt sympathy. She had brought a few lines of poetry, which she found in a newspaper, and read to him. Then she bade him good night. Two hours after he sprang suddenly from his bed in a convulsion, and expired almost instantly. Poor fellow! it was not the discharge he was looking for.

Another of her patients lived in St. Louis. He had been very ill, and was promised a furlough as soon he could bear the journey. He improved rapidly, and wrote home the good news that he would be strong enough to start in a few days. Two of his sisters had deferred their wedding days while he was in prison, but when he was so much better, concluded to wait no longer, and were married the same evening. All at once his disease assumed a new form, and he entered upon his rest. Touching and sad beyond comparison was the letter Miss Dupee received from his sisters in answer to hers, giving all the details of their brother's death and burial.

After passing nearly a year in these wards of the Naval School Hospital, Miss Dupee, early in the year 1865, went to City Point and joined Mrs. Mayhew and Miss Usher, who were devoted principally to ascertaining and relieving the wants of soldiers from Maine.

The association in Portland, though not large, was very active, and kept these noble women abundantly supplied with everything that could in any way add to the comfort and happiness of the men.

The Maine agency was a wonder in the army before Petersburg, and the care taken by that state of her volunteers a subject of remark among all the troops. "Next time I enlist," was a frequent saying with the boys, "it will be in a Maine regiment." Many belonging to other states came to the Maine agency. The ladies always helped them when they could do so without denying their own men. Sometimes those who claimed to be from Maine did not know whether it was the name of a town, a city, or a state. Some amusing revelations of geographical knowledge would often take place when Mrs. Mayhew or Miss Dupee would question them about their homes in Maine. But the rule of confining the supplies to men from that state was by no means strict, and few ever left the "log cabin" without taking with them something from Maine.

After the capture of Richmond the agency was removed to Alexandria, and there Miss Dupee and her associates continued to search for men from their state in the hospitals, and to supply the wants of the Maine regiments within their reach, until the grand armies of the Union were disbanded, and the great hospitals emptied.

In reviewing her camp and hospital labors, Miss Dupee says, "I look back upon my time passed in this work as being the most satisfactory of any period in my life. I shall ever be thankful that I was able to contribute in any degree to the comfort of our brave soldiers, for it is an experience that I prize above everything else. God grant that those who have been spared may never have cause to feel that they are neglected or despised by those in whose defence they gave up everything but life itself!"

MRS. ELIZABETH MENDENHALL,

AND OTHER WORKERS AT CINCINNATI.

IN most of the important cities near the border there were a large number of those who became, during the war, regular hospital visitors, devoting a part, and often the whole, of each day to the sick and wounded whom they found in the wards of the various military hospitals. In Cincinnati, where there were suffering soldiers from the summer of 1861 till the conclusion of the war in 1865, among the most active and constant in these labors was Mrs. Mendenhall. Though reared in Richmond, she was one of those Southern women whose natural kindness of heart and sympathy with suffering prevented her from ever defending or sustaining the social institutions of that portion of the country; and when the rebellion broke out, though her relatives were citizens of the South, a war for the perpetuation of slavery seemed to her so utterly unjust and iniquitous, that all her sympathies were enlisted on the side of the Union and its defenders. At the first call to arms she was active in suggesting and regulating the industry of those sewing circles which were organized in all loyal communities, and which were so useful in perfecting and renewing the wardrobe of our volunteers.

Early in the year 1862 Cincinnati began to be a hospital

centre for the army operating under General Grant, and in a few weeks was filled with the blood-stained heroes of Fort Donelson and Pittsburg Landing. For the two years and a half that followed, Mrs. Mendenhall was a constant hospital visitor and nurse. She always spent half, but more frequently the whole, of each day among the sick and wounded, working in any capacity that she could to increase their comfort. As her excellence in judgment and skill as a nurse became known, the surgeons in charge gave her great facilities and such needful authority to regulate the affairs of each ward as she thought best. She enjoyed, also, the entire confidence of the United States Sanitary Commission, and had an understanding with its agents, by virtue of which she could go to their rooms and take supplies of anything she found on hand suitable for her patients.

On the recurrence of the national, holidays, as Thanksgiving and Independence, she was specially active in securing, from a generous public, a bountiful supply of provisions, to enable the wounded and convalescent soldiers to forget the grim necessity that separated them from their own homes.

Labors and charities of this character occupied her time until the fall of 1863, when her activity took a larger range, and was exhibited on a more conspicuous theatre.

It was the pen of Mrs. Mendenhall that first stirred the citizens of Cincinnati to emulate the splendid enterprise of her sister and rival city, Chicago, in the inauguration of the Great Western Sanitary Fair. In that noble work she took among the lady managers the position of leader, as well by her natural force of charaeter, as by the excellent spirit which prompted her labors.

She prepared and sent abroad among the communities of the great North-West an appeal to all classes and ages, every trade and occupation, and all the professions, to contribute whatever they could to make the Fair a magnificent success, and give it the scope of a national enterprise.

Another and special appeal was also made by her to "Patriotic Young Ladies of the North-West, and of Cincinnati in particular, interested in the welfare of the soldiers," asking them that, "instead of laboring to make valuable presents, on the approaching holidays, to those who did not stand in need of comforts, that they make such articles and donate them to the Fair, for the benefit of those brave men who had sacrificed home, friends, and all that was dear to them, to defend *their* homes."

During the months of November, December, and January, Mrs. Mendenhall was wholly engrossed with the business of the Great Fair, and she and all her co-laborers were abundantly paid for their exertions in the unequalled success with which those splendid works were crowned. The princely sum of two hundred and fifty thousand dollars was realized, and paid over to the United States Sanitary Commission, as the result of the Great Western Sanitary Fair of Cincinnati.

After the excitement and labors of the Fair were ended, Mrs. Mendenhall resumed her customary round of hospital visits. This course of life continued till the war ended, and the military hospitals of Cincinnati were disorganized. While the war lasted, during four years, she had not been absent from the city, or failed of her customary hospital visits, for five days. Among the very great number of different soldiers whom she saw in her visits, many interested her very much by the patience with which they bore their sufferings, and by the spirit of unquestioning and unbounded loyalty which animated their breast, and inspired their actions.

One, in particular, who died in the hospital, seemed to her the most profoundly patriotic of all whose death she had witnessed.

His name was William Starr, a man in humble life, and a private in one of the Ohio regiments. He was brought in from the front very dangerously injured by the kick of a vicious horse. The blow had fallen upon the breast, and he had frequent and dangerous hemorrhages from the lungs. It did not seem possible that he could live many hours, and his sufferings were very acute. Mrs. Mendenhall, and other ladies in the hospital, paid him special attention, and soon had the satisfaction of seeing him much better, and able to walk slowly around the room. He improved gradually, and left the hospital, returning to service, so that his kind benefactor lost sight of him for three years. But the wound never fully healed, and his lungs at length commenced to bleed worse than at first. He was brought to the same hospital, and hearing the name of Mrs. Mendenhall mentioned by a lady who was standing over him, sent for her, at the same time speaking in the warmest terms of her former kindness. The tears started down his fine face, stamped with the noblest traits of manhood, but now fearfully pallid, as he grasped her hand, and prayed God to reward her in this life and the next for her kindness to him and other suffering soldiers. He lived a number of days, and each day, as long as he could lift his hands, wished to see the papers, that he might know how the battles were going. The only earnest wish that he expressed was, that he might live long enough to hear of the capture of Richmond.

One April morning the glorious news was proclaimed through the hospital wards that Richmond was evacuated, and Lee, with his army, in full retreat. "Now," said the dying soldier, "now I am ready to go." He had but one request to make — that, when he was stiff in death, he might have the American flag laid over his body, and then be buried in Spring Grove Cemetery on the soldiers' lot. Just before he drew his last painful breath, a little son of Mrs. Mendenhall went to bid him farewell, and carried in his hand a little flag, with which he was playing.

As the glazing eye of the patriot caught sight of the colors, he stretched out his hand, and taking the little banner from the boy, waved it several times, his eye meantime lighting up with the ardor of a soldier and the flush of victory. This was his last act; and when his tall figure was prepared for the grave, Mrs. Mendenhall went with a friend, and succeeded in finding a very handsome silk flag, which they laid over him till his coffin received the form of the dead soldier.

Associated with Mrs. Mendenhall in these voluntary and unsalaried labors for the soldier were other ladies of

Cincinnati, many of whom were as praiseworthy, though less prominent than herself.

Miss Elizabeth Morris, and her married sister, Mrs. Ellen Thomas, commenced their hospital visits as soon as there was any call for such work, and gave themselves wholly to these charities, refusing all offers of pay from the medical department, until, in 1864, a rule was passed excluding all unpaid nurses. Under these circumstances, they for some months drew a nurse's pay, half of which they gave to the hospital fund, and applied the other half towards furnishing substantial and palatable food for the private soldiers' table. They continued this Christian work and charity till the hospitals were emptied and dismantled by the culminating successes of the spring and summer of 1865.

The wife of Colonel C. I. Wright, of Cincinnati, was also among the first to assist largely in the hospitals, spending the greater part of her time in alleviating the sufferings and discomforts of the soldiers.

Her labors were not confined to the hospitals, as she was very efficient and untiring in preparing and distributing comforts in various ways to the soldiers of her husband's regiment in the field.

Mrs. C. W. Starbuck, Mrs. Peter Gibson, and Mrs. Jonas, all residing in the city, gave much of their time to the hospitals, and were extremely liberal in furnishing large supplies of various comforts and delicacies for the wounded.

Mrs. William Woods, Mrs. Cadwell, and Miss Eckstein were also frequent visitors. Miss E. C. Smith was a frequent, and, much of the time, a constant hospital visitor while the war lasted; and Mrs. Kendrick, a sister of General Anderson, proved herself worthy the name of that Christian patriot and soldier, by a devotion to the sufferers, that was equal to his fidelity to the flag in far-famed Sumter, where the war began.

LOYAL SOUTHERN WOMEN.

IN many parts of the South the sentiment of fidelity to the Union was cherished by both sexes with as much warmth as by any in the loyal states who volunteered their services for hospital duty, or gave up their sons and husbands to the call of patriotism.

Throughout the mountainous regions of Kentucky and Tennessee this spirit was in the ascendant; and when the rebel forces made their numerous raids through the Cumberland Mountains for plunder in the rich counties of Middle and Northern Kentucky, they were sure to encounter the most vigorous hostility from the scattered and persecuted, but unterrified, loyal men and women, whose cabins are nestled in the lonely coves and glens of that wild region.

In the fall of 1862, when Bragg and Kirby Smith made their swift and inglorious retreat from Kentucky through Cumberland Gap, they were sharply pursued by Rousseau. One morning the regiment in the van, the Twenty-third Kentucky, when about twenty-five miles east of Wildcat Mountain, were greatly surprised to see a squad of ragged Confederates come filing slowly into camp disarmed, and a woman walking behind them with a musket in her hands. There were eleven of the Confederates, and the woman handed them over to the colonel as prisoners of war.

She said they came to her house the night previous, and finding that her husband was a volunteer in the Union lines, proceeded to help themselves promiscuously to everything they fancied. Some ran down the chickens, and began to kill and eat, while others cut up her carpets for horse blankets, and committed wanton depredations about the house. The incensed woman remained quiet, but watched her opportunity. Presently they were all collected in the largest room, and making merry over the fire, having left their muskets in a stack near the door. Weary, and suspecting no mischief in a solitary woman, they relaxed their watch, while she quietly removed all the fire-arms but two loaded muskets, which she took in her hands, and, standing by the door, demanded a surrender. One of them, more alert than the rest, made a spring for the muskets, but fell dead on the floor with a ball through his body. She told them quietly that any further attempt to escape would be met by a similar fate. As they had a resolute foe to deal with, discretion now became the better part of valor: they submitted to the fortunes of war, and at daylight she marched them into the Union camp as described.

Noble Act of two Tennessee Women.

During the same autumn, when Grant was commanding in West Tennessee with headquarters at Jackson, the twenty-seventh Iowa was ordered to take the cars at Corinth and proceed to Jackson. It was night time and the train was crowded, men occupying the platforms and covering the roofs of the cars. As he approached a bridge, the engineer saw two lanterns in the distance swung to and fro with the greatest earnestness. He gave the signal of danger; the breaks were instantly applied, the train stopped, and men sent forward to ascertain the cause of the alarm. Two women were found at the bridge, who said the coming of the loaded train of Union soldiers was known to a gang of guerrillas which infested the neighborhood. In the early part of the night the assassins had fired the bridge, and allowed the string-pieces to burn nearly off, when they extinguished the fire, and left the structure standing, but so weak that it would go down as soon as a train came over it. Hearing of this piece of dastard villany, the women had left home in the dead of night, and travelled on foot several miles through the woods, to give an alarm and prevent the fearful consequences that would otherwise have ensued.

The officers and men whose lives were thus saved begged of these heroic women to accept a purse of money, which was made up on the spot. This they refused; and all the return they would permit was that a small squad of the soldiers might see them safely home.

Heroism of the Misses Taylor.

During the same campaign a scene took place at Danville, Kentucky, which illustrates the lofty courage which often inspires the soul of woman. This town was much divided in allegiance, many who had long been neighbors and friends espousing opposite causes. But there was no doubt as to the sympathies of Mrs. Taylor and her estimable family.

Broad and beautiful floated the striped bunting over her cottage, which proclaimed that their hearts, and hopes, and fears were all with the Union cause.

When Kirby Smith occupied Danville, he sent a squad of half a dozen men to take down that piece of bunting from Mrs. Taylor's house. They were met at the door by Mrs. Taylor's two daughters, Maria and Mattie, who politely, but firmly, announced their intention to resist any effort to remove the national emblem. The valorous squad returned, and reported that it would require a full company to remove the flag. The force was detailed. A captain marched a hundred men with loaded guns to the door, drew them up in "battle's magnificently stern array," and made a formal demand for the colors. The young ladies now came to the front door, each armed with a revolver, and holding the glorious banner between them. They replied to the Confederate captain that they had vowed never to surrender that flag to traitors, and declared their intention to shoot the first rebel that polluted it with his touch. After hesitating a few moments, the officer withdrew his force, and reported that in the exercise of his discretion he had not found it advisable to remove the colors referred to.

Bravery of Miss Schwartz.

A year later, in the summer of 1863, a party of guerrillas went in the night to the house of Mr. Schwartz, twelve miles from Jefferson City, Missouri, and, on demanding admittance, were refused by Miss Schwartz, a girl of fifteen years. They answered that they would come in, and commenced breaking down the door. Five or six men, who were in the house, now ran out by the back door, taking with them, as they supposed, all the fire-arms. In their haste a revolver was left, which the heroic girl seized, and pointing it at the head of the leader of the gang, said, "Come on, if you want to; some of you shall fall, or I will!" They then said they would kill her if she did not leave the door. She answered, "The first man of you that takes a step towards this door dies. This is the home of my parents, my brothers and sisters, and I am able to, and shall, defend it." After a brief consultation the ruffians left. Brigadier-General Brown, commanding the district, in a general order, after setting forth the facts of this instance of noble courage, concludes as follows: —

"It is with feelings of no common pride and pleasure that the commanding general announces this occurrence to the citizens and soldiers of his district. On the other hand, those miserable cowards who deserted this brave girl in the hour of danger, flying from the house and leaving her to her fate, are unworthy the name of men, deserve the scorn of the community in which they live, and should be shunned by every man who has a spark of honor or bravery within him."

Miss Oldom's Adventure.

Miss Cornelia Oldom, of Kentucky, displayed courage and address equally brilliant, in the recovery of her horse from a band of rebel marauders.

Her father lives near Mount Sterling, in the hills of Eastern Kentucky. The Confederates came to the house in his absence, and were about to take all his horses, including a large and beautiful animal belonging to the young lady. Notwithstanding her earnest remonstrances, they started off with her horse, when she sprang upon the back of another, which was standing near, and galloped to town as swiftly as possible to give the alarm. On her way home she saw, on the roadside, a pair of holsters containing pistols. Quickly dismounting, she found the weapons loaded, and taking them with her, hurried after the horse thieves. One of them was riding her beautiful pet. She dashed up to him, and ordered him to dismount, with a grace and decision worthy of Di Vernon. Finding he was dealing with a resolute character, and seeing something in her eye which looked dangerous, he surrendered her favorite steed. When she had regained his back and patted his neck, the noble creature seemed to know how much he owed to his fearless mistress.

Spirited Conduct of Mrs. Phelps.

John F. Phelps, a loyal Missourian, resides near Wilson's Creek, where the bloody engagement took place in which General Lyon met his untimely but heroic death. At the time of the battle he was away from home, in command of a Union regiment of Missouri volunteers. After Lyon's death the Union force retreated to Springfield, leaving the body of their general in the hands of the enemy. Mrs. Phelps determined to rescue it, and see that it had a Christian burial. It was reported also that some of the secessionists had threatened to cut out the heart of the dead soldier, and preserve it as a trophy.

Arming herself, she went out on the field, appalling as it was with the dead still unburied, and stood guard over the body of the hero all night. When ordered to give it up, she fearlessly refused; and when they insisted, she said they must sacrifice her before they could lay ruthless hands on the remains of that fallen brave.

After daylight she made the proper arrangements, and removed the corpse to her house, where it was duly laid out. To furnish him a funeral pall, she cut into breadths and sewed together in a proper form a magnificent black velvet robe, a part of her own apparel.

Though perfectly aware of her unprotected situation, the rebels surrounded the house in which the lifeless form of a gallant enemy was guarded by a solitary but heroic woman, and made the night hideous by savage screams, horrible oaths, and barbarous threats. In a short time, however, they retreated, and the body of General Lyon was taken in charge by the loyal army, removed to Connecticut, his native state, and there interred with the fullest military honors.

General Price soon after returned to the vicinity of Wilson's Creek, and called on Mrs. Phelps. He was about to enter the house, when she forbade his crossing her threshold. He remonstrated with her, and tried to cajole her by flatteries and amusing talk. When he again spoke of coming in, she addressed him in these words: "General Price, you are a man, at the head of twenty thousand troops. I am a helpless woman. You are armed. I am not. You have the physical power to take possession of my house. If you ever enter here, it will be simply by reason of my weakness, not by my consent. I ask you, as a soldier, whether you will use violence in such a case." Thus appealed to, Price did not insist, and whenever he came there, stood in the yard, and conversed with the lady of the house through the open door.

An Instance of Self-sacrifice.

When the lines of field-works were being established around the national capital, the military engineers in charge of their location came upon a lovely spot near Bladensburg, Maryland. A tasteful cottage home, standing on the verge of a gentle slope, was surrounded by orchard shade trees, grape-vines, a charming flower garden, a lawn of exquisite smoothness, and "shrubberies that a Shenstone might have envied." This little paradise was the residence of a lady and her daughters, whose husband and father was away fighting under the Union flag. The formation of the country was such as to require the line of earth-works to pass directly through these beautiful grounds and gardens. The position commands the country around for miles, and is the proper point for a battery. Yet the officers saw at a glance that the planting of guns on the hill would make terrible havoc of that charming rural home. Every tree in the orchard must come down, the shrubbery be torn away, a wide ditch cut through the flower garden, and the whole place, in fact, desolated and ruined. Other lines were run in the hope of avoiding this hill entirely, but in vain. No other eminence afforded such a tactical position, and to neglect it might be to throw the advantage thus afforded into the hands of the enemy. It became the unpleasant duty of the officers in charge of the survey to call on the lady and inform her of the military necessity that demanded the mutilation of her grounds, and the destruction of all that was loveliest on the premises. They stated their conclusion in as delicate a manner as possible, and told her how they had hoped to avoid an occupation of her land. She heard their statement in silence, arose, walked to the window, and gazed for a few moments on the tender lawn and the blooming garden. Then, with tearful eyes, she turned to the engineers and said, "If it must be so, take it freely. I had hoped to live here in peace and quiet, and never to leave this sweet spot, which my husband has taken so much delight in making beautiful. But if my country demands it, take it freely. You have my consent."

When the women of Tyre cut their long hair and braided it into bowstrings for the archers on the walls of the besieged city, their devotion was no greater than was here shown by this patriotic lady of Bladensburg.

A Loyal Richmond Girl.

The following story of "hair-breadth 'scape," illustrates at once the genuine loyalty of some of the citizens of the rebel capital, and the unequalled fertility of woman's wit in devising expedients.

S. R. McCullough, the hero of the story, is a Wisconsin soldier, who was captured at Chickamauga, and brought as prisoner to Richmond.

Being somewhat ill, he was sent to a hospital, and had not been there long before a young lady of the city made him a present in the form of a pretty bag filled with "Virginia fine cut." It occurred to young McCullough that possibly the bag might contain something besides tobacco; and sure enough, at the bottom he found a slip of paper with these words: "Would you be free? Then be prepared to act. Meet me to-morrow at ——." The meeting took place. In a few brief words she told him her plan for his escape, agreed upon a day for its execution, and the parties separated without being noticed by the guard. In a few days he received another note conveyed in a similar manner, giving further instructions, and saying that he might bring a comrade with him.

As the day approaches he can think of no way of passing the guard but by feigning to be dead. The details of this ruse were discussed with his fellow-prisoners; and on the eventful day four of them laid him out as a corpse, covered him with a blanket, and carried him to the dead house, where he lay, still as a log, and nearly smothered with his rude face-cloth, till dusk. At length he raised himself, made a hasty reconnoissance barefoot, and finding all right, sallied forth. Just at this time, as had been arranged, a sham fight was played off in the opposite part of the inclosure, by which the attention of all the guards was arrested, when his comrade slipped into a hut near the dead house, and McCullough, as had been arranged, when everything was favorable, threw a stone against the logs. His comrade came out; the two adventurers were together, and undiscovered. They quickly scaled the high board fence, one standing on the other's shoulders, and then drawing his companion up, and let themselves down on the other side in the same manner. Once outside the prison, they went to the place designated by the young lady, and found her waiting. She told them to follow her at a distance, keeping in sight her white handkerchief. Taking a circuitous route she led them twenty-five blocks, and waited for them on the steps of a house, which proved to be that of her father. Here they were kindly received by him, though he knew nothing of the plan of his daughter. In a few days he procured them passes by paying for them between two and three thousand dollars in Confederate money. The young lady provided them with suitable clothes; her father sent them away in his carriage, and he and his daughter gave them their blessing as they departed for the Federal lines, which they reached, with but little difficulty, on the 23d of December, 1863, just three months after they were made prisoners.

The Good Woman at Rome.

A large body of Union soldiers, that had been confined in a distant southern prison, reached the town of Rome, in Northern Georgia, on their way to Richmond. Weary, famished, and thirsty, they were halted in the middle of the streets, under a broiling sun, and exposed to the coarse jeers of the imbittered populace.

Handsomely dressed women came out with handfuls of little cotton bullets, which they threw at the poor, helpless fellows, with such words as, "So you have come to Rome — have you? How do you like your welcome?" Hour after hour of this tedious waiting and insult had passed, when a Union major, who was leaning wearily against a post, was lightly touched on the arm, and turned around expecting some fresh opprobrium. He saw a fine-looking boy, about twelve years of age, standing by his elbow, who, glancing at the guard, who was then looking the other way, pulled the major's skirt, and asked, "Are you from New England?" "I was born in Massachusetts," was the reply. "So was my mother," returned the boy, brightening up. "She was a New England girl, and she was what you call a school-ma'am; she married my father, and I'm their boy; but how she does love New England and the Yankees, and the old United States! and so do I."

The poor major was touched at finding this stray scion of the good old stock away here by "the rivers of Babylon." There was nothing he could give the boy to strengthen his loyalty but one of the buttons on his frock. As he was cutting this from his breast, the lad pulled a string of them from his pocket, and said, "See, I have a dozen just like it, gifts of other boys in blue. My mother would like to see you. I'll go and tell her."

"What are you doing here?" growled the guard, with an oath, as he turned upon him. But the little fellow slipped away through the crowd, and presently returned, walking beside a lovely lady, who moved slowly along the pavement, near the curb-stone, and quietly thrust bank notes into the hands of one and another of the prisoners.

As she approached the major, the bright-faced boy gave him a look that seemed to say, "This is my Massachusetts mother, Sir, who has taught me to love Yankees and the Union." The glances interchanged as the lady threw her eyes upon the war-worn New England soldier were hasty, for the suspicious guard was near, but how full of mutual admiration and esteem!

Mrs. Hetty M. McEwen.

Nashville, Tennessee, was the only city in the seceding states that contained a large number of genuine Unionists who had the courage to assert their sentiments openly and in defiance of southern sympathizers. This fearlessness was as often manifested by women as by men. The southern character, frank, ardent, and uncalculating, was never more aptly illustrated than by the high-spirited defiance with which they dared all danger and all criticism in manifesting their fidelity to the Union.

During the spring and summer of 1861, while Isham G. Harris and his co-traitors were plotting dishonor and disaster for Tennessee, and a majority in the middle and western districts sympathized with him, there were a few in Nashville who frankly characterized his conduct in no measured terms, and advertised their sentiments by keeping the national colors always flying from their house-tops.

Of these few, Mrs. Hetty M. McEwen was perhaps the most conspicuous, and her conduct in the defence of the flag upon her house is truly memorable.

She is an old lady, having been born during the Presidency of George Washington. She had six uncles at the battle of King's Mountain, four of whom wet that hard-fought field with their life-blood.

Her husband, Colonel Robert H. McEwen, fought under Jackson at Horseshoe, and his father was a surgeon in the revolutionary army. She could remember the time when there was no Tennesseean that did not live in a log cabin, no preacher that did not take his rifle into the pulpit with him as regularly as his Bible, and was as familiar with one as with the other. When secession was talked of, with her own fingers she stitched together the folds of bunting, and reared the Red, White, and Blue on a flag-staff in the yard of the residence that had been known as theirs almost from the time when Nashville was an Indian fort. As treason grew less and less odious, the flag was subjected to various insults. Boys threw stones at it. The papers noticed it, and advised its removal. Colonel McEwen received an anonymous letter full of plantation venom, and threatening assassination unless the odious colors were removed. When at length the machinations of Governor Harris culminated, and Tennessee was made to appear of secession preferences by forty thousand majority, Colonel McEwen fastened a pole into one of his chimneys, and nailed the national colors where they could float solitary, yet dauntless and defiant, over the rebellion-cursed city. The hostility now became fiercer than ever. He was told that the flag must come down from that roof if they had to fire the house to bring it down. He asked his wife what they had better do about the flag, adding that he would sustain her in any course she thought best to adopt. "Load me the shot-gun, Colonel McEwen," said the heroic old lady. And he loaded it for her with sixteen buckshot in each barrel. "Now," added she, "I will take the responsibility of guarding that flag. Whoever attempts to pass my door on their way to the roof for that star-spangled banner, under which my four uncles fell at King's Mountain, must go over my dead body!"

Not long after, Governor Harris issued an order for all fire-arms to be brought to him at the state-house, and enforced it by sending a squad of soldiers to Colonel McEwen's house. In reply to their demand she said, "Go tell your master, the governor, that I will not surrender my gun to any one but himself, and, if he wants it, to come in person and risk the consequences."

ANNA ETHERIDGE.

WERE our government to order a gold medal to be given to the woman who has most distinguished herself by heroic courage on the field, and by the most patient and effective service in the military hospitals, there can be little doubt that the united voices of the soldiers and of all the army nurses would assign the honor to Anna Etheridge, of Michigan.

In the great work of charity and self-sacrifice performed by the women during the late conflict, some have displayed organizing and executive talent truly wonderful. Others have become remarkable for the extent and duration of their labors — others for the admirable and Christian spirit they brought to the hospitals and the battle-field. Genuine courage and hardihood have been displayed by females, but not generally in connection with those finer characteristics for which woman is most prized.

But in our "gentle Anna" was combined that true heroism which is the highest boast of manhood, with the modesty, the quiet bearing, the deferential manners and unobtrusive worth which are the loveliest traits of the fairer and the weaker sex. Few soldiers were in the war longer, or served with so slight intermissions, or had so little need of rest.

When the first enlistments took place, in the summer of

1861, Anna Etheridge was in Detroit, on a visit to friends. There she enlisted in the Second Michigan volunteers, under Colonel Richardson. Nineteen young ladies are said to have offered to go with the regiment in the capacity of nurses; but in a few months' service every one but Anna had returned home, or lost her health, or been discharged.

She was with the regiment in the action at Blackburn's Ford, which was preliminary to the first battle of Bull Run, and continued with it through nearly all the great Virginia battles. She was furnished with a horse, side-saddle, saddle-bags, &c., and during a battle would often ride fearlessly to the front; and whenever she found a soldier too badly hurt to go to the rear, she would dismount, and, regardless of shot and shell, produce her lint and bandages, bind up his wounds, give water or stimulating drink, then gallop on in search of another sufferer. General Berry, who for a long time commanded the brigade to which her regiment was attached, and who was remarkable for his personal gallantry in all these engagements, declares that she has remained cool and self-possessed under as hot a fire as he ever saw or was exposed to himself. The brilliant General Kearney at one time commanded this brigade, and, in consideration of her dauntless courage and invaluable services, commissioned her as a regimental sergeant, and presented her the handsome cross that bears his noble and heroic name. When not actively engaged on the field or in hospital, she superintended the cooking at brigade headquarters; and when the brigade moved she would mount her horse and march with the ambulances and the surgeons, administering to the wants of the sick and wounded. At the nightly bivouac she wrapped herself in her blanket, and slept on the ground with the hardihood of a true soldier.

Her exploits at Antietam, Chancellorsville, Gettysburg, and in the battles of Grant's closing campaign, were a favorite theme with the soldiers. On one occasion a wounded man, to whom she was attending, was struck by a shell and torn in pieces, almost between her hands. Generally, during an engagement, she would remain a little in the rear with the surgeon; but often, when she saw a man fall she would dash forward into the hottest of the fire, lift him on her horse, and bring him safely to the rear, where he could have prompt attention. Many times she received balls through her dress, but was never hit. Many and many a soldier owes his life to "gentle Anna's" intrepidity. More than once, when the troops showed signs of retreating, she rushed to the front, seized the colors, and rallied them to a charge, shaming many into doing their duty. At the battle of the Wilderness, when the fighting was at its height, the balls raining like hailstones, theFifth Michigan and some other troops were surrounded and nearly cut off by the rebels. As the line of battle swung around, the enemy took the places our men had vacated. Anna was at that moment speaking to an orderly, a mere boy, when a bullet pierced his heart, and he fell against her, dead. For the first and only time during the war our heroine became "demoralized;" and laying the dead orderly on the ground, she ran towards what she took to be the Union troops. Too late she discovered her mistake, but kept on, dashing through the rebel line, and though several shots were sent after her, made her escape unhurt.

In demeanor "Michigan Anna" is thoroughly modest, quiet, and retiring, while her habits and conduct are correct and exemplary. Though on the battle-field she seems to be possessed and animated by the single desire of saving the lives of wounded men, she seldom speaks of herself, or refers to anything she has done. With strangers she is very reticent, and has a reserve and apparent pride of manner. With the soldiers, though sharing all their hardships, she never spoke familiarly, and was held by them in the highest veneration and esteem, as an angel of mercy. While the contest was going on, she took the deepest interest in the issue, eagerly reading all the newspapers that she could find in camp, and keeping well informed as to the progress of the war.

When general orders excluded her temporarily from the front lines, she engaged promptly in any hospital labors where aid was needed.

During a part of the Peninsula campaign she was on a hospital transport, and Miss Bradley speaks in warm terms of the constant, thorough, and effectual service there performed by her. So, also, at City Point she coöperated with Mrs. Husband and other ladies, working indefatigably, and winning the respect and admiration of all under her care.

No one of the noble women who have distinguished themselves during the war can furnish so rich, varied, and romantic a series of recollections as Anna Etheridge, more of which might have been employed for the embellishment of this brief sketch, were it not that the heroine is preparing a volume of her own, which is likely to prove one of the most interesting recitals connected with the history of the times.

A career so romantic has not failed to stimulate the enthusiasm of several of our poets to celebrate her exploits in rhyme.

Perhaps the lines which follow are the best tribute which the Muses have, as yet, made to this admirable character: —

TO MISS ANNA ETHERIDGE,

THE HEROINE OF THE WAR.

Hail, heroine of the battle-field!
  Sweet angel of a zeal divine!
Hail, maiden, whose device and shield,
  Sculptured in tears and prayers, will shine,
On Love's eternal column reared
  In memory of the martyred dead,
To be, through coming time, revered,
  And sacred to the pilgrim's tread!

Hail, dauntless maid! whose shadowy form,
  Borne like a sunbeam on the air,
Swept by amid the battle-storm,
  Cheering the helpless sufferers there,
Amid the cannon's smoke and flame,
  The earthquake roar of shot and shell,
Winning, by deeds of love, a name
  Immortal as the brave who fell.

Hail, angel! whose diviner spell
  Charmed dying heroes with her prayer,
Stanching their wounds amid the knell
  Of death, destruction, and despair.

Thy name by memory shall be wreathed
  Round many desolate hearts in prayer;
By orphan lips it shall be breathed,
  And float in songs upon the air.

And History's pages shall embalm
  The heroine's deeds in lines of fire;
Her life shall prove a hallowed charm,
  And every loyal heart inspire.
Press on, press on! in glory move!
  Unfading laurels shall be thine
To gem the victor-crown of Love,
  And sparkle in the realms divine!

MISS A. SHELTON,

AND OTHER NURSES AT CHATTANOOGA.

FEW places in the country are so rich in the historical associations of our great war as Chattanooga. Situated at the points where the Tennessee bursts through the barriers of the Appalachian range, romantic in its site, and sublime in mountain scenery, it is, at the same time, a commercial and railroad centre, and a key-point in military strategy. Its immense importance in the defence of southern territory is proved by the fact that it is the only point in America that has as yet been the theatre of two protracted and bloody battles, each fought for no other strategical object than the possession or occupation of this town.

The battles took place in the fall of 1863, and it can easily be seen that during the winter that followed, there must have been an untold aggregate of suffering concentrated there.

More than two hundred miles from Louisville, the base of supply, with railroad and wagon communication subject to constant interruption by raids and surprises, it was crowded with the severely wounded of two bloody battles, great numbers of whom died for want of sufficient and proper food, clothing, and the customary hospital supplies.

The heroic army-workers had done something to relieve

this suffering early in the season. Mrs. Harris, whom no difficulties ever appalled, whom no labors, though they might prostrate, seemed ever to exhaust, had, with Miss Tyson, of Baltimore, and Mrs. Beck, of Washington, penetrated to this point when it was at the front, and the scene of actual hostilities. But sickness followed the exposures and hardships to which they were subject, and they were without facilities for accomplishing much for the relief of the suffering. In early spring the subject was taken up by the ladies of the Sanitary Commission of the West, and a number of zealous workers went to Chattanooga, arriving there about the middle of April, 1864.

The deputation was mostly from Iowa. There were Miss Coggill, of Iowa City, Miss Hagan, of Muscatine, and Miss A. Shelton, the sister of Miss Mary E. Shelton, who acted as the secretary and hospital assistant of Mrs. Wittenmeyer. Four others, Mrs. Conrad and her sister, and the Misses Hanford, went to Knoxville on similar errands of mercy.

The three who remained at Chattanooga were for a few days lodged at the rooms of the Christian Commission; but about the 21st an ambulance drove up to the door to take them to the hospital by the foot of Lookout Mountain, at the point where Chattanooga Creek empties into the Tennessee. Their quarters they found rough and dirty, and the strict discipline of the camp appeared severe and arbitrary. But these discomforts and annoyances were soon lost sight of in the absorbing and tragical scenes of the hospital wards.

One of the first patients that Miss Hagan attended was raving with the delirium of fever. "Send across the field for my wife; just across the field there. She'll come as soon as you tell her; she has no idea how sick I am." When she laid her cool hand on the hot forehead, and stroked back the crisp, brown hair, the poor fellow thought "she" had come, and said, in a tone of satisfaction that was inexpressibly touching, "There, I thought you would come; I knew you would, as soon as you knew how much I needed you."

As soon as arrangements were completed, these ladies had in charge the special diet kitchen, where they prepared food for about two hundred patients. At first, these duties were found very exhausting; but they were steadily persevered in, and contributed greatly to the comfort and the rapid convalescence of the patients.

Their time was wholly engrossed with these labors of philanthropy and patriotism; yet the Chattanooga life, stern and exacting as it was, had its hours of romantic interest. Above the hospital where they labored towered the famous historic mountain peak, where the storming columns of the victorious Union troops had crowded up the rocky slope till the final volleys and the ringing cheers of triumph were far above the clouds. Near them rolled the blue waters of the Tennessee, whose banks had for three years been echoing to the fierce thunders of the fratricidal strife; while, from time to time, long columns of troops, with immense army trains, would file past the hospital, moving on southward at the command of the great Marching General, to earn imperishable renown in a series of bloody battles culminating in the most wonderful success in all history. The scenery, also, particularly at night, often realized all they had conceived of as the wild and romantic scenery of war. A corps or a division would encamp on Chattanooga or Chickamauga Creek, and their camp fires extend up the slopes of the grand old mountain, till it seemed all ablaze with the lurid glories of war.

In May began active operations against the enemy; and the hospital was soon filled with wounded men from the action at Dalton, Tunnel Hill, and numerous other points on the line of march through Northern Georgia.

Soon it became necessary to establish other special diet kitchens. On the 26th of May, Miss Hagan and Miss Shelton went to Hospital No. 1; and though there was everything to be done, and nothing to do with, by dint of perseverance, hard work, and Miss Hagan's uncommon executive ability, order soon came out of confusion, and an abundance of suitable and well-cooked food was supplied to all the wards in the hospital.

This was not abated during the month of June, after which Chattanooga was of less importance as a hospital centre. Then Miss Shelton went to Nashville, and co-operated with her sister in labors for the patients in Hospital No. 1 and Hospital No. 14. An account of these labors, and some very touching and tragical incidents that occurred there, will be found in the narrative and hospital sketches of Miss Mary E. Shelton.

These sisters continued their labors at Nashville, and afterwards at Wilmington, for months after the war ended, endeavoring to restore again to useful activity and cheerfulness the patriots who, during the last year of the terrible warfare, had made such vast sacrifices of their own health and life, to give vigor, unity, and permanence to the life of the nation.

Very truly yours
Georgiana Willets

MISS GEORGIANA WILLETS.

THIS accomplished and lovely young woman was one of that large number who for many months were kept back from serving their country in the military hospitals and on the battle-field by a misconception of the duties that nurses had to perform.

As soon, however, as it was apparent to her and her friends that very effective and important services could be rendered without the compromise of either delicacy or dignity, she entered heart and soul into the work.

Leaving her home at Jersey City in the spring of 1864, she repaired to Washington, holding herself in readiness to respond to any call that might be made for hospital labor. Early in May, Grant moved his powerful army across the Rapidan, and struck the first of those giant blows under which the Confederacy at length reeled to its downfall.

With this campaign was inaugurated in Virginia his peculiar mode of warfare, which consists in following up one battle with another, and this by a forced march, giving the exhausted enemy no time to collect, reorganize, or recuperate. Such fighting naturally created great suffering, and imposed heavy losses upon the forces of the North.

Into the midst of these unequalled and appalling scenes of bloodshed and hardship Miss Willets found herself suddenly plunged, when, on the 13th of May, she went to the scene of active operations, and entered the old war-battered city of Fredericksburg.

It was one enormous hospital; or rather it was a city of wounded and exhausted men, who had been rapidly collected from the rear of battles that had lasted with little or no intermission for seven days. But at no time throughout the war was there such a lack of adequate hospital appliances as at Fredericksburg after the battles of the Wilderness.

Immediately on her arrival, Miss Willets reported to Dr. Dalton, the Medical Director, and was assigned to duty in the Catholic Church, known as a ward of the First Division, Second Corps Hospital. Here she found a hundred and fifty wounded men, with literally nothing to make their condition comfortable, or even tolerable. Supplies could be had only by way of Belle Plain, a distance of twenty miles, over a road that, by a constant passage of army trains and frequent storms, had become one long quagmire, through which a horse could hardly drag a hundred pounds. All the available force, and most of the trains, had moved on towards Richmond, leaving this city of sufferers to be relieved as best they might. There were no beds in the ward where Miss Willets was engaged except such as were made by stitching two blankets together, and stuffing the sack thus made with straw that had been used for packing; no pillows for the dying, except such as were rudely formed by cutting off the sleeve of some poor soldier's shirt, and filling it with hay. Canteens, boots, and even bricks, were the uncouth bolsters for patients whose condition required the most careful attention. The only dishes were a rough and blackened tin cup for not one man in three; the only place for cooking, an open camp fire.

Thus rude was her introduction to army life. But the noble girl was neither repulsed nor discouraged. Why should a well person repine at anything, when men by the thousand lay suffering and dying around her, their battle uniform yet stiff with gore, bolstering their weary and aching heads on brickbats, yet never breathing a word of complaint? Here for two weeks she worked assiduously, using all a woman's wit and ingenuity to extemporize something having a semblance of comfort for her hundred and fifty patients. The transportation from Belle Plain had greatly improved, supplies were arriving every hour, and the prospect of seeing the wounded in a condition less pitiable was quite inspiring, when all their ameliorating plans were cut short by the progress of events and a military order.

Grant had advanced so far as to make his land communication with Washington too long a line to be held. He had established a new base on the York and James Rivers; the theatre of operations was now the close vicinity of Petersburg and Richmond, and Fredericksburg must be evacuated.

Here was a fresh breadth of canvas in the ever-shifting panoramas of a great war. Eight hundred patients were to be transferred immediately from their rude resting-places, and from cots, to the transports that lay by the river bank. Slowly and painfully the poor fellows were lifted upon stretchers, almost every movement giving exquisite torture, carried by two soldiers down the steep bank, and laid side by side along the decks of the vessels. Night fell moonless and stormy while the work was in progress; but the demands of war recognized no distinction between storm and sunshine; they made no allowance for darkness and midnight; the embarkation must go on. If the ladies had not the strength to lift wounded men and carry stretchers, they could at least hold the lights. Accordingly Miss Willets and her two associates, Miss Hancock and Mrs. Lee, took their positions along the path that led from the gangway to the hospitals, and stood hour after hour in the rain and deep gloom of midnight, as the grim procession of the wounded filed slowly past them.

All through the long, wet night, these true-hearted ladies continued at their self-assigned posts of duty, until, as morning dawned, they found themselves, with their shiploads of suffering men, moving slowly down the Rappahannock. When opposite Port Royal, an officer came aboard with the information that a thousand of the wounded in the last battle were lying on the ground, and in wagons, just as they had been brought from the field. He asked who would volunteer to go and do something for them. Miss Willets had come out from Washington in company with Mrs. Swisshelm; but in the darkness and confusion at the embarkation they were separated, and she was now quite alone. She not only had no acquaintance at Port Royal, but the town had very recently been evacuated by the rebels, and there was no certainty that she might not be subject tc insult by going so wholly unprotected into a place full of southern sympathizers. But considerations of this kind could not deter our heroine from the line of usefulness. Here were a thousand suffering soldiers, to whom a little attention might be of inestimable importance, and she went to work among them without hesitation. She found one of her own sex engaged in similar labors, Mrs. Spencer, state agent for New York, who hailed her with a genuine welcome. For four days she remained here, doing whatever she could as best she could. They were days of toil and discomfort so great as almost to reach suffering, when another shift in the grand kaleidoscope changed all plan and arrangements. White House was now the base, and thither Miss Willets went on the supply steamer Planter. Working here for two weeks, the next advance was to City Point, where she was permanently connected with the Hospital of the Second Division of the Second Corps. The wounded in the engagements of the 16th, 17th, and 18th June were brought in just as she commenced her labors; and for some time she had charge of eleven wards, and also of a low-diet kitchen, where food for the most dangerous cases was prepared. The arduous labors in which she was engaged through the summer were varied, not relieved, by a trip to Washington, on a hospital transport, in July. Two hundred and fifty men, wounded in the assault of the rebel lines before Petersburg, were on board, just as they were removed from that disastrous field.

One lady, Mrs. Price, was with Miss Willets to assist; but for all that number of patients they had but two basins with which to wash and dress wounds, almost no supplies, one small stove in charge of a testy and slatternly old negress down in the hold. With such desires as she had to do something for the poor men, and such inadequate means to operate with, well may she describe that trip from James River to Washington as "thirty-six hours of torture."

Excepting a short interval in September, when over-exertion had produced sickness, Miss Willets remained at the hospital of the Second Division, Second Corps, till late in the fall of 1864, when, the number of patients having greatly diminished, she went home for a short interval of rest, intending to return at the opening of the spring campaign. How soon that campaign closed, and with it the whole war, all the world knows.

Though some labored for a longer period than Miss Willets, few, from any part of the country, brought to the service more pleasing manners, more graceful accomplishments, or a kinder heart. She was one of those whose presence by their cots the soldiers gratefully recognized by calling them "sunbeams." The wounded who were so fortunate as to be under her care, as well as Mrs. Husband, and others who coöperated with her, conspire in their praises of her winning gentleness, the loveliness of her person, and the sweetness of her character.

WOMEN AS SOLDIERS.

DURING all periods of the war, instances occurred of women being found in the ranks, fighting as common soldiers, their sex remaining unsuspected, and the particular motive in each case often unknown.

Some went to avoid separation from those who were dearer to them than ease, or life itself; others, from a pure love of romance and adventure; and others, from a mental hallucination that victory and deliverance would come to the war-burdened land only by the sacrifice of their lives. As an instance of the latter kind, we cite the story of the young lady of Brooklyn, New York, who was killed at the battle of Chickamauga.

In the early part of the year 1863, when the national fortunes were darkest, and victory perched continually on the standards of rebellion, this young lady, then fresh from school, and scarce nineteen years of age, conceived the idea that Providence had destined her, as an American Joan of Arc, to marshal our discouraged forces, rally them to new efforts, and inspire them with a fresh and glowing enthusiasm.

Probably she had lingered too fondly over that most thrilling chapter of French history, where, as by a miracle, the obscure shepherdess leaps to the van of the demoralized but fiery Gallic army, and towers at once into the rarest heroism with the courage of an Amazon, the bearing of a queen, and the purity of a saint.

Her parents at first treated this fancy of hers as a harmless day-dream, produced by excessive study, and by hearing of the constant reverses of the Union arms. At length more active means were employed to disabuse her mind of an impression so idle, and to dissuade her from a plan of action so utterly impracticable; but in vain.

An eminent physician was consulted, her pastor called to converse with her, and her former associates at school brought to her, that by their united influence she might see the folly of her dream; but none of their representations could dissuade her from a determination that was every day becoming more fixed. Finally, in a family meeting, it was held the most judicious course to take her to Michigan; and a maiden aunt became the companion and custodian of the enthusiastic girl. But she was not improved by the change, for only the positive command of her aunt prevented her from going to Washington to seek an interview with the good president, and ask the command of the national forces. At length it was found necessary to deprive her to some extent of her liberty; but this made her quite unmanageable, and she determined to enlist at all hazards.

Escaping from her aunt, she disguised herself as a boy, and joined the drum corps of a Michigan regiment.

All efforts to trace her were unavailing; and after some weeks of search, she was mourned by her parents as dead, and was believed to have committed suicide.

The regiment to which she was attached being ordered

to reënforce General Rosecrans, she went with it to Tennessee, and marched under that accomplished strategist in all those skilful movements by which the rebel general Bragg was forced across the Cumberland Mountains and beyond the Tennessee River, at the sacrifice of hardly a man in the Union lines. Then followed the hard struggle for Chattanooga. Her regiment was in Van Cleve's division, and in the sharp but indecisive engagements of Saturday she was unhurt. But on the disastrous day which followed, as the fair young soldier was standing unterrified under a deadly fire, a minie ball pierced her side, and she fell. On being carried to the surgeon's tent, an examination of her wound revealed her sex. The surgeon told her that she could not live, and advised her to disclose her real name. This she was unwilling to do. But the colonel of the regiment, though suffering from a painful wound, at length prevailed upon her to inform her family of her situation; and just before she died she dictated the following telegraphic despatch which was sent to her father: "Mr. ———, No. — Willoughby Street, Brooklyn. Forgive your dying daughter. I have but a few moments to live. My native soil drinks my blood. I expected to deliver my country, but the Fates would not have it so. I am content to die. Pray, pa, forgive me. Tell ma to kiss my daguerrotype. EMILY.

"P. S. Give my old watch to little Eph."

The gentle enthusiast was buried under the shadow of the cloud-capped mountain, which a few weeks after echoed from base to summit with the victorious cheers of our triumphant host, and the broad blue Tennessee murmurs for her a requiem soft and sad. Grave more glorious or more fitting she could not have chosen.

Equally romantic, and more sad if possible, is the story of the Wisconsin girl, who, with a devotion of which only woman is capable, followed her soldier-lover through four years of active service, and at last closed his eyes in death in a Washington hospital a few days after Lee's surrender.

Her name is Ellen Goodridge, and the brave boy she loved so truly was James Hendrick. He volunteered for three months when the war broke out in 1861, and was at the first battle of Bull Run. Receiving a lieutenant's commission, he enlisted for three years, and wrote to that effect to his parents, and also to Ellen. When she told her parents that she had made up her mind to go with her lover and share the fortunes of war by his side, they were so incensed at what they considered her folly, that they turned her from their doors, and bade her never return. Going to Washington, she found young Hendrick's regiment, and obtained permission to remain at the colonel's headquarters and look after the cooking.

They were in every great battle that was fought in Virginia, and in the intervals she often went with him in skirmishes and raids, on one such occasion receiving a painful wound in her arm from a minie ball. His health remained good till after the fall of Richmond. Then he became very sick, and was taken to Washington, where she watched over his couch, bathed his hot forehead, read to him, wrote for him, and showed the most painful anxiety for his recovery; but all in vain. A day or two before he died, their marriage was solemnized by an Episcopal clergyman. The occasion was inexpressibly sad, he writhing in the grasp of a fatal disease, having survived all the great battles of the war only to die, and leave the noble girl, who had been so true to him, broken-hearted and a widow, and she almost wild with the terrible thought that, after giving up so much, and suffering so much, to be near him, death would leave her only his name and a bleeding heart.

The hardihood of "Irish Biddy" was probably not surpassed by any camp-follower during the war.

She sometimes went out with the men on picket, and remained all night on watch. At times, when sickness or hard service had thinned the ranks of the regiment, she would take the place of a soldier, and go out on a scouting or a raiding expedition, doing the full duty of a soldier.

At other times the part she acted was more fearless and sublime, taking then the place of an officer, and acting the commander rather than the companion.

One occasion of the latter class shows that "Irish Biddy" possessed the courage, if not the grace and poetry, of Joan of Arc.

The brigade was in Virginia, near Dinwiddie Court House, engaged in a series of skirmishes and actions with the enemy, the general object of which was to complete the investment and isolation of Richmond.

One of the captains in the regiment to which she was attached had fallen in a skirmish with a party of Confederate cavalry. The regiment was repulsed at the end of the action, and the body of the fallen officer left in the lines of the enemy. Bridget was near by during the fight, and knew that his body was abandoned by the men in their retreat.

She rode boldly in, and was not challenged or disturbed by the enemy, who may not have seen her, or who respected her sex and the sacred character of her errand too much to fire upon or capture the heroine. The lifeless body of the captain she lifted and laid over her horse, and with this double, and to most persons fearful, load, she rode alone for twelve miles before she found the majority of the regiment, and could deliver the corpse to those who would give it Christian burial.

During this ride of twelve miles she came upon a small wagon train, and rode along with it for some distance.

When some hostile demonstration was made, the teamsters, who were few in number and poorly armed, were on the point of making a sudden and what would have been a dishonorable escape and abandonment of their train to the enemy, when Bridget rode among them, rallied them, told them there was no real danger, and, in language less polite than forcible, called upon them "for God's sake not to run off and leave their wagons before the rebs were within a mile of the nearest of them."

Her efforts were successful, and the men were actually recalled to a sense of soldierly duty by a woman who was then in the act of rescuing the dead body of an officer who had fallen in a skirmish, and had been abandoned by his men, who sought safety in retreat.

The battle of Fair Oaks commenced by a vigorous charge of an overwhelming rebel force upon a single division of McClellan's army, which had advanced across the Chickahominy. As Casey's division, thus attacked, gave way, there was danger that the panic might spread and infect the troops that were hastening to the support. Among these was the Seventh Massachusetts, that, having advanced to within range of the rebel artillery, had just received the order, "Forward," that would in a few moments plunge them into the heat of the contest. They obeyed the command but slowly, for the enemy's fire was growing every moment more terrific. Just then "Irish Biddy" came along, supporting her husband, who had a ball through his leg. Swinging her soldier's cap over her head, she shouted, "Arrah! go in, boys, and bate the bloody spalpeens, and revinge me husband, and God be wid ye."

The effect was instantaneous and decisive. The regiment gave three cheers for "Irish Biddy," and three for the Seventh. Then joining the Tenth Massachusetts, and other troops, they made a gallant and successful charge on the enemy's centre.

Browned by exposure, and with sensibilities somewhat hardened by years of constant service in camp, a character like that of "Irish Biddy" may fail to interest us for its feminine characteristics, but it must, nevertheless, command our admiration for its strength, its fortitude, its dauntless courage, and the genuine and inextinguishable kindness of heart which led her ever to place the good and the comfort of the men above all demands of safety, and all considerations of personal ease.

NELLY M. CHASE.

A SOLDIER, who, though fearfully wounded, has survived that disastrous attempt to storm the enemy's intrenched lines at Fredericksburg in December, 1862, gives an admirable account of his sensations when marching "into the jaws of death," his sufferings on the field, and the touching kindness with which he was cared for and his life saved by one of those angels of mercy, a volunteer army nurse. Inquiry has hitherto failed to reveal more concerning the character and services of Miss Chase than has been given to the world in the story of this one-armed volunteer; but this alone is enough to enshrine her in the grateful hearts of every soldier, and win for her the blessings of all who love virtue and their country.

After describing the sensations with which he awoke from his sleep in the streets of Fredericksburg, at the sound of heavy cannonade, and the manner in which the division was marched out and pushed forward in the attack, "One-Armed" continues his narrative as follows: —

"'Steady, men — forward!' rang out the voice of our commander; and disentangling from the retreating fugitives, we steadily bore on till we neared the batteries, and with a cheer sprang forward. That instant a line of fire leaped from behind a stone wall close in our front, and — I don't remember anything more about it. My next recollections were of a confused and contradictory character; one instant I was fully conscious; the moment following, utterly lost.

"Then I would imagine I was at home and half asleep, while all the house was astir with some past or anticipated catastrophe with which I was in some way connected. Then all was dark, and a great load seemed to press me down and glue me to the ground in spite of all my efforts to rise. Then I heard voices, all strange and heartless but one; this had chords of human sympathy in it. I could feel something force open my jaws, and a fluid trickle into my throat, which I managed to swallow to prevent strangling: still it trickled down, and still I painfully swallowed, hoping, praying that it would stop; but it did not, until I recognized that it was some powerful stimulant that I was taking, and that I was becoming more able to swallow it. All this time I could hear the kind voice encouraging me; also some cold, unsympathizing voices. I could not distinguish what they said: only by the tone could I tell the sympathetic from the unsympathetic. At last I heard the words in part of one who said, 'It's no use working over him; he's dying now.' Quietly, but O, so earnestly and tenderly, the kind voice replied, 'No, doctor, he's not dying; he's coming to life; he will live if we don't give him up. This wound on his head won't amount to anything if we can get him warmed up. Don't you see he's been nearly frozen to death while faint from loss of blood? But he's coming on finely, and by and by you can take off his arm, and the man may get well. Who knows but he has a mother or a sister to love him, and thank you or me some day for a son or brother saved?'

"Yes, I was saved; I understood it all now: I remembered the battle, and that my present condition was in some way the result of it; and, for the sake of that dear mother and sister so strangely invoked, I made an effort to unclasp my eyelids, and opened my eyes once more to the light of the sun. At first the glare confused me, but soon I could distinguish three surgeons beside me, watching my symptoms with curiosity, if not with interest. On the other side of me, as I lay on the ground under a large hospital tent, there was kneeling a *woman:* her left hand was under my head; in her right she was holding a spoon, with which, at short intervals, she dipped some warm fluid from a cup held by a boy soldier, her attendant. I tried to speak, but could not; she merely shook her head, to discourage my efforts, and turning to the lad, said, 'Now, Johnny, the beef soup.' In a moment the soup was substituted for the toddy, and I gradually felt life, and the love of life, coming back to me. Looking around, I saw near me a basin of water, with a sponge, and the lady's hands covered with blood. I inferred, what I afterwards learned to be the case, that she had been washing the clotted gore from my hair and face, and had discovered that what looked like a fatal wound on the head was merely a scalp cut, which had bled profusely, and looked hopeless, but was not so in reality.

"Gradually I recovered sufficient strength to undergo the amputation of my shattered right arm, and then recovered entirely. I had been struck both on the head and arm at the same time, and lay senseless on the field till late in the night, when the stretcher-carriers found me, and bore me to the city, where I was thrown into an ambulance and taken across the river. After waiting my turn with hundreds of others, I thank God that, when that turn came, I fell into good hands — the blessed hands of a kind-hearted woman! Even here, amid the roar and carnage, was found a woman with the soul to dare danger; the heart to sympathize with the battle-stricken; sense, skill, and experience, to make her a treasure beyond all price. The choicest blessings of Heaven be hers in all time to come! Since my recovery I have observed her in her ministrations, and I see she is gifted in a wonderful degree for scenes like these. She has been in the army ever since the war broke out, and ever at the front. Rear hospitals are no place for this noble girl. Though not twenty-four when I first saw her on that memorable day, I do not believe, as an army nurse, she has an equal any where. The surgeon of the Seventy-ninth New York, stationed in the hospital from which this is written, has placed her in charge of our supplies and stores, and most efficiently does she deal them out.

"Many a poor wounded soldier would lack his timely stimulant, or food proper for his condition, if she did not pass through the tents at all hours of the day and night; for they say she seldom sleeps. For many months she was connected with the One Hundredth Pennsylvania, known as the Roundhead Regiment, and went with it to South Carolina. At the time of Benham's defeat on James Island, Dr. McDonald, who was there, says she performed incredible labors, as she does here. Among the many developments of character produced by this war, I have seen none that I consider more admirable than Miss Nelly M. Chase. She has never been a paid nurse, but considers herself a member of the regiment, and works for others only when she cannot accompany it. For all the labors, privations, and hardships of her campaigning life, her only reward is the consciousness of being so largely useful, and the unbounded admiration and gratitude of the private soldiers, who almost worship her."

WOMAN'S SACRIFICES.

IN one of the great battles of the war, among thousands of similar sacrifices, there fell a noble young man from Philadelphia. His body was taken up, embalmed, and forwarded to the house of his grandmother, Mrs. Ellet. Soon after its arrival two sympathetic and warm-hearted gentlemen, Mr. George H. Stuart, president of the Christian Commission, with the Rev. Robert Patterson, D. D., of Chicago, called upon her to condole with her upon the loss, and to offer the consolations of religion. Dr. Patterson expressed the hope that the Lord would sustain her under her bereavement. "I regret," answered the noble-spirited woman, "that I cannot give as largely of my means to this war as I might have done in other and better days. But I shall be happy to place in your hands, Mr. Stuart, two beautiful and very valuable shawls, the proceeds of their sale to be distributed among the widows and orphans of soldiers fallen in battle. Two sons I have already given, Commodore Ellet, of the Ram Fleet, and Brigadier-General Ellet, of the Marine Brigade, and four grandsons; nor do I regret the gift. Had I twenty sons, I would devote them all to the cause. Were I twenty years younger, I would go and fight myself to the last, for the country must and shall be preserved."

Shortly after the first call of President Lincoln, a regiment of volunteers was standing in the streets of one of the cities of Pennsylvania, nearly ready to take up their line of march for the national capital.

The troops were very gay and light-hearted. Many of them were boys, and thought it was only a ninety days' frolic they were starting on. In the midst of a small squad of hardy-looking men stood a tall, raw-boned youth, whose animal spirits seemed to be inexhaustible. He had been making fun for them all the afternoon. "Well, boys," said he, "we're going off—ar'n't we?" "Yes, we are," replied half a dozen voices. "When we get there, may be we won't give 'em fits, eh?" "May be we won't," was the response.

Just then an old woman in a thin, faded, woollen shawl, came elbowing her way among the men, and turning up a searching look to one after another of the tallest fellows, as though very anxious to find some one. In a moment she stood before this light-hearted young volunteer. His eyes dropped instantly; his face was covered with a flush; and as he turned his head, he lifted his finger to his eye, and shook it with a twirl as he said, "Now, mother, mother! you promised me that you wouldn't come out—didn't ye? Now you promised me. When I said 'Good-by' to ye, mother, I told ye I didn't want ye to come out here and unman me, and here ye've done it. Now I wish ye hadn't."

The old woman lifted up her wrinkled, labor-knotted hands, and laid them on the great, broad shoulders of her stalwart boy. The tears ran down her face as she said, "O, Jack, don't scold me; don't scold your poor old mother, Jack; you know you're all I have, Jack; and I didn't come out to unman ye; I didn't come out to unman ye, Jack; I have come to say, God bless ye, Jack; God bless ye;" and folding the little faded shawl over her breast, she slipped away between the men, and walked rapidly down the street. The big soldier boy drew his sleeve rudely over his face, and bringing down his arm with a sort of vexed emphasis, as though defying the emotion he could not control, blurted out, as a sort of apology for his wet cheek, "Hang it, boys, she's mother, you know."

In a few moments the band struck up a lively air, and the order, "Column, forward, march!" came down the long line from the mounted colonel.

"Just then," says a bystander, "I saw a little girl standing on a doorstep. She was ten or twelve years of age, I should judge. As I looked in her face, my attention was arrested. A deep cloud of sorrow came over and rested upon that young brow. She stood with her little hands clasped tightly, and the childish face seemed pinched with very agony. And I thought, 'Well, now, what can be the matter with that child?' I determined to watch her. So I took my stand near by. The sound of the music grew nearer and nearer. By and by the heavy tramp of the men was heard. As they approached us, I saw that little form becoming more fixed and rigid; the hands began to quiver; her neck was stretched with eager intensity, and her eyes were fairly riveted upon the men as they came marching slowly by the door. A moment after, I was startled by a penetrating little voice, as she cried out, "O, that's him! that's him! It's pa! it's pa! He's going! he's going! he's gone!" and with loud sobbings, as though she knew she would never see that sober-faced, broad-shouldered patriot again, she turned away and entered the house.

A Mother's Sacrifice.

The records and desolations of our great war do not appear alone in the empty sleeves which we see in every village, nor in the blackened ruins that mark the pathway of our great armies. The most incurable wounds, and the losses hardest to be supported, were suffered by the mothers who gave up darling and only sons to the sacrifice.

What mother can read the following story of the enlistment and death of "Little Eddie, the drummer boy," without feeling that neither glory nor public honors can ever make up her loss or heal her lacerated heart? We give the story as the soldiers tell it.

"A few days before our regiment received orders to join General Lyon, on his march to Wilson's Creek, the drummer of our company was taken sick and conveyed to the hospital, and on the evening preceding the day that we were to march, a negro was arrested within the lines of the camp, and brought before our captain, who asked him 'what business he had within the lines!' He replied, 'I know a drummer that you would like to enlist in your company, and I have come to tell you of it.' He was immediately requested to inform the drummer that if he would enlist for our short term of service, he would be allowed extra pay; and to do this, he must be on the ground early in the morning. The negro was then passed beyond the guard.

"On the following morning there appeared before the captain's quarters, during the beating of the *réveille*, a good-

THE MOTHERS SACRIFICE.

Engraved Expressly for the Women of the War

looking, middle-aged woman, dressed in deep mourning, leading by the hand a sharp, sprightly-looking boy, apparently about twelve or thirteen years of age. Her story was soon told. She was from East Tennessee, where her husband had been killed by the rebels, and all their property destroyed. She had come to St. Louis in search of her sister; but not finding her, and being destitute of money, she thought if she could procure a situation for her boy as a drummer for the short time that we had to remain in the service, she could find employment for herself, and perhaps find her sister by the time we were discharged.

"During the rehearsal of her story the little fellow kept his eyes intently fixed upon the countenance of the captain, who was about to express a determination not to take so small a boy, when he spoke out, 'Don't be afraid, captain; I can drum.' This was spoken with so much confidence, that the captain immediately observed, with a smile, 'Well, well, sergeant, bring the drum, and order our fifer to come forward.' In a few moments the drum was produced, and our fifer, a tall, round-shouldered, good-natured fellow, from the Dubuque mines, who stood, when erect, something over six feet in height, soon made his appearance.

"Upon being introduced to his new comrade, he stooped down, with his hands resting upon his knees, that were thrown forward into an acute angle, and after peering into the little fellow's face a moment, he observed, 'My little man, can you drum?' 'Yes, sir,' he replied, 'I drummed for Captain Hill, in Tennessee.' Our fifer immediately commenced straightening himself upward until all the angles in his person had disappeared, when he placed his fife at his mouth, and played the 'Flowers of Edinboro''—one of the most difficult things to follow with the drum that could have been selected; and nobly did the little fellow follow him, showing himself to be a master of the drum. When the music ceased, our captain turned to the mother and observed, 'Madam, I will take your boy. What is his name?' 'Edward Lee,' she replied; then placing her hand upon the captain's arm, she continued, 'Captain, if he is not killed'—here her maternal feelings overcame her utterance, and she bent down over her boy and kissed him upon the forehead. As she arose, she observed, 'Captain, you will bring him back with you—won't you?'

"'Yes, yes,' he replied, 'we will be certain to bring him back with us. We shall be discharged in six weeks.'

"In an hour after, our company led the Iowa First out of camp, our drum and fife playing 'The girl I left behind me.' Eddie, as we called him, soon became a great favorite with all the men in the company. When any of the boys had returned from a horticultural excursion, Eddie's share of the peaches and melons was the first apportioned out. During our heavy and fatiguing march from Rolla to Springfield, it was often amusing to see our long-legged fifer wading through the mud with our little drummer mounted upon his back, and always in that position when fording streams.

"During the fight at Wilson's Creek I was stationed with a part of our company on the right of Totten's battery, while the balance of our company, with a part of the Illinois regiment, was ordered down into a deep ravine upon our left, in which it was known a portion of the enemy was concealed, with whom they were soon engaged. The contest in the ravine continuing some time, Totten suddenly wheeled his battery upon the enemy in that quarter, when they soon retreated to the high ground behind their lines. In less than twenty minutes after Totten had driven the enemy from the ravine, the word passed from man to man throughout the army, 'Lyon is killed!' and soon after, hostilities having ceased upon both sides, the order came for our main force to fall back upon Springfield, while a part of the Iowa First and two companies of the Missouri regiment were to camp upon the ground and cover the retreat next morning. That night I was detailed for guard duty, my turn of guard closing with the morning call. When I went out with the officer as a relief, I found that my post was upon a high eminence that overlooked the deep ravine in which our men had engaged the enemy, until Totten's battery came to their assistance. It was a dreary, lonesome beat. The moon had gone down in the early part of the night, while the stars twinkled dimly through a hazy atmosphere, lighting up imperfectly the surrounding objects. Occasionally I would place my ear near the ground and listen for the sound of footsteps; but all was silent, save the far-off howling of the wolf, that seemed to scent upon the evening air the banquet that we had been preparing for him. The hours passed slowly away, when at length the morning light began to streak along the eastern sky, making surrounding objects more plainly visible. Presently I heard a drum beat up the morning call. At first I thought it came from the camp of the enemy across the creek; but as I listened, I found that it came up from the deep ravine; for a few minutes it was silent, and then, as it became more light I heard it again. I listened, the sound of the drum was familiar to me, and I knew that it was

> 'Our drummer boy from Tennessee,
> Beating for help the *réveille.*'

"I was about to desert my post to go to his assistance, when I discovered the officer of the guard approaching with two men. We all listened to the sound, and were satisfied that it was Eddie's drum. I asked permission to go to his assistance. The officer hesitated, saying that the orders were to march in twenty minutes. I promised to be back in that time, and he consented. I immediately started down the hill, through the thick undergrowth, and upon reaching the valley, I followed the sound of the drum, and soon found him seated upon the ground, his back leaning against the trunk of a fallen tree, while his drum hung upon a bush in front of him, reaching nearly to the ground. As soon as he discovered me he dropped his drumsticks and exclaimed, 'O corporal, I am so glad to see you! Give me a drink,' reaching out his hand for my canteen, which was empty. I immediately turned to bring him some water from the brook that I could hear rippling through the bushes near by, when, thinking that I was about to leave him, he commenced crying, saying: 'Don't leave me, corporal — I can't walk.' I was soon back with the water, when I discovered that both of his feet had been shot away by a cannon ball. After satisfying his thirst, he looked up into my face and said, 'You don't think I will die, corporal, do you? This man said I would not — he said the surgeon could cure my feet.' I now discovered a man lying in the grass near him. By his dress I recognized him as belonging to the enemy. It appeared that he had been shot through the bowels, and fallen near where Eddie lay. Knowing that he could not live, and seeing the condition of the boy, he had crawled to him, taken off his buckskin suspenders, and corded the little fellow's legs below the knee, and then laid down and died. While he was telling me these particulars, I heard the tramp of cavalry coming down the ravine, and in a moment a scout of the enemy was upon us, and I was taken prisoner. I requested the officer to take Eddie up in front of him, and he did so, carrying him with great tenderness and care. When we reached the camp of the enemy the little fellow was dead."

"That feels like Mother's Hand."

During the last year of the conflict a young officer in a Rhode Island battery received a fearful wound in his right leg from a fragment of a shell. A week of dreadful pain and hardship ensued, during which he was transported from the front, near Richmond, to Washington. The surgeons here, upon consultation, advised an amputation. He telegraphed home that all was well, and composed himself to bear whatever might be in the future, with the fortitude of a true soldier. The operation was performed; but the condition of the patient was critical. His constitution did not rally after the shock, and he was carefully nursed by one of those angels of mercy whose presence illuminated so many of our military hospitals.

His mother, in Rhode Island, who, with the intuition of a woman, had apprehended the extent of the danger, left home on the receipt of the telegraph, and reached Washington at midnight. As the surgeon had enjoined the utmost calmness and quiet as indispensable to the wounded hero, the mother was not allowed to see her suffering boy at once, but sat in an adjoining room patiently waiting for daylight and the permission of the surgeon to enter the ward where he lay.

As the nurse sat there fanning the patient and resting her fingers on the fluttering and feverish pulse, she was thinking every moment of that heavy-hearted mother in the next room, every fibre of whose heart was yearning to come and sit where she was sitting, and lay her hand on her boy. At length, when the ward was still and dark, she glided out, and told his mother that she might go in very softly and take her place; that he seemed to be sleeping, and probably would not know the difference. Gently and without uttering a word, she moved to his bedside, and laid her fingers on the wrist, as the nurse had directed; but the patient, though apparently asleep, perceived a change in the character of the touch. Nature was too strong to be deceived: opening his eyes, he said, "That feels like my mother's hand. Who is this beside me? It is my mother! Turn up the gas, and let me see mother!"

The gas was turned up. The true-hearted boy saw that he was right, and their faces now met in a long, joyful, sobbing embrace.

He rallied a little after she came, and seemed to try very hard, on her account, to feel stronger. But the stump showed bad symptoms, and another amputation, nearer the body, was decided upon, after which he sank.

As the end approached, weeping friends told him that it only remained to make his condition comfortable. He said he had looked death in the face too many times to be afraid now. He had just completed his twenty-first year, and the third of his service in the United States army, when the final bugle-call reached his ears, and the mother laid away the mutilated form of her soldier boy in a sleep from which no electrical touch of maternal love can ever waken him.

The Women of the Prairies.

A great number of the most genuine instances of heroism and self-sacrifice occurred under circumstances that render it impossible for the historian and the annalist to preserve any distinct record of them. The soldier, no matter what his regiment, or in which branch of the service he has enlisted, whether on land or on sea, moves in the eye of the world, and can hardly fail of due praise if he exhibits conspicuous gallantry on the field, or uncommon bravery on the deck of the man-of-war. But the wife and the mother, the sister and the daughter, who have been left without protection and without aid in the solitary cabin, in the lonesome cottage, — what "general order" can praise their self-sacrifice? what bulletin can herald their acts of devotion?

During the four years while the struggle continued, two millions of men in the loyal states were subtracted from the productive labor of the country, and for longer or shorter periods engaged in military service. In the manufacturing communities this deficiency could be supplied with little perceptible derangement. Machinery could do the work that had been performed by muscle, and the millions of Europe were separated from our shores by an ocean that seems ever to grow narrower. But in the West it was otherwise, for that part of our country is agricultural. Nothing could have enabled those magnificent regions to respond so promptly and enthusiastically to the successive calls for men as they did, had not the "lamp of sacrifice" burned on all those hearth-stones; had not the spirit of Christian heroism inspired the hearts of those women of the prairies.

In the absence of so large a number of farmers and farm laborers, agricultural production would in many sections have been cut short, in others almost suspended, had not the women, with a promptness and patriotism rarely equalled in history, volunteered to add field labor to their home employments. "Go," said they, as from time to time the Good President, his heart burdened with the woes of his people, felt the necessity of calling for fresh relays of men, "go at the country's call. We cannot, for we are women; but our sex does not prevent us from assuming your labors. Go, but your plough shall not rust in the furrow where you have left it; weeds shall not choke the corn; the potatoes will not be left to rot in the ground; the ripened wheat shall not be abandoned in the golden fields. With the hands that God has given us, and this fertile soil on which we walk, though none remain with us but boys and graybeards, neither we nor you in the army shall suffer for lack of bread." How nobly that pledge was redeemed is shown by the wonderfully prosperous condition of the loyal states at the end of four years of gigantic warfare.

When the scarred and swarthy veterans, the lines of whose marches had woven a network over the entire face of the Southern States, returned to their homes amid the green savannas of the broad North-west, there were no marks of neglect to be erased, no evidences of dilapidation and decay. They found their farms in as good a condition as when they enlisted. Enhanced prices had balanced diminished production. Crops had been planted, tended, and gathered, by hands that before had been all unused to the hoe and the rake. The sadness lasted only in those households — alas! too numerous — where no disbanding of armies could restore the soldier to the loving arms and the blessed industries of home.

But even these desolated families were not without those consolations that for the noble-hearted can rob widowhood of half its bitterness. Had they not fallen bravely? Were not their names forever linked with great battle-fields? And had not the cause for which they had shouldered arms, and for which they had poured out their lives, been carried by the united labors and sacrifices of all to a triumphant issue and a glorious peace?

MISS JANE BOSWELL MOORE.

SOME who gave themselves to the toils and excitements of army life, and did much for the relief of suffering in camp and hospital, were incited by the recollection of brilliant achievements and shining record of ancestors and kinsmen who figured conspicuously in the Revolution and in the old English wars. This was especially true of a young lady of Baltimore, Miss Jane Boswell Moore, who commenced her army labors in the early part of the war, and continued them, with but brief interruptions from sickness, until midsummer of 1865, after the capture of Richmond.

Her grandfather was a colonel under Wellington in the early part of his splendid military career, when he

> "in far Assaye
> Clashed with his fiery few and won."

Her ancestors on both sides fought at the siege of Derry, and distinguished themselves. Colonel Andrew Boyd, a maternal kinsman, was an officer who served with repute in the war of the Revolution. These family honors and traditions had so wrought upon a temperament naturally enthusiastic, that when our civil war began to mutter its thunders, and to rock the nation with the shock of arms,

Miss Moore regarded this as a summons to her to show by her self-imposed labors, by zeal and devotion, by courage in danger, and by patience in hardships, that she was not unworthy of the martial blood she inherited. The first service she performed was developed in the loyal press of the city to which she belonged, in a series of pungent and unanswerable rebukes to treason. When she entered upon her duties in the sanitary field of the war, her mother became her inseparable companion, and the story of their experiences, most of which is from their own lips, will be found in the words which follow: —

"Who can do justice to the heroism and endurance of our soldiers in this war? The patriotism of a *true* private seems to excel all others — it is so pure, so free from hope or expectation of gain or renown, so unselfish and real. Of the tens of thousands who have fallen, unknown, save to a few dear ones of the home circle, it may be truthfully be said, *Their* only record is on high, and in the eyes of Him to whom all thoughts and motives are open, surely no sight can be more pleasing, than the steady performance of noble, faithful deeds, without thought of, or reference to, earthly reward. No noble or heroic action can ever be without its measure of influence: to rescue, then, a few of these from forgetfulness, is no unworthy endeavor.

It is not often I allow myself to dwell on the fearful realities of the past, as they now rise before me; — from the first hospital, or barracks thrown open in Baltimore, after the battles of Bull Run and Williamsburg, to the closing scenes of the great struggle. A simple incident led us to one of these, — even as we heard convalescing patients allude to the battle-fields—I fainted. But they said our sympathy cheered them, and after a determined struggle our visits were constant. How little my mother or self *then* thought of the scenes awaiting us! Among returned prisoners at McKim's, we saw Samuel E. Smith, a Pennsylvania lad, the fragrant memorial of whose early death has since gone forth to many thousands of souls. By the light of a dimly-rising moon we rode over the burial trenches of Antietam to Smoketown Hospital, through whose scattered grove of trees the roaring of the December wind sounded like the notes of some great funeral organ. Our tent was daily visited by an ever coming and going throng of the maimed and sick. How humble their thanks for paper, ink, books, and little delicacies made us! We had no more welcome guest than the *then* boy-hero, James O. Ladd, of Massachusetts, whose right arm was gone. 'But O,' said he with gathering tears, 'it can't be that my days of helping the cause are over. I want to do more, O, so much more!' What a history was that of this gifted youth, who has been in the service ever since passing six months in southern prisons! A picture of desolate grandeur was Harper's Ferry, with its rude hospitals, its dead on the hill-side, whose march was over, and its tens of thousands of the living thronging every winding path on their way to Fredericksburg, Martinsburg, and Cumberland, in whose old mill, on a wild March evening, we watched the failing breath of Dutton, a New York soldier, dying away from 'an ever-loving and almost forsaken mother'; from Grafton and Wheeling to the old ruined town of Winchester, by whose desolate churches so many of our dead are sleeping, and our little room in Taylor Hospital then (under General Milroy) crowded with fever patients.

We hurried away from here to the wounded of Chancellorsville, those of a single corps covering a large plain at Brook Station. Our tents (for store-room, kitchen, and sleeping) were in a secluded ravine, overhung with laurel. We had sad music — the bands on the hill-side with their mournful 'dead march,' by open graves, and the plaintive cry of the whippoorwill, when our busy day was done. The hurried falling back, and Gettysburg with all its horrors, among whose dead and dying we passed a month, and then found ourselves encamped along the Rappahannock. In the midst of spring's early blossoms we watched Sigel's march up the Valley, visiting his forces just before they left Winchester, with stationery, pickles, &c., and hurried back over deserted roads, with our precious mail-bags bearing thirteen hundred letters, many of them the last messages to friends, and a large flag intrusted to us, and recaptured from the rebels, who took it from us at the time of Milroy's disaster. A deserted cabin formed our next quarters at Point of Rocks, close to the swamps of the Appomattox, where we saw the opening bombardment of Petersburg. The New Hampshire youth, Leonard Wiggan, fell asleep here as the guns were firing, with whispered words of his widowed mother, the shade of green trees, and the babbling brook at home.

"How distinctly memory recalls the night of his death — the doors, windows, and walls of our rude dwelling shook and rattled so under every gun, that we willingly left it, and stood by the stile in the light of a full moon, watching the exploding shells. We then made Leonard the lemonade he had enjoyed so much, for the *last* time. Before the morning broke, he heard the guns no more. His prayer, 'Lord, take me home from all my sufferings,' was answered.

"Half an hour after they were wounded, many of the victims of the fatal mine explosion were under our care, for, by a special order from General Grant, we were allowed to remove to the 'front,' something over a mile and a half from Petersburg. Our tent, which stood in the midst of a group of pines, was shaded with boughs, and the earth strewn with a carpet of pine needles, the dull, monotonous, awful sound of continued musketry firing being ever in our ears. The soul sickens with the horror of the scenes in those woods on and after July 30. What noble letters those brave, crippled, colored soldiers dictated, through us, to friends they were never to see!

"Amid the booming of guns from the neighboring battle-field of Cedar Creek, on an October morning, we entered our little room on Braddock Street, Winchester. How many times were the barrels and boxes of that crowded spot replenished by the Sanitary and Christian Commissions during the six long, busy months of labor among the regimental hospitals, as well as in the snowy tents of Sheridan, covering so many suffering and dying souls!

"O, the sad heart-rending letters written nightly to kindred far away, by that blazing fire of Virginia rails. Twenty messengers sometimes in a day, some to stricken parents, telling of the death of a first or youngest born; some wife would learn from another that strangers cared for and closed the eyes of a dying husband; while to others tidings of safety were gladly sent. That long, cold winter, with its varied and constant cares, passed away, and with tearful eyes, on a Sabbath morning in spring, we heard the church windows rattle amid the booming of great guns, and rejoiced, though in an enemy's country, that victory long delayed was ours. But the brave men who had earned it for us were weary; so we passed under Fort Drury's now silent guns, with our stores, into Richmond, for ten weeks' labor among worn-out troops. This seemed the hardest of all our campaigns; but the end was near: we saw it when the several armies passed through that city, bearing the tattered remnants of what had once been banners, intrusted to them by a redeemed people. Many were so worn out that we found it harder to cheer them than during the war. Are you weary, reader, even of the hasty record of these campaigns? Think, then, of the debt we owe to those who endured them for us. . . . Among the wounded at Brook Station, were many who were mere boys. I remember the names of three from far-off states, William Lauer, Hugh McDonald, and Edward Goodman. They had lost limbs, and I shall never forget their simple, childish joy, when I put aside their coarse hospital fare, and gave them instead, on their tin plates, soft crackers, butter, and nourishing food. They were too shy to speak but little. Hugh wiped his moist eyes with his one remaining hand. Edward was a little German boy. On my way to a dying soldier who thought I could make him tea, and custard, such as he had had at home, a nurse ran out to ask me to stop on my return at his tent, where a little boy, who had lost a leg, was anxious to see me. I went to his cot and offered him some delicacy, when he remarked, with great earnestness, 'It is not for the things you bring, though they are very nice, that I want to see you; but the sight of your face does me so much good! and here I haven't seen you in four days!' A burst of laughter greeted this speech, and I was obliged to explain that my absence had been through no neglect, but from the fact that there were hundreds in that corps to whom my visits were exceedingly desirable; but from that time, whenever it was at all possible, I went in and for a few minutes let him look at me, which he always did steadily, and with an expression of sincere childish satisfaction. The last time I saw him was on the morning of that hurried abandonment of Acquia Creek, as I distributed lemons, boiled eggs, and other articles among those waiting removal. He lay on a stretcher in the sun, by the rude freight cars, and I trembled, as I filled his canteen, for the poor maimed member, after its secondary amputation, having that rough ride in prospect. 'Are *you* going with us?' he asked. 'No,' I replied, 'we shall not leave until all the wounded are away.' 'Will you come and see me in Washington?' 'I am afraid not; there will probably be another battle, and other poor boys will need me.'

"On carrying to Dalton his daily meal, I found on the next cot an Ohio lad of nineteen, whose leg had been amputated the day before. He had not eaten anything all day, but took some crackers, fruit, and a cup of tea, and then told me he had two lemons in his knapsack, which he was afraid would spoil, as he could get no one to make him some lemonade. I made him a tin cup full, and heard him say it was the best he had ever tasted. One day he showed me a letter from home. 'Isn't it a nice long one? Father wrote a bit, and then mother; and then they were afraid it wasn't enough, and they wrote more.' And a noble letter it was, — every line of the four foolscap pages telling of yearning love, of sharp pain smothered for his sake; the mother's heart longing to have him with her, to show him how he should be nursed and cared for; but the father bade him be of good cheer; it would be strange if they would not look after him, and he would much rather have him crippled as he was, than have the taint of coward or copperhead on his name. I told Albert's soldier scribe to tell his mother, a southern woman who detested treason and who knew better than many its cost, had charge of him, and would do all in her power for him. 'I've just been having him tell her so,' was his pleased reply.

"Late at night our room in Taylor Hospital was closed, and amid the sound of nailing coffins in the next room, we sought sleep. But a constant hollow cough was heard from the opposite side, and one day a pale, consumptive boy handed us a handkerchief to hem, saying he had bought it, and 'paid money for it.' It was *his* cough we had heard; he was the only son of a poor widow in West Virginia. When we asked him if he would not like to die at home, his sad face assumed an almost hopeless expression, as he said, 'his mother would be the proudest woman in West Virginia if she could only see her boy; but he had no hope of it.' We said nothing to raise his hopes, for we well knew the character of the surgeon of his regiment, since gone to give account for much cruelty; but we lost no time in making his case known to General Milroy, whose indignation was almost as great as our own. In the evening I carried him the news, with his supper, filling his haversack with good things. He could hardly credit me, and was so weak that it seemed doubtful how he would travel the five miles from the railroad station to his home. 'Somebody will give you a lift,' I said as cheerily as I could; 'just tell them your story.' How long he lived I never knew.

"Not the least distressing sight, after a great battle, is that of friends in search of the wounded and fallen. Ofttimes the claims of those suffering are so great that the dead can scarcely be thought of. One evening a poor widow, with five little children at home dependent on her earnings as a seamstress, came from Philadelphia to look for her eldest boy on the field of Gettysburg. She had heard he was dead, but could not believe it. On reaching the hospital she was told he was in one of the tents. 'O,' she said, 'how my heart beat for joy! but when I went in, they told me he was dead.' He had written to her that nothing would induce him to miss this battle, as on it depended the fate of Pennsylvania, and perhaps the whole country. During the last day's battle he raised his head from behind a stone wall to fire, and being shot through the head, was instantly killed. 'O,' said the poor mother, 'if I could only know he was prepared!' She could be resigned to it all, she said, if her boy's body could go with her, and be buried where she could see his grave. And in perfect trust, she handed me fifteen dollars,—all she had,—and begged me to tell her what to do. I had not a minute to spare, save early in the morning; but I made diligent inquiry, and found a comrade of her son, who described his grave. Then we went together to the man who removed and prepared bodies for transportation. It was clear her money would amount to little. I said so while I was thinking what to do, and she fearfully caught at the words, assuring me she would sew at government tents and bags, any length of time after her return, to make it up. 'Such an idea never entered my mind,' I replied; 'I was only thinking what was best to do. We will arrange it some way.' So I told her story to the grave-digger, whose wife at once gave her her board in their humble house, while her husband reduced his charges. Then we walked to Adams express office, passing a great pile of rusty muskets lately gathered from the battle-field. I could hardly get her away from these. 'I wonder if *my* boy's is there,' she said sadly; and then, as she entered the express office, where her feelings overcame her, 'It was through it,' she said, 'my boy used to send me his little bit of money!' Only the beginning, thought I, of sad memories to haunt her after-life. Here I pleaded her case again, not doubting the result, as every facility possible had been afforded me during the war from the company. Transportation tickets to Baltimore were next procured, and I hurriedly wrote, in the office of the provost, a note to a friend who would pass her the rest of the way. Then she rode in the ambulance as far as it went on her way to search for the grave, and I promised to see her again in the evening. The excitement was then over; she had found the grave, and though unable to see her boy, a lock of his hair had been cut for her, and all was ready for her to leave on the morrow, a gentleman in Philadelphia having offered her burial-room in his lot. But words failed her when she tried to express her gratiude; she could only pour out blessings.

"As I moved in the midst of the appalling scenes on the day of the mine explosion at Petersburg, I heard many groans and prayers. One just brought from the 'table,' was saying, with all the fervor of a departing soul, 'I shall never see my home again; but, Lord, don't *you* forget me.' Colored citizens of Baltimore cried to us to give them 'only one cracker,' and our hearts melted when the appeal was enforced by their directing attention to the stump of an amputated arm or leg. The distress of one poor boy was great; yet he eagerly questioned all whom he saw as to the result of the battle. No one seemed able to soothe him; he mentioned the names of the boys in his regiment, and his great concern for them; then his eyes filled with tears, and he wept, unmindful of his own wound. I went to him, and told him how fearful I was that he would injure himself by excitement, which could do no good. 'Were we to give way to our feelings at such a time, what would become of us, or those around us? It is an awful day to us all; we can only trust in God. Now I want to do all I can to help these poor boys, and to do so I must be very calm; I *know* you will help me.' He smiled amid his tears, saying, 'I haven't seen a lady for months, and it does seem sweet to see one in this awful place.'

"When, in a drenching rain, we visited Haxall's Landing, on James River, with barrels of pickles for Sheridan's weary raiders, the brave and chivalrous Colonel Preston, of the First Vermont cavalry, tin cup in hand, dealt them out to his tired men, meeting our thanks with the reply, 'No, ladies, I feel that I cannot do too much for soldiers.' And then he proposed, and they all gave, three hearty cheers for their friends in Baltimore. But a short time after, riding in the cars, I saw chronicled in the morning paper the heavy loss of the First Vermont, and the death of the noble colonel, leading a charge at Cold Harbor. The same kind interest was shown by the brave Colonel Thoburn of the First West Virginia, on our somewhat perilous trip to Romney, and long afterwards, at the close of a weary day in Winchester, we saw his coffin borne through with tearful eyes.

"In ward twenty of Sheridan Hospital lay a soldier named Powers, who had a wife and six children in Connecticut. His wound was through the body. When I first saw him, he was weak and faint, emaciated almost to a skeleton, and so feeble and tremulous, that he could not raise a cup to his lips without assistance. His eyes were unnaturally bright; but his nurse, a kind, intelligent man, thought, with the best of food and care, he might yet be saved. 'But,' said he, 'where is he to get them?' His physician was a Scotchman, always grateful for attention paid his patients; and from that day I took this one under my especial care, driving daily to his tent with wine, milk punch, egg-nog, canned chicken, butter, jelly, tea, pickles, &c., varying his fare as often as possible, and his improvement fairly astonished us. At first it was a little jelly he craved, and that tasted 'so good' to him; but by and by he relished stronger food. For thirty years, we were told, Shenandoah Valley had not seen such a winter. Even in February the snow was a foot deep, and the cold was severely felt in those open tents on that bleak hill-side. Powers's clothes were cotton, and thin at that. But thanks to kind hearts somewhere, I was able to furnish him with a warm woollen outfit; and as I handed him each garment, he looked up earnestly, saying, 'Now, are you sure I am not taking too much from you?' I told him he must thank others for them, and that I only fulfilled my duty in giving them. One day the surgeon in charge passed through, and seeing him, exclaimed, 'Why, man, I thought you were dead long ago?' And so he would have been, but for those donations of friends intrusted to us. When I asked him to inscribe a line in my note-book by way of remembrance, he replied, 'I am too weak to hold the pen firmly; but write for me, and let it be, "You took me from death!"' What true Irish eloquence was that! His physician wrote under it, 'I fully indorse the above, and also thank you for your unwearying kindness. C. M. M'Laurie.'

"In the same hospital was Isaac Price, of the Fifteenth Virginia, a soldier of thirty-eight years of age, with a wife and nine children, the eldest of whom, a lad of nineteen, was in the Tenth Virginia. But the greatest of calamities had fallen upon him. Both his arms had been amputated; yet he was cheerful and patient, always greeting us with a smile. On the receipt of a bag of clothing at Christmas, he dictated a letter in reply from his home in Bealington, Barbour County, West Virginia. Nor was his the only case. After the battle of Antietam, in the hospitals of Frederick, we talked with Arias H. Young, a lad of seventeen, from Wisconsin, and Daniel Fuller, from Pennsylvania, both of whom were thus terribly stricken.

"In the hospital at Point of Rocks, on the Appomattox, two cases were peculiarly distressing. One was that of a soldier named Heskett, who left a mother, wife, and four little children, all very destitute. Two of his brothers had died in the army, one never having been heard from; another, William, was in the service, and Heskett was dying. In his delirium he frequently turned to his nurse, exclaiming, 'There's my wife! She came up here to see me! Why don't you let her come?' When I wished to write to his mother, 'O, no,' he said, 'my mother can't bear any more trouble. She has lost so much!' He was one of the hundred days' men from Ohio, and his sorrowing family was unable even to have his remains brought home. The other was Hummiston, who also volunteered for a hundred days. About an hour before his death, as he lay on the earth, with a knapsack for a pillow, a letter, once anxiously looked for, but now, alas! powerless to give consolation, was brought in and laid by his side. It was a cheerful, happy letter, from a loving, industrious wife, telling of household straits and cares, with all the sunshine of a glad spirit, enough to give the hardest heart a pang to read it, and then look at that unconscious, dying man! In it was the first child-letter of his little daughter, Flora, 'to dear pa.' In a subsequent letter, Mrs. Hummiston says, 'I have four children, the eldest about ten years old, and the youngest seventeen months. I feel I have a great responsibility resting upon me, not so much in supporting them, as in training them up for usefulness and future happiness. When I think of my lonely and helpless condition, I can but remember the many widows, made such by this terrible war, who have never been used to work, and are dependent on their own exertions for support.'

"In visiting one of the many houses in Winchester, over whose floors the wounded were strewn, the morning after they arrived from the front, I found, in a little up-stairs room, Sergeant Colby, of the Thirty-fourth Massachusetts regiment, wounded in the ankle. He looked dispirited, and we brought him reading, paper, and pencils, leaving him some delicacy daily. He whiled away some hours executing two beautiful drawings, now in the keeping of his bereaved mother, one a female figure of Hope, with uplifted finger, and an anchor grasped in a firm hand; the other a soldier, pacing his weary rounds as a sentinel in a heavy snow-storm. When I found him after his removal to the field hospital, I was startled by the frightful rapidity with which death had done his work. 'Write something cheering,' he feebly murmured, as a few lines were pencilled to his mother. It was no common offering that this Christian mother laid upon the altar of her country. We can ill spare such men as James Colby. I have never read more touching letters than those written while he was in the army. They breathe the fervent, earnest spirit of a devoted Christian, and a warmly affectionate and patriotic heart. It makes one shudder to think what our condition would have been, had not the blood of tens of thousands of dearly loved sons and fathers been thus poured out. His mother, who has a crippled son at home, and has lately buried two lovely daughters, says, 'His plastic nature answered my fondest hopes. Not only did he grow in all manly virtues, but God set his seal. James gave his heart to the Saviour ere he entered the service of his country. He writes just after battle, "I had no fear, for I knew that God was with me!" There was no need that he should make his profession of faith when he came upon his death-bed. His work was done — he had nothing to do but to die! *Years ago I longed and prayed that I might be permitted to do something for the poor slave. By terrible things in righteousness have I been answered. Yet I often rejoice, even exult, that I am permitted to suffer, to weep with those who have wept tears more agonizing than mine!'* Such is the spirit of one of the many American women to whose sacrifices our country owes its life. *Their full reward cannot possibly be here.*

"Riding out to regiments near Richmond, I met soldiers with knapsacks, lately mustered out, and on their way to Richmond to take the boat for home. One, to whom I gave the 'Christian Banner' for his child, said, with tears in his eyes, 'I'll not forget what a comfort your things have been to me. Many a time I've written home on the paper you gave me, when I hadn't a cent to buy any with.' My eyes filled. Truly this pay was very sweet!

"The war, with its opportunities of usefulness, has indeed passed away, but the work will never be done while a maimed or crippled soldier remains in our land. *And the widow and orphan — are they not with us?*"

Referring to this long series of exposures and exertions, Miss Moore says, "We drew liberal supplies from both Sanitary and Christian Commissions, as well as largely from individuals, but have ourselves belonged to no association, and received no compensation from any quarter. None of our expenses were defrayed, except in the matter of government passes. As southern women who had no relatives to give to the cause, we have endeavored to be behind none in our devotion."

In not a few instances Miss Moore was engaged in the hazardous work of ministering to the wounded even before they were removed from the battle-field. She has braved danger of every kind short of actual presence in a battle, in relieving the sufferings of our wounded braves.

General Emory says of her and her mother, "The names of Miss and Mrs. Moore are on the lips of thousands to whom they have ministered in camp and hospital." General Grant also testifies to their remarkable usefulness. The health of Miss Moore has been seriously impaired by the hardships she has suffered, and by the agitations of those four years of unremitting military service. But are not such sacrifices of ease and health balanced, and more than compensated, by the consciousness of having discharged, to the utmost degree of her ability, the duty of a patriot, and by the affection and gratitude of thousands ready to perish to whom she brought such timely succor?

WHAT SANITARY LABORERS HAVE ACCOMPLISHED.

THE question of the right of a state to secede, and of slavery to make itself perpetual, though on the ruins of theRepublic, were not the sole issues that our war has submitted to the arbitrament of the sword.

Up to the year 1860 — we may say till the year 1865 — European monarchists, while admitting the efficiency of the Great Republic as against foreign enemies, professed a doubt as to its ability to outlive the assaults of an intestine foe. That question is now and forever put at rest.

No one circumstance or fact has done more to establish this great result than the vast, the untiring, and the systematic contributions which the American people, of their own free will, and with cheerful alacrity, made to sustain the soldier in the field, and the widows and orphans of those who fell. The history of the world had seen nothing like it before. It marks an epoch in civilized warfare. It has shown, as nothing else could, the intense patriotism of our people. It proves that though the constitution is but an abstract and intellectual statement of our views of government, that parchment is as dear to the American heart as the person and living presence of any king ever was to the most enthusiastic loyalist.

The generation to whom the giant questions of 1861 were submitted was essentially and thoroughly peaceful. The Mexican war was remote and unimportant. It was not waged to avenge a great wrong, or vindicate a great principle, and therefore it never laid hold upon the hearts of the people; it never roused the enthusiasm of the masses.

It had been almost fifty years since the blood in American veins had been thrilled by the war-trumpet, pouring its stern and stirring notes across the continent, and calling the nation to the defence of everything worth living for and worth dying for.

And when that summons came, how promptly and heroically was it answered! The entire nation, as by a common and simultaneous impulse, resolved itself into a committee of the whole, to vindicate the national unity and save the national life. Twenty millions of people divided themselves into two grand classes — those who shouldered the musket and marched to fight the great battles of the issue, and those who, by reason of their age or sex, or those immediately dependent on their industry, could not fight, but who commenced at once to do all in their power to provide for, to sustain, to cheer, to encourage the soldiers in active service.

The question is unimportant as to which city or which state was the first to organize those societies for soldiers' relief which were eventually merged and comprehended in the great national systems of beneficence known as the Sanitary and the Christian Commissions. Those noble, self-sacrificing, and far-reaching organizations were the natural growth and the logical development of a desire common to ten thousand hearts. Large credit may be due to this or that organizing brain for the skill with which the popular zeal was utilized, and made to bear uniformly and with success upon the sufferings created by war; but the popular zeal, the devotion and self-sacrifice, were kindled by no eloquence, they were manufactured by no daily press, they emanated from no metropolitan centre. Even before one hostile gun had been fired, and while the national flag was still afloat, without challenge or insult over the defences of Charleston harbor, here and there busy hands, prompted by saddened hearts, were scraping lint and rolling bandages — the first fruits of woman's thoughtfulness and woman's love. In April, 1861, it was known that war must be; how vast, how long, or how bloody, was known only to the Creator of the universe.

Cleveland, probably, can claim the honor of calling the first public meeting with the view of organizing a Soldiers' Aid Society. This was five days after the fall of Sumter. Six days later, on the 25th of April, a company of women assembled at the Cooper Institute, in New York, and organized themselves into what was so long known as the "Woman's Central Relief Association of New York." Miss Louisa Lee Schuyler became the president of this organization, and prepared the circular, which was sent out over all the land, as an appeal to the women of the country, already engaged in preparing against the time of wounds and sickness. For week after week, till the eventful months became years big with the records of a nation's sacrifice, did this accomplished and energetic young woman devote herself to the wide field of home labor which the presidency of this association opened for her. It was in a great measure due to the breadth, the wisdom and practical efficiency of her plans, that the organization expanded, taking on a form worthy of the great metropolis where it originated, and became the United States Sanitary Commission. Early in the summer of 1861, Miss Schuyler and the ladies whom she represented felt that there was wanting a system to act for the soldier with the government, and in harmony with the established modes of sanitary relief. To accomplish this, an address was made to the Secretary of War, by the Woman's Central Relief Association, the advising committee of the Board of Physicians and Surgeons of the hospitals of New York, and the New York Medical Association, for furnishing hospital supplies.

After some natural delay and hesitation, not without some opposition from red-tape routinists, it was established under the authority, but not at the expense, of the government, on the 9th of June, 1861, and went into immediate operation.

The general ideas which it strove to carry into effect, and upon which its great usefulness was based, were as follows: —

1. The system of sanitary relief established by the army regulations to be taken as the best, and the Sanitary Commission is to acquaint itself fully, and see that all its agents are familiar, with the plans, methods of care and relief, of the regular system.

2. The Commission should direct its efforts mainly to strengthening the regular system in every practicable way,

and securing the favor and coöperation of the Medical Bureau, so as to win a cheerful and unobstructed pathway for the mercy and charities of a great and loyal people, in their desire to sustain the soldier in the field.

3. The Commission should know nothing of religious differences or state distinctions, distributing without regard to the place where troops were enlisted, in a purely Federal and national spirit.

With these cardinal, and, as it were, constitutional provisions, the Sanitary Commission in the summer of 1861 completed its organization. It constituted, when in operation, a colossal network of charity, a system of beneficence as broad as the theatre of the war, an aqueduct of continental proportions, with complicated yet smooth running appliances, whose blessed function it was to bring to the tent, and to the hospital of the weary, the sick, the bleeding, or the ragged soldier, that moral and material comfort and sympathy, which had their origin in thousands of distant villages, by ten thousand solitary hearth-stones.

It is somewhat remarkable, that while the volunteering enthusiasm of the Northern States died out in the first year of the war, so that drafting, and at length large bounties, were necessary to keep up the armies in the field, the liberality and self-sacrifices of the loyal women of the North continually increased, so that, after the rage and desolation of three years of warfare, it was as easy to raise a hundred thousand dollars for the soldier as it had been to collect ten thousand for the same objects in 1861.

No feature of the war was more extraordinary than that series of Sanitary Fairs that were so wonderfully successful in producing abundant supplies for the Commission in the years 1863 and 1864. For more than two years the appeals for money had been made to be paid directly, and on principle, for the benefit of the soldier, and the returns thus realized, though small in detail, gave a magnificent amount in the sum total. More than seven millions had been sent from the people to the soldiers, through the agency of the Sanitary Commission, before the battle of Gettysburg and the fall of Vicksburg. Chicago was the first of the great metropolitan cities to begin this splendid series. She was the pioneer in these enterprises, and though the year following she was surpassed by St. Louis, and by Pittsburg and Philadelphia and others, yet, considering that all they did was to use to a broader extent, and under a warmer popular enthusiasm and rivalry, the machinery first brought into use *there*, Chicago deserves all praise for the incentive of her brilliant example.

Mrs. Hoge and Mrs. Livermore, ladies who devoted themselves throughout the war to every loyal word and work, and every good deed by which the soldier could be cheered and sustained, entered upon this enterprise with a zeal and a largeness of heart and comprehensiveness of plan which were worthy alike of the magnificent region in which they operated, and of the heroic army for which they labored. None of the great fairs was so entirely the offering of the gentle hands and pure hearts of patriotic women as this at Chicago.

Their executive committee covered the whole North-west from Detroit westward to the cities of Iowa, and northward to St. Paul. And yet, so little accustomed were the people to the princely munificence of later months, that they would have thought their success brilliant if they could have been certain of realizing twenty-five thousand dollars. Their returns were far beyond this modest estimate, and they were enabled, at the termination of their labors, to pay over to the Sanitary Commission more than three times twenty-five thousand as the net profits of the Chicago Fair.

Cincinnati was the next of the western cities to follow in the path that had been blazed out by the vigor and loyal enterprise of her sister emporium. Here, too, woman was the first to suggest, and the most efficient and unwearied in the labors that ensued.

The first step taken in the originating of the great western Sanitary Fair was the following appeal from the pen of Mrs. Elizabeth Mendenhall, which appeared in the Cincinnati Times of October 31, 1863, and a day or two afterwards in most of the daily prints of that city:—

"Editor Times: I wish to call the attention of the patriotic ladies of Cincinnati to the fair that is now progressing in Chicago for the benefit of the soldiers, and which is realizing a handsome sum of money. Taking into consideration the fact that the winter is fast approaching, and that the soldiers will stand in need of much assistance, would it not be well for our Cincinnati ladies to rouse themselves in the same cause, and in the same way? We should not let Chicago, or any other place, be in advance of us in our efforts. I know we have ladies here who are devoted friends of the soldiers, and now is the time for them to be up and doing."

In two weeks from the publication of this suggestion, a

public meeting was called, and very largely attended, at which managers of both sexes were appointed, who proceeded at once to organize, on a scale of greater magnitude, and to embrace a greater number of interests and classes in the community, than any charitable enterprise that had ever been set on foot in America.

If the honor of the original conception of a magnificent fair belongs to Mrs. Hoge and her co-laborers at Chicago, Mrs. Mendenhall and her assistants at Cincinnati are entitled to the credit of carrying into execution the true plan upon which such enterprises should be conducted. They saw that, in order to obtain a complete success, the effort must be general, appealing to all classes, calling the farmer from his golden harvest-field to come and bring with him the first fruits of the earth, as a free-will offering on the altar of his country, appealing to the artisan to give from his workshop his most cunning and elaborate handicraft. The soldier, also, could send from battle-fields that are now famous in history his trophies and his flags, his relics and his mementos. The men of position and genius, who, by their pens or tongues, had won national repute, could advance the cause by furnishing their autographic poems, or other articles of literary value. Upon this comprehensive plan the organization was effected, and rarely has machinery so complicated been adjusted with greater skill, or worked in harmony more admirable. Enlarging thus amply the original idea of Chicago, the executive committee of Cincinnati proposed to raise two hundred and fifty thousand dollars — just ten times the sum proposed at Chicago; and the result showed that the liberality of the people, when appealed to in the manner suggested, had not been over-estimated. The Cincinnati Fair was in all its features, and in its returns, a magnificent success. It was the true beginning of those noble enterprises that afterwards astonished Europe, and by whose operation over five millions of dollars were, in a little more than a twelvemonth, contributed to promote the sanitary condition of the armies in the field.

The Christian Commission, as well as its predecessor and co-laborer, owes its efficiency mainly to the zeal, the patience, and the generosity with which it was sustained by the loyal ladies of the country.

Organized in November, 1861, at first as a Christian enterprise for evangelical labors among the soldiers, its operations became each year more and more sanitary in their character. It was found that to feed the hungry, to clothe the naked, and to bind up the wounds of battle, were the surest way of reaching the heart of the soldier for spiritual suggestions.

The system of special diet kitchens, that in the latter part of the war was extended so as to reach every corps, every division, and often every brigade in the whole army, was especially the product of the organized benevolence of the Christian Commission. Mrs. Anne Wittenmeyer had this work under her special superintendence, with Miss Mary Shelton and Miss Goodale for assistants. It proposed to supply to the sickest in each hospital food as nearly resembling as possible that which his mother and sisters would have furnished him at home. It was a gospel of suitable and delicate food, administered with Christian kindness and "in the name of a disciple," the effect of which in relieving suffering and saving life is alike beyond estimation and above praise.

In the third year of the war, Ladies' Christian Commissions were organized, and went into operation so as speedily to assume a tangible form and give practical results. In 1865, there were in all two hundred and sixty-six branch or auxiliary societies in various parts of the land, mostly connected with the evangelical churches. There were eighty in the city of Philadelphia alone, and the aggregate receipts from all at the end of the war were found to be considerably over two hundred thousand dollars.

In their closing report, made January 1, 1866, the officers express their acknowledgments for the aid furnished by patriotic women: "They have fed the flame of piety and patriotism in our homes, through heavy hours, for successive years, and with busy fingers and devices of love have kept the hands of our agents and delegates in the field full of comforts for suffering patriots. To them, under God, the Commission owes its success. We only anticipate the verdict of the future when we say that thus far in human history such work is exclusively theirs — a work that could have been wrought only by praying wives, and mothers, and sisters, in behalf of an imperilled country."

Though the amounts in cash furnished for sanitary purposes came mainly through these great fairs, contributions from other sources and in other material did as much, and, in many cases, more than money for the substantial well being of the volunteer.

Soldiers' Aid Societies were formed in almost every large

town throughout the Northern States. In these, ladies assembled weekly, and sometimes more frequently; sometimes at the public rooms of the association, but oftener at private houses; and made clothing for the soldiers. These garments, together with various articles of food, such as pickles, dried fruit, jellies, and wine, were securely packed, and sent to the nearest large city where the Sanitary and Christian Commissions had depots of supply. No computation has been made, and none can be, of the entire amount and value of articles thus furnished.

As a specimen we may take the State of Wisconsin, where there is no metropolitan city, and which held no great sanitary fair. In her final report, Mrs. Joseph S. Colt, of Milwaukee, corresponding secretary of the Wisconsin Soldiers' Aid Society, a most admirable and praiseworthy home laborer, says, "We present our last report with devout thankfulness, not unmixed with a degree of pride in our state. We are thankful that the war is over, the republic saved, human freedom established over the whole land. We are proud that Wisconsin, without the excitement of a fair, and remote from the seat of war, has done her part so well.

"Gifts to the amount of two hundred thousand dollars; packages numbering six thousand; bureaus whose success has been unexampled; a society for forwarding supplies; a bureau for getting state pay for the families of soldiers; another for securing pensions and arrears; another for obtaining employment for the wives and mothers of volunteers through government contracts; still another for securing work for those partially disabled in the war; still another for supplying the wants of those who have been permanently crippled in the service, and thrown upon wives and mothers for support, — these, and more, have been our work."

The Chicago branch of the Sanitary Commission had one thousand Aid Societies constantly sending in money and material, by which its treasury was kept full, and its shelves loaded. Five hundred societies united in supporting the Cleveland and the Cincinnati branches. The memorable services rendered by Mrs. Hoge and Mrs. Livermore in the extreme North-west, and by Mrs. Mendenhall and Mrs. Hoadley at Cincinnati, are elsewhere described.

At Cleveland, also, these magnificent results were almost wholly the work of women. Mrs. Rouse, president of the Cleveland branch, is a lady who unites the charity of the Christian to the force and judgment of a woman of the world. A descendant of Oliver Cromwell, she has proved herself not unworthy of the heroic blood of those splendid old Puritans who brought to civil and military affairs a coolness of judgment and an immutability of purpose which some writers have thought inconsistent with their religious zeal, but which were, in fact, the necessary effects of it. For more than forty years she has been at the head of every philanthropic enterprise in that city, and her advanced years and delicate health did not prevent her from acting a truly noble part in this, the most magnificent of all modern charities.

Mrs. Rouse was very effectively sustained by her secretary, Miss M. C. Brayton, a young lady of fine capabilities and acquirements, of easy fortune, and superior business faculties. She was for Cleveland what Louisa Lee Schuyler was for the parent society in New York. Miss Ellen Terry, the treasurer, with an admirable turn for affairs, kept the books, and handled the finances of a business that amounted to more than a million of dollars, with skill that would have done credit to the largest of mercantile houses.

Detroit, also, was a large contributor to the sanitary stores. Here, as at Cleveland, the work was mainly performed by fair hands. Miss Valeria Campbell and Mrs. Adams, Mrs. Brent, Mrs. Sabine, and Mrs. Luther B. Willard, were incessant in their exertions throughout the rebellion. Mrs. Huzz and her two daughters, Susan and Ella, devoted much of their time to the cause.

The case of another admirable friend of the soldier in Detroit, and the circumstances of her death, so sudden and appalling, are such as to require special mention. Miss Mary Dunn, a young lady of about twenty summers, endowed with every Christian and every female grace, beloved by all who knew her, while in the act of bearing food to some sick soldiers at the barracks, where she was a frequent visitor, was killed instantly on the street by a stroke of lightning. At the very hour this occurred, her two brothers were in a distant part of the country, in the midst of a hard battle with the Southern foe. The soldiers were so affected by the peculiar death of Miss Dunn, and so warm in their admiration of her virtues, that they turned out to a man, and buried her remains with full military honors.

Aside from her activity in Detroit, which lasted during

the war, and was wholly gratuitous, Mrs. Willard went to Chattanooga as a volunteer nurse; but severe and lengthened illness cut short her service in the field.

At Buffalo the head centre of sanitary charities was Mrs. Horatio Seymour; and her aids were Miss Grace Bird and Miss Babcock. The contributions made through these ladies were very large, a great number of packages having been sent directly to agents at the front. Mrs. Price, who represented this society at the Naval School Hospital, was constantly supplied with clothing and comforts of all kinds for distribution there and at City Point, where she afterwards went.

In concluding her report, Mrs. Seymour illustrates the spirit in which the contributions from Western New York were made by the following instances and figures: "We cannot shut out from our memories the scenes which will always hallow these rooms to us — the sister, whose brother had gone out in his country's defence, coming to us one bleak, cold day, having rode twelve miles in a stage with her two little children, to ask for shirts to make up for the soldiers. She was poor, had no money to give, but with tearful eyes said she must do something for the boys.

"Nor can we forget the old, true-hearted, patriotic farmer, who drove to the door, one of the severest days in November last, with a load of potatoes, which 'wife and I' had dug, and wished there were ten times as many for the boys.

"We have sent nearly three thousand packages to Louisville, and six hundred and twenty-five to New York. We have cut and provided materials, at our rooms, for over twenty thousand shirts and other articles for the army, amounting in all to more than two hundred thousand pieces. Little children, mostly girls under twelve years of age, have given us over twenty-five hundred dollars."

In Philadelphia the three leading societies were the "Soldiers' Aid," represented in the field for a long time by Mrs. Brady; the "Ladies' Aid," whose secretary was Mrs. John Harris, and the "Penn Relief Association." The operations of the two first named are described in the memoir of Mrs. Brady, and the account of Mrs. Harris's wonderful activity in behalf of the soldier.

The Penn Relief dispensed clothing and delicacies to the value of fifty thousand dollars. Most of their packages were forwarded directly to representatives at the front. Mrs. Husband received a great amount of clothing, of a superior quality, from the Penn Relief. Mrs. Fales, of Washington, Mrs. Hetty K. Painter, and Miss Anna Carver, all drew largely from the same source.

The Woman's Central Relief Association of New York, throughout the struggle, represented the metropolis of the continent in the breadth of country from which it drew its supplies, the largeness of its contributions, the admirable foresight, comprehension, and energy, with which its plans were laid and its finances handled. Replenished from time to time by private contributions, and by the returns of the great Sanitary Fairs of Brooklyn and New York City, its treasury was able to report its monthly disbursements by tens of thousands, and the sum total of its income by millions.

Of the New England States, Connecticut and Rhode

Island sent their contributions mostly to New York. The New England Women's Auxiliary Association of Boston, acting for Massachusetts and the three states to the northward, represented more than a thousand towns, and furnished, in cash and various garments and stores, more than the value of three hundred and fourteen thousand dollars, the Music Hall Fair alone netting about a hundred and fifty thousand dollars.

Miss Abby W. May, of Dorchester, occupied the chair of the executive committee in this Association, and did for Boston what Mrs. Hoge did in Chicago, and Mrs. Seymour in Buffalo.

In the final report of that committee, made in July, 1865, the manner in which every class in the community, and all ages, united in their sympathies for the soldier in the field, is thus set forth: "From the representatives of the United States government here, who remitted the duties upon soldiers' garments sent to us from Nova Scotia, down to the little child diligently sewing with tiny fingers upon the soldiers' comfort-bag, the coöperation has been almost universal. Churches of all denominations have exerted their influence for us; many schools have made special efforts in our behalf; the directors of railroads, express companies, telegraphs, and newspapers, gentlemen of the business firms with which we have dealt, have befriended us most liberally; while private individuals, of all ages, sexes, colors, and conditions, have aided us in ways that we cannot enumerate, and that no one really knows of but themselves."

During the latter part of the war, the ladies in different

points over the land, where several railroads converge, established Soldiers' Homes and Soldiers' Rests, where the worn, hungry, ragged, and sick soldier could pause, sometimes only a few moments in changing trains, and sometimes days or weeks, according to his condition, have his various wants supplied, and be sent forward to his destination.

In June, 1865, many of these noble institutions were distributed over the country, from Boston to New Orleans. The daily scenes within them, and the manner in which they afforded aid and comfort to the travelling soldier, can be understood from the following description of the Home at Columbus, the capital of Ohio, written by an army officer in the spring of 1865: —

"How few of our citizens have taken the pains to turn the corner of the Union Depot to give a passing look at the flourishing Soldiers' Home, stretching its white length along the pier! The last few days have brought an unusual number of guests to its door — on Wednesday one hundred and fifty, and on Thursday one hundred and seventy, more having been entertained there.

"Eastern hospitals are in process of depletion to make room for new arrivals from Sherman's army of those who have fallen by the way in the grand march. *Convalescents* they call these weary men, who hobble on crutches about the door, and crowd every available space within the Home limits; yet each bears his marks of disease or wound, either in pale face or feeble gait, in useless arm or crippled limb. But all differences in individual cases are merged in the one absorbing interest with which the still closed dining-room door is watched. Behind that protecting barrier all is now bustle and active preparation, and under the influence of quick fingers the meal is in readiness, soon enough for the patience even of the hungry crowd waiting beyond the door. Now the word is given, and in troops the first instalment of men, very slowly and feebly, — not as they marched away with Sherman, — for these must be carefully helped to their places at the bountiful table, with crutches stowed away in close proximity; this one must have some kind hand to supply the place of the arm now hanging useless by his side, and another's morbid appetite craves some variation from the ordinary fare. The guests' names must be recorded as accurately as the warfare of knives and forks will permit, rough government crutches exchanged for the comfortably-padded ones furnished by the Sanitary Commission, and many little deficiencies in clothing noted and remedied, while the men do justice to the fare before them. No wonder the faces brighten under the combined influence of kind words and good cheer. Did the maker of these marvellous cookies realize the exquisite relish with which the appetite of a convalescent regards them? These vegetables and apple-butter, with which some thoughtful country Aid Society has furnished the Home larder, are delicious beyond belief to men so long consigned to salt beef and hard tack; while the butter and soft bread receive such special attention, that reënforcements are speedily required. A low hum of applause and approving comment runs round the tables; one and another says, audibly enough to rejoice the attendant ladies, 'Well, this looks like home!' or, 'I haven't seen anything like this since

I left home!' Many pay only the compliments of full justice to the meal, while here and there one summons up courage to make a neat little speech of thanks as he rises from the table. But whether silent or complimentary, the feeling of all, we believe, is expressed in the words of the tall, pale sergeant, who, rising with difficulty on his crutches, says, 'Ladies, kind friends! it is worth the little we have suffered for our country to meet such a warm reception at home.'

"Now the room is finally emptied of its first guests, and the tables hastily prepared for the second instalment, and then for a third and fourth. All honor to the worthy matron that her larder stands bravely such repeated attacks, and her coffee-boiler stoutly replies to all drafts made upon it. What a relief, that the last poor fellow who lingered near the table has fared as well as the first who rushed eagerly in to the assault! The same programme is repeated on each occasion, with variations in individual cases. One forever-helpless man is carried in the arms of a brother soldier, that he, too, may have the pleasure of sitting at the table with the rest; and he pulls out the fatal bullet which 'ruined' him, as he says, to exhibit. Meanwhile there are many in the sleeping ward too feeble to care to leave its comfort, whose taste must be consulted, and to whom food must be carried. Here one man's wound needs dressing, another asks for a fresh bandage; here a slipper is wanted for a swollen foot, and another sickly soldier must have some strengthening remedy from the medicine-chest. At last all are fed, all rested, and all wants attended to; the whistle of the train is heard, and the soldiers depart, with strength enough gained to carry them on their journey, leaving behind them a blessing for the Home. But their departure brings little rest to the Home corps. The *débris* must be removed, and fresh preparations made for the arrival of the later trains, which may bring as many more guests, to be entertained again and lodged over night."

On the first day of May, 1861, two weeks after the fall of Sumter, a large number of Union troops, passing through the city of Philadelphia on their way to the national capital, landed at the foot of Washington Avenue, on Delaware River. While here, awaiting transportation, a number of ladies, residing in the immediate vicinity, spontaneously formed themselves into a committee, and with the assistance of the neighbors generally, distributed among these men such quantities of hot coffee as could be prepared.

These ladies, Mrs. Wm. M. Cooper, Mrs. Sarah Ewing, Mrs. Grace Nickles, Mrs. Catharine and Mrs. Elizabeth Vansdale, Mrs. Turner, and some others, formed the nucleus of the Cooper Shop Volunteer Refreshment Committee.

Near by the place where these gallant volunteers received these first hospitalities stood an old cooper shop. The ladies interested their husbands in the cause; a portion of the shop was partitioned, and so arranged that soldiers could conveniently partake of coffee and other refreshments. From that time till the summer of 1865, for a period of four years and two months, this saloon was constantly sustained and kept in activity by the patriotic citizens of Philadelphia and its vicinity. A hospital was established in connection with the saloon, through the untiring exertions of Miss Anna M. Ross — exertions so strenuous as in the end to consume her vital powers, and add her name to the long roll of martyrs in the good cause. The whole number of soldiers furnished with substantial meals at the saloon was about three hundred and seventeen thousand.

A dispensary of medicines was connected with the cooper shop, a bathing-room, and an arrangement for supplying necessary clothing.

These descriptions of the two, which are taken simply as specimens, located in Columbus and at Philadelphia respectively, will apply to the Homes at Buffalo, Detroit, Washington, Boston, and the various other points where they were established.

With these facts, the question is natural, How were these unequalled largesses disbursed? and what was the practical result to the sick, the wounded, or the destitute soldier, of systems of relief so varied and so copious?

We have in answer the testimony of one of the ablest of our commanding officers, that the two most effective ways in which our armies in the field were sustained in the long struggle, were, first, by the general assurance that was felt, that neither the wives, children, parents, nor others dependent on those in the field, would suffer for the necessaries of life, while their supporters were in the service of the country; second, that the sick and wounded would not lack for any of those things, which, though not provided by army regulations, might conduce to comfort, expedite recovery, save the lives, and sustain the morale of the soldier.

Another and more perfect answer may be found in sanitary statistics. Before this war of ours, it was considered as inevitable that for every soldier killed in battle, four must die of disease. In the Crimean war, seven eighths of the mortality of the British troops during the entire campaign was due to disease, and one eighth only to deaths from wounds received in action. In January, 1855, the month of the greatest mortality of that campaign, ninety-seven per cent of the mortality was from disease. During our national struggle, *two hundred and eighty thousand four hundred and twenty* men — good, true, and loyal — sealed their patriotism by death in the service. Of these over sixty thousand died in battle, while *thirty-five thousand* survived the day of the conflict to die of their wounds, and *one hundred and eighty-four thousand three hundred and thirty-one* died of disease. Thus two persons died of disease for every one that fell by the enemy's weapons. With ordinary sanitary and medical appliances, such as Napoleon had in his armies, and such as the English had in the Crimea, our deaths by disease would have reached the fearful aggregate of more than *three hundred and sixty-eight thousand.* Thus it appears that the result of all these labors and sacrifices by our loyal women, of the abundant returns from our sanitary fairs, and of the constant, loving, unremitting care for the brave champions of the Union, has been a saving of *more than a hundred and eighty-four thousand lives*, that would otherwise have been victims of the malaria of southern climates, the exposures of the camp, the transport ship, and the bivouac, the infection of hospitals, the depression consequent upon being forgotten and neglected among strangers, homesickness, and the slow corrosion of constant anxiety for the loved ones left behind, and all the other horrors and hardships of terrible war.

In conclusion, the author of this volume of sketches feels it due to himself to allude to the great difficulty he has experienced in obtaining his materials.

It was only by overcoming extreme reluctance to anything like publicity on the part of many, by a voluminous correspondence, and by numerous personal interviews, that he has collected the facts of which the foregoing pages are a recital. Now, however, as the compilation has reached the limits to which he is circumscribed, he finds his table loaded with a surplus of material so large, interesting, and valuable, that he cannot claim that this volume, as the record of female heroism and self-sacrifice, is either complete or exhaustive.

Those who, in person or by their friends, responded with promptness, and furnished abundant material, may seem to have a mention too prominent. This, however, is entirely the result of circumstances, and was not done with the view of making invidious distinctions.

Among those who labored long and faithfully in the army of the Potomac, Miss Bradford and Miss Gilson, of Massachusetts, were, perhaps, not equalled by those whose record is fully given. The story of the army life, and of the death of Mrs. General Barlow, is full of interest and romance.

The work of Clara Barton is known from Maine to Missouri. The close of the war has not terminated her industry nor furnished an opportunity to complete her admirable record.

In the hospitals of Georgia and Tennessee, Mrs. Cameron, formerly of Chattanooga, now of Philadelphia, acted a noble part, and has endeared her name to thousands of destitute and suffering refugees.

Miss Hancock, of New Jersey, Miss Bissell, Miss Lucy Chase, Mrs. Painter and Mrs. Carver, and Miss Mary Duncan, of the fifth corps, are gratefully remembered by hundreds who bled in the great battles of the final campaign. Among hospital visitors in Washington, none was earlier in the service, or labored with zeal more unwearied, than Mrs. Almira Fales; none displayed a finer union of the graces of womanhood than Mrs. Pomeroy. When bowed with crushing sorrow over the loss of his favorite boy, it was from the lips of this Christian lady that our late martyred president received words of the truest consolation and the suggestions of celestial hope.

Mrs. Harlan, wife of the Hon. James Harlan, United States senator from Iowa, and more recently Secretary of the Interior, is another shining instance illustrating the value of woman's work during the great conflict. She was with the army at Pittsburg Landing, and hundreds of men are alive to-day, who, but for her ministering visits to the field of Shiloh, for her energy, or for her "outranking Halleck," might have been rudely buried on that bloody field. She at first devoted her energies to caring for the volunteers from her own state, but afterwards gave her time and labor to the general cause, for the good of which she braved the storms of ocean, many journeys to the army, but lived to see her efforts crowned with splendid success, and her name blessed in nearly every city, town, and hamlet in the land.

Though a number of charming hospital scenes and stories are related in the present volume by some of the large deputation from Maine, there are others whose record is as rich in incidents and as valuable for the display of fine character as any already given. Mrs. Preble and Mrs. Sampson did a noble work, for which thousands in the army of the Potomac will never forget them.

Some there were who went out from homes the most luxurious, and gave themselves to lives of loyal sacrifice, in the spirit of Him who said, "Whosoever is chief among you, let him become your servant."

The spirit that prompts self-forgetfulness — and is, for that reason, the more admirable — suggests, also, entire reticence as to the details of benefactions. It is on this account that so little will be found here as to the army experience of the Misses Woolsey, of New York city, and their relative, Miss Green, of Norwich.

Nor has the subject of the good done and the heroism displayed at the Naval School Hospital been exhausted by what has been written of Miss Hall and some of her assistants. The administration of Mrs. Tyler at Annapolis was eminently successful, and her career highly interesting. So, also, Miss Noye, of Buffalo, and Miss Howe, of Brookfield, Massachusetts, with many others, whose period of service there was shorter, will never be forgotten by hundreds of the skeleton victims of southern barbarism, who here learned to forget the horrors of their long imprisonment amid the kindly graces and sympathetic attentions of Christian ladies.

The Charter Oak.

www.ingramcontent.com/pod-product-compliance
Lightning Source LLC
LaVergne TN
LVHW021105110826
845150LV00001B/172

9781425565183